BIBLICAL HERMENEUTICS IN HISTORICAL PERSPECTIVE

Biblical Hermeneutics in Historical Perspective

Studies in Honor of Karlfried Froehlich on His Sixtieth Birthday

Edited by

Mark S. Burrows and Paul Rorem

William B. Eerdmans Publishing Company
Grand Rapids, Michigan

255 Jefferson Ave. S.E., Grand Rapids, Mich. 49503

Printed in the United States of America

The publisher expresses its gratitude to the following for permission to reprint articles that originally appeared in their publications:

To *The Princeton Seminary Bulletin* for Karlfried Froehlich, "Church History and the Bible," 4 (1978): 213-24.

To *Lutheran Quarterly* for the articles by Bart D. Ehrman, John V. Fleming, Eric W. Gritsch, Blake R. Heffner, David W. Johnson, and Bruce McCormack, and for the bibliography compiled by Amanda Berry Wylie, all of which appeared as a special issue in the summer of 1991 (vol. 5, pp. 143-231).

ISBN 0-8028-3693-3

Contents

V. Modern Questions of Biblical Hermeneutics

Foreword

This *Festschrift* is a particularly convincing testimony to the significant role which students play when measuring the life's work of a scholar. The large number of substantial studies in Karlfried Froehlich's special field, written by colleagues and especially his students, demonstrates the depth of this teacher's lasting influence. Without his guidance and the stimulation of his own work, the history of biblical exegesis as an important branch of theological research would not have experienced the progress in his circles which we observe in this symposium.

Especially welcome is the fact that this gathering brought together specialists of all periods of Christian thought, which is deeply influenced by the Bible. In this way, both the exposition of the Bible and the wide-ranging study of church history are enriched in fruitful ways. This publication ensures that this dimension of historical studies, so necessary to all theology and now well linked to the name of Karlfried Froehlich, will continue to produce additional fruit in the future.

The mutual enrichment of teacher and student, which Professor Froehlich enjoys today, I myself have experienced with him. I can hardly imagine my own work without the encouragement of my former student and assistant. Through his collaborative thinking and concrete cooperative work, Karlfried Froehlich provided me with valuable services in the drafting of many of my publications.

I also remember the encouragement and help he gave me in the realization of my project, "Studies in the History of Biblical Exegesis," a series which was summoned to life partly by him. The publisher, Mr. Siebeck (Mohr, Tübingen), to whom I had originally presented the suggestion, undertook its foundation with considerable interest, an initiative which has been continued by his son in laudable ways. It is a great joy to me that I can hand over to Karlfried Froehlich the responsibilities as Editor-in-Chief of this series, which by now includes many volumes.

The honoree is especially suited to work in the history of interpretation because of his own scholarly method, which does not avoid exacting detailed work and the use of sources which are hard to get at. He also has the sense needed in this field for locating the decisive texts. In particular, I would like to emphasize an especially valuable charism, which serves his research well: the gift of *hearing* others, taking their questions seriously, engaging their thoughts positively. This has enabled him to derive appropriate benefits from the reading of others' works and to lead them forward decisively. He goes about it not with the false attitude all too common among scholars which only asks "what can I criticize in the other?" but rather with the right understanding of the test which St. Paul recommends — "test everything; hold fast what is good" (1 Thess. 5:21) — asking first of all, "what can I learn and affirm from someone?" and only then "what can I not accept?"

I would like to say plainly that this charism of *hearing others* explains why Karlfried Froehlich, having begun his work in the field of biblical exegesis, has subsequently devoted himself more specifically to the history of biblical exposition, a field created by the great theologians of the past and the present.

I have made special mention of his readiness for hearing in this Foreword since this charism expresses itself so fruitfully in his research. But it also bears other fruit: his gift for languages, his international and above all his ecumenical relationships, and, last but not least, his untiring readiness to help — in sum, the atmosphere of *friendship* in which he pursues teaching and research. This seems to me a necessary condition for a productive scholarly career. All the contributors to this book and all his other students and colleagues can testify that the honoree — supported by his wife, Ricarda — knows how to create this atmosphere. He is, therefore, a great teacher of the church.

Oscar Cullmann
Chamonix, 1 August 1990
translated by Paul Rorem and Mark S. Burrows

Dr. Karlfried Froehlich
Benjamin B. Warfield Professor of Ecclesiastical History
Princeton Theological Seminary

Introduction

In his inaugural address as the Benjamin B. Warfield Professor of Ecclesiastical History, Karlfried Froehlich commented on the "immense power of biblical language," and argued that

> I have become convinced myself that historical "understanding" of a biblical text cannot stop with the elucidation of its prehistory and of its historical *Sitz im Leben*, with its focus on the intention of the author. Understanding must take into account the text's post-history as the paradigm of the text's own historicity, i.e., as the way in which the text itself can function as a source of human self-interpretation in a variety of contexts, and thus, through its historical interpretations, is participating in the shaping of life.[1]

It is this conviction that has both inspired the manner in which Prof. Froehlich has exercised the church historian's vocation and also guided his work as mentor to a generation of younger scholars in the general area of the history of biblical interpretation. Not surprisingly, his conviction has stimulated these studies, which explore from a wide variety of perspectives and on a sweeping range of topics how Scripture has functioned as a "living voice" and how it has informed the character of witnessing communities of faith during almost two millennia.

The Church's proclamation and mission from the earliest stages of its oral tradition attempted to make sense of a language of immense power and, often, obscurity. At times that obscurity has only appeared as the unspoken presumptions and unrecognized premises of one generation lost their voice and became incomprehensible or suspect for another. At other

1. See "Church History and the Bible," below, p. 9.

times, obscurity prevented readers of an earlier period from penetrating the meaning of texts which only became evident through the insights and discoveries of subsequent readers, the harvest in fields as diverse as archeology, sociocultural studies, and linguistic analysis. In both cases, the concrete horizon of readers of biblical texts provides the occasion for the communal act of interpretation, an act that informs the community's self-understanding as one component of its grasp of the scriptural witness. In other words, the elucidation of the truth lodged within or behind the text is at one and the same time a charting of perceptions rooted within or behind the communities of readers. And yet the power of this language resides, as Prof. Froehlich has reminded us, not only in the receptive community but also in the texts themselves: in the complex world of biblical narrative which formed traditions of faith and life. These interrelated convictions have stimulated Prof. Froehlich's sustained scholarly work on exegetical history, not only as a historical but also as a theological discipline. As he argued in his inaugural address, "church history has as much to do with the Bible as systematic or practical theology and as the academic discipline of biblical studies," precisely because it is a history of communities of interpreters for whom Scripture has functioned as the foundational document. Communities for whom biblical texts have been received as "sacred" have both informed and been reformed by this witness.

This realization prompts us to ask whether it is any longer sufficient to speak of Scripture with uncritical confidence as a univocal source in shaping Christian faith and life. If it is true, as form and redaction critics have often demonstrated with remarkable skill and technical dexterity, that texts have histories which precede their settled canonical form, it is also true that texts continue to have living "histories" insofar as their reception in communities shapes their common life. This could be measured in many ways, such as the manner in which institutional life emerges, pastoral advice is given, and theological arguments are conducted. Scripture is always a text living within ecclesial communities which both interpret and are interpreted by these particular texts; just as we have no immediate access to a "bare" original, a text "behind" the text, our recognition of that text in its canonical shape compels us to ask about the text's own voice exercised in its reception history. Thus, we have various forms of records — e.g., in biographies, commentaries, sermons, letters, artistic and architectural creations — which chart this process of interpretation by which some obscurities are clarified and others introduced with the passage of time. The history of biblical interpretation thus serves as one means of unravelling a broader textual "history," if we might call it that, in this case the story of communities for whom Scripture provided the constitutive narrative for self-understanding and self-criticism. This reception history thus serves as a vital tradition by which texts function as "sacred scripture" insofar as they receive a "voice," as it were, and are received by communities of readers. This is the question of a "traditioning" process by which these texts have lived and continue to live within witnessing communities of synagogue and church.

John Henry Newman once characterized Scripture as "needing completion," because the Bible "cannot . . . be mapped, or its contents catalogued; but after all our diligence, to the end of our lives and to the end of the Church, it must be an unexplored and unsubdued land, with heights and valleys, forests and streams, on the right and left of our path and close about us, full of concealed wonders and choice treasures."[2] If we have learned anything from the extensive formative period when sacred texts took shape within communities, both Jewish and Christian, it is that these texts convey a message which has not been exhausted. Despite the best efforts of historical critics, theologians, and the faithful but technically untrained readers, the Bible still remains a largely "unexplored and unsubdued land." Why is this the case? Is it because of the character of these texts as what Karl Barth once called a "strange new world"?[3] Yes, in part. And is it because of the witnessing character of these texts, which sustain a genuine conversation among communities who behold the One who both transcends all names and yet has appeared in Jesus of Nazareth as the enfleshed *logos* of God? Again, yes, in part. But must we choose between these two? Wherever we locate the reasons for the unchartable depths of these canonical texts, we do recognize in the history of their reception the "mysteries and treasures" of which Newman speaks. And it is this that continues to hold our attention not only to "the word" but to Scripture as a language that exists between the revelation proclaimed and the revelation received, between the Word spoken and the Word as it continues to speak.

The essays included in this volume explore various chapters in the history of biblical hermeneutics. These contributions are the product of a symposium cosponsored by Princeton Theological Seminary and the Center of Theological Inquiry (Princeton, NJ) held in May 1990. Entitled "*Viva vox scripturae:* Symposium on the History of Biblical Interpretation," this gathering brought together a host of scholars who worked with Prof. Froehlich over the last three decades, during his first years as a teacher at Drew

2. *An Essay on the Development of Christian Doctrine* II.1.6 (1845; reprint, Harmondsworth: Penguin, 1973), 162.

3. See "The Strange New World Within the Bible," in *The Word of God and the Word of Man*, trans. Douglas Horton (Boston, Chicago: Pilgrim, 1928), 28-50.

University (1960-68) and subsequently during his tenure at Princeton Theological Seminary. Participants joined once again in a common and now quite expanded "workshop," a root metaphor descriptive of the shared responsibilities of research undertaken in Prof. Froehlich's doctoral seminars through the years; the product of these wide-ranging presentations and discussions form the substance of the essays which follow. Joining this group were many of Prof. Froehlich's colleagues from the Princeton community, particularly members of the seminary's theology and church history departments. One invited guest who could not attend in person eagerly submitted the foreword to this volume: Prof. Dr. Oscar Cullmann, Karlfried Froehlich's own teacher at Basel whose foundational work in the area of biblical interpretation needs no further comment.

The scope of these pieces and the sweeping variety of perspectives, both of substance and method, is particularly noteworthy. These chapters explore issues of textuality and contextuality, of exegetical detail and theory, of theological style and method, and of the shifting social, cultural, and intellectual horizon in which Scripture has been received and studied. As a whole they are impressive in demonstrating the staggering and at times exasperating difficulty of this project, since one must employ in this task the diverse tools of exegete and hermeneutician, text critic, historian, and theologian, and do so in varying configurations. This is the consequence, of course, of the peculiar role "sacred scripture" has played in the Church's life and witness, as both the object and in an important sense the ongoing subject of theological discourse. If Prof. Froehlich's insight into the "immense power" of biblical language is correct, a claim that these essays would amply corroborate, then it is equally true that this language and these texts demonstrate a stubborn resilience and surprising multivocality through the centuries of reception and transmission. Indeed, here the living voice of the biblical texts *(viva vox scripturae)* has had much to do with what one might well call the *viva vox ecclesiae,* the living voice of the Church. It is this conjunction of text and ecclesial context that establishes the critical and constructive parameters for the essays printed in this volume.

We have arranged these essays into five broad sections determined largely by chronological order rather than according to thematic concerns that often established a different "conversation" among the authors during the symposium as in their published form. These points of convergence and continuing debate, which were substantial yet always convivial, will become evident enough to the reader who surveys the whole as well as sampling the parts. The volume is bracketed, as it were, by two of Prof. Froehlich's own contributions, one old and one new: first, his inaugural address, delivered at Princeton Theological Seminary in 1977, and subsequently published in the *Princeton Seminary Bulletin* under the title "Church History and the Bible"; and, finally, his own concluding reflections on the state of this field of study as a postscript to the symposium and a signpost for future work. The volume concludes with a full bibliography of Prof. Froehlich's publications, both as an aid to the interested scholar and as a chronicle of the remarkable breadth and significance of his scholarly contribution, both to the Church and to the academy.

The first section explores the dynamics of early Christian exegesis from a variety of perspectives. In the opening essay Bart Ehrman examines the complex question of textual transmission and suggests how theological convictions might have shaped the texts as they were "passed on" by scribes. Kathleen McVey considers the theological character of Theophilus of Antioch's early commentary on the creation account (Gen. 1) which she locates within the broader intellectual world of the second century. Finally, Amanda Berry Wylie analyzes John Chrysostom's homilies on the Acts of the Apostles, delineating Chrysostom's historiographical perspective by which he interpreted not only this narrative but also the Church's fundamental character within the wider historical context.

The second section turns from the interpretive world of the Greek East to the Western Augustinian tradition. Paula Fredriksen's chapter on "vile bodies" sketches the way Paul and later Augustine understood the resurrection of the body, with particular interest in how the latter reconsidered corporeality within a millenarian framework. Robert Bernard explores the function of *figura* in Augustine's thought, and particularly the bishop's use of nonliteral exegesis to define the logic and comprehensibility of the "rhetoric of God." Finally, David Johnson traces the "myth" of the Augustinian synthesis in the later Middle Ages by analyzing the structure and consequences of Cassiodorus's "Augustinian" revision of Pelagius's Pauline commentary.

The third section leaves the world of late antiquity and enters the realm of medieval exegesis in the West. Blake Heffner surveys the interpretation of the Mary/Martha pericope (Luke 10:38-42) across a millennium of readers, focusing particular attention upon Meister Eckhart's masterful reception of this story at the end of that trajectory as a call to the active life. Christopher Ocker returns to the pericope Prof. Froehlich had focused upon in his early research, the classic text used for papalist arguments (Matt. 16:18-19), and examines the fusion of exegesis and ideology among several fourteenth-century readers of this Petrine text. Mark Burrows explores the broad question of exegesis in the late medieval context, focusing specifically upon Jean Gerson's argument in the early fifteenth century for a "traditioned sense" of Scripture residing not in the magisterium, nor even among contemporary theologians, but in the legacy of the early fathers. Finally, John Fleming brings us up to date as we approach the quincentennial celebration of Columbus's pioneering voyage to the "new world" by taking us on an exploration into the exegetical world of this navigator, a world replete with intricacies and carefully constructed codes that were more than an intellectual pastime for this would-be scholar.

The fourth section turns to a variety of exegetical traditions of the Reformation era. Eric Gritsch leads the way by considering how Luther's humor, as manifested in his lectures on Genesis and Galatians, enabled him to receive and proclaim the biblical witness by linking laughter and poetry, humor and music. David Steinmetz's essay approaches Calvin's theology and the possible Thomistic influences upon it, an argument that brings Calvin's exegesis of the "hardening of Pharaoh's heart" (Rom. 9) into conversation with relevant passages in the writings of Thomas Aquinas and the Dominican convert to the Protestant cause, Martin Bucer; on the basis of this analysis, Steinmetz eventually dismisses an argument for a common (Thomist) school tradition in favor of a deeper agreement with an Augustinian heritage. Elsie McKee examines the relationship of theology and exegesis in Calvin's thought, focusing in particular on the order of teaching, what she calls the "traditioning" of Scripture, and the unified dimensions of practical theology found in this Reformer's thought. Jane Douglass probes Marie Dentière's exegetical construction of a theology of history, one that interpreted contemporary events of the Genevan reform against the backdrop of biblical narrative to produce a story at once apologetic and prophetic in scope. Finally, Rodney Petersen explores Heinrich Bullinger's view of prophecy, and the Zurich Reformer's conviction that the dramatic events of the Church's renewal in his age point to the inbreaking of the final restitution promised in the Apocalypse.

The fifth and final section moves from the Reformers to their heirs, sampling several "conversations" arising out of the Church's more recent encounters with the Scriptures. Klaus Fröhlich offers a thematic and cultural analysis of a selection of sermons preached during the 1860s by Prof. Froehlich's great-grandfather, Heinrich Fröhlich, exploring the manner in which this Saxon preacher utilized history as a tool for teaching purposes and in order to mobilize historical memory against the apparently shifting cultural climate of this transitional period. James Moorhead samples a wide variety of sources interpreting — often in heated exegetical arguments — eschatological themes and texts among nineteenth-century American scholars and preachers, concluding that postmillennialist arguments in particular had run their course by the early twentieth century. Cornelius Plantinga, Jr., explores the Gospel of John as it has been used for trinitarian theology, moving from the early fathers to consider the way in which the Fourth Gospel supports a "social analogy" of the Trinity and in turn how this theological tradition has been received and reworked among contemporary sources. Finally, Bruce McCormack charts the hermeneutical revolution effected by the young Karl Barth, whose unswerving commitment to "dogmatic interest" established both the starting point and the continuing logic governing exegesis conducted within and for an ecclesial context.

What began some four years ago as a celebration designed to mark Prof. Froehlich's sixtieth birthday has thus borne abundant fruit. This gathering brought together a collection of scholars whose work in various disciplines and fields and in diverse locations and settings (university departments of religion, classics, philosophy, history; seminaries; denominationally aligned colleges; etc.) has a common source of inspiration, intellectual and personal, in this former teacher whose particular charism is the gift, as Oscar Cullmann so rightly notes, of genuinely "hearing" the other. And, although it is perhaps a natural coincidence, the name of this teacher (*fröhlich* is German for "joyful") provides a hermeneutical clue into the personality: this is a man for whom the rigors of scholarship are a joyful responsibility, and it is this spirit which has — for better! — influenced and often infected those privileged to have worked alongside him. Karlfried Froehlich is also one of those remarkable teachers for whom his fundamental concern for *die Sache* (subject matter) makes of him an ongoing student, and his students "teachers" in their own right. Indeed, Chaucer's description of the clerk, "and gladly would he teach, and gladly learn," characterizes this scholar with appropriate force. It was in the presence once again of this great teacher, and in the context of a common intellectual task that was as serious as it was convivial, that the *"Viva vox scripturae"* symposium took place in late May 1990; it has been in that same spirit that these essays have now acquired a final redaction in their varied transmission histories, often on the basis of particular comments and the larger dialogue of that event. Alongside the hard work involved in these sessions, each participant brought another story of how the meticulous mind and generous spirit of this teacher contributed to the zeal *and* discretion with which their own work matured. Prof. Froehlich participated in each of the seminar sessions in characteristic style: intensely curious about every detail, concerned about the foundations and conclusions of larger arguments, and restlessly committed to the fundamental question of the "immense power" — historical and actual — of biblical language.

We offer these essays to Prof. Froehlich now as a tangible memory of this scholarly celebration of his sixtieth birthday, and as a gift of gratitude to him during his final year of teaching (1991-92) at Princeton Theological

Seminary. With equal measures of gratitude and respect, we dedicate these essays to his honor, hoping that he might now also be known not only by his own fruits, to rework the biblical claim, but also by those of his students and friends! One final word must be said about the supporting cast in all of this. On the personal side, this symposium became for Prof. Froehlich something of a family reunion as well: present throughout the days of this symposium as during all the years of their North American pilgrimage was his wife and colleague in things of the spirit, soul, and body, Ricarda; in addition, there was a considerable witness of the Froehlich family — their own children, and members of the German family not part of this trans-atlantic diaspora. The presence of these family members brought the whole event into domestic focus, reminding us that scholars depend not only on archives, libraries, and studies, but on the day-to-day strength found in those with whom we make our homes.

In bringing this three-year project to a close, there are several persons who deserve special recognition for support, encouragement, and concrete assistance, and without whom this project would not have flourished as it has. First, we wish to thank President Thomas Gillespie of Princeton Theological Seminary, the primary host for this event. When we first approached President Gillespie to explore whether the seminary would assist in what we had then conceived as a much less ambitious celebration, he responded with immediate enthusiasm and generous promises of support, both financial and institutional. This was surely a measure of his respect for Prof. Froehlich, as well as an indication of his own commitment to the significant role that hermeneutical and biblical studies hold for the Church's life and witness. Alongside President Gillespie, the late James I. McCord, former president of the seminary and then chancellor of the Center for Theological Inquiry, offered financial and institutional support for the project; and, in the years following Dr. McCord's death, acting chancellor Roland Frye and current chancellor Daniel Hardy have continued to demonstrate the Center's enthusiastic support of this project. William B. Eerdmans himself showed immediate interest and support for this project, and to him we express here our thanks. With such backing, and given the identity and nature of the honoree, we knew that we could only succeed in our initial plan. Subsequently, President Gillespie offered further financial subvention to see that the fruit of this event would reach a wider audience, first as an issue of the *Lutheran Quarterly* (Summer 1991) which includes several of the papers and subsequently in the form of this full volume of the symposium's proceedings. It is with enduring gratitude that we note here the generosity of these institutions and their chief executives, as well as their staffs, whose competence was matched only by their faithfulness and humor. Without this supporting cast of characters, many of whom must (and will) remain known primarily to its organizers, this symposium would be a memory cherished by the few rather than the object of wider study and use. We must also acknowledge the patience and more modest levels of support offered by the institutions in which we, the cochairs of the symposium, have lived, worked, and had at least a part of our being during these years: Wesley Theological Seminary (Washington, DC) and the Lutheran School of Theology at Chicago. We are particularly grateful to Andrew F. Weisner of LSTC and Michael Ponder Jones of WTS for preparing the indices.

This symposium and its fruits here published are the result of a gathering of scholars committed to the ways in which Scripture has been a text functioning as "a source of human self-interpretation in a variety of contexts," to echo Prof. Froehlich's description of the church historian's vocation. It was also a gathering of persons located within the often estranged worlds of academy and Church for whom this text is not merely the object of disinterested study, but the "subject" — the "living voice" *(viva vox)* —which continues to participate in "the shaping of life." Within the horizon of these shared boundaries, it is our hope that these essays might take their place as a contribution not only to "historical science among the theological disciplines" but also to "the ongoing dialogue with the historical disciplines outside the seminary," to recall Prof. Froehlich's profession of his own scholarly commitments. In this manner we hope that these chapters on "biblical hermeneutics in historical perspective" might contribute in some measure, to recall words from one of Charles Wesley's hymns, to "unite the pair so long disjoin'd: knowledge and vital piety." If so, our efforts would yield fruits worthy of one like Karlfried Froehlich for whom these are but different points of entry into a shared source of human self-understanding, in this case the world of the biblical text situated within ecclesial context.

Mark S. Burrows and Paul Rorem
Washington, DC, and Chicago
July, 1991

Abbreviations

AHR	*American Historical Review*
ANF	Ante-Nicene Fathers
ANRW	*Aufstieg und Niedergang der römischen Welt*
BARev	*Biblical Archaeology Review*
BETL	Bibliotheca ephemeridum theologicarum lovaniensium
BGBH	Beiträge zur Geschichte der biblischen Hermeneutik
Bib	*Biblica*
BQ	*Baptist Quarterly*
BT	*Bible Translator*
CCSL	Corpus Christianorum Series Latina
CD	*Church Dogmatics*
ChH	*Church History*
CSEL	Corpus scriptorum ecclesiasticorum latinorum
CTJ	*Calvin Theological Journal*
HBT	*Horizons in Biblical Theology*
HTR	*Harvard Theological Review*
JAH	*Journal of American History*
JBL	*Journal of Biblical Literature*
JEH	*Journal of Ecclesiastical History*
JJS	*Journal of Jewish Studies*
JR	*Journal of Religion*
JSNT	*Journal for the Study of the New Testament*
JTS	*Journal of Theological Studies*
LCC	Library of Christian Classics
LCL	Loeb Classical Library
LW	Luther's Works
LXX	Septuagint

MQR	*Methodist Quarterly Review*
NEB	New English Bible
NICNT	New International Commentary on the New Testament
NPNF	Nicene and Post-Nicene Fathers
NTS	*New Testament Studies*
NTTS	New Testament Tools and Studies
PAPS	Proceedings of the American Philosophical Society
PEQ	*Palestine Exploration Quarterly*
PG	*Patrologia graeca,* ed. J. P. Migne
PL	*Patrologia latina,* ed. J. P. Migne
PSB	*Princeton Seminary Bulletin*
RE	*Realencyklopädie für protestantische Theologie und Kirche*
REAug	*Revue des études augustienennes*
RGG	*Religion in Geschichte und Gegenwart*
RSR	*Recherches de science religieuse*
SC	Sources chrétiennes
SJT	*Scottish Journal of Theology*
SPAW	Sitzungsberichte der preussichen Akademie der Wissenschaften
ST	*Summa Theologiae*
SVF	Stoicum Veterum Fragmenta
TB	Harper Torchbooks
TToday	*Theology Today*
TU	Texte und Untersuchungen
TynBul	*Tyndale Bulletin*
USQR	*Union Seminary Quarterly Review*
VC	*Vigiliae christianae*
Vulg.	Vulgate
WA	Weimarer Ausgabe
WA.TR	Weimarer Ausgabe, Tisch Reden
ZKG	*Zeitschrift für Kirchengeschichte*
ZTK	*Zeitschrift für Theologie und Kirche*

Church History and the Bible

Karlfried Froehlich

It seems appropriate that an inaugural address should present some basic methodological reflections about the field of study which, by virtue of my appointment, I have the duty, joy, and honor of teaching among you. This expectation is not only a venerable tradition of this venerable institution, but, I am happy to say, constitutes a direct link to the venerable Middle Ages. In the heyday of the medieval university, the master in theology began his first course of lectures with a *principium,* an inaugural speech of methodological scope. We have dozens of such *principia* preserved in manuscript, written both by well-known theologians and by the many obscure teachers from the 13th through the 16th centuries. Only recently has scholarly interest begun to turn to this body of material which may well present a major clue to the development of the late medieval treatise on biblical hermeneutics. Since all masters had to lecture on the Bible first, the conventional form of the *principium* seems to have been a *laus sacrae scripturae,* a praise of Holy Scripture. I see myself at least in formal contact with this host of academic fathers when I propose as the topic of my reflections "Church History and the Bible."

I

Church history is a *theological* discipline. It is this not by choice but by definition. To speak of "church" always implies a theological decision, a

This essay is reprinted, with permission, from PSB *n.s. 1 (1978): 213-24. It is the text of Prof. Froehlich's inaugural lecture as the Benjamin B. Warfield Professor of Ecclesiastical History at Princeton Theological Seminary (Feb. 23, 1977).*

theological principle of identification. Specifically implied is a judgment about the limit, nature, purpose, and even the social reality of the phenomenon one regards as "church." In one word: implied is an ecclesiology. Even though today one's ecclesiology may be quite ecumenical, covering a wide, almost infinite range of what one is willing to endorse as "church," the term always reflects a prior commitment to a reality which, from the standpoint of secular society, must appear as "sectarian," however value-free the adjective may be used.

That church history is a theological discipline has to be reclaimed today. When Karl Barth started to rethink the structure of the entire theological enterprise in his *Church Dogmatics* from the angle of the priorities for the church of his day, church history seemed to get a seat in the very back row. The famous quote from vol. I/1 of his *Church Dogmatics* reads: "So-called church history does not answer a question which must be raised independently, concerning the Christian talk about God. It is therefore not to be regarded as an independent theological discipline. It is *the* indispensable *auxiliary science* of exegetical, dogmatic, and practical theology."[1]

Of course, no self-respecting intellectual wants to run just an auxiliary enterprise for others, and even if he does, resents being told so. The loud protest of professional church historians has claimed that Barth's devaluation of church history was the inevitable consequence of its theologization. If church history is seen as a *theological* discipline, so it seemed to many, it must needs become the servant of any prevalent dogmatism, the propaganda tool of churches who will want to bend the patient historical facts, which can no longer defend themselves, to their sectarian purposes. However, this protest did not just arise from the hurt pride of professionals or from the moral posture of defending a defenseless past against manipulative misuse. It arose from the immense respect for monument and document, for historical evidence and its contingent character, which the age of historicism had taught historians and should have taught theologians as well. This respect had always driven church historians into seeking closer contacts with secular historical scholarship during those decades, in the hope of finding greener pastures of freedom to investigate sources and of "objectivity" in interpreting them — of an objectivity which seemed to be the only appropriate attitude for the one who respected the past.

The inner emigration of church history from the theological disciplines and the concomitant radical secularization of ecclesiastical histori-

1. See *Die Kirchliche Dogmatik*, I/1: *Die Lehre vom Wort Gottes. Prolegomena zur kirchlichen Dogmatik* (Zürich: Theologischer Verlag, 1975), 3 (author's own translation).

ography has become a characteristic feature of the academic scene in America. The American Church History Society is holding its meetings in conjunction with those of the American Historical Association, and even if it were to change this practice, the major option would be joining hands with the American Academy of Religion, one of the most powerful constituents of the Council on the Study of Religion, whose membership is drawn from all settings in which religion is taught as an academic subject. Church historians accordingly tend to define their work in terms of a descriptive science, for which any theological commitment has at best an extracurricular function. It is even more likely to be regarded as forcing one's discipline into a circle of dogmatic chronicle where everything is self-explanatory, or as obscuring the much more important keys to its interpretation which are offered by social history, psycho-history, or the history of culture. Church historians are uneasy with their task in this company and often enough prefer to teach the "history of Christianity" or other, more neutral and objective titles. Much of this tendency no doubt is due to the peculiar sociology of academe in America which, in its supremely tolerant approach to *all* subject matter, including religion, as a possible subject for scientific investigation, has a distinct advantage over the traditional framework of central Europe, where theological schools still hold the first place among the "faculties" of a university, while in the public mind the very place of anything that smells of religion has long since become questionable and plainly anachronistic.

It is this situation of polite invitational peer pressure to fill a predetermined slot that makes it necessary to reclaim church history as a theological discipline. Respect for the monument and document, respect for evidence, is certainly an irrevocable heritage of the era of historicism. But respect is not just the result, it is the presupposition of a fruitful relationship, the precondition for a fair and equitable encounter between engaged and engaging partners.

It must be remembered that Karl Barth's dictum about church history as an auxiliary science was not meant to be a defamation of a reputable branch of learning. It was meant as an attack on the oppressive weight of the historical sciences, quite specifically against the imperialism of a church history from whose pontifications in the name of scientific method there seemed to be no recourse in the church or in the other fields of academic theology. It was an attempt to restore at least some fair balance out of respect for the church and its integrity, and out of the realization that even in history method does not in itself assure the knowledge of truth.

Thus, to speak of church history as a *theological* discipline, despite all the dangers, is not just a predicament. In the face of the ever-present threat of an imperialism of historical scholarship in a scientific age it is also a blessing which saves the church historian a great deal of unfruitful apologetic, by giving his dialogue with the past a necessary place and focus and a primary audience within a much wider potential range of people who might want or find it necessary to listen. Obviously, historians wish to know *wie es eigentlich gewesen* (Ranke's phrase), what has actually happened, but they want to know it *in a perspective*; as Father Georges Florovsky once put it, "Commitment is a token of freedom, a prerequisite of responsiveness."[2]

II

Church history is also a historical discipline. It is part of the far more comprehensive enterprise of historical study, and again it is this not by choice but by definition. As church *history* its material participates in the universal scope of the totality of the humanly experienced past which is properly subjected to investigation by the critical methods developed in this particular brand of knowledge.

Thus, church history cannot claim a special category of holy history which would not be open to investigation by historical criticism. Some thirty-five years ago, Oscar Cullmann reintroduced the term *Heilsgeschichte* in the theological debate. He never understood *Heilsgeschichte* as describing a group of specially elevated, inherently sacred events whose nature is inaccessible to the general historian's mind. Rather, *Heilsgeschichte* describes a faith judgment on the coherence of specific events within the scope of universal history, which judgment can be traced by historical-critical analysis of the evidence, beginning with the New Testament. With all historical disciplines church history shares fully not only the potential but also the problems of the historical-critical method about whose limits much has been written since Croce, Collingwood, and Löwith. There can also be no difference in the kind of subject matter. Church history's subject is always part of universal history, of the totality of humanly experienced past, event as well as interpretation. Regardless of what exact segment church history will have to treat, it is and remains part and parcel of this totality. This has consequences. For the church historian to emigrate from the theological disciplines does not mean that the task will ever be anything less than the grasping of this totality. If there is no sacred corner for church history, there is no sacred corner for any other

2. "The Predicament of the Christian Historian," in *Religion and Culture: Essays in Honor of Paul Tillich*, ed. Walter Leibrecht (New York: Harper, 1959), 156.

kind of history either. All such unassailable corners are eventually passed by as utterly irrelevant in the historical process of life, if they do not face up to the challenge of the "horizon of universal history" (Pannenberg), the "*whole amplitude* of human concerns" (Florovsky).[3]

That church history is a historical discipline has to be repeated today with unequivocal clarity. We experience much pious romanticism in churches, ecclesiastical bodies, and Christian individuals. It seems that about any plausible account of church history by any properly endorsed expert in pulpit or teaching chair can be and is being mistaken for that history itself and serves as sectarian self-justification or as the reenforcement of communal prejudice, particularly when it comes in the reassuring garb of modern scientific jargon. Today, the historicizing of myth is perhaps a greater danger than the mythicizing of history has ever been, and pious fraud in this regard is often hard to detect in a community, Christian or not, which is struggling for self-identity and a definable place in a pluralistic society.

In the years around the Second World War, several students of Karl Barth in Germany took Barth's definition of church history as an auxiliary science and applied it rigorously to the task of separating right from wrong in the church struggle and its aftermath. Church history was relevant only insofar as it helped to separate the sheep from the goats. It had become a "decisional," an existential, discipline. Such an application may have its relative right in this and other times of crisis. But it only underscores the precarious position of an "auxiliary science," a *Hilfswissenschaft,* and its modern Protestant proponents are seldom aware of the closeness to the attitude of Cardinal Manning, who hailed the decrees of the First Vatican Council as the much needed "victory of dogma over history."

Against any such imperialism of dogma and present ephemeral need it is necessary to hold the fact that church history is by definition a historical discipline which remains responsible for the totality of the humanly experienced past, not just for any convenient segment. In this context, the legitimate call of history may come through not so much by listening to the "engaged" historians of our time who make no apology for their standpoint because everybody has one anyway. It may come through, more importantly, by hearing those less fervent voices of the quiet workers who are carrying on the great legacy of historicism in their application of the historical-critical methods to the production of critical editions, the correc-

3. See, e.g., Pannenberg, "Hermeneutic and Universal History," in *Basic Questions in Theology: Collected Essays*, 2 vols., trans. George Kehm (Philadelphia: Fortress, 1970), 1:98; Florovsky, "The Christian Historian," 156.

tion of historical detail, the retracing of the biographical steps of this or that seemingly obscure figure. As a matter of fact, every good historian has started somewhere in this kind of terrain. The church historian can spare him- or herself considerable trouble in constructing a plausible argument if he or she keeps close to results and procedures of a lot of dull but solid scholarship.

Looking once more at Karl Barth's controversial dictum, we should point out that Barth in fact acknowledged the importance of historical method and critical research. Church history, he said, is *the* indispensable auxiliary science for all other aspects of the theological enterprise. This can only mean that he presupposed its use without any question. On this point, times may have changed. Against the pious ostracism of history rampant in our time we may have to spell out again the absolute requirement of sober historical research as the basis for any ever so relevant approach to church history. There is no shortcut to relevance.

Of course, there can be no doubt that the discipline of history itself has fallen on evil days: not in terms of output or of manpower tied down by it in academe, but in terms of its place in the public consciousness. The posture of the historian as a scientist has quite naturally led to the demand for "scientific proof" in history, and no subsequent disclaimer that there really is no presuppositionless, objective history could ward off the resulting confusion, when historians failed to deliver the original promise. For many people, history has become too difficult and too unprofitable to get excited about. It is no longer fiction but it is not science either. The spectacular rise of structuralism in recent years may be a good indication of this general mood: for its approach to reality it no longer uses a historical model, with all the concomitant hermeneutic ambiguity, but a linguistic one. Whatever the value of the movement may be, it seems today to satisfy better than the historical disciplines the hunger for scientific or pseudoscientific method in the mind of the time. History is in a deep crisis of meaning.

But to speak of church history as a *historical* discipline is not just a predicament. In the face of the ever increasing tendency to use history for apologetics, to ride it as an easy vehicle to pious relevance, it is a blessing to be confronted with the unpredictable otherness of the historical past such as critical and honest scholarship encounters it. To do church history in terms of confronting humanly experienced past in its givenness holds out the promise of something really *new,* of seeing really *new* light, of becoming open to truly *new* horizons, of experiencing change in ourselves, precisely because we cannot change the past. History itself in its inexhaustible universal horizon is the given, and as such the best dialogue partner to help us discover that life never needs to be dull.

III

Both as a theological and a historical discipline church history has to do with the Bible: as a *theological* discipline because church and Bible belong inextricably together. One of the fundamental tenets of the ecclesiology of the Reformers was that there can be no church without the Bible as the central witness to the Word of God in Jesus Christ. On the other hand, one of the fundamental results of the modern ecclesiological debate in the ecumenical context has been the insight that there is no Bible without the church — the church which received the apostolic witness, selected the canon, and gave the biblical witness unity by its interpretation. As a *historical* discipline, church history has to do with the Bible because church history cannot be entered at any arbitrary point. It is unalterably oriented toward a fixed point, the primary document of which is the New Testament and its interpretative annexation of the Old Testament. Thus, from both sides, the theological and the historical, the task of reflecting on the relationship of church history and the Bible is an intrinsic methodological necessity.

It seems to me that the major contribution to this task in recent decades has come from Gerhard Ebeling, now of Zürich, Switzerland, and it may be appropriate to mark an anniversary today. It was thirty years ago almost to the day that Gerhard Ebeling delivered his inaugural lecture as a *Privatdozent* in the field of church history at Tübingen University. The title of his essay was: "Church History as the History of the Exposition of Holy Scripture."[4]

Ebeling proceeded by first analyzing the place of church history in the theological enterprise, stressing like Barth (but without the note of an auxiliary science) the interdependence of all of its branches since the advent of a pervasive critical methodology. He then characterized three conceptions of church history — the Catholic, the enthusiastic, and the one represented by the Reformers — as an outgrowth of different understandings of the relation between church and history, squarely placing his own formula in the line of the Reformers. However, he found a difficulty with even the Reformers' stance in their lack of a clear definition of the relation due to their *ecclesiological* distinction between "visible" and "invisible" church. His own formula was then not meant simply to tie church history to the discernible manifestations of the concrete word of the Bible, or to

4. First published as "Habilitation Lecture" in 1947; republished in *Wort Gottes und Tradition: Studien zu einer Hermeneutik der Konfessionen* (Göttingen: Vandenhoek & Ruprecht, 1964), and as "Church History Is the History of the Exposition of Scripture," in *The Word of God and Tradition: Historical Studies Interpreting the Divisions of Christianity*, trans. S. H. Hooke (Philadelphia: Fortress, 1968), 11-31.

any speculative history of the "Word of God." Particularly the former point has often been overlooked. For Ebeling, church history was not just Bible history, but the extremely complicated history of a self-interpreting and an interpreted Bible. In the third part, Ebeling spelled out the help he expected from the formula: It would assist in delimiting the exact province of church history, it would help define its nature in terms of the ongoing stream of traditioning throughout the centuries, and it would determine its theological character (in good Barthian terms) as "the radical critical destruction" of tradition as a barrier instead of a pointer to Christ.

The context in which the proposal has to be seen was no doubt Karl Barth's theology of the Word of God, and the rise of the hermeneutical question in New Testament exegesis which owed much to Barth's impulse. Particularly in Barthian circles, the enthusiasm for the Ebeling thesis was considerable. Ebeling had not found it necessary in his lecture to touch on biblical hermeneutics directly, repudiating an understanding of the Bible without history. As a matter of fact, the hermeneutical situation at the front seemed to be far beyond such concerns for a student of Rudolf Bultmann. The exciting thing for his readers was that he now seemed to fight an understanding of church history without the Bible in the framework of a historical-critical approach to both. Thus his title (and often no more than that) was read as a program asking for a new method in historiography: *Auslegungsgeschichte,* the history of the exposition of Scripture. At the First Patristic Conference at Oxford in 1955, two young church historians, David Lerch and Lukas Vischer, presented an outline of how such a "discipline" might function.[5] It is interesting that there is no reference to Ebeling in their paper. This suggests that different interests were riding the crest of the wave. Soon after this initiative, two new monograph series started to be published in the new field: "Beiträge zur Geschichte der biblischen Exegese" and "Beiträge zur Geschichte der biblischen Hermeneutik," but again without Ebeling among the editors. Lerch and Vischer had argued as follows: By understanding a particular interpretation as part of a history-of-exegesis process, on the one hand, the discipline could shed light on the exegesis of the text itself; on the other hand, it could open up ways into a largely unexplored area of primary materials in the commentary literature of all centuries, and it could also be of corrective value in the history of theology, where the quest for "immanent development" and "influences" dominated too much. It could finally open a new hermeneutical vista on the Bible itself: "The

5. "Die Auslegungsgeschichte als notwendige theologische Aufgabe," *Studia Patristica* 1 (1957): 414-19.

history-of-exegesis material becomes a mirror of the mystery which the text itself is witnessing to."[6]

While the (otherwise Barthian) sentence is deficient in failing to include the history of possible distortions of the text, I have become convinced myself that historical "understanding" of a biblical text cannot stop with the elucidation of its prehistory and of its historical *Sitz im Leben,* with its focus on the intention of the author. Understanding must take into account the text's post-history as the paradigm of the text's own historicity, i.e., as the way in which the text itself can function as a source of human self-interpretation in a variety of contexts, and thus, through its historical interpretations, is participating in the shaping of life. I still regard making accessible the sources of early and medieval exegesis as an enterprise well worth my own time and effort as a scholar. But I have become aware that more than the biblical exegetes who all too often have their very restricted agenda of squeezing the text for meaning, it is art historians, literary historians, political scientists, and church historians who want and know how to read these materials as sources.

IV

Thirty years after the initial event it seems wise to assess the situation. For this purpose I have found helpful a review article on the Ebeling thesis by Friedrich De Boor, published in 1972,[7] and a 1971 issue of the journal *Verkündigung und Forschung,* with contributions by younger church historians such as Wolf Dieter Hauschild, Gustav Adolf Benrath, and Klaus Scholder, who survey the field of the history of exegesis. The reviewers agree in their basic impression that the results of work in the new discipline have been disappointing and have not fulfilled the high expectations of the early years. Exegesis itself did not profit much, since it has not been clear for exegetes studying the history of biblical interpretations what exactly they could and should be looking for in the "pre-critical" materials. The commentaries of the fathers with their own rich and varied agendas did not answer the precise critical questions that were raised, and the tracing of random texts in their history of exposition yielded at best interesting details and the impression of a bewildering zigzag course. The same impression of a certain helplessness and aimlessness prevails when one uses the first recent commen-

6. Ibid., 418 n. 1.

7. "Kirchengeschichte oder Auslegungsgeschichte?" *Theologische Literaturzeitung* (June 1972): 401-14.

tary on a biblical book which, by design, includes sections on the history of exegesis, Brevard Childs's *The Book of Exodus: A Critical, Theological Commentary,* Old Testament Library (Philadelphia: Westminster, 1974). The history-of-exegesis sections, while presenting most interesting material from Jewish and Christian sources, look somewhat contrived and respond to the requirements of a principle more than to an organic need. In fact, Childs wants to reeducate scholarly and pastoral exegetes whose training he thinks has rendered them incapable of making sense of pre-critical materials so that these could in a meaningful way inform the living interpretation of the Bible in the church today. I find the intention highly laudable and the implicit encouragement to biblical scholars to become church historians existentially appealing. But good intentions are no assurance of success. The church historian will have to remain doubtful of the value of random selections of sources which can hardly provide a plausible developmental picture. He will have to ask himself, however, how much more would in fact be needed. Perhaps this would differ with every passage. But if no solid critical attempt is made to sort out the diffuse material, the developmental organization can hardly hide the fact that we have here no more than a modern *catena.* Of course, *catenae* are most interesting sources if one knows how to read them, but to teach this reading skill was supposedly the purpose, not the presupposition, of this commentary. I personally think that without much more detailed study independent of the production of commentaries and without effective teamwork, similar single-handed enterprises have little chance of success, particularly when an exegete is doing the whole job. In the meantime, the value of such efforts, however limited, for a new generation of exegetes may lie exactly in the confrontation with strikingly different patterns of exegetical thought and practice which have a logic of their own, and in the timely warning that historical method must lead into ever increasing contacts with other disciplines rather than to an ever greater concentration on a restricted specialty.

Historians of doctrine or of theology who have contributed to the history of exegesis seem to have achieved somewhat better results. Yet here, too, the overall value of the work is judged to be rather limited. No really new aspects have come to light, though individual insights have been deepened and guesses have been corrected. Dissatisfaction seems to center on various diachronic attempts to trace the history of a passage through the centuries. The success, it is maintained, depends entirely on the selection of a good passage, one which *has made* history rather than just *having* one. But who would have known that Prov. 8:22-25 was the touchstone of the Nicene controversy on the Arian side! And how *can* one know? On the other hand, in cases which would have seemed logical choices, the outcome has been quite unexpected or disappointing, as in one case where the conclusion of a thorough study on Rom. 13 was that the exegetical literature contributed little or nothing to the formation of medieval political theory and ethics. The reviewers find this hit-and-miss game distressing. I must confess that I am more optimistic here. In his delightful 1964 presidential address on "Theodosius' Horse," the church historian Albert Outler said: "Every segment of the human maze sprawls past the boundaries of reason and marches with infinity."[8] What we need first is a knowledge of the material regardless of its aimed usefulness, inroads into the vast maze the coherence of which we can only guess. The surprises in the field are normal for work in relatively unknown sources, and much initial effort has to be wasted as long as there is no glimpse of a pattern as yet. It is the cumulative effect of surprises that removes surprise and will make a surer approach possible. We may still need quite a number of less successful studies tracing the history of specific texts as well as the underlying history of hermeneutics before we will really know what questions to ask and how to make selections.

Finally, despite positive response to Ebeling's thesis, there seems to be no comprehensive attempt anywhere to write church history from the angle of the history of the exposition of Scripture. Ebeling himself, one author noted, has never tackled the task. Hauschild frankly doubts the potential of the Ebeling thesis as a historiographic device: Ebeling's program, he writes, "has not produced a corresponding treatment of the history and doctrine of the ancient Church, because this would even hardly have been possible." I am still wondering about this flat denial of historiographic relevance for the thesis. Is it the last word? Could such a treatment be tried? Should it?

Early critics have charged, and the meager results of the more recent work have reinforced the impression, that Ebeling's thesis cannot stand unrevised today. On the one hand, his definition was "too narrow." The history of the exposition of Scripture does not yet make church history. The history of the *means* by which God calls together his people is no surrogate for the history of this people. On the other hand, Ebeling's understanding of "exposition" as including the historical expression of Christian life in many forms has been criticized as being much "too wide." It "blurs the contours," leads into limitlessness, and allows for no clear principle of selection any more. Even De Boor, who is generally sympathetic toward Ebeling's stance, regards "all attempts to substitute the history

8. See "Theodosius' Horse: Reflections on the Predicament of the Church Historian," *ChH* 34 (1965): 257.

of hermeneutics or of the exposition of scripture for church history or the history of doctrine . . . as an error."[9]

V

One critic, Hauschild, at least allows the possibility that this may not be all Ebeling's fault. Contrary to the use some enthusiasts have made of his slogan for *their* agenda, Ebeling's title did not propose a clear definition of church history in identity terms. The English translation in the volume of his essays: "Church History *Is* the History of the Exposition of Holy Scripture," if it is not a typographical error, is a mistranslation of the German: "Kirchengeschichte *als* Geschichte der Auslegung der Heiligen Schrift."[10] Hauschild suggests that rather than being read as the charter of a new discipline or a program for church history writing, Ebeling's definition should be seen as the "interpretive horizon," the *Deutehorizont,* within which church history can be properly understood. Not a developmental history of exposition but the continuous event of such interpretation is what Ebeling drew attention to.

If Hauschild is correct, then Ebeling's start, despite all the interest in a theological foundation, may well have been the *history* side of church history. History was the basic given, the proper subject matter to be understood; history in its widest sense as the sum of the humanly experienced past, yet in a historical perspective. And Ebeling's proposal may then have been to approach this vast realm of the given with the ordering question of the manifold encounter with the Bible, a historical phenomenon itself; an encounter which is undeniable for most of Western history and can serve as the basic principle of selection. Church history as the history of the exposition of Scripture would then not start with a concept of the *church,* however defined theologically or sociologically, a church whose story could be traced just under the aspect of its carrying the biblical message. Nor would it start with the *Bible,* either as the seed for the story of a growth process or as a supra-historical norm dividing history at any given cross section into legitimate and illegitimate events. Church history would have to start with history in its widest possible sense. We remember the charge by critics that Ebeling cast the net too wide, that the limits of a manageable discipline were blurred. But this is precisely the point: *Anything* in Western culture could be the start for church historical concern. The limit is set solely by the direct or indirect

9. "Kirchengeschichte," 411.
10. See n. 4 above.

encounter with the historical Scriptures, presupposed or suspected in a specific case. The revolutionary aspect of Ebeling's thesis was that it drew attention to an interpretive horizon in Western history which historians so far had no use for: the immense power of biblical language (understood or misunderstood) that not only shapes now but has shaped a great deal of human life and action in a decisive manner.

It is my opinion that such an approach does hold considerable historiographic potential. It may not lead (except marginally) to diachronic histories of the exegesis of particular passages by themselves, nor to a history of hermeneutics, but, using partial results of both, it could encourage a style of history writing that would expose this normative power of the biblical language not only as a post-factum reflection or rationalization but also as the historical start for thought and action.

Let me give an example. I think that the early history of Mariology, the devotion to the Virgin Mary, may be written as a history of biblical interpretation. As far as we can tell, there are no early independent sources of information about Mary in second-century Christianity except what we find reflected in the canonical Gospels and writings. Therefore, all of the later tenets of mariological doctrine must be somehow related to the interpretation, under the impact of other historical forces, of the hints to Jesus' mother which we have there. This applies already to the creation of the earliest writing with an independent interest in Mary, the apocryphal *Protoevangelium of James.* From the late second century on, its stories about Mary's childhood and Jesus' birth set the pace for a growing veneration of Mary as well as for specific features of Marian doctrine. But the *Protoevangelium* itself should be understood as a pious reflection upon the slim biblical basis. According to the most recent critical editor and interpreter, the author's method was to enrich the canonical birth stories by a deep and devout imagination nourished everywhere by biblical types and allusions, but not by independent sources. Here we find already the concept of Mary's virginity in giving birth and after birth, both likely to be expansions of the meaning of the title "virgin" in Matt. 1:27 (quoting Isa. 7:14) and Luke 1:32, where it refers to a virginal conception only. To support this particular expansion, Jesus' brothers, who are mentioned in the Gospels, are declared to be the sons of Joseph's former marriage, a standard explanation which (on the basis of a specific interpretation of Luke 1:34) was later replaced by Jerome. It seems easy to trace the late tradition of Mary's house in Ephesus which even affects tourist traffic today to an imaginative combination of Jesus' word on the cross: "Woman, behold your son" (John 19:27) with the assumed Johannine authorship of the Fourth Gospel and the tradition of this John's later residence in Ephesus. After all, John 19:28

says that the disciple took her "into his own." But even the unfavorable details about Mary which Origen quotes from the pagan, Celsus, are traceable, it seems to me, to interpretations of the canonical basis of the *Protoevangelium.* Jesus' illegitimate birth from a soldier named Panthera, while perhaps reflecting early Jewish polemics, in fact interprets the scriptural account of the virgin birth. The portrayal of Mary as a poor peasant girl rests on Celsus's understanding of Nazareth as a small Jewish village, her "spinning for hire" seems to be an unfriendly reading of the skills the *Protoevangelium* attributes to her, just as the emphasis on Mary as a "nobody" may polemicize against the same book's legend of her noble, wealthy, and well-known family background.

To be sure, Mariology is an example from the history of Christian thought and doctrine where the connections to the biblical language can be most easily seen. But it would be equally possible to investigate other historical phenomena from this angle: a movement such as early Franciscanism, a political event such as a medieval tyrannicide, a work of Romanesque art, a group of pieces of early English vernacular literature. As a matter of fact, art historians and literary historians seem to have felt the need to get into church history in the horizon of a history of biblical interpretation long before church historians have been awakening to its potential.

If the history of the exposition of Scripture is suggested as no more than the "interpretive horizon" for church history, it need not be the only historiographic device in the field. Other approaches would remain equally valid and must constantly be tried. All of them are partial and provisional and remind us that it is in the nature of history as a given that it presents its understanding as a never-ending task. Those who expected the Ebeling thesis to provide a universal key expected too much. In fact, they probably misread his argument. What should be clear, however, is that the concrete form of historiography which writes history from the angle of the history of biblical exposition does have a place in historical studies and will therefore have a future in church history, notwithstanding its problems of scope and method and the justified criticism of its results to date.

VI

Our theme was: Church History and the Bible. There was once a time when church history reigned as queen among the theological disciplines. For Harnack, biblical studies were part of church history, and theology was in the category of belles lettres. There was another time when systematic theology wore the crown. For Karl Barth and many of his friends, church history was an auxiliary science, and exegesis appeared in small print in the *Church Dogmatics*.

There was still another time when biblical studies seemed to be queen. Bultmann saw theology as part of the hermeneutical task of interpreting the Bible, and critical history was the tool. Who will be next? Which queen will be elected? Let us face it. Ours is no time for royalty. There will no longer be queens. As in so many other branches of knowledge, all parts of the theological enterprise have become so interlocked, so interdependent, that the lines are drawn mainly for the division of labor. Despite the stubbornness of our structures, we have no other choice but to cross lines, to become "dialogical" in our professional work. Other disciplines in the theological community may already be far advanced in the experience of this mode of existence. Church history still has a long way to go in order to be truly itself in this dialogical situation. We spoke of the dilemma of the church historian. On the one hand, there is the constant temptation of inner emigration which often hampers the dialogue with his theological peers. On the other hand, there is the commitment to a "sectarian" stance in the eyes of the other historical disciplines which leaves him as somewhat of a stranger in the dialogue with them.

I think that on this long way the Ebeling thesis can assume a significant role. It seems to have the advantage of focusing the discipline's attention on a central point. Within the theological disciplines all dialogue has an open or hidden point of reference, the dialogue with the Bible as the primary "document" of the Christian faith. To say this is no endorsement of a hierarchical curricular sequence of "Bible and Church History." Rather, church history has as much to do with the Bible as systematic or practical theology and as the academic discipline of biblical studies. To see church history in the interpretive horizon of the history of the exposition of Scripture seems a proper answer to the challenge of this situation. But as an interpretive horizon it also provides the distinctly historical basis for the dialogue with the other historical sciences. I regard doing church history in this way as a singular opportunity for the field in which I have chosen to teach to find its valid place as a historical science among the theological disciplines, but also to contribute in the ongoing dialogue with the historical disciplines outside the seminary something of the very essence of my and of any theological discipline.

I. EARLY CHRISTIAN EXEGESIS

1. The Text of Mark in the Hands of the Orthodox

Bart D. Ehrman

The history of biblical interpretation cannot be understood as a field of investigation sui generis. For since it has as its subject matter literary texts, it is in fact a subfield of literary criticism. Developments within this wider discipline can naturally be expected to have some relevance to the history of scriptural exegesis. Furthermore, the texts studied by this particular subdiscipline are themselves uncertain: while we have literally thousands of biblical manuscripts (MSS), none of them is an autograph and all of them contain mistakes. This means, among other things, that the texts of the biblical books have to be reconstructed prior to exegesis, and, more significantly for our purposes here, that anyone interested in knowing how these books have been interpreted through the ages must know something about the forms of text prevalent in various times and places. This study will explore some of the ways these fields of literary criticism, textual criticism, and the history of interpretation — fields which on the surface may appear quite disparate — relate rather closely to one another.

I. Literary Criticism and the History of Interpretation

There have always been scholars who have studied the history of interpretation for narrowly exegetical reasons, viz., to assist in the determination of the "original meaning" of a text — whatever the term "original," and even more problematic, the term "meaning," might be understood to signify. Others of us, however, see these historical data as more than handmaidens of exegesis. For the history of interpretation is equally significant in providing insights into the act of interpretation itself, i.e., by showing us what actually has happened and does happen when texts are read and construed.

Of the numerous developments within the broader field of literary criticism, one of the most fruitful for approaching this matter of the history of biblical interpretation is reader response criticism.[1] For unlike some of its predecessors in the field — one naturally thinks of new criticism and structuralism — reader response criticism is not narrowly concerned with the text per se, i.e., with a document as some kind of "objective" entity from which meanings can be culled like so many grapes from a vine. It is instead interested in the process of interpretation. For its more radical representatives, such as Stanley Fish, meaning does not at all inhere in a text, because texts in themselves simply do not mean anything. Meaning is something that results from reading the text; it is an event that occurs when the reader constructs an understanding from the linear arrangement of words on the page.[2]

This view represents a direct and conscientious challenge to one of the founding principles of the so-called new criticism, as laid out by W. K. Wimsatt and M. Beardsley some forty years ago in their seminal essay, "The Affective Fallacy."[3] Wimsatt and Beardsley insisted that a text's meaning is independent of its effect, psychological or otherwise, on the reader; to tie a text's meaning to its effect is to commit the affective fallacy. For them, meaning resides within the text, and it is the task of the critic to discover that meaning by applying objective interpretive criteria in the process of analysis.

Reader response critics object to this "myth of objectivity," and argue to the contrary that meaning does not exist independently of readers who

1. Two recent anthologies can serve as a nice entrée into this field: Susan R. Suleiman and Inge Crosman, eds., *The Reader in the Text: Essays on Audience and Interpretation* (Princeton: Princeton University Press, 1980); and Jane Thompkins, ed., *Reader-Response Criticism: From Formalism to Post-Structuralism* (Baltimore: Johns Hopkins University Press, 1980).

2. See his two recent collections of essays, *Is There a Text in this Class? The Authority of Interpretive Communities* (Cambridge, MA: Harvard University Press, 1980); and *Doing What Comes Naturally: Change, Rhetoric, and the Practice of Theory in Literary and Legal Studies* (Durham, NC: Duke University Press, 1989).

3. "The Affective Fallacy," 1949; reprinted in Wimsatt, *The Verbal Icon: Studies in the Meaning of Poetry* (Lexington: University of Kentucky Press, 1954), 21-39. The other guiding principle of the new criticism was the "intentional fallacy." The new critics maintained that it was a fallacy to ask what an author intended his or her work to mean, both because such knowledge is generally unattainable and because texts take on a life of their own once they are written, so that they can mean something quite different from what an author might have intended.

construe texts. For them, the words of a text do not in themselves determine the text's meaning. This is shown by the fact that the same words can mean radically different things in different contexts, and by the related fact that readers with different assumptions typically assign different meanings to the same text. Even the same reader will frequently understand a text differently at different times. Thus, for reader response critics, every time a text is read its meaning is construed; every time it is reread it is reconstrued, and reconstrued more or less differently. In this sense, reading — the process of construing a text — differs not substantially from writing, so that every time we read a text, whether we know it or not, we re-create or rewrite the text.

One does not have to agree wholeheartedly with Stanley Fish and his devotees to see something useful in this understanding of readers and texts. For in some measure it represents a development of the conventional wisdom that there is no such thing as exegesis without presuppositions, and that one's presuppositions — indeed, all of one's dispositions, ideologies, and convictions, not only about the text but about life and meaning itself — cannot possibly be discarded, removed like so much excessive clothing, when coming to a text. The reader-response view goes beyond this exegetical commonplace in asserting that there is in fact no such thing as an "objective" text to which a reader brings his or her "subjective" predispositions: texts do not exist apart from those who read them, and meanings cannot be located anywhere outside those who bring them to the texts.[4]

The significance of these views for the history of biblical interpretation should be rather self-evident. In studying how the text of the Bible has been interpreted over the ages, we see how the process of constructing meaning has taken place among different readers in different contexts. And we ourselves can then reconstruct the hermeneutical process that has been at work, i.e., we can see how pre-understandings have shaped texts in such a way as to produce their meanings. What is not as self-evident is how these two fields relate to the third, New Testament textual criticism, and more specifically, to the study of the transmission of the texts of the New Testament.

4. See esp. Stanley Fish, "Normal Circumstances and Other Special Cases," "Is There a Text in this Class?," "How to Recognize a Poem When You See One," "What Makes an Interpretation Acceptable?," and "Demonstration vs. Persuasion: Two Models of Critical Activity," all in *Is There a Text in this Class?*

II. Literary Criticism, Textual Criticism, and the History of Interpretation

If it is true that everyone who reads a text will understand it somewhat differently, i.e., that every rereading of a text is a re-creation of the text, or a rewriting of the text, then in textual criticism we have abundant evidence of precisely this phenomenon at our fingertips, although we have scarcely recognized it for what it is. All of us interpret our texts and ascribe meaning to them, and in that sense we "rewrite" them. The scribes, somewhat more literally, actually did rewrite them. And not infrequently it was precisely their understanding of their texts that led them to rewrite them — not only in their own minds, which all of us do, but actually on the page. When we rewrite a text in our mind so as to construe its meaning, we interpret the text; when scribes rewrite a text on the page so as to help fix its meaning, they modify the text. On the one hand, then, this scribal activity is very much like what all of us do every time we read a text; on the other hand, in taking this business of rewriting a text to its logical end, scribes have done something very different from what we do. For from the standpoint of posterity, they have unalterably changed the text, so that the text that is henceforth read is quite literally a different text. It is only from this historical perspective that one can apply the standard text-critical nomenclature to this scribal activity and call it the "corruption" of a text.[5]

The deliberate modification of the New Testament text is a widely attested phenomenon. It occurs, of course, in a somewhat innocuous way whenever a scribe tries to make sense of the grammar of a text that otherwise appears incorrect or needlessly obscure. But it also occurs when a scribe changes a text in order to make what it says coincide more closely with what, in the scribe's view, it has to mean. The Gospel of Mark provides an interesting testing ground for the thesis that the pre-understandings of scribes — their "theology" — led them to read the text in certain ways and that their reading of the text led them to rewrite the text, or to use the text-critical term, to corrupt the text, at significant points. For unlike the other Gospels, Mark begins with Jesus' baptism as an adult. It does not mention his birth, let alone a virgin birth, or anything about his preexistence. Furthermore, the Gospel does not conclude with accounts of the bodily appearances of the resurrected Jesus, but only with the proclamation that Jesus has been raised. Given this beginning and this ending one can well imagine how Mark's story could be

5. The terms "corrupt" and "corruption," while problematic for the reasons I discuss here, are the standard designations used by biblical scholars and classicists to refer to the accidental or intentional modification of a literary text.

variously read by Christians of the early church, especially before orthodoxy finally established a normative reading. As far back as our earliest records we find Christians who claimed that Jesus was adopted to be the Son of God at his baptism, that his anointing by the Spirit at his baptism was the Christological moment par excellence.[6] Mark's narrative does little to discourage such a view. And we know of other Christians, at least by the mid-second century, who maintained that Jesus and the Christ were two different entities, that at his baptism the man Jesus received the heavenly Christ, who indwelt Jesus and empowered him for his ministry, before leaving him at some time prior to his death on the cross.[7] Irenaeus specifically tells us that some such persons used Mark's Gospel to the exclusion of all the others (*Adv. haer.* 3.11.7).

As is well known, Christians of the orthodox persuasion recognized and denounced these adoptionistic and Gnostic Christologies.[8] And, as we shall see, it was precisely this orthodox opposition to heretical readings of Mark that led to some of the textual corruptions still evident in the manu-

6. This is the view of the so-called Dynamic Monarchianists of the 2d and 3d centuries, including Theodotus the Cobbler, his disciple Theodotus the Banker, and Artemon. For these, Adolf von Harnack's treatment is still quite useful (*Dogmengeschichte;* ET, *History of Dogma,* 7 vols. in 4, trans. Neil Buchanan [New York: Dover, 1961], 3:1-50). A similar view was espoused earlier by the Ebionites, a Jewish-Christian sect. On these, see esp. A. F. J. Klijn and G. J. Reinink, *Patristic Evidence for Jewish-Christian Sects* (Leiden: Brill, 1973). Whether this view was intended by the author of Mark is difficult to say. It is striking, however, that both Matthew and Luke have gone to some lengths to eliminate the possibility by recording narratives of Jesus' virgin birth, narratives typically rejected by adoptionists. This makes it all the more interesting that in a significant portion of the textual tradition of Luke's account of Jesus' baptism (i.e., in the Western text), the voice from heaven quotes the words of Ps. 2 that proved so amenable to an adoptionistic construal: "You are my son, today [!] I have begotten you."

7. This is a typically Gnostic view, about which we have always known, e.g., from reports of the early heresiologists (see, e.g., Irenaeus *Adv. haer.* 1.7.2; 21.2; 25.1; 26.1; and 3.16.8). Now we have independent access to these notions in the writings of the Gnostic library discovered near Nag Hammadi in Egypt in 1946. See, e.g., the *Second Treatise of the Great Seth,* in *The Nag Hammadi Library in English,* ed. James M. Robinson (San Francisco: Harper & Row, 1978), 329-38.

8. The term "orthodoxy" is anachronistic for the ante-Nicean age, but is used here simply to designate the theological views espoused by Christians who were later claimed as forebears by the orthodox party of the 4th and following centuries. In the 2d and 3d centuries, such "orthodox" Christians did not at all constitute a monolithic group with a unified theology; but they did evidence certain clear tendencies and theological predilections. Prominent among the theological views they rejected, e.g., were Christologies that were perceived to be docetic (Christ was God, and only "appeared" to be a human), adoptionistic (Christ was a flesh-and-blood human being who was only "adopted" by God to be his Son, usually at the baptism), or Gnostic (Christ is the heavenly being who descended upon the man Jesus, usually at his baptism, and who left him sometime prior to his death).

script tradition of this Gospel. It is striking that several of the most intriguing occur exactly where one might expect, at the beginning and near the end of the narrative.

Mark 15:34

One of the most interesting variant readings in Mark's Gospel occurs at a climactic point of the story, in Jesus' cry of dereliction from the cross (15:34). The reading of several Western witnesses has attracted considerable attention, especially since Adolf von Harnack championed it as original.[9] In these MSS, rather than crying out "My God, my God, why have you forsaken me?" the dying Jesus cries, "My God, my God, why have you reviled me?" The change makes some sense in the context, for as Harnack notes, everyone else — Jewish leaders, Roman soldiers, passersby, and even the two crucified robbers — has reviled or mocked Jesus. And now the scene ends with Jesus bearing the reproach of God himself for the sins of the world. Nonetheless, the overwhelming external support for the more common reading has led nearly all critics since Harnack to reject the Western variant as a corruption. It would probably be a mistake, however, to construe the change as a simple attempt to provide a consistent motif throughout the context. For the earlier form of the text, εἰς τί ἐγκατέλιπές με, normally translated "why have you forsaken me," could readily be construed in spatial terms: "why have you deserted me," or "why have you left me behind," a reading not at all unrelated to the Gnostic view that the man Jesus died alone after the divine Christ had left him in order to return into the Pleroma. Interestingly, the tradition of Jesus' last words was construed precisely in this way by the apocryphal Gospel of Peter, in which the dying Jesus cries out, "My power, Oh power, you have left me!" (Gos. Pet. 19). In addition, Irenaeus claims that certain Gnostics used Mark 15:34 to portray Sophia's irretrievable separation from the Pleroma (*Adv. haer.* 1.8.2). Orthodox scribes seem to have recognized the real possibility of a Gnostic reading of the text, and consequently changed it in line with their own reading by providing a paraphrastic rendering of the Hebrew of Ps. 22. The change was a real tour de force: it successfully maintained the allusion to the Psalm, while conforming the cry to the events ad loc and circumventing the possibility of a Gnostic misconstrual.

9. "Probleme im Texte der Leidengeschichte Jesu," in *Studien zur Geschichte des Neuen Testaments und der alten Kirche,* vol. 1, *Zur neutestamentlichen Textkritik* (Berlin: de Gruyter, 1931), 86-104.

Mark 1:10

A similar kind of change occurs at the very outset of Mark's narrative. According to codices Vaticanus and Bezae, along with several other important witnesses, when the Spirit descends upon Jesus at his baptism in 1:10, it comes as a dove εἰς αὐτόν, "unto" or "to" him. But the preposition εἰς, of course, can also mean "into" him, which naturally coincides rather well with the Gnostic notion that the Christ came into Jesus at his baptism. Both Matthew and Luke give the preposition as ἐπί in their accounts, providing subsequent scribes just the grounds they needed to accommodate Mark's text to its Synoptic counterparts. But it would be a mistake to see this as a thoughtless harmonization when a historical explanation is ready to hand: without the change the Gnostics who were maligned by Irenaeus would indeed have had a convenient prooftext for their own reading of the Gospel accounts, a reading that asserts that the heavenly Christ came into Jesus in the form of a dove at his baptism.

Mark 1:3

Other variant readings serve to counter not the Gnostic but the adoptionistic reading of Mark's Gospel, i.e., the view that Jesus became God's Son only at his baptism. Scribes could circumvent this reading of Mark by making a variety of changes in the text. For example, any variant reading which affirms that Jesus himself was God would counter such a view, as would any reading suggesting that Jesus was already God's son prior to his baptism. Interestingly, both kinds of orthodox corruption occur within the first three verses of the Gospel.

When Mark put the words of Isa. 40:3 on the lips of the Baptist, he, or his source, somewhat modified the LXX text with an interesting Christological result.[10] Whereas the LXX had said "Prepare the way of the Lord, make straight the paths *of our God,*" Mark's modification serves to identify more closely who "the Lord" is: "Prepare the way of the Lord, make *his* paths straight." John is portrayed here as the forerunner of Jesus, who is understood in this Gospel to be the κύριος. But strikingly — and here Mark stands in good company with other early Christian writers — Jesus is not called God, either here or anywhere else throughout the narrative.

Later scribes, however, saw both the opportunity and the importance of reading Jesus' divinity in this text. The opportunity was provided by the

10. See the discussion of Erich Fascher, *Textgeschichte als hermeneutisches Problem* (Halle: Max Niemeyer, 1953), 17.

LXX, the importance by the controversy over Jesus' divine status. And so the change represented by Codex Bezae and the early Latin witnesses is not merely a Septuagintalism: it is a theological statement that Jesus, even prior to his baptism, can rightly be called divine. "Prepare the way of the Lord [i.e., Jesus], make straight the paths of our God."

Mark 1:1

One of the most frequently debated texts of the second Gospel occurs in its opening verse, which serves as something of a title over the whole. Given the importance of the textual issue, and its particular relevance to our problem, we would do well to consider this passage at somewhat greater length. The vast majority of MSS read: "The Beginning of the Gospel of Jesus Christ, the Son of God." But the final phrase, "the Son of God," is lacking in several important witnesses, including codices Sinaiticus and Koridethi, MSS 28ᶜ and 1555, the Palestinian Syriac, Armenian, and Georgian versions, and Origen. In terms of numbers the support for this shorter text is slight. But in terms of antiquity and character, this is not a confluence of witnesses to be trifled with. It frequently is trifled with, however, and here is where one finds no little confusion in earlier discussions of the problem. Thus one scholar discounts the evidence as deriving entirely from Caesarea, and as therefore representing merely a local corruption — even though the supporting witnesses include the early Alexandrian Codex Sinaiticus and the part of Origen's Commentary on John written in Alexandria.[11] Another scholar maintains that since Sinaiticus has some affinities with the so-called Western textual tradition (he must have in mind the opening chapters of John, which have no relevance to the issue here), it is to be grouped with the Western text, so that we have only secondary Western and Caesarean support for the reading.[12] Other scholars argue that since Origen and Sinaiticus are otherwise so similar, their support must be counted as one witness instead of two, a solitary Alexandrian witness not to be given much weight.[13] In point of fact, we have two of the three best Alexandrian

11. Jan Slomp, "Are the Words 'Son of God' in Mark 1:1 Original?" *BT* 28 (1977): 143-50.

12. Alexander Globe, "The Caesarean Omission of the Phrase 'Son of God' in Mark 1:1," *HTR* 75 (1982): 209-18.

13. Thus C. H. Turner, "A Textual Commentary on Mark 1," *JTS* 28 (1926-27): 150, followed, e.g., by William Lane, *The Gospel According to Mark,* NICNT (Grand Rapids: Eerdmans, 1974); and Wolfgang Feneberg, *Der Markusprolog: Studien zur Formbestimmung des Evangeliums* (Munich: Kosel, 1974), 151-52.

witnesses supporting this text. Furthermore, Origen quotes it in this form not only in Alexandria but also in the *Contra Celsum,* which he wrote in Caesarea.[14] He may, of course, simply have remembered or used his Alexandrian MSS after his move, but it is to be noted that the reading also occurs in other so-called Caesarean texts, including its best representative, Codex Koridethi, and the Palestinian, Armenian, and Georgian versions. Furthermore, the reading is found in a later witness that otherwise attests an essentially Western text (1555).[15]

This slate of witnesses is early and diverse in terms of both textual character and geography. It is this that poses the greatest difficulty for the normal explanation of the problem. Most commonly it is explained that the shorter reading was created by accident: because the words Χριστοῦ and θεοῦ end in the same letters (-ου), a scribe's eye accidentally skipped from one to the other, leading him inadvertently to leave out the intervening phrase.[16] But the view short-circuits on several grounds. It is made somewhat unlikely by the occurrence of the shorter reading in a range of textual witnesses that are early, widespread, and unrelated.[17] This means that the omission would have had to have been made independently by several scribes, in precisely the same way.[18] The view is made even more difficult by the circumstance that the same error, so far as our

14. *Comm. on John* 1.13 and 6.24; *Contra Celsum* 2.4.

15. Thus Globe, "Caesarean Omission," 216.

16. The technical terminology for this kind of error is that it occurred because of parablepsis (an "eye-skip") occasioned by homoeoteleuton (words "ending in the same way"). It is sometimes argued that this kind of mistake is particularly likely here, because the words Ἰησοῦ Χριστοῦ υἱοῦ θεοῦ would have been abbreviated as *nomina sacra,* making the accidental skip of the eye from the word Χριστοῦ to the following θεοῦ more than understandable. See, however, n. 19 below. This explanation is given, e.g., by Feneberg, *Der Markusprolog;* Turner, "A Textual Commentary"; Joachim Gnilka, *Das Evangelium nach Markus,* vol. 1 (Zürich: Benziger, 1978); Carl Kazmierski, *Jesus the Son of God: A Study of the Markan Tradition and Its Redaction by the Evangelist* (Wurzburg: Echter, 1979); and Vincent Taylor, *The Gospel According to St. Mark* (London: Macmillan, 1953).

17. "Unrelated" in this context means that several of the witnesses belong to different textual families, so that the textual variants they have in common cannot be attributed simply to a corrupt exemplar that they all used. The precise agreement of otherwise unrelated MSS therefore indicates the antiquity of a variant reading.

18. The same can be said of the other reading as well, of course: a substantial addition to a text can never be purely accidental, and this variant likewise boasts early and widespread attestation. But this means that whoever made the change, whichever change was made, must have made it intentionally. Once that is conceded then the issue becomes, which of these two readings is better explained as a conscientious alteration? And here, as we will argue, there can be little doubt that the longer reading, which happens both to coincide with Mark's account otherwise and to help circumvent a heretical construal of that account, is the more likely corruption.

evidence suggests, was not made by later scribes of the Byzantine tradition, many of whom are not known for their overly scrupulous habits of transcription.[19]

Finally, and this is a consideration that to my knowledge no one has brought forth, it should strike us as somewhat odd that this kind of careless mistake, the omission of two rather important words, should have happened precisely where it does — within the first six words of the beginning of a book. It is certainly not too difficult to see how such carelessness might otherwise occur; indeed, its occurrence is virtually ubiquitous throughout the tradition. Copying texts was a long and arduous process, and fatigue could lead to carelessness and as a result to a host of readings that prove to be utterly nonsensical. But here is a reading that occurs at the outset of a text, independently attested in a number of witnesses, that makes perfectly good sense. This raises an interesting question: *Is* it less likely that a scribe — or rather that a number of scribes — would make this kind of careless error at the beginning of a book rather than in the middle? It is a difficult question to answer, since we know so little about the mechanics of how scribes actually operated, especially in the early centuries.[20] But it seems at least antecedently probable that a scribe would begin his work on Mark's Gospel only after having made a clean break, say, with Matthew, and that he would plunge into his work with renewed strength and vigor. So that this does not appear simply to be the romantic ramblings of a twentieth-century critic, it should be pointed out that the scribes of our two earliest MSS attesting the omission, Sinaiticus and Koridethi, have in fact gone to some lengths to decorate the end of the previous work on Matthew and to note afresh the beginning of the new work at hand.

For all these reasons, it appears that the textual problem of Mark 1:1 was not created by accident: whether the phrase "Son of God" was added to a text that originally lacked it or deleted from a text that originally had it, the change was apparently made intentionally.

This in itself makes it more likely that the earliest form of Mark's Gospel lacked the phrase. For one can understand why a scribe who did not read the phrase in the book's opening verse might want to add it —

19. Yet more curiously, the words Ἰησοῦ Χριστοῦ, which have the same potential for omission as *nomina sacra* ending in *omicron-upsilon,* are not omitted in the tradition, either individually or as a phrase, except in the first hand of 28, which has been corrected.

20. On this issue, see E. C. Colwell, "Method in Evaluating Scribal Habits: A Study of p^{45}, p^{66}, p^{75}," in *Studies in Methodology in Textual Criticism of the New Testament,* NTTS 9 (Leiden: Brill, 1969), 106-24; and James A. Royse, "Scribal Habits in the Transmission of New Testament Texts," in *The Critical Study of Sacred Texts,* ed. Wendy D. O'Flaherty, Berkeley Religious Studies Series, 2 (Berkeley, CA: Graduate Theological Union, 1979), 139-61.

and indeed, as we shall see, there may have been more than one reason to do so. But it is very difficult to see why scribes who read the longer phrase might deliberately seek to shorten it.

A number of scholars have insisted, nonetheless, that the longer text (i.e., including the phrase "Son of God") must have been original, because it coincides so well with Mark's Christology otherwise. This is an interesting claim, since it assumes that if a scribe were to change the text of Mark, he would do so in a way that stands at odds with the rest of Mark's account. Needless to say, this assumption is not at all necessary: the way scribes understood Mark's Gospel in antiquity naturally coincides at a number of points with the way it is commonly construed today. Thus even if the variant reading does evince Mark's understanding of Jesus, it still may not be original.

Other scholars have claimed that since Mark ends his story of Jesus, for all practical purposes, with the centurion's proclamation that Jesus is the Son of God (15:39), that he likely would have begun the Gospel on the same note in 1:1. This also is not persuasive, because the opening bracket for which 15:39 provides the closing is not 1:1 but 1:10, where, as in 15:38-39, there is a "ripping" (σχίζομαι, only in these two verses in Mark: of the heavens and of the temple veil), a "voice" (from heaven, from the centurion), and the affirmation of Jesus' divine sonship (by God, by a Gentile).[21]

Thus while most interpreters agree on the importance of the phrase

21. It could be pointed out in reply, however, that 1:1 and 15:39 are the only occurrences of υἱοῦ θεοῦ in Mark without the use of the article. This is of course true, but it scarcely counts as evidence for the longer reading in 1:1. On the one hand, it is somewhat difficult to conceive of an author indicating an *inclusio* simply by omitting an article at two points of his narrative, as opposed say to structuring two entire scenes around parallel motifs (such as in 1:9-11 and 15:38-39). And there may in fact have been other reasons for the phrase to be left anarthrous in both places. If it was not original in 1:1, a scribe who wanted to add it would no doubt have sought to make the insertion as unobtrusive as possible, and could have accomplished his goal simply by adding the four letters YYΘY. It is to be noted that the name Ἰησοῦ Χριστοῦ which immediately precedes is anarthrous as well. With respect to the occurrence in 15:39, it may be of some significance that this is the only time in the Gospel that a pagan calls Jesus "Son of God," and it may well be that the author left the phrase anarthrous to effect a nice ambiguity: it is not altogether clear whether the centurion is proclaiming Jesus to be "the Son of the only true God" (as it is normally taken), or a "Divine Man," i.e., one of the sons of the gods. Furthermore, it should be noted that if an *inclusio* is formed by 1:1 and 15:39 it would be somewhat out of joint, since it begins at the very beginning of the story but concludes before its very end — before this Son of God has been raised! If on the other hand the *inclusio* is formed by 1:11 and 15:39, it brackets Jesus' public life with proclamations of his divine sonship, first by God at his baptism, after the ripping of the heavens, then by the Gospel's first real convert, the Gentile centurion, at Jesus' execution after the ripping of the temple veil.

"Son of God" to Mark's narrative otherwise, this in itself provides no evidence for the text of 1:1. To the contrary, the centrality of the phrase actually highlights the hermeneutical problem confronted by early interpreters of the narrative. For Mark does not indicate explicitly what he means by calling Jesus the "Son of God," nor does he indicate when this status was conferred upon him. This makes the interpretation of his Christology a somewhat precarious matter, as even the most recent investigations provide ample witness.[22] In the early church, this Gospel could be read by adoptionists who believed that it was at his baptism that Jesus became the Son of God, as well as by the orthodox, who believed that Jesus had always been the Son.

Since the textual situation in Mark 1:1 appears not to have been created by sheer accident, and since the longer text appears in relatively early, unrelated, and widespread witnesses, we can now draw a tentative conclusion concerning the status of the text. Scribes would have had little reason to delete the phrase "the Son of God" from Mark 1:1, but they would have had reasons to add it. Just as was the case in the other variant readings we have considered (Mark 1:3; 1:10; and 15:34), it may well have been precisely the orthodox construal of Mark's Gospel that led to the corruption of 1:1. Mark entitled his Gospel "The Gospel of Jesus Christ" (RSV), and proceeded to narrate that first significant event of Jesus' life, his baptism and the accompanying revelatory experience. In order to circumvent an adoptionistic reading of this inaugurating event, early orthodox Christian scribes made a slight modification of Mark's text so that it affirmed Jesus' status as the Son of God prior to his baptism, even prior to the mention of John the Baptist, his forerunner. Now even before he

22. The issues pertaining to Mark's messianic secret have proved thorny since Wilhelm Wrede's *Das Messiasgeheimnis in den Evangelien* was first published in 1901 (ET *The Messianic Secret,* trans. J. C. G. Grieg [London: T. & T. Clark, 1981]). See James L. Blevins, *The Messianic Secret in Markan Research, 1901-1976* (Washington: University Press of America, 1981); and the essays collected in *The Messianic Secret,* ed. C. Tuckett (Philadelphia: Fortress, 1983). Furthermore, for nearly two decades many scholars have seen in Mark a kind of "corrective" Christology, i.e., a conscientious attempt to rectify a flawed understanding of Jesus found otherwise in the Markan community, and probably represented in Mark's own Gospel sources. According to this view, these sources, which no longer survive, provided a glorified portrayal of Jesus as a Hellenistic divine man ("son of god") whose powers were evident particularly in his miracles and whose Passion was of little or no salvific significance. Mark then was written to oppose such a view by stressing the Christological importance of Jesus' death. This view, popularized by Theodore Weeden, *Mark: Traditions in Conflict* (Philadelphia: Fortress, 1971), has been challenged in more recent research. See, e.g., the balanced statement of Jack Kingsbury, *The Christology of Mark's Gospel* (Philadelphia: Fortress, 1983). For a more general account, see Frank Matera, *What Are They Saying About Mark?* (New York: Paulist, 1987).

comes forward to be baptized, Jesus is understood by the reader to be the Christ, the Son of God.

III. Conclusion

The various changes we have examined in the MS tradition of Mark's Gospel evidence the orthodox tendency to read all four canonical Gospels in the light of each other and in the light of orthodox theological views. They thus represent milestones on the road to a complete orthodox harmonization of the Gospels, a harmonization in which the Jesus who hears of his divine sonship at his baptism (in Mark) comes to be identified with the Jesus who is the Son of God by virtue of his virginal conception (in Luke), who is in turn identified with the Son of God in the bosom of the Father who has seen God from eternity past and now has made him known (in John).

This kind of scribal corruption, however, is not at all unlike what all readers do whenever they construe the meaning of their texts. To the contrary, as the reader response critics have argued, no one can give an "innocent" or "objective" reading of a text, because texts are never read in isolation but always in interpretive contexts, and the contexts within which interpreters live determine the meanings of the texts that they read. In this sense, the meanings readers derive from their texts are in fact responses determined by what they bring to these texts. This was no less true of scribes in antiquity than it is for exegetes today. Similar to the way we all "re-create" or "rewrite" texts whenever we construe them, the scribes, who reproduced their texts conscientiously by hand rather than mechanically by machine, actually did re-create them, so that their orthodox construals, their orthodox corruptions, actually determined the way these texts have been transmitted to us, their future readers.

2. *The Use of Stoic Cosmogony in Theophilus of Antioch's* Hexaemeron

Kathleen E. McVey

The Christian *hexaemera,* interpretations of the biblical "Six Days of Creation," often in the light of a philosophical or scientific framework, comprise an intriguing body of literature that stretches in an unbroken line from antiquity through the medieval period, and the line continues even into the present. The authors of these works range from Philo Judaeus, Basil of Caesarea, Ambrose, and Augustine to Milton and Cotton Mather.[1] Even the more recent Christian response to the Darwinian theory may be seen as a form of hexaemeral literature.[2]

Theophilus's apology *Ad Autolycum* (later 2d century C.E.) contains the first extant Christian use of the word *hexaemeron,*[3] and it is also the

1. See F. E. Robbins, "The Hexaemeral Literature: A Study of the Greek and Latin Commentaries on Genesis" (diss., University of Chicago, 1912), 1; Winton U. Solberg, "Science and Religion in Early America: Cotton Mather's *Christian Philosopher,*" *ChH* 56 (1987): 73-92.

2. Both situating the "creationists" in historical and literary context and disputing their claim to represent the only theologically authentic Christian position are two articles by R. M. Frye, "So-Called 'Creation-Science' and Mainstream Christian Rejections," *PAPS* 127 (1983): 61-70; and "The Religious Case against Creation-Science," in *Is God a Creationist? The Religious Case against Creation-Science,* ed. R. M. Frye (New York, 1983), 1-29.

3. *Ad Autolycum* 2.12. Reference will be made to Grant's text (Theophilus of Antioch, *Ad Autolycum,* ed. and trans. Robert M. Grant, Oxford Early Christian Texts [Oxford: Clarendon, 1970], henceforth cited as *Autolycum*) and usually to his translation, except when

It is a happy privilege to contribute to this volume in honor of Karlfried Froehlich, my dedicated colleague, generous mentor, and dear friend. To him, as well as to J. Christiaan Beker, P. Corby Finney, and Robert Grant, I am indebted for encouragement and for bibliographic and other suggestions for improvement on earlier drafts of this paper.

oldest example of a Christian *hexaemeron* which survives in full.[4] Study of this work will provide insights into the origin and nature of hexaemeral literature.[5] These insights may then be tested by comparison with contemporaneous works surviving only in fragments to establish a firm foundation for understanding later developments, especially insofar as they draw upon or react against Theophilus. His presuppositions and intentions, however, are not easily discerned. Like other early Christian apologists he constructs polemical characterizations of philosophical views based on doxographies; his arguments depend on such a wide variety of philosophical positions that he has been repeatedly accused of lacking any notion of consistency — philosophical or otherwise.[6] Nevertheless, many precise parallels to Stoic ideas are evident in his thought; for example, a strong and consistent emphasis on the role of providence,[7] an anthropocentric view of the world,[8] the two-stage logos,[9] and the cosmic conflagration.[10]

Still, those who have sought to show coherence in Theophilus have

---

a change in translation seems appropriate to make a point more clearly. Philo had already used the term ἑξαημέρον and perhaps invented it; cf. Monique Alexandre, *Le Commencement du Livre Genèse I–V: La version grecque de la Septente et sa réception,* Christianisme Antique 3 (Paris: Beauchesne, 1988), 47; for three senses of the word, ibid., 215-16.

4. For discussion of other Christian writers from the first two centuries, fragments of whose discussions of the *hexaemeron* survive or to whom other early writers allude as having composed such works, cf. Alexis Smets and Michel van Esbroeck, Basile de Césarée, *Sur l'origine de l'homme,* SC 160 (Paris: Cerf, 1970), 94-96; and Arthur Droge, *Homer or Moses? Early Christian Interpretations of the History of Culture,* Hermeneutische Untersuchungen zur Theologie 26 (Tübingen: Mohr, 1989), 102.

5. The most important recent contribution to the task of understanding this literature as a whole is the work of Alexandre, *Commencement.*

6. For example, Johannes Geffcken remarked, "Er hat keine einzige selbständige Idee" (*Zwei griechisches Apologeten* [Leipzig, 1907], 250). More damning, since he seems to want to give Theophilus the benefit of the doubt, are Gustave Bardy's observations in *Théophile d'Antioche: Trois Livres à Autolycus,* trans. J. Sender, SC 20 (Paris: Cerf, 1949), 10-32, esp. 22: "Il n'a pas la moindre idée de la philosophie," and 32: "Théophile n'est pas le moins du monde un penseur original et nous nous en rendrons compte mieux encore que nous ne l'avons fait jusqu'à présent en étudiant sa position à l'égard des grands problèmes de la foi, de Dieu, de l'homme." More recently, cf. Robert Grant's discussion in *Greek Apologists of the Second Century* (Philadelphia: Westminster, 1988), 148-56.

7. Cf. Michel Spanneut, *Le Stoïcisme des Pères de l'Église de Clément de Rome à Clément d'Alexandrie* (Paris: Seuil, 1957), 325-31; on 93-94 he notes Theophilus's use of "un texte très précis" of Aristo in *Autol.* 3.7. Theophilus's purpose there is to insist on the doctrine of providence despite the persecution of the wise — a particularly poignant issue for a Stoic Christian in a context of persecution. For this theme and its use by the early Greek apologists, cf. Geffcken, *Zwei griechisches Apologeten,* 229-31; further, K. McVey, "A Fresh Look at the Letter of Mara Bar Sarapion to His Son," *Orientalia Christiana Analecta* (forthcoming).

8. Spanneut, *Stoïcisme,* 380-85, esp. 382.

9. R. Grant, "Theophilus of Antioch to Autolycus," *HTR* 40 (1947): esp. 229, 245-49, but overall Theophilus's "first book is an example of confused rationalism" (ibid., 229).

10. Cf. ibid., 252-54.

looked at him mainly in terms other than the philosophical. He has been seen as an anti-heretical writer, addressing himself to Marcionite errors, or as a Jewish-Christian writer close to rabbinic Judaism in his methods and arguments.[11] Some recent studies have taken more seriously the traditional claim of apologetic literature to address a pagan audience. So some have found coherence in his arguments as catechesis, ignoring the question of the philosophical viewpoint of those to be catechized.[12] Vermander has argued that the coherence and competence of his argument, at least his third book, is best appreciated if it is seen as an answer to Celsus.[13] Droge has extended this argument to say that, when seen within the context of Hellenistic historiography, the full value and consistency of Theophilus's arguments become apparent.[14] The general significance of the "argument from antiquity" in the Christian apologists of the second century has long been recognized.[15] Droge has drawn attention to the roots of this argument in the historiography of the Hellenistic period, not only within the context of Hellenistic Judaism but more broadly in the culture of this period. He has argued convincingly that Theophilus's presentation of biblical history is a cultural history, specifically a heurematography — an account of human progress through discovery — in this case, an account in which Hebrews, not Greeks or any others, have led the way.[16]

My argument here is an expansion of Droge's, but the focus is on Theophilus's views on origins of all kinds — of the cosmos, of plant and animal life, of human beings — rather than only on the origins of human culture. First, his apology in its final form emerges as an eclectic form of philosophy dominated by Stoicism,[17] and it is an integral whole within

11. On the former see principally Adolf von Harnack, *Marcion: Das Evangelium vom fremden Gott,* 2d ed., TU 45 (Leipzig: J. C. Hinrichs'sche, 1924); the Eng. trans. by J. E. Steely and L. D. Bierma, *Marcion: The Gospel of the Alien God* (Durham: Labyrinth, 1990), lacks the appendices; also, Grant, *Apologists,* 160. On the latter see Grant, "Theophilus," esp. 237-41; idem, "Jewish Christianity at Antioch in the Second Century," *RSR* 60 (1972): 97-108, esp. 104-8; idem, *Apologists,* esp. 157-60. Yet he sometimes stresses the prior Hellenistic Jewish appropriation of Stoic concepts; cf. Grant, "Theophilus," 243-56.

12. J. Bentivegna, "A Christianity without Christ by Theophilus of Antioch," TU 5.61 (Studia patristica 13) (1975), 107-30; F. Bergamelli, "Il linguaggio simbolico delle immagini nella catechesi missionaria di Teofilo di Antiochia," *Salesianum* 41 (1979): 273-97.

13. Jean-Marie Vermander, "Théophile d'Antioche contre Celse; A Autolycos III," *REAug* 17 (1971): 203-25.

14. Droge, *Homer,* 102-23.

15. The issue is most thoroughly presented in Carl Andresen, *Logos und Nomos: Die Polemik des Kelsos wider das Christentum* (Berlin: de Gruyter, 1955), esp. 108-45, 312-44.

16. Droge, *Homer,* esp. 102-18.

17. The complex question of his use of earlier sources cannot be thoroughly discussed

which various notions of genesis are central.[18] Second, just as the Hellenistic historians provide an appropriate literary context for Theophilus as historian, they also provide the framework for Theophilus as proto-scientist,[19] since they, too, prefaced their presentation of human cultural development with their views of cosmic, botanic, zoological, and human origins. Third, the context for Theophilus's *hexaemeron* must be set by a summary of the basic principles of Stoic cosmogony and cosmology and Chrysippus's "physiological" reading of Greek mythopoetic tradition.[20] Fourth, Theophilus's interpretation of Gen. 1–3 is best understood as a Stoicizing revision of the biblical original; specific parallels to the first two stages of Chrysippus's cosmogony will be demonstrated. Fifth, defending the biblical account in the light of the historiographic conventions of Diodorus Siculus, Theophilus stresses the historicity of the account of Adam and Eve in Paradise. Finally, I conclude that Theophilus's guiding principles in questions of cosmic and human genesis are Stoic, especially as this tradition is represented by Chrysippus and Diodorus. Yet in emphatic disagreement with these two authors, he insists that these principles be read out of (or into) the biblical text rather than the earliest Greek (or any other) literature.

---

here. Perhaps with Dillon we should avoid the use of the term "eclectic" given its negative connotation of an incapacity for systematic thought (John M. Dillon, *The Middle Platonists: 80 B.C. to A.D. 220* [Ithaca: Cornell University Press, 1977], xiv). Nor do I wish to be understood as advocating a return to the practice deplored by Dillon of "ferreting out 'Aristotelianisms' and 'Stoicisms' " from the works of Middle Platonic thinkers (ibid., xv). I mean to stress instead that the philosophical framework within which Theophilus operates may be the mirror image of Middle Platonism, a Stoic doctrine which has been "modernized" by the introduction of certain Platonic and Aristotelian doctrines but which remains to its proponents quite definitely "Stoic," not "eclectic"; cf. Dillon, xv.

18. Grant has drawn attention to the importance of cosmological ideas here; cf. "Theophilus," 254: the "most important part of Scripture to Theophilus was the cosmogony in Genesis," and he notes that this was an important discussion in his time, perhaps alluding principally to the Marcionite discussion. He calls it a "literal" cosmogony, though he identifies some Stoic ideas therein. The discussion of human origins has been stressed by Droge, *Homer,* 102-23.

19. Noticing Theophilus's penchant for the use of scientific illustration, Grant has nevertheless taken a dim view of his philosophical consistency and scientific accomplishment in his *Miracle and Natural Law in Graeco-Roman and Early Christian Thought* (Amsterdam: North-Holland Publishing Company, 1952), 100-102. He notes that several of Theophilus's views are drawn from Epicurus despite the fact that "his philosophical background is a strange combination of Platonism and Stoicism with the scepticism of Carneades" (ibid., 100). His opinion of Theophilus's use of Greek learning seems to have remained fairly constant; cf. Grant, *Apologists,* 149-56.

20. For this tradition of allegorical exegesis, cf. Jean Pépin, *Mythe et Allégorie: Les origines grecques et les contestations judéo-chrétiennes,* 2d ed. (Paris: Etudes Augustiniennes, 1976), esp. 97-98, 103-4, 121-33, 141-43, 152-55, 181-88, 232-33, 239-43, 291-307, 317-23.

I. The Relation of Theophilus's *Hexaemeron* to the Apology as a Whole

Theophilus's discussion of Gen. 1–3 occurs in the middle of his apology, is clearly germane to it, and is fully integrated into the more familiar apologetic themes. The principal question of the first book of *Ad Autolycum* is epistemological: how do we know God? Theophilus gives a twofold answer: (1) the ethically pure can know God directly through the "ears of the heart" and the "eyes of the soul"; (2) "God cannot be seen by human eyes but is seen and apprehended through his providence and his works" (*Autol.* 1.2, 5). Although the inner noetic path has intellectual priority, showing the more Platonic side of Theophilus's epistemology, the second path, a Peripatetic-Stoic argument through external evidence, is more important to his apologetic purpose. This way is itself twofold, encompassing the natural world on the one hand, and the historical arena on the other. These two are so intimately related for Theophilus that his argument moves easily from cosmogony, cosmology, and natural history to human history.

Closely related to the question of how God can be known is the question of the nature of the God known. Theophilus prefers to speak of the divine attributes and epithets rather than speaking of God directly: "he is in glory uncontainable, in greatness incomprehensible, in loftiness inconceivable. . . . If I call him Light, I speak of his creature; if I call him Logos, I speak of his beginning."[21] Although Theophilus applies the epithets "ineffable" (ἄρρητον) and "inexpressible" (ἀνέκφραστον) to the "form" (εἶδος) of God, suggesting a Platonic philosophical framework (*Autol.* 1.3), he stresses the invisibility[22] of God rather than God's incorporeality. Simultaneously he emphasizes knowledge of God through providence[23]

21. *Autol.* 1.3; cf. Grant, *Apologists,* 167; Grant has argued elsewhere that the list is based in the NT and anti-Marcionite polemic ("Scripture, Rhetoric and Theology in Theophilus," *VC* 13 [1959]: 33-45, esp. 33-36). Theophilus's appellations of God overlap somewhat with the hypostases of Basilides' God; cf. Bentley Layton, "The Significance of Basilides in Ancient Christian Thought," *Representations* 28 (1989): 135-51, esp. 138. Jewish parallels come to mind, an aspect of Theophilus's thought emphasized by Grant; cf. esp. his *Apologists,* 157-59, 165-68. My intent here is not to contrast overly much the biblical with the Stoic notions, but to draw the greatest possible attention to Theophilus's philosophical consistency by stressing the Stoic interpretations insofar as possible.

22. Cf. Cicero *De natura deorum* 2.45 *(consuetudo oculorum);* cf. Geffcken, *Zwei griechesches Apologeten,* 250 n. 5; also Th. Korteweg, "The Reality of the Invisible: Some Remarks on St. John XIV 8 and Greek Philosophic Tradition," in *Studies in Hellenistic Religions,* ed. M. J. Vermaseren, Études préliminaires aux religions orientales dans l'empire romain 78 (Leiden: Brill, 1979), 50-102, esp. 82-84; and P. C. Finney, *The Invisible God: The Earliest Christians on Art* (forthcoming).

23. Cf. n. 7 above.

and through the order and beauty of the visible creation:[24] "Just as the soul in a man is not seen, since it is invisible to men, but is apprehended through the movement of the body, so it may be that God cannot be seen by human eyes but is seen and apprehended through his providence and his works."[25]

To illustrate this invisible presence of God he chooses the traditional Stoic images of the pilot, the sun, and the king.[26] Equally characteristic of Stoicism is his notion that God surrounds and contains the creation — an idea which he illustrates strikingly: "As the pomegranate seed, dwelling inside, cannot see what is outside the rind since it is itself inside, so man, who with the whole creation is enclosed by the hand of God, cannot see God."[27] All these features suggest that Theophilus belongs more on the Stoic than the Platonic side of the eclecticism of his time.[28]

Consideration of the creation leads Theophilus to ponder the majesty of the Creator, the impending judgment, and the vision of God which will be available to those resurrected thanks to faith and the ethical life it elicits (*Autol.* 1.6-7). This leads him to defend the doctrine of bodily resurrection, using the maxim that trust of the teacher must precede learning,[29] as well as the analogy of human conception and other evidences (τεκμήρια) from the natural world (*Autol.* 1.13).[30] He then contrasts Autolycus's skepticism

24. Spanneut, *Stoïcisme,* 270-88, 362-85; Geffcken, *Zwei griechesches Apologeten,* 250.

25. *Autol.* 1.4. The analogy between human ensoulment and the soul or spirit of the cosmos played a central role in Stoic cosmology; cf. Michael Lapidge, "Stoic Cosmology," in *The Stoics,* ed. John M. Rist (Berkeley: University of California Press, 1978), 168-76; David E. Hahm, *The Origins of Stoic Cosmology* (Columbus: Ohio State University Press, 1976), chap. V, "Cosmobiology," 136-84.

26. The pilot, pomegranate (cf. n. 27 below), and king images were noted by Bardy, *Théophile,* 39, cited by Spanneut, *Stoïcisme,* 283-85; Geffcken, *Zwei griechesches Apologeten,* 250 n. 5, observed only the pilot image. On the sun as ἡγεμονικόν of the cosmos for Cleanthes, cf. Hahm, *Origins,* 150-52.

27. *Autol.* 1.4-5. Unlike Cleanthes, Chrysippus taught that the cosmic ἡγεμονικόν was in the αἰθήρ, thus surrounding the cosmos; cf. Lapidge, "Stoic Cosmology," 179-82; SVF 2:144-46. As Bardy notes (*Théophile,* 62 n. 2), the Stoics use συνέχω, whereas Theophilus uses περιέχω here; but cf. *Autol.* 2.13 and n. 93 below. Schoedel's discussion of this concept gives little attention to Stoic precedent, emphasizing instead Hellenistic Jewish and early Christian originality and their use of other philosophical traditions in this regard; cf. William Schoedel, "Enclosing, Not Enclosed: The Early Christian Doctrine of God," in *Early Christian Literature and the Classical Intellectual Tradition: In Honorem Robert M. Grant,* ed. W. R. Schoedel and R. L. Wilken, Théologie Historique 53 (Paris: Beauchesne, 1979), 75-86. Most interesting is Grant's parallel between the image of the pomegranate and the Stoic use of the honeycomb ("Theophilus," 230-31).

28. Cf. n. 17 above.

29. From Carneades; see Grant, *Apologists,* 151.

30. On the analogy of human conception cf. Justin *Apol.* 1.19. On τεκμήρια, cf. Nicole

about bodily resurrection with his gullibility about pagan myth, idolatry, and worship of the emperor (*Autol.* 1.9-12). At this point he is ready to offer the counsel that will lead him into the second and third books: "If you will, you too must reverently read the prophetic writings. They will be your best guides for escaping the eternal punishments and for obtaining the eternal benefits of God. For *he who gave the mouth for speech and formed the ear for hearing and made eyes for vision* will examine everything and will judge justly, *rewarding each one in accordance with what he deserves*. . . . Since you made this request, my friend, 'Show me your God,' this is my God. I advise you to fear him and believe him."[31] Theophilus has moved the discussion from epistemology to Scripture. He has also claimed that God is creator, providential ruler, and judge of the world.[32] In the subsequent books he will argue that this God is best described by the Bible rather than by Greek literature in any form.

The second book of *Ad Autolycum* begins with a paragraph recollecting the contents of the first book and identifying the nature of the argument which is to follow. He promises to demonstrate the falsity of pagan religion through the use of "history books."[33] His argument begins not with human history but with a series of philosophically motivated criticisms of the mythological accounts of the origin of the gods and the cosmos.[34] First is a Euhemeristic argument, that the stories of the births of the gods, no less than their images, have been fashioned by humans.[35] If gods were once

---

Zeegers-Vander Vorst, "Les citations du Nouveau Testament dans les Livres à Autolycus de Théophile d'Antioche," TU 5.60 (Studia patristica 12) (1975), 371-82, esp. 381.

31. *Autol.* 1.14, quoting Exod. 4:11, Ps. 93:9, and Rom. 2:6, as Grant notes ad loc.

32. At the end of the second book (2.37) he will reinforce the notion of divine judgment in Stoic terms by using the technical term ἐκπύρωσις and collecting biblical prophecies of judgment under the imagery of fire; for this eminently Stoic doctrine in other early Christian writers, cf. Spanneut, *Stoïcisme,* 358-60. God as judge is equally at home in Stoic and in Jewish and Christian contexts, as Grant has observed, citing Plutarch, *Stoic Contradictions* 1050E, in *Apologists,* 168 n. 13. Connecting the periodic cosmic conflagration with judgment, however, seems to be a result of the marriage of Stoic with biblical conceptions that Theophilus is promoting.

33. τὴν ματαιοπονίαν καὶ ματαίαν θρησκείαν ἐν ᾗ κατέχῃ. . . . δι' ὀλίγων τῶν κατά σε ἱστοριῶν ὧν ἀναγινώσκεις, *Autol.* 2.1.

34. For discussion of Theophilus's view of creation in the context of other early Christian writers, cf. Grant, *Miracle,* 135-52, esp. 142-43.

35. *Autol.* 2.2. On Euhemerus and his critique of polytheism, cf. G. Vallauri, *Euemero di Messene: Testimonianze e frammenti con introduzione e commento,* Universita di Torino Pubblicazioni della Facolta de lettere e Filosofia VIII.3 (Torino: Cuneo, 1956). In his attack on pagan myth in the first book Theophilus had begun with an inverted Euhemeristic argument but shifted quickly to an attack on the irrationality and ethical deficiencies of Greek (and Egyptian) myth: "The names of the gods you say you worship are the names of dead men. What men were they? What kind? Is not Kronos a child-eater who consumes his own

generated, moreover, the process should still be seen now, and since they are immortal, they should far outnumber people.[36]

He turns next to brief doxographical parries against a variety of philosophical views that, he alleges, deny the existence of God, of providence, or of the world's coming into existence; here he mentions by name or uses commonplaces of the Stoics (mentioning Chrysippus explicitly), Aristotle, and Epicurus.[37] Here, too, he focuses on the question of origins. Linking the notion that "God is uncreated" with the Platonic phrase that God is "Father and Maker" (πατὴρ καὶ ποιητής)[38] of the universe, he proceeds to reproach the Platonists with inconsistency for their failure to subscribe to an ex nihilo doctrine of creation.[39] Despite their use of the title, their God is not really the Maker of the universe, he argues. By assuming that both God and matter are eternal, they have undermined the sovereignty of God; they have assumed, in effect, "that uncreated matter is also God . . . immutable and equal to God" (*Autol.* 2.4).

Still more important than the inadequacies of the philosophers' views on creation is the fact that their views "are inconsistent with those of other writers" (*Autol.* 2.5). Theophilus is determined to drive a wedge between the Greek mythopoetic tradition and Greek philosophy especially on the question of cosmogony. The God who is Father and Maker of the universe

---

children? And if you should mention his son Zeus, you must learn his deeds and his manner of life" (*Autol.* 1.9). Similar arguments are in *Autol.* 2.8, and again, at 2.3; in other second-century apologists, cf. Grant, *Apologists,* 37, 121; and on Euhemerism inverted, cf. J. W. Schippers, *De Ontwikkeling der Euhemeristische Godencritiek in de Christelijke Latijnse Literatuur* (Groningen: J. B. Wolters, 1952), esp. 103-8.

36. *Autol.* 2.3; Theophilus quotes the Sibyl here; cf. Grant, *Autolycum,* 25.

37. Grant has noted parallels in both Plutarch and Carneades (*Autolycum,* 27 n. 1; idem, *Apologists,* 151-52). In closing, I will address the problem these attacks on Stoic views pose for my thesis.

38. Cf. *Timaeus* 28 c. As Philo and Plutarch sometimes do, Theophilus reverses Plato's order; cf. Philo *De opif. mundi* 10.21; for discussion of this phrase in Philo and Plutarch, cf. D. T. Runia, *Philo of Alexandria and the "Timaeus of Plato"* (Kampen: Vrije Universiteit Boekhandel, 1983), 1:82-85. Unlike Philo, Theophilus seems to avoid the use of the term "Demiurge" (δημιουργός) here, but he uses it later in 2.34 and again in 3.9, in a passage that Grant, following Goodenough, sees as reflecting in some degree a Hellenistic Jewish consensus; cf. Grant, *Apologists,* 167.

39. *Autol.* 2.4; cf. 2.10, 13; and cf. Grant, *Miracle,* 142-43. On the question whether the notion of creation ex nihilo is present in Hellenistic Jewish sources and in Christian sources prior to Theophilus, cf. Gerhard May, *Schöpfung aus dem Nichts: Die Entstehung der Lehre von der Creatio ex Nihilo,* Arbeiten zur Kirchengeschichte 48 (Berlin: de Gruyter, 1978). May has emphasized the importance of Basilides' views (as portrayed by Hippolytus) in the development of the philosophical notion of creation out of nothing. Layton's recent interpretation of Basilides' cosmology as essentially Stoic (based on an argument for the superiority of the accounts of Irenaeus and Clement over Hippolytus) necessitates a review of May's conclusions; cf. Layton, *Representations* 28 (1989): 135-51.

is not Zeus or any of the gods of Greek myth. Speaking of Ocean as "origin of the gods" (θεῶν γένεσιν), Homer has confused God with water.[40] By his own account, Hesiod's gods originate after the world; yet the Muses, "daughters of Zeus," tell the story of the world's origin. "How," Theophilus asks, "did the Muses know these things when they originated later than the world? [μεταγενέστεραι οὖσαι τοῦ κόσμου] How could they describe them to Hesiod when their father had not yet been born?"[41] He continues his critique of the *Theogony:*

> In a certain way he assumes the existence of matter and the origin of the world [ὕλην μὲν τρόπῳ τινὶ ὑποτίθεται, καὶ κόσμου ποίησιν] when he says:
>
> > First Chaos came to be, and then
> > Wide-bosomed earth, ever-sure foundation of all
> > The immortals, who hold the peaks of snowy Olympus . . .
> > . . . .
> > From Chaos came Erebus and black Night.
> > And Earth first bore, equal to herself, to cover her everywhere,
> > Starry heaven, that there might be an ever-sure abode for the blessed gods;
> > . . . and afterwards
> > She lay with Heaven and bore deep-swirling Ocean.
>
> He says this, but he still does not explain by whom they were made [ὑπὸ τίνος ἐγένοντο]. If originally there was chaos, and a certain uncreated matter already subsisted [ἦν χάος, καὶ ὕλη τις προϋπέκειτο ἀγένητος οὖσα], who was it who reshaped, remodelled, and transformed [μετασκευάζων καὶ μεταρρυθμίζων καὶ μεταμορφῶν] it? Did matter itself reshape and arrange [μετασχημάτιζεν καὶ ἐκόσμει] itself? Zeus came into existence [γεγένηται] much later, not only after matter, but even after the world [τοῦ κόσμου] and great numbers of people, and so did his father Kronos. Was there not instead some sovereign principle that made matter

40. This is also directed against Zeno's interpretation of the *Theogony,* according to which "Hesiod's precosmic chaos was simply water" (SVF 1:104; cited by Lapidge, "Stoic Cosmology," 161-85, esp. 165; cf. n. 67 below. Both Droge and Grant note and discuss Theophilus's attack on Hesiod's cosmogony over against Celsus's attack on Genesis; Droge, *Homer,* 121, and Grant, *Apologists,* 134, 155. While Droge argues that Theophilus's apology is an answer to Celsus, or at least to some such anti-Christian polemic, Grant rejects this possibility in favor of its being an answer to Marcionite views; cf. Grant, *Autolycum,* xv and 67-69, notes; and idem, *Apologists,* 157. Andresen has also addressed the importance of cosmological discussion for Justin's and Celsus's apologetic arguments in *Logos und Nomos,* esp. 276-91, 312-20. Grant has also suggested Theophilus has Stoic opponents in mind here (*Miracle,* 143), and elsewhere (ibid., 37) he notes this same statement is attributed to Zeno.

41. Grant notes a parallel in Sextus Empiricus *Adv. math.* 10.18 and a general similarity between Theophilus and Clitomachus here (*Miracle,* 143).

> [κύριόν τι τὸ ποιῆσαν ἀυτήν] — I mean God, the one who set it in order? [κατακοσμήσας ἀυτήν][42]

Theophilus proceeds to ridicule the genealogies of the Greek and Egyptian gods, the Titans, Cyclopes, and Giants, dismissing in an aside the notion of a cosmic egg as origin of the universe.[43] After a Euhemeristic argument that the derivation of the Alexandrian demes from Dionysus, Heracles, Apollo, Poseidon, and Zeus proves that the so-called gods of mythology are not gods, he completes his attack on the cosmological deficiencies of Greek literary tradition with a demonstration of the inconsistencies among poets and tragedians on the doctrine of providence.[44]

Having leveled this anachronistic barrage against the literary classics of Hellenism, Theophilus must, of course, answer the same objections with regard to the Mosaic cosmogony. He is well prepared for this challenge. Prior to his discussion of the poets, he had insisted on creation ex nihilo as the only notion worthy of God, as we have seen. Now he can proceed to refute the objections implied by his own critique of the Greek writers. Unlike the Muses the Jewish prophets need not antedate the creation of the world or any of the historical events they describe since they are inspired by the Logos of God who not only existed before the entire cosmos but created it ex nihilo.[45] The assertion that these prophets are all consistent with one another not only puts him on the right side of this old rhetorical ploy, but it also allows him to search the rest of Scripture for attestations of the Logos and Sophia (sometimes = Holy Spirit)[46] to

42. *Autol.* 2.5-6; quoting, as Grant notes, *Theog.* 116-23, 126-33. Grant notes a significant parallel in Aelius Aristides' *Oration to Zeus* in "Scripture, Rhetoric and Theology in Theophilus," *VC* 13 (1959): 33-45, esp. 42. For discussion of the argument here and its basis in skeptical argument against the Stoic "physiologists," cf. Grant, *Miracle,* 33-35; idem, *Apologists,* 155. The parallels here to the Stoic cosmogony will become evident in III-IV below.

43. *Autol.* 2.7; on this cf. Grant, *Miracle,* 35, 143, and n. 50 below.

44. *Autol.* 2.7-8. Among the few early Christian writers who know Aratus's *Phainomena* Theophilus alone recognizes that its theme is providence; cf. Annewies Van de Bunt-Van den Hoek, "Aristobulos, Acts, Theophilus, Clement Making Use of Aratus Phainomena: A Peregrination," *Bijdragen* 41 (1980): 290-99, esp. 297-99.

45. *Autol.* 2.8-9; cf. n. 39 above. On this point, cf. Adelbert Davids, "Hésiode et les prophètes chez Théophile d'Antioche," in *Fides Sacramenti Sacramentum Fidei: Studies in Honour of Pieter Smulders,* ed. H. J. Auf der Maur et al. (Assen: Van Gorcum, 1981), 205-10. As Grant has observed, Autolycus could make the same claim to inspiration by the Logos on behalf of Hesiod; cf. *Miracle,* 143.

46. On the inconsistencies in Theophilus's trinitarian doctrine, cf. Bardy, *Théophile,* 38-45, esp. 44, versus Grant, *Apologists,* 169-71, and esp. Nicole Zeegers-Vander Vorst, "La Création de l'Homme (Gn 1,26) chez Théophile d'Antioche," *VC* 30 (1976): 258-67, esp. 258-60.

supplement the creation story of Gen. 1–3.[47] Once the Logos, Sophia, and Spirit have been firmly inserted into the narrative, he proceeds to a fairly detailed and consecutive discussion of the text of Gen. 1–3 in the Septuagint version.[48]

Theophilus's *hexaemeron* leads directly into his brief exposition of the rest of the Genesis narrative and, more sketchily, of the remainder of Hebrew Scripture. Although his account is somewhat confused, the essential point, made clear by occasional, often disparaging, allusions to Greek, Egyptian, and Assyrian literature and history, is that the biblical account is the earliest record for all humankind.[49] Other historical records are valuable only insofar as they can be harmonized with and fitted into this history. Since he clearly assumes that the antiquity of the biblical account makes it a superior source of religious truth, the extensive chronological argument of the third book is essential to establishing his view.

Cosmological knowledge is closely related to historical and ethical forms of truth, as he shows by his remarks just after he has described the settlement of the world by humans: "Writers who do not know these things want to call the world spherical or to compare it with a cube. How can they speak truthfully in these matters when they do not know how the world was created or how it was inhabited?"[50] In other words, only those who know both cosmogony and the earliest history accurately are able to speak with authority about cosmology. Conversely, the prophets' ethical precepts and opposition to idolatry were based on knowledge of the obligation to worship "the real God who made the universe" (τῷ ὄντως θεῷ καὶ ποιητῇ τῶν ὅλων) rather than the invented gods of idol-makers and

47. *Autol.* 2.9-10. Essentially he combines Ps. 109:3; John 1:1; Prov. 8:22, 27-29 with Luke 1:35 and Gen. 1:1-2 to establish that God's Logos and Sophia were present before the creation of the world. Philo had introduced the Logos through a different tactic: if humans are created in the image of God, then the whole of which they are part must also be an image of God, i.e., the Logos; cf. *De opif. mundi* 6.

48. *Autol.* 2.11. For the moment I will pass over the discussion of this part of the work to continue consideration of the place of Theophilus's cosmological concerns within the apology as a whole.

49. *Autol.* 2.29-32. Grant suggests that Theophilus has incompletely accommodated an ethnographic source with a fourfold scheme of migration to his threefold biblical scheme based on Noah's sons, in *Miracle,* 101.

50. *Autol.* 2.32. The idea of a spherical cosmos is attributed to the Stoics and Epicurus by Plutarch and to the Stoics, Leucippus, and Democritus by Stobaeus; Plutarch adds that others consider it conical or egg-shaped; Theophilus seems to have misunderstood a view ascribed to Pythagoras (and Plato; cf. *Timaeus* 55) that each of the four elements came to be out of the geometrical solids, earth being made up from cubes; see H. Diels, *Doxographi Graeci* (Berlin: G. Reimeri, 1879), 329 a 2-8, b 6-9; 334 a 17-335 a 4, 334 b 8-335 b 2; both cited by Grant, *Autolycum,* 83 n. 4.

myth-makers.[51] Knowledge of this God and the world created by God also implies awareness of providence and just judgment.[52]

In his third and final book Theophilus's multifaceted argument for the superiority of Christian teaching recommences with attacks on the ethical uselessness of traditional Greek literature. Here the Mosaic law rather than the Mosaic cosmogony is the center of attention. The Decalogue is presented as given by "the real God" through Moses "not only to all the world but especially to the Hebrews" to teach "justice, piety, and beneficence."[53] After further ethical discussion, he returns to historical and chronological arguments, and the book culminates with his universal chronology.[54]

II. Theophilus, the Hellenistic Historians, and Stoic Cosmology

Theophilus's juxtaposition of cosmogony with chronography may appear strange. But this sequence has roots both in the Genesis narrative and in the conventions of the universal histories and "antiquities" of the Hellenistic period.[55] Theophilus believed that the antiquity of his tradition not only validated the religious insights of Christianity, but it also conveyed the stamp of authority on the cosmological information contained in the first chapters of Genesis as he understood them. A brief consideration of the place of cosmogony in Hellenistic historiography will illustrate his convictions on this subject.

51. *Autol.* 2.34-35, with confirmation from the Sibyl in 2.36.

52. Imperfectly taught by the poets, correctly by the prophets, *Autol.* 2.37-38.

53. *Autol.* 3.9. Further, cf. Grant, *Apologists,* 160-61, as well as his earlier discussion, "The Decalogue in Early Christianity," in *HTR* 40 (1947): 1-17, esp. 13-14. In "Theophilus," 243-44, Grant notes that the virtues specified here show Stoic influence.

54. For its sources and structure, cf. Grant, *Apologists,* 155-56. For the argument that book 3, unlike books 1-2, is Theophilus's response to Celsus, cf. Vermander, *REAug* 17 (1971): 203-25; Grant rejects this idea, *Apologists,* 134-35; Droge, *Homer,* 119-23, who accepts some but not all of the parallels adduced by Vermander, nonetheless thinks the whole apology is an answer to Celsus. Whether or not Theophilus has addressed Celsus specifically, Vermander and Droge have shown that the two are involved in the same essential argument and that Theophilus has addressed questions left unanswered by other second-century Christian apologists.

55. Droge has noted (*Homer,* esp. 108-18) the connection between the interest in cultural history in Theophilus and in the Hellenistic historians. He has also noted the juxtaposition of cosmogonic with cultural historical arguments in Theophilus and Celsus (pp. 119-23). But his conclusion that Theophilus must have been answering Celsus overlooks the fact that cosmogony and cultural history are linked more generally in Hellenistic historiography.

Although a movement toward universal history is to be found in the earlier Greek historiographic tradition, especially in Herodotus and Polybius, Stoic notions of natural law and of the *cosmopolites* provide the rationale both for the writing of universal history and for prefacing such a history with a cosmogony.[56] Diodorus Siculus's *Historical Library* (composed ca. 66-44 B.C.E.) is the earliest surviving history of this sort.[57] Diodorus began his history with the earliest Egyptian materials, and these he prefaced with a brief but comprehensive account of origins.[58] His book 1, chaps. 7-13, tells the story of the origin of the world, of animals, of humans, of the first elements of civilization, including religion. The cosmogony in chaps. 7-8 is a reinterpretation in Stoic terms of traditional cosmogonic material drawn from the pre-Socratics as well as from Egyptian sources.[59]

56. Anne Burton, *Diodorus Siculus, Book I, A Commentary,* Études préliminaires aux religions orientales dans l'empire romain 29 (Leiden: Brill, 1972), 35-38.

57. For the dating, cf. ibid., 42-44.

58. The traditional view that Diodorus's first book is essentially borrowed from Agatharchides of Cnidos and Hecataeus of Abdera has been supplanted by the view that it is Diodorus's reworking of materials derived from Hecataeus, Agatharchides (possibly via Artemidorus), Herodotus, and Manetho, the last two again via later sources; cf. Burton, ibid., 1-34.

59. Spoerri has argued that the cosmogony described by Diodorus in book 1, chaps. 7-8, belongs to a general class of "διάκρισις cosmogonies" in which the Deity acts upon a disorderly chaos to bring about the creation of the four elements, a notion which presupposes a mixture of Platonic with Stoic ideas and thus presumes the philosophical developments of his own time, the 1st century B.C.E. (Walter Spoerri, *Späthellenistische Berichte über Welt, Kultur und Götter: Untersuchungen zu Diodor von Sizilien,* Schweizerische Beiträge zur Altertumswissenschaft 9 [Basel: Friedrich Reinhardt, 1959], 107-8). On the materials in book 1, chaps. 7-13, and for the argument that the Stoicism specifically of Posidonius is the source of Diodore's cosmogony, cf. ibid., 1-117, esp. 107-17. Either Diodorus himself or a slightly earlier contemporary such as Posidonius would then have interpreted traditional cosmogonic material from the pre-Socratics and possibly Egypt as well by enlarging, excerpting, or "modernizing" it. (As suggested by Burton, *Diodorus,* 16, 45-46, who accepts Spoerri's critique of the earlier views [esp. pp. 1-7, 15-16], but she is skeptical of the specific attribution to Posidonius and even to Stoicism, accepting rather a view of Diodorus as thoroughly eclectic; pp. 35-73, passim, esp. 51. She provides a straightforward summary of the issues, pp. 44-47.)

This view needs reevaluation in the light of current studies of Stoic cosmology which indicate that the Platonic influence alleged by Spoerri in the διάκρισις cosmogonies is inherent in the early Stoic cosmogonies and need not imply a transcendent or incorporeal deity. Lapidge describes the early Stoic cosmogony in terms closely parallel to Spoerri's definition of "διάκρισις cosmogonies" (Lapidge, "Stoic Cosmology," 166). Hahm has argued on behalf of essentially the same early Stoic cosmology and has addressed the questions of earlier influences on the first Stoics, particularly the role of views derived from the pre-Socratics, Plato and Aristotle. He has demonstrated that although the influence of Plato's *Timaeus* can be discerned in the early stages of Stoic cosmological thought, this influence along with others has been brought into a coherent system of thought, the central metaphor of which is biological (Hahm, *Origins,* esp. 29-90). There is no need on the grounds

Likewise important are the *Antiquities,* an apologetic genre of historical writing, which also flourished in the Hellenistic period, and which was rooted in the native histories composed by such writers as Manetho and Berossus.[60] Most begin with mythology treated with at least a pretense of critical distance.[61] Some, such as the *Phoenician History* by Philo of Byblos and Josephus's *Antiquities,* begin with an updated and Hellenized cosmogony purporting to be the ancient system of the people whose history and customs are related in the remainder of the book.[62]

All these Hellenistic historians show particular interest in cultural history, polemically interpreted as the accomplishment of the historian's people — Greek or "barbarian."[63] I contend that the cosmogonies also fit into this picture for those historians who begin with them. In this case the writer shows the philosophical acumen of his people by demonstrating that an up-to-date cosmogony is implied in their ancient cosmological documents. Thus the Stoics at least from Chrysippus onward read their views into Hesiod, Homer, and the pre-Socratics to such an extent that it has been

---

introduced by Spoerri, then, to insist on a 1st century B.C.E. *terminus post quem* for Diodorus's cosmogony. This reopens the question of Hecataeus of Abdera's authorship of the cosmogony as it stands. More important to my purpose here is that this new picture of Stoic cosmogony provides a more coherent picture of a more consistently Stoic philosophical background for the cosmologies of both Diodorus and Theophilus of Antioch.

60. Tessa Rajak, "Josephus and the 'Archaeology' of the Jews," *JJS* 33 (1982): 465-77, esp. 472f.

61. Ibid., 470.

62. Philo (late 1st century–early 2d century C.E.) begins with a cosmogony he attributes to Sanchuniathon of Beirut, allegedly an ancient figure antedating not only Hesiod and his *Theogony* but also the Trojan War, hence belonging to the late 2d millennium B.C.E. Cf. Albert I. Baumgarten, *The "Phoenician History" of Philo of Byblos: A Commentary,* Études préliminaires aux religions orientales dans l'empire romain 89 (Leiden: Brill, 1981), 94; also Harold W. Attridge and Robert A. Oden, *Philo of Byblos: The Phoenician History: Introduction, Critical Text, Translation, Notes,* Catholic Biblical Quarterly Monograph series 9 (Washington, D.C.: Catholic Biblical Association, 1981), 3-6. In fact, his cosmogony uses early Phoenician tradition but interprets it through the lens of Greek rationalism; cf. Baumgarten, 94-129, esp. 123, and Attridge and Oden, 1, 75 n. 22. Like Diodorus's account, Philo's account includes not only cosmogony but also zoogony, the origin of humans, a primitive cultural history, early kings, and the origin of religion. Josephus's (d. ca. 100 C.E.) *Jewish Antiquities* likewise begins with his summary account of the Hebraic cosmogony, attributed, of course, to Moses, who lived, according to Josephus's calculations, a full millennium before the Trojan War; this assertion and its importance for Josephus are discussed by Droge, *Homer,* 35-48, esp. 44. Josephus, too, shows a tendency to rationalize and reorganize the biblical materials. The principles underlying Josephus's interpretation of the cosmogony have not yet been clarified, but many important details have been noted by Thomas W. Franxman, *Genesis and the "Jewish Antiquities" of Flavius Josephus* (Rome: Biblical Institute Press, 1979), esp. 37-64.

63. R. A. Oden, "Philo of Byblos and Hellenistic Historiography," *PEQ* 110 (1978): 114-26, esp. 120-21.

difficult for scholars to differentiate their views from those of Heraclitus.[64] Similarly the hybrid cosmogonies of Diodorus Siculus and Philo of Byblos have produced a seemingly endless debate about their sources.

Theophilus's early history has the essential features common to Hellenistic histories.[65] In view of this context, it is likely that his treatment of the biblical cosmogony would be a Stoicized updating presented as if it were nothing more than a literal rendering of the ancient text. With this hypothesis in mind, we can proceed to a brief survey of the basic principles of Stoic cosmology, followed by a detailed analysis of some sections in *Ad Autolycum* 2.10-28, his treatment of Gen. 1–3. Finally, we will draw some conclusions about his intentions.

III. Basic Principles of Stoic Cosmogony and Cosmology

The monistic system of the Stoics begins with a single material substance (οὐσία), "a finite natural continuum" which has two "aspects" or principles (ἀρχαί).[66] The first is the active principle (τὸ ποιοῦν) and is also known as the word (λόγος), or god (θέος) as well as "creative fire"; the second is the passive (τὸ πάσχον), known also as "inert" or "unqualified matter" (ἄποιος ὕλη) and as chaos or water.[67] When the logos as "creative fire" acts upon the inert matter construed as moisture (= phase one),[68] the cosmos as a differentiated and ordered being is generated (= phase two) in a manner which owes as much to Aristotelian notions of biological reproduction as to the pre-Socratic philosophers.[69] From this action the four elements are produced and arranged in "spherical tiers": earth, water, air, and fire.[70] The

64. Cf. Pépin, *Mythe,* esp. 125-31; Hahm, *Origins,* esp. 57-90.

65. Droge, *Homer,* esp. 1-11, 33-35, 102-23; for the five main features of Hellenistic historiography, cf. Oden, *PEQ* 110 (1978): 114-26.

66. The phraseology is from Robert B. Todd, "Monism and Immanence: The Foundations of Stoic Physics," in *The Stoics,* ed. John M. Rist (Berkeley: University of California Press, 1978), 137-60, esp. 139. Similarly, Lapidge suggests one should think of "one primal substance with two aspects, one active, one passive" ("Stoic Cosmology," 164, citing SVF 1:87; 2:308, 313).

67. For "inert" rather than the more usual "unqualified" or "qualityless," cf. Todd, "Monism," 140-41.

68. Lapidge notes this as the first of two stages ("Stoic Cosmology," 166); cf. Hahm, *Origins,* 76.

69. Cf. Todd, "Monism," 143-46; Lapidge, "Stoic Cosmology," 165-66; Hahm, *Origins,* 57-90.

70. This is the second stage according to Lapidge, "Stoic Cosmology," 166; for the arrangement and the phrase quoted, cf. ibid., 177. This is Zeno's arrangement; for Chrysippus's modification, cf. n. 73 below.

result is a cosmic embryo.[71] The thoroughgoing application of this biological metaphor to the cosmos is the central concern and vital innovation of Stoic cosmology and cosmogony.[72]

The production and arrangement of elements in the cosmic embryo is understood differently by Zeno, Cleanthes, and Chrysippus. Most important for our purposes is Chrysippus's modification of Zeno's scheme. Whereas Zeno supposed that first the earth settled out from the liquid, then the air evaporated from the water, and then some of the air changed by rarification to fire, Chrysippus modified the sequence so that αἰθήρ rather than fire is produced in the final stage.[73] Whereas Zeno seems to have supposed the production of compounds and further individuation of beings in the cosmos took place through a growth process governed by "nature" (φύσις) defined as "a craftsmanlike fire, proceeding methodically to genesis" (πῦρ τεχνικὸν ὁδῷ βαδίζον εἰς γένεσιν),[74] Chrysippus introduced a new entity, the spirit (πνεῦμα) to continue the generative action of the logos (= phase three).[75] Closely related to Logos, thus virtually another principle, the spirit is also a sort of fifth body emerging from the αἰθήρ to bring the fiery principle of life to the sublunar world.[76] Heavenly bodies and vegetable, animal, and human forms of life are understood to have come into existence through similar processes of generation. Once in existence and located in the environment to which each is suited, they are governed by the same nature which created them and guides them toward the purpose for which they were brought into existence. Thus the familiar Stoic notions

71. Cf. SVF 1:102 and its citation and discussion by Todd, "Monism," 143-44; also Hahm, *Origins,* 76-78.

72. See Lapidge, "Stoic Cosmology," esp. 163-66; Hahm, *Origins,* esp. 43-48, 60-78. According to Hahm, "The Stoics . . . seem to have begun with the widespread, venerable, ancient idea that the cosmos is a living being and that its origin was a birth exactly like the birth of living things. . . . the biological character of the cosmos was interpreted according to the latest scientific theories of the biologists. The result was a synthesis of the current theories of cosmology and biology. In this synthesis the original elements, drawn largely from Plato and Aristotle, were so tightly welded that they lost most of their Academic and Peripatetic character, and resulted in a philosophical system with a soul of its own. The Stoic doctrine of *archai* shows resemblances to Aristotle's theory of reproduction, his four causes, and his prime mover, as well as to Plato's receptacle, demiurge, and world soul. Yet there was originality in the Stoic doctrine; for it was the Stoic achievement to combine these apparently disparate elements and to give them a new direction, so that they might serve as the foundation of a new cosmological system" (pp. 47-48).

73. Cf. SVF 1:102 and 2:579, as cited and discussed by Lapidge, "Stoic Cosmology," 166-67.

74. For this translation of SVF 1:171, cf. Hahm, *Origins,* 200; further on Zeno's definition of nature, cf. Todd, "Monism," 143-48, 154-55; and Hahm, *Origins,* 200-208.

75. Todd, "Monism," 148-55, esp. 149.

76. Ibid., esp. 150, 153.

of the beauty of the cosmic order, of providence, and the linking of the two through astrology are closely related to the common origin of the entire cosmos.

For Chrysippus the spirit is present in the world in a manner analogous to the wind or breath in the human body.[77] In addition, although the cosmic spirit permeates the cosmos, as in the case of the human spirit in the human body, it has a center of consciousness and decision (ἡγεμονικόν) identified with the αἰθήρ and situated above and around the four elements.[78] In its role as permeating the cosmos as the human spirit permeates the body, the cosmic spirit gives life and movement to the cosmos by providing a tension (τόνος) which holds all existents in inherent relation to one another.[79] The well-known Stoic concept of cosmic sympathy (συμπάθεια) is thus clearly rooted in this "cosmobiology," the understanding of the cosmos as a huge living being.[80]

Just as the elements and subsequently the rest of the world and its inhabitants have come into existence, they are destined to pass out of existence.[81] On the biological model this may be seen as both a cosmic death and a cosmic reproduction.[82] In the periodic cosmic conflagration (ἐκπύρωσις) the cosmos reproduces itself by the same fiery generative process by which it first came into existence. The cycle will repeat itself exactly without limit.

Both the pre-Socratic philosophers and the mythology of Homer and Hesiod were interpreted, especially by Chrysippus, in a harmonizing manner to show the compatibility of Stoic cosmogony with these earliest Greek literary traditions.[83] Thus the Ionians, especially Heraclitus, along with Homer and Hesiod, were seen as effectively "Stoics before their time." On the one hand, the Ionian cosmogonies were treated as fundamentally the same as their Stoic counterparts. On the other hand, the anthropomorphic deities of Homer and Hesiod were "physiologized" — that is, interpreted as actually symbolic of natural forces. Especially the tales of divine copulation and reproduction were readily harmonized with the Stoic cosmobi-

77. Lapidge, "Stoic Cosmology," 168-80. The spirit may permeate only the sublunar world, producing either a needed link or a problematic break in Stoic monism; cf. Todd, "Monism," 150-55.

78. Lapidge, "Stoic Cosmology," 178-80; cf. Hahm, *Origins,* 150.

79. Lapidge, "Stoic Cosmology," 172-76; Hahm, *Origins,* 136-84, esp. 164-74.

80. Lapidge, "Stoic Cosmology," esp. 176.

81. Hahm, *Origins,* 185-99.

82. Both in Lapidge, "Stoic Cosmology," 180-85, but only reproduction in Hahm, *Origins,* 194.

83. Cf. Hahm, *Origins,* esp. 79-82, 211-12; also Pépin, *Mythe,* 125-31.

ology.[84] In many respects Hesiod's *Theogony* had provided the basic insight here, but the Stoic use of Platonic and Aristotelian philosophical notions vastly increased the philosophical cohesion and credibility of the system.

IV. Theophilus's Reading of Genesis 1–3 as a Modification of Stoic Cosmogony

In the course of his second book Theophilus quotes verbatim and in sequence every verse of Gen. 1:1–3:19. While his approach gives the impression of deferring to the biblical text, in reality it allows him to comment with considerable latitude, highlighting some materials, rearranging or ignoring others,[85] even at times contradicting the Scripture he has just quoted.[86] Here he follows a clear pattern: he quotes some short passages of Scripture in the midst of commenting on them; then he quotes a long section of Scripture verbatim; then he comments on it at some length, selecting the issues he deems worthy of comment and sometimes subdividing his comments.[87] His reordering and subdivision of the text and commentary contribute to his complex compromise between accepting the organization of the biblical material itself and imposing a framework derived from Stoic cosmogony and protohistory. On the one hand the "Six Days of Creation" (deliberately) and the two accounts of creation (despite his best efforts) produce seams in Theophilus's treatment. On the other hand, the influence of Chrysippus's three-phase cosmogony and of the stages of Diodorus's cosmogony, zoogony, and protohistory is also evident in Theophilus's arrangement of his discussion.[88] An outline of this portion of the work will help to illustrate these points:

I. Gen. 1:1-4 as Chrysippus's phase one: Word (λόγος) acts on Matter (ὕλη)

84. Cf. Hahm, *Origins,* 61-63; Lapidge, "Stoic Cosmology," 166; and n. 20 above.

85. Passages on which he makes no comment are Gen. 1:27b; 2:3, 11b-12, 18-20, 22, 23b, 25; 3:1a, 2-5, 7, 8b, 10b-14a, 15, 16b, 17-19. He does not quote Gen. 3:20-24, although he alludes to 3:23-24.

86. He contradicts Gen. 2:15 in his comments in *Autol.* 2.24. On the importance of subtle forms of "retelling and reshaping" biblical materials, cf. Franxman, *Genesis,* esp. 25-27. Despite the fact that Josephus, unlike Theophilus, does not quote the Scripture but only paraphrases it, the insights and method of Franxman are quite helpful in analyzing Theophilus's use of Scripture.

87. The pattern of quoting extensive consecutive passages of Scripture, then commenting on them, is followed only in this section of Theophilus's work.

88. Given limitations of space I will address only the influence on Theophilus of two of Chrysippus's three cosmogonic phases and a few aspects of his treatment of human origins.

Quotation mixed with brief comments on each verse for Gen. 1:1-4a (*Autol.* 2.10.21-34)

II. The "Six Days of Creation"

Simple quotation of Gen. 1:4b–2:3 (*Autol.* 2.11)

III. The "Six Days of Creation" as Chrysippus's phases two and three: Separation of the elements in the cosmic embryo and generation by Spirit (πνεῦμα) of the sublunar world

Comments on Gen. 1:1–2:3 (*Autol.* 2.12-19)

A. Rhetorical praise of the "Six Days" followed by attack on its Greek imitators (*Autol.* 2.12)

B. Phase Two: Separation of the elements in the cosmic embryo

Comments on Gen. 1:1-13, the work of the first three days of creation, taken together (*Autol.* 2.13-14)

1. Work of the first three days (*Autol.* 2.13)
2. Typological interpretations (*Autol.* 2.14)

C. Phase three: Generation by Spirit (πνεῦμα) of the sublunar world

Comments on Gen. 1:14-31, the works of the fourth, fifth, and sixth days treated in clear sequence, each with extensive typological interpretations (*Autol.* 2.15-18)

1. On Gen. 1:14-19: Work and typology of the fourth day: Luminaries (*Autol.* 2.15)
2. On Gen. 1:20-23: Work and typology of the fifth day: Fish and birds (*Autol.* 2.16)
3. On Gen. 1:24-31: Work and typology of the sixth day: Land animals and man (humans? male and female?) (*Autol.* 2.17-18)
   a. On Gen. 1:24-25: Land animals and typology (*Autol.* 2.17)
   b. On Gen. 1:26-31: Man and his dignity

D. Comment on Gen. 2:1-2: The repose of the seventh day merely noted without interpretation (*Autol.* 2.19.1-3)

IV. Transition from generation to history (*Autol.* 2.19.4-23)

Quotation mixed with comments for Gen. 2:4-7

A. Gen. 2:4-5 as an alleged summary of Gen. 1:1–2:3

B. Formation of man and placement in Paradise: Gen. 2:6-7

Mixed quotation and comments to avoid double account

V. Biblical protohistory

Simple quotation of Gen. 2:8–3:19 (*Autol.* 2.20-21)

VI. Commentary on protohistory (*Autol.* 2.22-28)

Comments on Gen. 2:8–3:19

A. Problems of anthropomorphism and anthropopathism

Discussion of Gen. 3:8a and 3:10a in the light of λόγος doctrine (*Autol.* 2.22)

B. Unity and historicity of cosmogony and protohistory

Discussion of Gen. 2:7-14 (*Autol.* 2.23-24)

C. Problem of divine jealousy and punishment

Discussion of Gen. 2:16-17 in relation to Gen. 3:23-24 (*Autol.* 2.25-27)

D. Woman, sin, and the serpent

Discussion of Gen. 2:21, 23a, 24 (*Autol.* 2.28)

Theophilus's comments on Gen. 1:1-4 in *Ad Autolycum* 2.10.21-34 serve to bring the biblical text into conformity with phase one of Chrysippus's cosmogony. "In the beginning [ἐν ἀρχῇ] God made heaven and earth," Theophilus explains, means that "by his Word God made heaven and earth." In other words, the Word (λόγος) of God is the Principle (ἀρχή) by which "heaven and earth" were created. When he subsequently asserts that the first verses teach that "the matter [ὕλη] from which God made and fashioned the world came to exist in some way, having been produced by God," he seems to equate "heaven and earth" with matter produced ex nihilo by the Word of God. So, like the early Stoic cosmogony, Theophilus's cosmogony begins with a Principle, the Word, acting upon matter. But in contrast to their ideas, his matter is neither another Principle nor eternally linked with the Word; it is not merely inert but has been produced ex nihilo by the Word. He understands Gen. 1:2 as an explanation of the production of matter by Word: "Then after mentioning their creation [i.e., the creation of heaven and earth], he gives us an explanation: 'And the earth was invisible and formless, and darkness was above the abyss and the Spirit of God was borne above the water.'" Just as the Stoics identify the Word-Principle (ἀρχή-λόγος) with creative fire, Christian tradition had already identified Jesus with both Word and Light (John 1:1-12). So it seems natural that Theophilus proceeds to the next verse, prefacing the scriptural quotation with a remark that identifies Light (φῶς) with ἀρχή: "Light is the beginning [ἀρχή] of the creation, since the light reveals the things being set in order. Therefore it says: 'And God said, Let there be light.'"

Theophilus's comments in *Ad Autolycum* 2.13-14 on Gen. 1:1-13 depict the biblical text as phase two of Chrysippus's cosmogony, the separation of the elements in the cosmic embryo. After the extensive quotation of Scripture and his rhetorical praise of the "Six Days of Creation," he explains Gen. 1:1-2 again, this time defining four terms in order from the bottom up: (1) earth is equivalent to a base and foundation (ἔδαφος καὶ θεμέλιον); (2) the abyss is the multitude of waters; (3) darkness is caused by the heaven which covers the earth and waters; (4) the spirit is life-giving and nourishing and permeates the creation like the soul in a human being,[89] but simultaneously it holds the place of light separating the water and the darkness from heaven.[90] So "heaven" is the uppermost layer, or, as we shall see in a moment, the outermost layer, the container. With only slight interpretation these are the four elements of Chrysippus's cosmogony in their proper order: earth, water, air (identified with darkness),[91] and πνεῦμα = αἰθήρ.[92] Above and around the four elements is heaven: "Like a vaulted ceiling [καμάρα], then heaven [οὐρανός] surrounded [συνεῖχε] matter [ὕλην], which was like a clod of earth [βώλῳ]."[93] He fortifies this statement with a quotation of Isa. 40:22, to show the consistency of the prophet's description with Gen. 1:2.

The separation of the elements into their container would seem to be completed. Yet as he moves on to Gen. 1:3, the command "Let there be light!," Theophilus continues to describe a separation. The "Word, shining like a lamp in a closed room, illuminated the [matter] under the heaven, making it separate from the cosmos."[94] Now the Word-Light-Principle has assumed the position previously held for it by the Spirit. Diodorus Siculus

89. Cf. n. 77 above.

90. Contrary to Nautin's assumption, both aspects of Theophilus's Spirit are compatible with Stoic notions; cf. Pierre Nautin, "Ciel, Pneuma et Lumière chez Théophile d'Antioche (Notes critiques sur Ad Autol. 2.13)," *VC* 27 (1973): 165-71, esp. 167. For evidence that for Chrysippus the spirit is both in and above the world, see nn. 77-78 above. For an argument in favor of keeping the manuscript reading τύπον, "type, figure, symbol," rather than altering it with Sender and Grant to τόπον, "place," cf. Nautin, 168.

91. Cf. SVF 2:429, 430, understood as a fragment of Chrysippus's *Physics* where Hesiod's *Theogony* is allegorized, as per the discussion of Hahm, *Origins,* 239. For an important parallel in Aelius Aristides' *Oration to Zeus,* cf. Grant, *VC* 13 (1959): esp. 42. An inexact but interesting parallel occurs in Bereshit Rabbah i.13; cf. Grant, "Theophilus," 237. Nautin, missing the equation of darkness with air, sees only three elements here (*VC* 27 [1973]: 167).

92. Cf. nn. 71, 76 above.

93. *Autol.* 2.13. Note the use of συνέχω here; cf. n. 27 above. As Nautin has observed, Theophilus's heaven is spherical, and is only compared with a roof in its function, not in its shape (*VC* 27 [1973]: 171); but his textual emendation earlier in *Autol.* 2.13 (from τρόπον to τύπον) is not necessary since the prophet's words may be *interpreted* figuratively.

94. *Autol.* 2.13. Cf. Nautin, *VC* 27 (1973): 165-71, esp. 168-69, for the modification of Grant's translation here.

has a similar culmination to the separation of the elements: "When in the beginning . . . the universe was being formed, both heaven and earth were indistinguishable in appearance, since their nature was mixed: then, when their bodies separated from one another, the universe took on in all its parts the ordered form in which it is now seen; the air set up a continual motion, and the fiery element in it gathered into the highest regions, since anything of such a nature moves upward by reason of its lightness."[95]

This completes the work of the first day, but Theophilus does not mention this division of time. Nor will he note the passing of the second and the third days in his succeeding remarks on the activities which belong to them: the creation of the firmament, separating the waters, and the separation of the dry land from the water and the adornment of the earth with plants. So he seems to ignore or obscure the structure of the Genesis account here. Possibly the reason for this is that the Stoic accounts would draw a clearer line between the genesis of the heavenly bodies and the origins of the sublunar world.[96] The biblical account, in moving from the origin of plants to the origin of stars, causes some difficulty for Theophilus.[97]

V. Theophilus on Genesis 2–3 as Protohistory Rather Than Myth

Diodorus began his universal history by contrasting "two opinions" which he ascribed to "the best authorities both on nature and on history": "Some [Peripatetics], supposing that the universe did not come into being and will not decay, have declared that the human race has also existed from eternity; the others [Stoics], holding that the universe came into being and is corruptible, have said that, like it, people had their first origin at a definite time."[98] He then proceeded with the second (Stoic) view, sketching a process which corresponds to Theophilus's Stoicized treatment of Genesis as we have discussed it thus far. Diodorus's cosmogony was followed by a description of the origin of life on earth and then by the description of the first human beings and their life. In order to maintain the entire Genesis

95. Book 1.7.1-9, *The Library of History of Diodorus of Sicily,* trans. C. H. Oldfather, LCL, vol. 1 (= books 1 and 2.1-34) (London: William Heinemann Ltd., 1933), book 1.7 = pp. 24-29. In the quotations that follow, I have followed Oldfather's translation with slight modifications.

96. Cf. esp. Todd, "Monism," 152-55.

97. Cf. his remarks in *Autol.* 2.15.

98. Diodorus *History* 1.6.3. For the former as a Peripatetic view, cf. Oldfather, LCL, pp. 24-25 n. 1; for the latter as a Stoic view, cf. Hahm, *Origins,* 211-12.

narrative on a level of scientific and historical truth equal to Diodorus's, Theophilus must show that the biblical account proceeds smoothly from cosmogony to protohistory without mythological interruptions. He begins this task by addressing the problem of anthropomorphism and anthropopathism in Gen. 2–3.

Theophilus is concerned to safeguard the philosophical acceptability of the sacred text despite anthropomorphism and anthropopathism in the narrative. Thus he ostensibly addresses the question how God "walked" in the Garden, and indirectly how he "spoke" by stating that the Logos, or Word, of God is the one present in all theophanies (*Autol.* 2.22). The "hands" with which God formed man are Logos and Sophia (2.18). God is said to have "planted" the Garden only to show how good everything was there (2.24). God questions Adam not out of ignorance but out of patience (2.26). To the difficulty of divine jealousy or anger implicit in the punishment of Adam (and Eve?),[99] Theophilus responds with a thoroughly elaborated understanding of the divine pedagogy. Neither mortal nor immortal by nature, man was created with the capacity for immortality dependent on obedience to God's commands (2.26).[100] Immortality and divinization were the intended end for man, who was "obviously" permitted to eat from the tree of life in the Garden (2.24). The tree of knowledge was not death-dealing but only the wrong food for infants such as Adam was (2.25). Since Theophilus does not quote the final verses of Gen. 3, he avoids the passage most suggestive that the expulsion from the Garden was motivated by divine jealousy.[101] On the contrary, expulsion from the Garden offers the best opportunity to expiate the sin and to attain immortality; this is the explanation of the apparent inconsistency in Adam's being placed in the Garden twice (in Gen. 2:8 and 2:15); the second represents the eschatological return to paradise after the resurrection and judgment (*Autol.* 2.26). The subsequent biblical history is the story of human progress toward that goal.[102]

Equally important to Theophilus is the unity and historical reality of the paradisal narrative. Although he is clearly aware of the disjunction and repetition in the two creation stories (Gen. 1:1–2:4a and 2:4b–3:24), he

99. Theophilus seems to avoid referring to Eve in 2.25-28, and several times refers to Adam by name, so that it is unclear to what extent his observations here are applicable to all human beings as opposed to men.

100. Again, it is unclear whether Eve is meant to be included here and in the following places where I have translated ἄνθρωπος as "man."

101. Gen. 3:20-24 is not quoted, and the only allusion to any part of this pericope is in the remark that Adam knew his wife Eve only after being expelled from the Garden (*Autol.* 2.28).

102. This point is ably argued by Droge, *Homer,* esp. 102-18.

addresses the difficulties by harmonizing the divergences to produce a single narrative.[103] Furthermore that narrative is history, not myth. After the quotation of Gen. 2:8–3:19 he observes, "Such are the words of holy scripture which contain the *history* of the human being and paradise" (2.21, emphasis added). The reality of the punishments meted out to the woman and to the serpent serve as proof of the story.[104] That this is a story that happened in a historical sense is further corroborated by the fact that paradise is on earth: "To show that paradise is of earth and was planted on the earth, the scripture says: 'And God planted paradise in Eden to the east . . . , and he set man there; and God also caused to come up from the earth every tree which was beautiful to see and good to eat.' By the expressions 'also from the earth' and 'to the east' the divine scripture clearly teaches us that paradise is under this very heaven under which are the east and the earth."[105]

On the one hand, then, the narrative must not violate notions of the goodness and power of God: A good God must have originally placed humans in "a better place and a finer location" (2.23); as created, animals were neither ferocious nor carnivorous.[106] On the other hand, the narrative must be consistent with actual historical conditions. Thus when Theophilus depicts the pre-fallen state of Adam and Eve in terms of the contem-

103. For example, although fruit trees are explicitly included among the plants created on the third day and given to humans for food on the sixth day (Gen. 1:12, 29), the second account of the creation indicates there was no vegetation before God formed Adam from the clay and then planted the garden with various trees (Gen. 2:5-9). Theophilus solves the difficulty by treating Gen. 2:4-5 as a recapitulation of the narrative to that point and then by asserting, in contradiction of the Scripture as he has himself quoted it, "God then caused to come up from the earth every tree which was beautiful to see and good to eat, for originally there were only the plants, seeds and herbs produced on the third day" (*Autol.* 2.24; cf. 2.19). Likewise he harmonizes the two accounts of the creation of man by asserting that "God made man on the sixth day but revealed his formation after the seventh day, when he also made paradise" (2.23), or elsewhere, " 'Let us make man' had been spoken by God but the formation of man had not yet been manifested" (2.19) — apparently drawing a distinction between the word spoken by God and the deed of creation. In any case, the whole account is a unit.

104. καὶ ὅτι ταῦτα ἐστιν ἀληθῆ, αὐτὸ τὸ ἔργον δείκνυσιν (*Autol.* 2.23); here only woman's pain in childbearing and the serpent's crawling and eating the dust, respectively, are mentioned.

105. *Autol.* 2.24. He adds some details about the four streams that flow from the river of paradise that can be affirmed out of his own and his reader's knowledge of geography: the "Geon, which encircles the whole land of Ethiopia is a river which they say appears in Egypt, where it is called the Nile. [The Tigris and Euphrates] . . . are well-known to us because they are on the edge of our own regions" (ibid.).

106. *Autol.* 2.17; for herbivorous and carnivorous birds, cf. 2.16, and for the vegetarian diet of humans, too, cf. 2.18.

poraneous discussion among philosophers of the original condition of human beings,[107] the fall produces a change from a state of "soft primitivism" to a state of "hard primitivism."[108] That is, God's original intent was that humans enjoy the carefree primitive state free from toil: "When God set the man in paradise to work it and guard it, he commanded him to eat of all the fruits, obviously including the tree of life; he commanded him not to taste of the tree of knowledge alone. . . . The expression 'to work' implies no other task than keeping the commandment of God" (2.24; cf. 2.19). But after the fall the conditions of life are harsh: men have been cast out of paradise and so must toil, women must bear children in pain, some animals imitate the viciousness of humans. Human disobedience alone brought pain, suffering, sorrow, and death.[109]

Like the Stoics, Theophilus is clear that man is the center of the cosmos.[110] He understands the special dignity of man in the created order as related both to immortality and to dominion; but he gives particular emphasis to the latter, again in agreement with the Stoic preference for metaphors of sovereignty.[111] Where the Septuagint says, "Increase and multiply and fill the earth and dominate [κατακυριεύσατε] it and rule over [ἄρχετε] the fish . . . birds . . . flocks and all the earth and all the reptiles," Theophilus explains, "When he had made him and had blessed him so that he would increase and fill the earth, he subordinated all other beings to him as subjects and slaves [ὑπέταξεν αὐτῷ ὑποχείρια καὶ υπόδουλα τὰ πάντα]" (2.18; cf. 2.11). It is unclear that the

107. Droge, *Homer,* 103, et passim.

108. The language and notions are from Arthur O. Lovejoy and George Boas, *Primitivism and Related Ideas in Antiquity* (New York: Octagon, 1965), esp. 9-11; their work is cited by Droge, but not precisely in the way I use it here.

109. *Autol.* 2.25. Theophilus's silences are as telling as his statements. He passes over the coats of skin made for Adam and Eve by God in Gen. 3:21, perhaps because acquiring them would mean killing animals, an action inappropriate to God. (Cf. *Autol.* 1.9, where Theophilus relates disapprovingly an unusual story, possibly from Musaeus via Chrysippus, that Zeus killed and skinned a goat that had fed him; see Grant, *Autolycum,* p. 13 n. 1; idem, *Apologists,* 149). The punishment of the woman by desire for her husband and subjection to him is also omitted, perhaps because this would suggest God intended the situation to be otherwise. (For these ideas based on the silence of Josephus in the same two instances, cf. Franxman, *Genesis,* 62-63.)

110. On this theme in Stoicism, cf. Spanneut, *Stoïcisme,* 380-85.

111. He makes no direct statement about the nature of the image and likeness with reference to Gen. 1:26, but he stresses the special dignity in God's making man with his "hands" — Logos and Sophia. Man was created with the potential of immortality — a potential capable of actualization only pursuant to obedience in the garden (*Autol.* 2.27; his earlier apparent suggestion that God's breathing the breath of life into the face of Adam was the bestowal of an immortal soul [cf. 2.19] should probably be read in the light of 2.27). Since he states that if man were either created or became immortal, he would then be a god, one might expect that Theophilus would identify the image and likeness of God as the potential for immortality, but he does not do so (2.27; cf. 2.18). For sovereignty as a Stoic motif, cf. n. 26 above.

woman participates in this dominion. Theophilus gives very little attention to Eve, and the attention he gives is rather negative. After noting the formation of Adam, his placement in paradise and companionship with God,[112] he proceeds immediately to discuss the consequences of sin; the detailed narrative surrounding the sin receives scarcely any comment.[113] He discusses the formation of Eve from Adam's side only after he has completed his discussion of paradise and the fall: "It was when Adam had been cast out of paradise that he knew his wife Eve, whom God had made out of his side to be his wife" (2.28). She is clearly and forcefully associated with sexuality, which is, in turn, dissociated from the paradisal state. Although he does not address the questions how Eve knew the command or who was more to blame, he emphasizes her association with the serpent.[114] He omits the etymologies pertaining to "woman" as "taken from man" and "Eve" as "mother of all the living" and substitutes one which links her name with her sin "because she was at first deceived by the serpent and became the pioneer of sin."[115] Despite these negative associations, women have some positive value. God's creation of Eve from Adam's rib is meant to oppose polytheism by showing that a single God made them both and to assure the strength of men's love for their lawful wives (2.28).

In sum, for Theophilus man's pre-fallen relation to God and his rule over the creation are clearly delineated, but women are to be associated with sin and sexuality. Marriage belongs to the post-paradisal state, but it is good in that context. Although many of these elements are in the Genesis narrative itself, Theophilus is not anxious to subvert them. His perspective throughout the protohistory is consistent with Stoic conceptions of God as well as with

112. *Autol.* 2.22-23. In his discussion of the human condition in paradise, sin, and its punishment, he mentions Adam by name three times, never refers to Eve by name, and always uses ἄνθρωπος in the singular, suggesting that he may mean only or primarily Adam and hence "man" rather than "humankind."

113. *Autol.* 2.19, 22-27; Theophilus has no comment on Gen. 3:1-7, 8b, 10b-14a, 15, 16b, 17-19. Theophilus has passed over in silence the loneliness of Adam, the naming of the animals, and the themes of nakedness and shame, as well as the content of the conversations of the serpent with Eve and of Adam with God.

114. Although he has little to say about the details of the conversations of Eve with the serpent or God with Adam and Eve, he does allude twice to God's conversations with Adam and once to the serpent's speaking to Eve (Autol. 2.22, 26, 28).

115. Gen. 2:23b; 3:20; cf. *Autol.* 2.28. This cannot be explained entirely by the fact that the rejected etymologies are based on Hebrew rather than Greek. The etymology chosen by Theophilus alludes to a triple pun attested in the rabbinic literature by which her name is fundamentally related to "proclamation" of sin, "calamity," and "serpent." For the argument that these are Theophilus's allusions rather than the Bacchic cry "Euan" (as per Droge, *Homer,* 107, and others), cf. N. Zeegers-Vander Vorst, "Satan, Ève et le serpent chez Théophile d'Antioche," *VC* 35 (1981): 152-69.

Stoic emphasis on anthropocentrism, on marriage, with its implied subordination of women, and on the family as the natural basis of society.[116]

VI. Conclusion

I have argued that Theophilus's treatment of Gen. 1–3 is not a systematic, verse-by-verse commentary, but as befits its literary context, an apologetic argument, designed to address the question of its truth in the light of contemporaneous philosophical and proto-scientific thought. In this case, the intellectual disciplines which are assumed to be "scientific" are cosmogony, anthropology, history, geography, etymology, and ethics. His philosophical and literary world is eclectic but nonetheless dominated by Stoic notions of reality; it is the world of Hellenistic historiography and Stoic physical allegory of Homer and Hesiod, the "physiologists." He has shaped his discussion of the cosmogony and protohistory in the first chapters of Genesis specifically to address the concerns of Stoic philosophy as developed by Chrysippus and as applied to historiography by Diodorus Siculus.

Yet he does not always follow their views in every detail, and he is sometimes anxious to differentiate his view from theirs. Moreover he frequently argues against Stoic allegorizing, especially of Hesiod's *Theogony,* and he sometimes makes explicit reference to Chrysippus in this regard (*Autol.* 3.8). So it is reasonable to think of him as consciously anti-Stoic. Yet I have contended that the main lines of his argument as well as his presuppositions are Stoic. This is not the blatant contradiction it first appears to be. Although he has many quarrels with the representatives of these traditions who are neither Jewish nor Christian, he has paid them the tribute, at times perhaps unconsciously, of allowing many of their assumptions and commonplaces to function as the foundations of his argument. He assumes that most of the Stoic doctrines are simply scientific; they are valid. But the attempt to read these cosmological, geographic, anthropological, and etymological views into Homer and Hesiod is absolutely wrong in his view. Chrysippus, as the clear proponent of this approach to the epic tradition,[117] must be the principal enemy after Homer and Hesiod themselves. Theophilus is nonetheless clearly intent on reading many Stoic notions of genesis into the biblical book of Genesis. So the crucial question for him is *whose* ancient text will be reinterpreted in the light of contemporaneous science.

116. Cf. Emile Brehier, *Chrysippe et l'Ancien Stoicisme,* 2d ed. (Paris: Presses Universitaires de France, 1951), 259-79, esp. 260-61.

117. Cf. n. 83 above.

3. *The Exegesis of History in John Chrysostom's* Homilies on Acts

Amanda Berry Wylie

In the second century Lucian of Samosata complained that because of the political situation and the Parthian war, every single person was writing history, "nay more, they are all Thucydideses, Herodotuses and Xenophons to us."[1] Lucian, remaining safely out of range of the hazards of war and the hordes of ambitious historians, took it upon himself to give advice to those who thought that anyone could write history. From his work *How to Write History,* we see that there are certain conventions of historiography that endured despite differences of opinion regarding priorities and style. An educated person who picked up a work of history in the Hellenistic world had an idea of what to expect.

When John Chrysostom picked up the Acts of the Apostles and began to preach fifty-five homilies on the text to the church in Constantinople (A.D. 400), he saw Acts as a kind of history. This is not surprising since it is generally considered one of the more historical books of the Bible — one that tells the story of the earliest history of the church. Much discussion has raged in the field of New Testament studies over the literary context of Luke-Acts and the capability of Luke as a historian. A spate of works have been produced that seek to place Luke within the tradition of Hellenistic historiography.[2] In

1. Lucian, *How to Write History* 1.2-5. Cited from *Lucian,* vol. 6, trans. K. Kilburn, LCL (Cambridge: Harvard University Press, 1959), p. 5.

2. The bibliography on the subject is vast and the issues of main concern vary. For only a few of the more recent and helpful studies of Luke and history, see: David E. Aune, *The New Testament in Its Literary Environment* (Philadelphia: Westminster, 1987), chap. 3, "Luke-Acts and Ancient Historiography," 77-115, which gives additional bibliography on the subject; F. Bovon, *Luke the Theologian: Thirty-three Years of Research (1950-1983)*

Chrysostom's homilies we find that he too recognized Luke within this context. He did not try to prove that Luke was intending to write a history of one type or another — a project that has presented problems for some New Testament scholars. Luke's intention seemed obvious to John, who refers quite casually to Luke as "the historian."[3]

John's background clearly shaped his view of history. When making such claims about a writer of the Antiochene school, it is necessary to distinguish between what John was reading and how he was interpreting it. It does not suffice to say that he was just explaining the text in the historical (and not the allegorical) sense, as has come to be expected from writers in the tradition of Antioch. A more precise study of the exegetical method that raises critical questions about the usual boundaries of genre is truer to the work of Karlfried Froehlich. John had an idea of what history was, and that idea was shaped by his study of the Bible, his rhetorical training, and at least a general awareness of the literature of his day.[4] It is clear that the Old Testament had a strong historical significance for John.[5] Without denying that this may have affected his reading of Acts, it will be helpful to open up the field of possibilities to see what other sources John may have had for his ideas about history.

The homilies themselves reveal evidence as to what John meant when he called the book a work of history. In *Hom.* 29, John vents some frustra-

---

(Allison Park: Pickwick, 1987); L. R. Donelson, "Cult Histories and the Sources of Acts," *Bib* 68 (1987): 1-21 (on p. 2 he proposes that "Luke operated as any respectable Greco-Roman historian would have operated"); W. Ward Gasque, "The Historical Value of Acts," *TynBul* 40 (1989): 136-57; Colin J. Hemer, *The Book of Acts in the Setting of Hellenistic Historiography,* ed. Conrad H. Gempf (Tübingen: Mohr, 1989); M. Hengel, *Acts and the History of Earliest Christianity* (Philadelphia: Fortress, 1980); E. Plümacher, *Lukas als hellenistischer Schriftsteller* (Göttingen: Vandenhoeck & Ruprecht, 1972); W. C. van Unnik, "Luke's Second Book and the Rules of Hellenistic Historiography," in *Les Actes des Apôtres: Traditions, rédaction, théologie,* ed. J. Kremer, BETL XLVIII; Journées Bibliques de Louvain 28, 1977 (Louvain: Leuven University Press, 1979), 37-60.

3. John refers to Luke as the ἱστοριογράφος in *Hom.* 21, PG 60:163, NPNF 11:134-35; cf. *Hom.* 28, PG 60:211, NPNF 11:180; *Hom.* 35, PG 60:254, NPNF 11:220.

4. It is not clear exactly which historical writers, if any, John had read in full. See Chrysostomus Baur, *John Chrysostom and His Time,* vol. 1, trans. M. Gonzaga (Westminster, MD: Newman, 1959), 306, where he says that Chrysostom knows and cites Thucydides among other classical writers. He notes a reference in which Thucydides is mentioned only briefly, but there is no real indication that John has read his work (*De Sacerdotio* 4:6, 70, PG 48:669). Other historians are not cited by name, with the exception of Josephus, whose work is acknowledged in the Acts homilies in *Hom.* 5, NPNF 11:32, 35; *Hom.* 14, NPNF 11:89; *Hom.* 27, PG 60:206, NPNF 11:175.

5. See *Hom.* 29, PG 60:219, NPNF 11:187; *Hom.* 38, PG 60:274, NPNF 11:237-38; *Hom.* 38, PG 60:276, NPNF 11:239; *Hom.* 49, PG 60:342, NPNF 11:295; *Hom.* 54, PG 60:377, NPNF 11:322.

tion that his listeners are not reaping enough benefits from his preaching. He says that the Scriptures should provide cures for the maladies of the soul, both in its histories (ἱστορία) and in its exhortations (παραίνεσει). He then proceeds to give examples from the two forms of edifying material found in Scripture. When giving examples from the histories, John can merely mention key names that will remind his hearers of the whole stories. He names as illustrations the tales of Pharaoh, the Assyrian, Gehazi, Judas, and the devil, and explains that these stories yield the same messages that are proclaimed directly in other parts of the Bible.[6] Both forms are there to teach, says John, who cites Paul, "Now these things . . . were written down for our instruction" (1 Cor. 10:11).

While both forms of biblical material are instructive, John does make a literary distinction between them. The Acts of the Apostles are a kind of history, which is primarily the acts or πράξεις of Peter and Paul. When he reaches Acts 13, John indicates that up to this point he has been dealing with Peter, and from now on we will be learning about the history of Paul's deeds.[7] John recognizes Acts as only the second book of a two-part work.[8] Having told of Christ's works in the first book (Luke's Gospel), the historian now picks up the story of the apostles. John cautions that it is not just history as narrative that the book presents, but it is a witness to the experiences of the apostles.[9] Even this purpose, as we shall see, is part of the function of the book as history.

I. Luke and the Standards of Historiography

John indicates throughout the homilies that he is reading the text of Acts as history when he remarks on Luke's use of standard historiographical methods. Naturally, with his high regard for the inspiration of the text, John is eager to praise Luke's worthiness as a historian. Bearing this prejudice in mind, we nevertheless see that John makes an effort to qualify his estimation of the evangelist's writing by following traditional standards for the virtues and characteristics of historiography.

6. *Hom.* 29, PG 60:219, NPNF 11:187.

7. *Hom.* 28, PG 60:210, NPNF 11:179; cf. *Hom.* 33, PG 60:239, NPNF 11:205; *Hom.* 55, PG 60:383, NPNF 11:327.

8. John says that Luke divided his work into two parts for lucidity (σαφήνεια), *Hom.* 1, PG 60:17, NPNF 11:4. Dionysius considers σαφήνεια one of the essential rhetorical virtues by which he judges Thucydides *(De Thucydide);* see S. F. Bonner, *The Literary Treatises of Dionysius of Halicarnassus* (Amsterdam: Adolf M. Hakkert, 1969), 18-20.

9. *Hom.* 1, PG 60:15-18, NPNF 11:2-3.

One concern that was common among historiographers of the ancient world was the authenticity of the history, which is guaranteed by the sources used. Oral sources were preferred to written ones, and being an eyewitness to the events one described was best of all. Most of the historiographers wrote annals or accounts of events within their own lifetime.[10] In the very first homily, John discusses Luke's credentials as a historian. He says that Luke has already explained his authority in his Gospel, having learned about the life and work of Jesus from the apostles as eyewitnesses. He is even better qualified to relate the events that he has experienced personally as Paul's companion, where he himself becomes the eyewitness. Luke discerningly emphasizes that truths were delivered to eyewitnesses (Luke 1:2), asserts John, who himself echoes the conventional view of historical accuracy: "because, in matter of belief, the very thing that gives one a right to be believed, is the having learned from eyewitnesses: whereas the other appears to foolish persons mere parade and pretension."[11]

John upholds the integrity and truthfulness of Luke as a historian, saying that he does not hide facts in the history even when the full truth might not be flattering.[12] In one instance John explains that Luke describes Cornelius fully in order that no one would doubt the truth of the story.[13] He is also said to report names and numbers in his accounts in order to show that they are true.[14] In all things he seems to be consciously following certain methods of historical reporting. The emphasis on truth in historical writing is found throughout Greek literature, but was particularly expressed by Thucydides.[15]

According to Greek historiographical standards, not all facts and events are included, but only those that are useful or pertinent. When the narrative of Paul's travels seems inconsistent with Paul's own account, John explains that the writer here has omitted incidents and condensed the account for conciseness, or that he mentions the larger cities on the itinerary while passing by the smaller towns, "as relating a history." Luke leaves

10. Both Herodotus and Thucydides were interested in recent events and preferred oral sources to written ones. See Arnaldo Momigliano, "Greek Historiography," *History and Theory* 17 (1978): 1-28, esp. 4-5.

11. *Hom.* 1, PG 60:18, NPNF 11:3.

12. *Hom.* 51, PG 60:351, NPNF 11:303; *Hom.* 27, PG 60:205, NPNF 11:174; *Hom.* 34, PG 60:246, NPNF 11:213.

13. *Hom.* 22, PG 60:171, NPNF 11:142.

14. *Hom.* 27, PG 60:206, NPNF 11:175; *Hom.* 41, PG 60:290, NPNF 11:252; cf. *Hom.* 47, PG 60:329, NPNF 11:284, where both names and deeds are given in order to bear witness to the facts.

15. Hemer, *Book of Acts,* 79. The importance of truthfulness was echoed by many historiographers. On Lucian see Aune, *New Testament,* 95.

out certain details or parts of the story as the "heathen authors" do, according to John, either because he does not know the details personally, or because giving too much information makes the reader dull.[16] In another homily John judges that the historian seems to be epitomizing the events of many years by giving only the most important facts.[17] He praises Luke for his conciseness.[18]

As a writer of history Luke points out the function of that history for his readers. John commends him for demonstrating, as historians do, that the events narrated in Acts bring about certain results — there is a causality behind the deeds. When he tells of the apostles preaching to the Gentiles, Luke then shows the quick results by saying that many believed.[19] Again, Luke tells how churches were established in the faith as a result of Paul's circumcising Timothy, even though the action was contrary to Paul's own opinion. The decision did not work against Paul, but instead produced the greater good.[20] We see in the history that events consistently work out in some logical or providential way. John constantly points to the role of divine providence in the way things happen, even if they should not immediately appear to be positive results.[21] John seems to downplay the miraculous events and instances of direct divine intervention in Acts. John

16. *Hom.* 21, PG 60:163, NPNF 11:135; *Hom.* 34, PG 60:248, NPNF 11:215; cf. *Hom.* 43, PG 60:305, NPNF 11:265, where he explains why Luke has changed his method and reports details of the travel; *Hom.* 55, PG 60:382, NPNF 11:326. See also van Unnik, "Luke's Second Book," 52-54. Dionysius lists among the five tasks of a historian the decision whether to include or omit events. The discussion was part of his essay *On Imitation,* found only in fragments or in the summary in his letter to Gnaeus Pompeius; see Dionysius of Halicarnassus, *The Critical Essays,* vol. 2, trans. Stephen Usher, LCL (Cambridge: Harvard University Press, 1985), 379.

17. *Hom.* 45, PG 60:317, NPNF 11:275.

18. *Hom.* 28, PG 60:211, NPNF 11:180.

19. *Hom.* 30, PG 60:222, NPNF 11:189.

20. *Hom.* 34, PG 60:249, NPNF 11:216.

21. John refers to Providence (as NPNF translates it) or a divine plan to history throughout the homilies, using οἰκονομικῶς: *Hom.* 21, PG 60:166, NPNF 11:137; *Hom.* 23, PG 60:177, NPNF 11:148; *Hom.* 25, PG 60:191, NPNF 11:162; *Hom.* 33, PG 60:242, NPNF 11:209; *Hom.* 42, PG 60:298, NPNF 11:259, etc.; or οἰκονομία: *Hom.* 22, PG 60:172, NPNF 11:142; *Hom.* 24, PG 60:183, NPNF 11:155; *Hom.* 25, PG 60:195, NPNF 11:165; *Hom.* 32, PG 60:234, NPNF 11:201; *Hom.* 34, PG 60:245, NPNF 11:212; *Hom.* 47, PG 60:327, NPNF 11:282, etc.; or forms of οἰκονομέω: *Hom.* 22, PG 60:173, NPNF 11:143; *Hom.* 25, PG 60:194, NPNF 11:165; *Hom.* 31, PG 60:229, NPNF 11:197; *Hom.* 39, PG 60:276, NPNF 11:240, etc. When he does use πρόνοια for Providence, it reflects the use of an OT text (see LXX for Jer. 5:24): *Hom.* 31, PG 60:228, NPNF 11:196. While chance (τύχη) is an important factor for Thucydides, Dionysius prefers to speak of the involvement of the gods in a providential way. See Hemer, *Book of Acts,* 82-85; see also Glenn F. Chesnut, *The First Christian Histories: Eusebius, Socrates, Sozomen, Theodoret and Evagrius,* 2d ed. (Macon, GA: Mercer University Press, 1986), 37-60.

exults in Paul's human activity, e.g., building a fire by hand, noting that miracles are saved for times of emergency.[22]

When he reads the book as history, it is more important to John to see that God is working in all things, and that God more often allows or plans for good things to come about "in a human way."[23] God does not need to change the course of nature in order to guide Paul's ship to safety despite unfavorable winds.[24] In fact, when a person gives in to the belief in Fate and the accuracy of omens, that person is enslaved to those beliefs and is in chains more than Paul was. John does not guarantee that bad things will not happen to good people, but that the saints will not suffer in adversity which they know to be for their benefit and for the glory of God.[25]

II. John and the Didactic Purpose of History

John treats both the events of history and the writing of history with utmost seriousness, but the distinction between them is not always clear. In his estimation it seems that history happens with a purpose and histories are written according to certain rules, rules which also have a purpose. One thing that events and the records of events have in common is their pedagogical function. We can learn from our own experiences and from the experiences of others. We can also learn from reading about what happens to other people, especially when it is written in a way that is most instructive to us. This is the main function or utility (ὠφελεία) of history — to teach.[26] Especially as part of Scripture, the accounts in the book of Acts are not to be picked out merely as facts or details, but with the purpose of teaching.[27] We may learn from Luke, who was not ashamed to tell us about Lydia's occupation as a seller of purple, that we should not be ashamed of anyone.[28] In Acts we hear of the many trials and tempests through which Paul suffered, and since we have heard the stories, we are spared from having

22. *Hom.* 54, PG 60:373, NPNF 11:319.

23. *Hom.* 48, PG 60:333, NPNF 11:288; *Hom.* 26, PG 60:201, NPNF 11:171, where it has καὶ τοῦτο δὲ γίνεται ἵνα μάθωμεν ὅτι καὶ ἀνθρωπίνως πολλὰ ᾠκονόμηται.

24. *Hom.* 53, PG 60:367, NPNF 11:315.

25. *Hom.* 53, PG 60:372, NPNF 11:319.

26. The utility of history, particularly for its pedagogical function, is a common theme in Greek historiography. While Herodotus made it a rule to explain events in order to learn from them, and Thucydides, Dionysius, and Lucian all refer to it, the emphasis on ὠφελεία is considered particularly "Polybian." See Aune, *New Testament,* 95-96; Hemer, *Book of Acts,* 79; van Unnik, "Luke's Second Book," 49-50.

27. *Hom.* 34, PG 60:250, NPNF 11:217; cf. *Hom.* 46, PG 60:324, NPNF 11:281.

28. *Hom.* 35, PG 60:254, NPNF 11:220.

to suffer the same troubles ourselves. If we have learned something from his experiences, we can avoid similar trials.[29] We are not only informed by these lessons of history but also find comfort and assurance by remembering the evidence of God's providence.[30]

The insistence upon the utility of history, a common theme in Hellenistic historiography, provides the key for understanding John's hermeneutic of history that seems to guide much of his interpretation of the book of Acts. Granted, with all of his preaching John is homiletically oriented and never abandons exhortation completely when looking at the Bible exegetically. In fact he has often been dismissed as more of a preacher than an exegete, and he is seldom chosen to exemplify the Antiochene school of exegesis, that honor going more likely to Theodore of Mopsuestia.[31] John does take the preaching task seriously and often addresses the pressing issues of his day, such as the lack of churches for the peasants, the desires for luxury, and the horse races and theater that compete with his worship services for the attention of his congregation.

Even the two-part format of his homilies may help to clarify John's hermeneutic of history. The preacher gives a running discourse on the elements of each verse of the text. He explains the relevant points, both those of difficulty and those that are well known but central to the text. After the synopsis of the text for the sermon, Chrysostom repeats the process, giving precedence to points that he feels need to be emphasized by repetition. He then follows this first section with the exhortation where he addresses specific issues of moral or practical application. Many of his homilies, including the fifty-five on Acts, are divided abruptly between the exegesis or commentary and the exhortation.

The apparent disjuncture between the two parts of the homilies presents some problems for those who look for continuity between the text and the message preached.[32] One illustration of this difficulty is the problem of swearing taken up by John in four homilies in a row. He continues to expound on the text of Acts in order, but returns to the same moral issue for several homilies. He tells his congregation that he will continue to

29. *Hom.* 53, PG 60:371, NPNF 11:318.

30. *Hom.* 38, PG 60:274, NPNF 11:238.

31. For example, M. F. Wiles, "Theodore of Mopsuestia as Representative of the Antiochene School," in *The Cambridge History of the Bible,* vol. 1, ed. P. R. Ackroyd and C. F. Evans (Cambridge: Cambridge University Press, 1970), 489-510.

32. John may in fact give some clue as to the basis for the two-part procedure in his commentary on Galatians, where he comments that Paul himself divides his epistles into two parts. First he discusses doctrine, then he carries on a moral discourse in the second part. It may be that the apostle who has so inspired Chrysostom in many ways has also given him cause for following a certain structure in his own work. See *Gal. Comm.* 5, NPNF 13:39.

preach the same message until they hear him. Even when it appears that he is ready to continue with a subject indicated by the text, he returns to his favorite issue. We will not necessarily find the connections we seek as good homileticians between the first and second parts of John's homilies, but within his own framework there seems to be a continuity. In the first half of each homily on Acts, John follows the biblical text, resolving difficulties and explaining why things were said or done in a particular way. He emphasizes the actions and the personalities of the apostles as patterns or models for all Christians. The second half of each homily then addresses specific moral virtues or the way that we ought to live. One part shows us by example, the other tells us directly. It corresponds to what John in *Hom.* 29 calls either history or exhortation.

The two sections do not need to address identical subjects, but they do work toward the same purpose: the shaping of the soul toward true philosophy. John continues to preach on swearing, because he has selected that problem as the first lesson, which must be learned before the congregation is ready to go on to the next lesson.[33] Moral education is to be orderly so that the foundation is strong. These lessons deal directly with perfection of the soul, which is taught in the historical sections by giving models of such perfection. The first Christians did not resort to tears and grievances when faced with troubles, but they continued to preach and teach, and as a result much was accomplished. They grew stronger and more vigorous through their suffering, unlike the softer members of John's church. He lamented, "What tears do not these things call for! Think what they suffer, while we live in luxury, we in theatres, we perishing and drowning in dissolute living, seeking always idle amusement, not enduring to suffer pain for Christ."[34] Thousands chose faith and decided to live a virtuous life instantly when the church was young. They did not resist the faith or its demands but willed their way to virtue. No longer are people like them, says John, because the people of his day are reluctant and cold.[35] Often he begins the second half of his homily with a simple cry to imitate the virtuous behavior just seen in the text.[36]

33. *Hom.* 11, PG 60:98, NPNF 11:75.

34. *Hom.* 35, PG 60:255, NPNF 11:221.

35. *Hom.* 7, PG 60:68, NPNF 11:48.

36. *Hom.* 30, PG 60:225, NPNF 11:192; *Hom.* 39, PG 60:279, NPNF 11:242; *Hom.* 50, PG 60:348, NPNF 11:299; see also the emphasis on imitation in *Hom.* 9, PG 60:81, NPNF 11:60; *Hom.* 14, PG 60:117, NPNF 11:92; *Hom.* 21, PG 60:169, NPNF 11:140; *Hom.* 26, PG 60:202, NPNF 11:172; *Hom.* 43, PG 60:305-6, NPNF 11:265-66; *Hom.* 45, PG 60:319, NPNF 11:276; *Hom.* 52, PG 60:364, NPNF 11:312; *Hom.* 53, PG 60:372, NPNF 11:318; *Hom.* 55, PG 60:384, NPNF 11:328.

The deeds and human models in history work in the same way as text — they are text in action. The apostles are the embodiment of the new laws given by God: "not pillars of brass did He raise up, and engrave letters thereon, but twelve souls raised He up for us, the souls of the Apostles, and in their minds has He by the Spirit inscribed this writing." Christ wills that we not only look at these pillars, says John, but that we also should be like them.[37] The lives and acts of the apostles in this history are to be read as living text, and the lessons are invariably practical: "Nothing ruffled Paul, nothing discomposed Peter. When thou hast convincing proofs, why lose thy temper, to render these of none effect? It is impossible for one who is out of temper ever to persuade. Yesterday also we discoursed about anger: but there is no reason why we should not today also; perchance a second exhortation coming directly after the first will effect somewhat."[38] In *Hom.* 39 John begins his parenetic section by exhorting his hearers to imitate Paul. He states his plan to make a similar enquiry with words to the proof that he has just shown in the exposition of the text. The proof by action and experience is surer than words, but he wants to make it even plainer with words.[39] The acts speak more loudly than words.[40]

III. The History and Identity of a People

We have seen that John used terms that were common in describing historiography and its rules. He recognized Luke's writing in the context of Hellenistic historiography and gave his estimation of Luke's work within that context. We have also seen that historical exegesis has particular relevance for John as an interpreter of Acts, because he saw it as a historical book. To get even closer to the question, we need to probe this category of history to see more precisely what John thought he was reading. The results, if any, will not be readily applicable to ascertaining Luke's intention, but will further enhance our understanding of John's view of the text as history.

The specific way in which John interprets the purpose or utility of history may help to identify a narrower field of history in which the text was seen. The most central aspect of history for John seems to be its utility. This alone does not ally him with any particular school or genre of histori-

37. *Hom.* 5, PG 60:56, NPNF 11:37.
38. *Hom.* 32, PG 60:237, NPNF 11:204.
39. *Hom.* 39, PG 60:279, NPNF 11:242.
40. Paul uses both, *Hom.* 45, PG 60:314, NPNF 11:273.

ography, but shows an understanding of the common view of history. For John, the usefulness of history is obviously not in the way it teaches military tactics for generals, as we would find in Thucydides. John does not seek to find lessons for political life like Polybius, although he does apply the lessons of history toward building oneself up to endure the changes of fortune.[41] For John, the history in Acts primarily teaches us by providing moral models from the early Christian church for later generations. The apostles and other worthy persons in the earliest church are depicted as patterns to be emulated.

The earliest Christians are not just saints to be admired and imitated, but ancestors who are organically linked to the saints of later years. The apostles are the founders of the church that still thrives in John's day, and which he wants to make more mindful of its heritage. The book of Acts tells the history of these founders. John sees in the beginning of Acts the story of how "our people" (ἔθνος) was instituted.[42] The challenges that faced the Acts community have been inherited by the church of the fourth century. In Acts 12, John sees that the history of this community is the intertwining of rest and troubles, of good and bad events. When Peter is miraculously released from prison, he goes to find the other members of the church singing and praying through the night. For John this courage and faith in the sight of adversity is the ideal for the church: "With women, and children, and maidservants, they sang hymns to God, made purer than the sky by affliction. Nothing ever was more splendid than that Church. Let us imitate these, let us emulate them."[43]

As a group, the earliest church was a virtuous body. Unlike John's contemporaries, the disciples had great respect for their leaders, and yet rather than be conceited, the entire body of the church was in harmony.[44] The apostles were not contentious.[45] The saints in the church cared for one another as a large family.[46] They gave alms in greater abundance, both money and acts of service.[47] The saints of the early church were strong in fellowship, not only spiritually but in social relations as well, having despised wealth and

41. See Momigliano, "Greek Historiography," 7. Van Unnik cites Polybius (*Pol.* 1.1.1) who wrote that the lessons of history are the "school in which the right spirit for enduring the change of fortune can be acquired" (van Unnik, "Luke's Second Book," 38).

42. πῶς οὖν συνέστη τὸ ἔθνος τὸ ἡμέτερον; the English translation in the NPNF has "our religion," but the reading of τὸ ἔθνος as a religious group instead of a nation or people is not easily substantiated. See *Hom.* 1, PG 60:19, NPNF 11:5.

43. *Hom.* 26, PG 60:202, NPNF 11:172.

44. *Hom.* 37, PG 60:265-66, NPNF 11:231.

45. *Hom.* 24, PG 60:185, NPNF 11:156.

46. *Hom.* 25, PG 60:193, NPNF 11:164.

47. *Hom.* 25, PG 60:196, NPNF 11:166.

decided to "have all things in common."[48] Since none of them called anything their own, John praises them as an "angelic commonwealth" (πολιτεία ἀγγελικὴ).[49] When they realized that both spiritual and material things were in common (Acts 2:44), they became angels all at once.[50] Throughout the homilies, John refers to the apostles as angels. Lydia was even better than Abraham for the hospitality she showed the apostles, her heavenly visitors.[51] By speaking like the apostles we are speaking like the angels.[52] It is in our power also to become angels by living a life of virtue. We will be angels in will if not by nature. Even in the matter of mortality, with Christ's victory over death, there is nothing to prevent us from becoming close to the angels.[53] Since the apostles shared the same human nature with us, the only thing that separates us from them is in their will and purpose.[54] John says that Paul, the greatest of the apostles, is a kind of angel, and even like God, again not by nature but by will, by moral choice.[55]

John extols the community in Acts in order to encourage his people to imitate them and by doing so to become a part of the same community. For this social image of founders that are both leaders of society and models of virtue and behavior for their followers, John uses a metaphor that is common in Hellenistic literature: kingship or royalty. The ruler is often seen as divine, an earthly reflection of the ruler of heaven. The rulers of the Hellenistic world were considered to be chosen by the gods, and thus were intimately connected with the notion of divine providence.[56] As embodiments of the virtues and as true philosophers the rulers were supposed to serve as examples and models for their subjects. Under Neoplatonic influence, writers emphasized this imitation that would lead the imitators up toward divinity themselves. The apostles exhibit a royal courage. When John reads in Acts 5 that Peter and the other apostles courageously stood up in the temple to teach in the name of Christ, having been warned to refrain from doing so, he urges his congregation to imitate them and be undaunted in the face of danger. In fact, John sees that the apostles acted this way in order to instruct others by their bold example.[57] The apostles

48. *Hom.* 7, PG 60:64, NPNF 11:45.
49. See *Hom.* 7, PG 60:65, NPNF 11:47.
50. *Hom.* 7, PG 60:65, NPNF 11:46.
51. *Hom.* 35, PG 60:255, NPNF 11:221.
52. *Hom.* 9, PG 60:84, NPNF 11:63.
53. *Hom.* 32, PG 60:238, NPNF 11:205.
54. *Hom.* 43, PG 60:306, NPNF 11:265.
55. *Hom.* 51, PG 60:356, NPNF 11:306.
56. Francis Dvornik, *Early Christian and Byzantine Political Philosophy*, vol. 2 (Washington, D.C.: Dumbarton Oaks Center for Byzantine Studies, 1966), 501-10.
57. *Hom.* 13, PG 60:107-9, NPNF 11:83, 84.

are more convincing in their preaching, teaching, and presence than the emperor would be with a royal mandate.[58]

In his homilies on Acts John uses the image of royalty to describe faithful Christians in general and the apostles in particular. Peter's visit to the church at Lydda in Acts 9 inspired John to depict him as the commander of an army who went about inspecting the ranks to see what was in good order and what needed his presence.[59] It was only because the need for leadership arose that Peter assumed this role. Paul is the true general in John's eyes. Paul chose Silas to accompany him into Syria (Acts 15) just as a general chooses a "baggage-bearer."[60] It was Paul who fought the good fight and arose from all of his trials and shipwreck to enter triumphantly into Rome. "Like an emperor that has fought a naval battle and overcome, he entered into that most imperial city."[61] In *Hom.* 30, after urging his hearers to imitate the apostles and to practice philosophy as the apostles did, he asks for the stillness of a painter's studio, for in his descriptions of the apostles he is employed in painting royal portraits. He applies the colors of virtue to the literary paintings so that the images might inspire others to imitate their leaders.[62]

In a later homily John says that his listeners can make "royal portraits" for themselves, too, by putting others before themselves and by being true friends to all. He now applies the royal image that he used for the apostles to all who are gracious and virtuous like them. Honoring others, speaking good things, and forgiving are the colors of these royal portraits — they are the purple and gold that mark the emperor.[63] Portraiture provided a strong symbol of the person portrayed. The metaphor was used not only in biographies but in other historical works when a description of personality and character was painted.[64] John paints portraits of the apostles in a similar fashion, to show the true colors of the founders of his people. In his *Natural History,* Pliny describes how families would keep wax likenesses of their ancestors to have the whole clan on hand. Painted portraits were hung as a family tree, with lines spread between them to trace the pedigree.[65] Anxious to encourage such practices, Pliny even excuses those

58. *Hom.* 13, PG 60:110, NPNF 11:85.
59. *Hom.* 21, PG 60:165, NPNF 11:136.
60. *Hom.* 34, PG 60:247, NPNF 11:213.
61. *Hom.* 55, PG 60:382, NPNF 11:327.
62. *Hom.* 30, PG 60:227, NPNF 11:194.
63. *Hom.* 40, PG 60:288, NPNF 11:249-50.
64. The image of the painter is used in various ways by Plutarch, Polybius, and Lucian. See Hemer, *Book of Acts,* 81 n. 61, and p. 92.
65. *Nat. hist.* 35.2.6-7; see Pliny, *Natural History,* vol. 9 (Books 33-35), trans. H. Rackham, LCL (Cambridge: Harvard University Press, 1952), 265. Pliny describes the

who lay false claims to portraits of famous people, because it demonstrated a love for their virtues.[66] The family portraits painted in the homilies on Acts are descriptions of a royal heritage for the church, and the actions and virtues of the apostles themselves are no less than regal.

John reads the history of the earliest church in Acts and sees in it the story of the founders of his people. The deeds and words of the apostles and the saintly Christians who knew the powerful activity of the Holy Spirit when the church was new provide a philosophic heritage for believers of all times. In his preaching, John points out that Luke has supplied the history that can teach believers to live more virtuous lives. The form that this history takes is not purely biographical, but it is concerned with both the character of a few people and the foundation of a new institution.

The way that John has read the text is reminiscent of the "antiquities" of historians such as Dionysius of Halicarnassus, who rewrote the founding of Rome to highlight the Greek heritage, or even of Flavius Josephus and his history of the Jewish people. John shares their form, their emphasis on the role of divine providence in history and on the utility of the antiquities for the benefit of the community of their descendants. Dionysius shows the Romans as true Greeks, especially in their πολιτεία — the whole life and attitude of the city.[67] Dionysius also describes the noble figures of his history as becoming almost divine through the immortality of their deeds, which should inspire their descendants to live nobly as well.[68] The overall similarity is striking and seems to indicate a common intention in writing. John and Dionysius also have in common that rhetorical training, style, and skill have influenced the way they operate in their respective fields, John in his preaching and Dionysius in his historical writing.[69] Part of this proximity may come from the preaching task. This is not to say, however, that the similarities are only a matter of style. Both writers recognized the func-

old practice of keeping likenesses of ancestors which were carried in processions so that the entire family could be present.

66. Pliny *Nat. hist.* 35.2.8 (ibid., 267).

67. Rather than a commonwealth of angels (see above, p. 69), Dionysius sees a commonwealth of true Greeks. See p. 133 in Clemence Schultze, "Dionysius of Halicarnassus and his Audience," in *Past Perspectives: Studies in Greek and Roman Historical Writing,* ed. I. S. Moxon, J. D. Smart, A. J. Woodman (Cambridge: Cambridge University Press, 1986), 121-41.

68. Dionysius *Roman Antiquities* 1.3.6.

69. John was trained by rhetors in Antioch. Both Dionysius and Josephus are, according to Hemer, in a "specifically rhetorical tradition of Greek historiography" (*Book of Acts,* 64). For that matter so is Lucian (ibid., 67). See also van Unnik, "Luke's Second Book," 46-47.

tion of the ancient history of a people for the maintenance of that community within a changing society.

What we mean by history affects how we interpret a text historically. John was reading the book of Acts as history in the context of the Hellenistic (not the modern) sense of the word. Many of the methods and values of Greek historiography influenced John's reading of the text. If we are to speak of a historical school of exegesis, we must be aware of the full implications the term holds within that context. Although ultimately John was still a Christian preacher whose main goal was to interpret the biblical text for his church, his interest in moral interpretation should not be divorced from his recognition of the text as history and his Hellenistic perspective on what that means. His reading of Acts as the story of the church's ancestry provided the means to relate the history to his congregation.

II. THE AUGUSTINIAN TRADITION

4. *Vile Bodies: Paul and Augustine on the Resurrection of the Flesh*

Paula Fredriksen

The body that you gave breakfast to this morning, the body that helped you navigate your automobile, the body with which you at this moment occupy your chair is, according to Augustine, the very same body that will dwell in the heavens and see God. This is an extraordinary claim. It was scarcely coherent, and it was certainly unscientific, when he presented it in A.D. 428, in the closing book of *City of God.* And he was scarcely helped in formulating it by having to base his position on an exegesis of Paul, especially 1 Cor. 15:50: "Flesh and blood cannot inherit the kingdom of God."

I propose, in this paper, to investigate the significance of the body as a theological concept. Christian thought on the human body reveals the fundamental orientation of its ideas of redemption: What is a person? What is his ultimate fate? What is salvation (and saved *from* what)? I shall proceed by presenting an antiphonal exegesis of Paul and of Augustine — Paul, because his letters stand as our earliest statement of a redemptive mythology that we (though not he) could deem "Christian"; Augustine, the fountainhead of Western Christianity, because he based his notions (virtually contrary to those of Paul) on close and careful readings of the apostle. To do this, however, I shall first have to sketch the contextual parameters of their respective religious cultures: Hellenistic science on the one hand, and Jewish restoration theology on the other.

An earlier version of this paper was delivered in November 1989 to the Senior Seminar at King's College, London. I thank Professor Graham Stanton for his invitation, and the participants for their comments.

To begin with the Greeks: Antiquity's picture of the physical universe passed through the writings of Aristotle and the Hellenistic astronomers, though the speculations of Plato and of the Stoics also come into play.[1] We trace their influence in the West through such writers as Cicero and Seneca; later, Celsus, Ps.-Aristotle, and Plutarch; finally, in the concise pagan catechism of Sallustius, *On the Gods and the World.* Popular expressions of philosophical and scientific high culture appear in astrological handbooks and the magical papyri; we see them in the stone star-map encoded in the tauroctonies of the empire's mithraea; in the Jerusalem Temple the outer curtain was embroidered with the map of heaven, and near Tiberias, pious Jews placed the sky gods of the zodiac on their synagogue's mosaic floor.[2] This imagined architecture of the cosmos, in other words, was apparently ubiquitous and, in a sense, theologically ecumenical. It could accommodate the various mythologies of antiquity — pagan, Jewish, and eventually Christian.

We should envisage a series of concentric glass spheres. The outermost and uppermost is also the most divine, the realm of celestial ether and the fixed stars. As we move inward, or downward, we encounter motion: the spheres of the five planets known to antiquity, the sun, and the moon. Below the moon, in contrast to the harmony and increasing perfection of the upper spheres, matter grew thick, sinister, maddeningly mutable; demons, the souls of the dead, Necessity congested the sublunar atmosphere. Below this, finally, at the center of the world where the heaviest matter had sunk, stood earth. This model of the universe was presupposed and confirmed by science and astrology, by astral tours, by dreams and visions.

Its architecture encoded a consistent hierarchy of order and of value: the good was "up"; the less good, indeed the bad, was "down." But simple experience imposed an anomaly, for on the earth was man. Various myth-

1. The theory of the spheres can be traced to Eudoxus, a younger contemporary of Plato; Aristotle assumes it in the *Metaphysics* (11.8), and in *De caelo* chap. 5. Good introductions to this literature may be found in J. L. E. Dreyer, *A History of Astronomy from Thales to Kepler* (New York, 1953), 9-206; and P. Duhem, *Le Système du Monde,* vols. 1 and 2 (Paris, 1954-59, orig. pub. 1908). On the religious implications of this model of the universe, see E. R. Dodds, *Pagan and Christian* (New York, 1970), esp. 5-29; Hans Jonas, *The Gnostic Religion* (Boston, 1963), 3-47.

2. On the temple's outer curtain, which "portrayed a panorama of the heavens," see Josephus *J.W.* 5.212, 214. He notes that this curtain did not display the signs of the zodiac — presumably, as David Ulansey speculates, to avoid any implication of astrology ("The Heavenly Veil Torn: Mark's Cosmic *Inclusio,*" *BARev* [forthcoming 1991]). On the Beth Alpha mosaic, see esp. E. R. Goodenough, *Jewish Symbols in the Greco-Roman Period* (New York, 1953- 68), 1:241-53; plates in vol. 3, no. 640; on astronomical symbols more generally, including evidence from Jewish inscriptions and amulets, see vol. 12.2, chap. 12.

ologies attempted to explain what he was doing there — a hostage taken in a cosmic border skirmish, a terminus to the fall of the soul — but the fact that he was there at all disrupted the elegance of this picture. Man had mind; his true self, the soul, if properly trained, was drawn to reason, virtue, and the (literally) higher realities. But this true self was trapped in the immediate material environment of the body, with its demeaning and distracting urges. Cosmology and anthropology were thus coordinate realms: man was a miniature and reversed image of the cosmos. The truly real and spiritual was inner; and the soul, trapped in uneasy juxtaposition to the body, individually expressed that same fault line that divided the universe in two at the moon. And this anthropology implied, in turn, a soteriology. Salvation was *from* life in the sublunar realm; it lay in ascent to (or back to) the divine realm of the upper world.[3]

This model of both man and the universe, then, implied a redemption that would be *in principle* nonterrestrial and nonsomatic. It is both individual (the fate of each person after death) and, in the more sophisticated versions such as that of Plotinus, nonindividual (man's soul is part of Soul; it may be oned with the One, and so on). It is also nonhistorical. Time and the cosmos do not alter; man moves through them. The cosmos is a medium for redemption, but the focus of redemption is the soul.

Jewish restoration theology presents a different map of reality, a different concept of salvation, a different arena of redemption, and, concomitantly, a different view of the human and the divine. The Jewish Bible begins with God creating the universe and ends, at 2 Chronicles, with a call to rebuild the Temple and to make *aliyah.* "Thus says Cyrus king of Persia: The Lord, the God of heaven, . . . has charged me to build him a house at Jerusalem. . . . Whoever is among you of all his people, may the Lord his God be with him. Let him go up" (36:23). These two narrative poles of the Bible establish the typological field of later Jewish eschatology. Put plainly: when final redemption comes, it will come as a renovation of creation, and a new Temple and new Jerusalem figure prominently.[4]

3. See, e.g., Sallustius *On the Gods* 4, on the Milky Way as the zone at which body subject to passion begins; cf. 13, where he comments, given the incorporeal nature of divinity, that "the World *ought* to be incorporeal too." Porphyry *De antro nymph.* 22-28, relates that the soul descends to earth through the port of entry at the northeast point of the zodiac, at Cancer, and ascends again through Capricorn; see D. Ulansey, *The Mysteries of Mithras* (New York, 1989), 61; on this topic generally, see Alan Segal, "Heavenly Ascent in Hellenistic Judaism, Early Christianity, and their Environment," *ANRW* II.23.1 (1980), 1334-94.

4. On Jewish restoration theology, see esp. E. P. Sanders, *Jesus and Judaism* (Philadelphia, 1985), 77-119, 212-41; more recently, my briefer discussion, *From Jesus to Christ: The Origins of the New Testament Images of Jesus* (New Haven, 1988), 77, 81-86. See too J. Jeremias, *Jesus' Promise to the Nations* (Nashville, 1958), 55-72; for a systematic presen-

The historical anchor for this verse in 2 Chronicles was the end of the Babylonian Captivity and all it implied: exile from the land, the destruction of the (first) Temple and of Jerusalem. These events had evidently, and quite naturally, threatened a commonsense construal of Israel's covenant with God: if God had promised the land, and Israel was now driven from it, then the election and the covenant had been impermanent or conditional. We see how the classical prophets turn the Exile from disconfirmation to confirmation, weaving God's promises to Israel and the inviolability of the covenant into the texture of physical reality itself. So, for instance, Jeremiah:

> Thus says the Lord, who gives the sun for light by day and the fixed order of the moon and the stars for light by night, who stirs up the sea so that its waves roar . . . : "If this fixed order departs from before me, says the Lord, then shall the descendants of Israel cease from being a nation before me for ever. . . . If the heavens above can be measured, and the foundations of the earth below can be explored, then I will cast off all the descendants of Israel." (31:35-37)

Through the principle that God is just and constant, that he works his purpose through and in history, the prophets distilled from this combination of tradition and current events a dialectic at once historical and religious. Exile would always imply return; sin, repentance *(teshuvah);* destruction, rebuilding.

From the Hellenistic through the Roman imperial period, the claims of this prophetic affirmation of God's redemptive purpose swell into a vision that ultimately has in view all peoples and the entire world. In the later prophets and the Pseudepigrapha, in the Apocrypha, in synagogue prayers and later rabbinic discussion, we see the traditional elements of the conclusion of the Babylonian Captivity writ large. At the End, when God establishes his Kingdom, all the forces of evil, human and cosmic, will be overthrown. The twelve tribes will be reconstituted and all the exiles gathered in to Jerusalem. There the "mountain of the Lord," the Temple, will be rebuilt or renewed in splendor. It will in any case of necessity be greatly enlarged, since not only all Israel but also the Gentiles (no longer idolatrous) will gather there to worship "the God of Jacob." Together on the mount, Jew and Gentile will partake of the feast that God himself will

---

tation, see E. Schürer, *A History of the Jewish People in the Age of Jesus Christ,* rev. G. Vermes et al. (Edinburgh, 1979), 2:488-544. Other Jewish traditions speak of a final nonterrestrial period after the messianic age, *ha-olam ha-ba,* the world or age to come: see n. 6 below.

have prepared (Isa. 25:6).[5] In some of the literature, this earthly redemption is made prefatory to a yet further stage, *ha-olam ha-ba,* the world or age to come — a notoriously indistinct concept that I note but shall not discuss here.[6] Whether as history's ultimate or penultimate stage, then, God's rule will be marked by social and natural harmony. The land will bring forth fruits in abundance, war will be vanquished, death defeated; God will wipe away every tear.

It is within this particular, and peculiarly Jewish, idea of historical redemption that we must place the hope of *teḥiyat ha-matim,* the resurrection of the dead. I will start by saying the obvious: there was no universal agreement. In the late Second Temple period, belief in physical resurrection was most associated with the Pharisees; but it is probably more accurate to say that (almost) everyone but the Saduccees so believed. The idea has no secure pre-Hellenistic scriptural attestation but does grow prominent or explicit in the writings of the Maccabaean period, the heyday of apocalyptic eschatology as well. Once articulated, it becomes, as Moore notes, the sole article of dogma in early Jewish eschatology.[7] The second benediction of the Amidah praises God for raising the dead; and in chap. 10 of Mishnah *Sanhedrin* we find this anticipation of Pascal: "All Israel has a share in the world to come. . . . And the following have no portion: one who says, There is no resurrection of the dead."

Jewish opinions on the resurrection are so varied and so numerous that Schürer-Vermes prescinds from reviewing them.[8] So shall I. But I would emphasize the following. First, the idea of personal physical resurrection represents and affirms a particular theodicy, declaring that God is

5. On these themes, and their resonance with the tradition's view of the Babylonian Captivity, see Fredriksen, *Jesus,* 77-86. As usual far from univocal, Jewish texts (even the prophetic writings speaking of ultimate gentile inclusion) also anticipate the destruction of unrighteous gentiles or their subjugation to Israel, e.g., Isa. 49:23; 54:3; Mic. 5:9, 15; 7:16-17; Zeph. 2:1–3:8). For other florilegia of prophetic and pseudepigraphic texts, see Sanders, *Jesus,* 214; T. L. Donaldson, "The 'Curse of the Law' and the Inclusion of the Gentiles: Galatians 3.13-14," *NTS* 32 (1986): 110 nn. 43-50; Jeremias, *Jesus' Promise,* 46-75; for discussion of the entire issue, see my essay "Judaism, the Circumcision of Gentiles, and Apocalyptic Hope: Another Look at Galatians 1 and 2," *JTS* 42 (1991): 1-33. I emphasize the "inclusive" tradition here because that apparently is the one in which the first generation of Jesus' followers placed themselves and which figured most prominently in their improvised eschatology.

6. See W. D. Davies, *Paul and Rabbinic Judaism* (Philadelphia, 1980), 285-320, esp. 316ff.

7. G. F. Moore, *Judaism in the First Centuries of the Christian Era,* 3 vols. (Cambridge, 1927-30), 1:172; see also Davies, *Paul,* 300.

8. *History of the Jewish People,* 2:539. For a recent survey, see A. J. M. Wedderburn, *Baptism and Resurrection* (Tübingen, 1988), 167-80.

just and thus will vindicate the righteous (and, in those writings that hold to a general resurrection and final judgment, punish the wicked). Second, the medium of this redemption is history, the focus both the human person and the earth itself. From this, two further observations. The person is identified not with the soul, but with soul and body taken together. This anthropology is dichotomous but not dualistic.[9] And the insistence on terrestrial redemption, the insistence that the quality of physical existence, but not the fundamental fact of physical existence itself, would be changed, serves to affirm Creation. Further, while individuals rise and are judged as individuals, the fundamental metaphors are social — eating together, worshiping together, living at peace with one another. Finally, given the idiom of the Babylonian Captivity, in which much of this construct is expressed, Jewish restoration theology is, at least implicitly but often explicitly, political. The image of eschatological society serves as a counterpoint to and commentary on current unrighteous kingdoms that will be displaced by the Kingdom of God.

I have reviewed this familiar material, the Hellenistic and the Jewish, in order to draw as sharply as possible a contrast between them. The vector of Hellenistic redemption is vertical, from "down here" to "up there." The vector of Jewish restoration theology is emphatically horizontal, historical: "now" and "then," or, in its apocalyptic expression, "now" and "soon." Their respective energies drive in two quite different directions, not so much opposite (for opposed pull would result in stasis) as perpendicular. To continue borrowing from the language of mechanical physics: their intimate juxtaposition would guarantee maximum torque. It is with this metaphor in mind, then, that we turn first to Paul and then to Augustine on Paul.

In his extant letters, Paul the Pharisee presents a variant but nonetheless recognizable version of apocalyptic Jewish restoration theology. He proclaims a coming messiah, the resurrection of the dead, the imminent arrival of God's Kingdom, the redemption of all Israel on the basis of the covenant's inviolability, the redemption of the Gentiles apart from the Law — all standard Jewish stuff, modified, where necessary, in the light of his conviction that the messiah had already come and would soon come again. Paul lived within Jewish history — indeed, according to his convictions, in its very last days.[10] But Paul also inhabited the Greco-Roman cosmos, and the architecture of this cosmos very much affects his presentation of historical redemption.

9. See Davies, *Paul,* 17-19, 20-30.

10. On the deeply traditional quality of Paul's eschatology, as well as his modifications of specific items, see Fredriksen, *Jesus,* 165-76; with particular reference to Gentile salvation, see my essay "Judaism, the Circumcision of Gentiles . . . ," esp. pp. 17-31.

The sidereal piety that marks some Hellenistic philosophy and science has given way for Paul (as for others) to a sense of oppression, a view that the cosmic powers stand in an essentially adversarial relationship to humanity. Paul alludes very briefly to the biblical story of Adam's fall to account for this adversity (Rom. 5:12), though elsewhere in the same epistle he says simply that creation's futility and bondage are part of some (otherwise unexplained) divine plan (8:20ff.). In any case, his Gentiles in Christ wage no σαρκικός battle (2 Cor. 10:3-4): they oppose, with and in the Spirit given to them through baptism, the same rulers (ἄρχοντες) of this age (τοῦ αἰῶνος) who crucified the "Lord of glory" (1 Cor. 2:6-8). Ranged now between them and God stand the elements of this universe, the enslaving στοιχεῖα (Gal. 4:3, 9; cf. 5:1); the "god of this world" (Satan?) who blinds the minds of unbelievers (2 Cor. 4:4); the ἀρχή, ἐξουσία, and δύναμις of this age (1 Cor. 15:24); demons (sometimes identified with pagan gods, 1 Cor. 10:20; Gal. 4:8-9); angels and principalities (Rom. 8:38).[11] Through baptism into Christ's death and resurrection, the Christian, though still in this cosmos (the form of which is "passing away"), has entered into a demilitarized zone. These powers can no longer control him.

Ranged on the side of these hostile forces we find, as well, the flesh. Paul speaks of "flesh" sometimes as a moral category: the Christian is to live not κατὰ σάρκα but κατὰ πνεῦμα. At other times — most conspicuously in Rom. 7 — he speaks of it both as an almost independent force of evil ("I know that nothing good dwells within me, that is, in my flesh," 7:18), and as a medium through which sin and death work to undermine even the Law. The tensions between the flesh and the spirit which the Christian continues to feel will be resolved only when his body is redeemed (Rom. 8:23). This, as Paul explains most clearly (and how clearly is that?) in 1 Cor. 15, will occur shortly, at the Parousia, when the Christian's fleshly body, whether living or dead, will be transformed, like Christ's, into a spiritual body.

In his thoughts on the impending redemption and the nature of the resurrection, Paul is both at his most and his least Pharisaic. The nature of redeemed life, he insists to his puzzled Corinthian hearers, will be somatic (1 Cor. 15:35-53). The messiah as liberator will appear at a given moment in historical time, announced "with a cry of command, with the archangel's call, and with the sound of the trumpet of God" (1 Thess. 4:16). He will defeat every enemy, and finally death itself, before handing over the king-

11. For the definition of these terms as referring to astral forces, see W. Bauer, *Greek-English Lexicon of the New Testament,* rev. F. W. Gingrinch and F. Danker (Chicago, 1979); see also W. Meeks, *First Urban Christians* (New Haven, 1983), chap. 8.

dom to God (1 Cor. 15:24ff.). But flesh itself is emphatically *not* redeemed: it cannot inherit the Kingdom. And this is, perhaps, because the Kingdom will not be on earth, centered around Jerusalem and a new or renewed Temple. The Kingdom will be "in the air" (1 Thess. 4:17), "in heaven" (Phil. 3:20), where no flesh can dwell. Is redemption social? Hard to say. Paul's metaphors for redeemed humanity — whether the proleptic community currently represented by the *ἐκκλησία,* or the ultimate one, Jew and Gentile, at the End — tend to be organic, corporate rather than social. Individuals (and their egos) are knit together, integrated, into the body of Christ. Politics too drop from sight: Christ defeats not the current unrighteous imperial order, nor the apocalyptic Babylon (as he does in Revelation), but the cosmic archons of the age.[12]

In the centuries between his time and Augustine's, Paul had his greatest influence among Christian dualists, Gnostics and Manichaeans. The very various nondualist Christians tended to look past Paul to the great Jewish prophetic texts within their Bibles and without — Isaiah, Daniel, Jubilees, and Baruch — to construct their image of final redemption; and that image, accordingly, was more classically Jewish than Paul's had been. Irenaeus of Lyons approvingly cited an earlier father, Papias, for preaching "an approaching millennium after the resurrection, and a corporeal reign with Christ here on earth" (*Adv. haer.* 5.33.3). According to Papias, who had it from "the elders," who in turn had it from John, Jesus himself had taught that "the day will come when each vine will have a thousand branches, each branch 10,000 twigs, each twig 10,000 shoots, on each shoot 10,000 clusters, and each cluster 10,000 grapes" — a passage appearing almost verbatim as well in the Jewish *Apocalypse of Baruch* (2 Bar. 29:5). Justin Martyr, appealing both to Isaiah and to Revelation, likewise spoke of a coming period of terrestrial superabundance, ubiquitous peace, a fleshly resurrection of the saints, and their thousand-year rule in the renewed Jerusalem (*Dialogue with Trypho* 81 on Isa. 65 and Rev. 20).

Throughout these intervening centuries, many Christians asserted that Christ's second coming would occur soon. But when was "soon"? How could one know? One way was to study the prophets' and evangelists' catalogue of apocalyptic disasters, and their cryptic descriptions of kings, armies, and empires, and see whether these matched the times. Particularly in periods of persecution, such interpretations, promising as they did the vindication of those suffering, were both powerfully persuasive and pointedly political. John's apocalyptic Babylon, seated on seven mountains,

12. On Paul's peculiar denationalizing of Jewish eschatological traditions, see Fredriksen, *Jesus,* 173-75.

is clearly Rome (Rev. 17:9). Irenaeus sees the fourth beast of Dan. 7 and the beast from the sea of Rev. 13 as the *imperium qui nunc regnat;* the name of the two-horned earth-born beast, encoded in the numbers 666, is *Latinus.*[13] If that empire persecuted, then clearly the End was at hand.

Already by the early second century, however, the wait was fatiguing some. "Where is the promise of his coming?" complains a group in 2 Pet. 3:4. "For ever since the fathers fell asleep, all things have continued as they were from the beginning." "Peter," both to console and to exhort his congregation, recalled to them a line from Psalms: "With the Lord, one day is as a thousand years, and a thousand years as one day" (2 Pet. 3:8; Ps. 90:4). This verse, together with the days of creation sketched out in Gen. 1 and the thousand-year reign of the saints promised in Rev. 20, became the churches' support for a key eschatological concept: the cosmic week, or the ages of the world. As God had created the world in six days, and rested on the seventh, and as a day to him is as a thousand years, so too would the world endure for six ages of one thousand years each. Then at the end of the sixth age, six thousand years since creation, Christ would return in glory to inaugurate the first, fleshly resurrection and the thousand-year Sabbath rest of his saints. To know the time of the End, one had only to calculate the age of the world.[14]

This approach to millenarianism, developed particularly by Christian chronographers, permitted a traditional, historical interpretation of apocalyptic texts while at the same time gaining a control over the enthusiasms they inspired. The date for the year 6,000 in Western tradition fell in the equivalent *annus domini* of 500. When Hippolytus and Julius Africanus, writing in the third century, estimated that Christ had been born in the 5,500th year since the creation, they pushed the date of the Parousia well out of their own and their communities' lifetimes. In an age that saw the rise of the New Prophecy, Montanism, an age when Catholic bishops, inspired by Scriptures, dreams, or prodigies, might believe that the End was at hand and urge their congregations to drastic action, such an exegetical strategy had much to recommend it.[15]

13. *Adv. haer.* 5.26,1; 30,3. Cf. Victorinus of Pettau (ca. 300), who awaited the *ruina Babylonis, id est civitatis Romanae* (*In Apoc.* 8.2; 9.4). On early Christian millenarianism generally, see my essay, "Apocalypse and Redemption in Early Christianity: From John of Patmos to Augustine of Hippo," *VC* 45 (1991): 151-83.

14. On the cosmic week in Western theology, see Richard Landes, "Lest the millennium be fulfilled: Apocalyptic expectations and the pattern of Western Chronography, 100-800 CE," in *The Use and Abuse of Eschatology in the Middle Ages,* ed. W. Verbeke, D. Verhelst, and A. Welkenhuysen (Leuven, 1988), 137-211.

15. Hippolytus *In Danielem* 4.23-24; cf. 4.18-19, on these apocalyptically minded

This tradition, however, was fated not to age gracefully. Its intrinsic anti-imperialism became increasingly awkward after 312. And as the target date of 500 *anno domini*/6000 *anno saeculi* drew ever nearer, we can detect a certain nervousness in ecclesiastical reports of plagues, battles, eclipses, and military campaigns. But the vision of the reign of the saints on earth continued to inspire Christians, and this was nowhere more true than in the Bible belt of Latin antiquity, Roman North Africa.

The popular expression and celebration of this millenarian hope was the cult of the saint. The pious anticipated their impending earthly reign by repairing, on the saint's day, to his tomb, to feast, dance, and get splendidly drunk. The martyr's relics would work cures (a form of restoration of bodily integrity) while the reading of his *passio* inspired the faithful. These celebrations — known as *laetitiae,* or "jolly-ups" — infuriated Augustine, who condemned them (and very nearly lost his job in the effort). But in the abandon round the martyr's *mensa,* in the drinking and feasting of the faithful at the shrine of the saint, we glimpse ancient Christian hopes for life after the *prima resurrectio;* an affirmation through enactment that the Kingdom would come on earth, and that once it did, status distinctions would dissolve, labors would cease, life would be joy, food and drink abundant and attained without effort.[16]

So we come, finally, to Augustine. To his one side stood the Scylla of popular millenarianism (as well as its erudite counterpart, the chronographical tradition: in 395 his fellow Catholic bishop, Hilarianus, affirmed that the End was a scant century off).[17] To the other, the Charybdis of Manichaean dualism, with its emphasis on the soul's escape from this universe as the measure of redemption. And behind him lay the ruins of Origen's reputation: unlike his learned Eastern counterpart, Augustine was

---

bishops; Julius Africanus, *Chronographia* (fragments), ANF 6, 130-38, on the age of the world and implied date of the Parousia; see too the discussion in Robin Lane Fox, *Pagans and Christians* (New York, 1987), 265-67.

16. That these celebrations of the saints' cults express popular anticipations of millenarian bliss needs to be argued rather than simply asserted: I cannot do that here. I will observe, however, that Augustine criticized both these celebrations *and* popular millenarian interpretations of the first resurrection in precisely the same terms: they were "carnal"; they focused over-much on material pleasures, particularly eating and drinking (cf. *Civ. Dei* 20.7.1; *Ep.* 29.11 [where he complains that the riotousness of the saints' celebrations was a pagan corruption]). Interestingly, in *Civ. Dei* 22, when Augustine repudiates both popular millenarianism and the conduct of the faithful at the saints' feasts, he identifies the *praesentia* of the saints with their thousand-year reign on earth (Rev. 20:1-6) — a deft de-eschatologizing of a key traditional millenarian idea. See esp. F. van der Meer, *Augustine the Bishop* (New York, 1961), 471-526; Fredriksen, "Apocalypse and Redemption," 155-56, 161.

17. *De cursu temporum,* in *Chronica Minora,* ed. C. Frick (Leipzig, 1892), 1:155-74; Fredriksen, "Apocalypse and Redemption," p. 156 and nn. 33 and 34.

no longer free to radically allegorize prophetic texts or to present apocalyptic thought as a mere *façon de parler*.

Augustine confronted these problems head-on. Against inferring the nearness of the End from current catastrophes (such as the fall of Rome),[18] he argued that things have been worse, and that they could always get worse. A named date, he notes, causes embarrassment once it slips by, and the Bible explicitly prohibits eschatological calculations: Only the Father can know the time. But Augustine's most imaginative and innovative strategy is to redesign the cosmic week, and so redefine the relation of God's kingdom on earth to resurrection and eschatology. *Augustine relocates the 1000-year reign of the saints.* It comes not at time's edge, with the Parousia, but with Christ's first post-Resurrection coming in his glorious body, the Church. The saints, through their relics, reign *now*, within normal history.

Thus, Augustine can insist, the first resurrection *is* fleshly: it occurs while the Christian still lives in this body. But its chief import is spiritual, the passage from "death" to "life" accomplished now, through baptism, within the Church. The saints, who rule within the Church, will indeed reign for one thousand years. But one thousand, notes Augustine, is actually 10×10×10: the number clearly signifies not a fixed period of time but the quality of fulness and perfection. The actual hour of the End none can ever estimate or know.[19]

In view of this radical agnosticism, history cannot serve for Augustine as the prime medium of salvation. He emphasizes, rather, the individual as the locus and focus of God's saving grace and so, exegetically relocating the center of gravity of Paul's letter to the Romans from chaps. 9–11 to chap. 7,[20] Augustine plays stunningly creative variations on the theme of Christian millenarianism. The fleshly body will be raised spiritual, he insists with Paul; but spiritual, to Augustine, refers not to the body's substance so much as to its moral orientation.[21] The risen body will be morally trans-

18. " 'Behold, from Adam all the years have passed, and behold, the 6000 years are completed . . . and now comes the day of judgment!' " (*Serm.* 113.8, registering the popular reaction to Alaric's invasion of Rome in 410).

19. Augustine is deeply indebted to Tyconius, the lay Donatist theologian, for this interpretation of Revelation which enables him to "de-eschatologize" current events; see my "Apocalypse and Redemption," parts 2 and 3.

20. In so doing, he likewise de-eschatologizes Paul's letter, shifting the emphasis away from its crescendo in chap. 11, the summation of salvation history, to the self-doubts of the introspective individual, whom Augustine identifies, after 418, with Paul himself (*Contra ii epp. Pelagianorum* 1.8.13-14). I discuss this refocusing, and its lingering effect on Pauline studies, in "Paul and Augustine: Conversion Narratives, Orthodox Traditions, and the Retrospective Self," *JTS* n.s. 37 (1986): 3-34, esp. 25-28.

21. "Our spiritual body [1 Cor. 15] is called 'spiritual' because it will be subject to

formed, but it will be corporeal. It will even have gender: women, too, shall as women be raised.[22]

But this raised and morally perfected body will not dwell on a transformed earth. Defying both ancient Christian tradition and contemporary scientific thinking, Augustine insists that these corporeal bodies will dwell in the heavens: the Kingdom of God will *not* come on earth. Apocalyptic traditions of agricultural and human fecundity and social harmony thus drop out of Augustine's picture: no food, sex, or social relations in the Kingdom. His saved individuals in their perfected, thirty-three-year-old's bodies stand in comradely contemplation of the beatific vision of God.

For both Paul and Augustine, then, salvation involves the body. But I take Paul's spiritual body as undergoing a transformation of substance, from flesh to something else. Augustine's, as we have just seen, moves from "fleshly" flesh to "spiritual" flesh, but corporeality remains. On this point more classically Pharisaic than was Paul himself, Augustine insists that body and soul are made by God with such an appetite for each other that the soul without the body is imperfect, less than whole: the soul without the body, he argues, cannot see God.[23]

Augustine, further, must come to terms with the Christian tradition of the double resurrection, and in so doing allows for an earthly redemption of "bodies" in the Church through baptism, reserving final redemption for heaven. The similar Jewish distinction between the messianic age and the *olam ha-ba* may stand behind Paul's depiction — the ἐκκλησία, life in the Spirit, standing for the earthly messianic age; life after the Parousia, for nonterrestrial absolute redemption — but we lack the evidence to push this very far.[24] Neither system has in view, as did ancient prophets and Christian millenarian texts, any sustained political commentary. This may be simple prudence; but it seems to me that, for both, the final location of the saved

---

the Spirit, vivified by the Spirit alone. But it will still have corporeal substance" (*De gen. ad litt.* 7.7.18; cf. 35.68, quoted in n. 23 below); "The spiritual body will be subject to the Spirit; but it will be flesh, not spirit" (*Civ. Dei* 22.21, insisting on the raised body's corporeality). Augustine of course is not dealing with a tabula rasa: fleshly resurrection had been a traditional aspect of "orthodox" Christianity for centuries. What interests us here is how he manages to de-couple the idea from millenarianism.

22. Women will be raised as women, *Civ. Dei* 22.17; against scientific arguments on the weight of the elements telling against physical bodies dwelling in the heavens, see 22.4; 22.11; on physical perfection and the age of those raised, see 22.15.

23. "The soul possesses a kind of natural appetite for managing the body. By reason of this appetite it is somehow hindered from going on with all its force to the highest heaven so long as it is *not* joined with the body, for it is in managing the body that this appetite is satisfied" (*De gen. ad litt.* 12.35.68).

24. Davies too suggests this correlation, *Paul,* 308-9.

in heaven turns their concern away from earth and the relatively narrow compass of contemporary politics.

But despite the strong verticality of their respective systems — a pull they come into, I have argued, through their picture of the universe — both men stress, as does the Bible itself, that God redeems as a historical act.[25] Paul insisted, on the basis of his experience of the Risen Christ, that he knew "how late the hour [was]," how redemption was "nearer to us now than when we first believed" (Rom. 13:11). Three hundred and fifty years later, Augustine insisted with like urgency that that hour was unknowable, and probably far off: nothing — whether Christ's resurrection, current catastrophes, or universal chronology — reveals the hour of history's clock. But Christ's resurrection does drive him, as it drove Paul, to assert that the believer's body will likewise be redeemed. Whether changed substantially or morally, then, the flesh's transformation will mark for both the hour of historical redemption.

25. See Wedderburn's comments on the relation of eschatology, spirit, and resurrection, in *Baptism,* 233, 269.

5. *The Rhetoric of God in the Figurative Exegesis of Augustine*

Robert W. Bernard

Introduction

In his remarkable autobiography, the *Confessions,* Augustine of Hippo presents not only his pilgrimage in the faith but also in the Scriptures. As for the latter, in books 11-13 of this work he presents an exegesis of the opening verses of Genesis; he demonstrates there both a concern for philosophical and theological questions and a mastery of nonliteral exegesis of the sacred text. It is that "nonliteral" or figurative exegesis that is the subject here; book 13 of the *Confessions* presents an extensive and figurative exegesis of the first several verses of Genesis, and one portion of that exegesis is presented below. As will become clear, this passage not only presents an excellent example of Augustine's figurative exegesis, but also sets a foundation for understanding the rhetoric of God,[1] the role of *figura* or "symbol" in that rhetoric, and the reason why "figurative" is the most appropriate word to describe Augustine's nonliteral exegesis of Scripture.

I. Augustine's View as Presented in *Confessions* 13.15.16-18

In *Conf.* 13.15.16-18, one finds a nonliteral interpretation of Gen. 1:6: "Let there be a firmament in the midst of the waters."

1. The rhetorical nature of the message of Scripture is the major theme of the work by Gerhard Strauss, *Schriftgebrauch, Schriftauslegung, und Schriftbeweis bei Augustin,* vol. 1, BGBH (Tübingen, 1959); see esp. chaps. 3-4. Strauss's concerns were more general; mine were more focused on terminology specifically pertaining to figurative exegesis.

> And who but you, our God, made for us the firmament, that is, our heavenly shield, the authority of your divine Scriptures? For we are told that "the sky shall be folded up like a scroll," and that now it is spread out like a canopy of skin above us.
>
> O Lord, "let us look upon the heavens of yours, the work of your hands." Clear away from our eyes the cloud with which you have covered your firmament.
>
> Above this firmament of your Scripture, I believe that there are "other waters," immortal and kept safe from earthly corruption. They are the peoples of your city, your angels, on high above the firmament. Let them glorify your name and sing your praises, for they have no need to look up to this firmament of ours or read its text to know your word. Forever they gaze upon your face and there, without the aid of syllables inscribed in time, they read what your eternal will decrees. They read, they choose, they love it. They read it endlessly, and what they read never passes away; for it is your own unchanging purpose that they read, choosing to make it their own and loving it for themselves. The book they read shall not be closed; for them, the scroll shall not be unrolled; for you yourself are their book, and you are that forever. You allotted to them their place above this firmament of ours, this firmament which you established to protect the weakness of your peoples here below, so that they might look up to it and know this work of your mercy which proclaims you in time, you who are the creator of time.
>
> For, "O Lord, your mercy is high as the heaven, and your faithfulness reaches the clouds." The clouds pass, but the heavens remain. Those who preach your word pass on from this life to another, but your Scripture is outstretched over the peoples of this world to the end of time. "Though heaven and earth should pass away," your words will remain. The "scroll shall be folded," and the mortal things over which it was spread shall fade away, "as the grass withers and the beauty thereof; but your word stands forever." Now we see your Word, not as he is, but dimly, through the clouds, "in a riddle, through the mirror" of the firmament, for though we are beloved by your Son, "what we shall be hereafter is not known as yet." Wearing the tissue of our flesh, he turned his eyes to us. He spoke words of love and inflamed our hearts, and now "we hasten after the sweet fragrance of him." But "when he comes, we shall be like him, for we shall see him as he is." It will then be ours to see him as he is, which is not yet our ability to see him.

The passage is extremely intricate, wide-ranging, and poetic. OT and NT passages are interwoven to produce a tapestry presenting both the present glory of God's kingdom and the future hope of the believer in Christ. The temporal and passing order is contrasted starkly with the eternal God and his angelic hosts; dim perception of God in this life is pitted against immediate and complete angelic comprehension of the Deity.

II. The Verbal Nature of God's Revelation

In the midst of these themes, one point comes to the fore: God's revelation is indeed seen as primarily verbal in Augustine's exegetical theory.[2] One obvious example of that verbal nature is the Scriptures, which Augustine sees symbolized by the "firmament" of Gen. 1:6. In them, we read the will of God.

The bishop, however, makes a striking comparison between us and the angelic host; we are not the only ones who read that will. Even the angelic creation in a sense "reads" it, according to Augustine. "Forever they gaze upon your face and there, without the aid of syllables inscribed in time, they read what your eternal will decrees." Thus, both they and we read God's message. Augustine's point, however, is that human beings need the Scriptures; angels do not. Yet the verbal nature of the revelation even to the angels is striking; they are reading something, and that is the face of God himself: "for you yourself are their book. . . ." Thus, by analogy, God's revelation is the same in both realms; its essence in both, of course, is extremely different. There it is direct; here it is indirect.

This passage, furthermore, makes clear that it is a specific Person of the Triune God that the angels are "reading" — it is the Son of God, the Word of God: " 'But your word stands forever.' Now we see your Word, not as he is. . . ." Again, while in separate levels of reality, both human beings and angels receive the message of God through the same source. For Augustine, the Son is central to the communication of the message of God. The bishop reinforces this point in *Confessions* 11.8.10, by quoting a Latin paraphrase of John 8:25, "Who is the beginning, for he speaks to us."[3] In this context, Christ's ministry is seen as that of the communicator of the Father's will; once again, the revelation is seen in verbal terms. For the angels, that communication is by gazing directly at the Son. For humanity, however, both Scriptures and the Incarnation are necessary. In *The City of God* 11.2-3, Augustine speaks of Christ's revelation to human beings through both the Incarnation and the Scriptures; concerning the latter, he

2. This point has been noted by other authors as well, including Strauss, *Schriftgebrauch.*

3. The Latin of this verse from John, as quoted by Augustine in *Confessions* 11.8.10, is "Quia principium est et loquitur nobis."

says that Christ spoke not only through his own ministry but also through the human authors of the Scriptures.[4] The verbal nature of God's revelation, then, is established by Augustine on the basis of God's communication of his will through Christ the Son; the importance of the human author's role in that communication will be examined later on.

III. The Problem of Human Understanding of Scripture

The essential difference between angelic and human understanding of God and his will has been mentioned above; the difference is also one of access. The angels' access is direct; that of human beings is indirect. As the bishop states it in *Conf.* 13:

> O Lord, "let us look upon the heavens of yours, the work of your hands." Clear away from our eyes the cloud with which you have covered your firmament . . .
>
> Above this firmament of your Scripture, I believe that there are "other waters," immortal and kept safe from earthly corruption. . . . Now we see your Word, not as he is, but dimly, through the clouds, "in a riddle, through the mirror" of the firmament, for though we are beloved by your Son, "what we shall be hereafter is not known as yet."

The passage contains phrases that shed light on Augustine's analysis of the reason why human beings need the sort of revelation which the angels clearly do not. They are kept free from death and corruption. For the bishop, the dilemma of human beings in the light of God's communication is the problem of sin — it clouds the Scriptures and clouds human eyes. It appears

4. In chap. 2, Augustine discusses the problem of human knowledge flawed by sin and states concerning the human condition, "In qua [sc. fide] ut fidentius ambularet ad veritatem, ipsa Veritas, Deus, Dei Filius, homine adsumpto, non Deo consumpto, eandem constituit et fundavit fidem, ut ad hominis Deum iter esset homini per hominem Deum. 'Hic est enim mediator Dei et hominum, homo Christus Iesus.' " (Truth Itself, God, the Son of God, by taking on humanity without thereby destroying his deity, established and made firm the same faith by which humankind might come to the truth, so that human beings might have a way to humanity's God through one who was both human and God. 'This is the mediator between God and human beings, the man Christ Jesus' [1 Tim. 2:5].) The emphasis here is on the Incarnation. Immediately following the discussion of the mediatorial role of the incarnate Christ, Augustine states in chap. 3, "Hic [sc. Christus] prius per prophetas, deinde per se ipsum, postea per apostolos, quantum satis esse iudicavit, locutus, etiam Scripturam condidit quae canonica nominatur." (Christ, having spoken first through the prophets, then through himself, and finally through the apostles, as much as he judged to be sufficient, also established the Scriptures which are called canonical.) Augustine thus places the Incarnation in a continuum with the revelation made by Christ in Holy Scripture.

that Augustine's concept of communication by means of "signs," as presented in *On Christian Teaching* and discussed below, is based upon the bishop's concept of the Fall, in which human beings lost the ability to communicate directly with God and thus were compelled to hear his eternal will indirectly, through words.[5] Humanity is now compelled to read words, which enunciate in time the eternal will of God.

There is, moreover, yet another difficulty for human beings in reading the Scriptures. Not only are they indirect, through signs; they are also obscure. Again, in the passage quoted above from *Conf.* 13, Augustine states: "Now we see your Word, not as he is, but dimly, through the clouds, 'in a riddle, through the mirror' of the firmament." The message is thus not only indirect (through the mirror), it is also obscure (in a riddle); through Paul's words from 1 Cor. 13, Augustine expresses an apparent necessity for God to "encode" his message by framing it in human words. Such "encoding" involves indirect expression, and it is here that *figura* or "symbol" finds its place in Augustine's interpretation of Scripture.

IV. The Theory of Signs and Figurative Speech

In order to understand more fully the linguistic theory behind this view of Scripture, and the role which *figura* plays in it, one must turn to the theory of signs in *On Christian Teaching.* A close examination of this theory shows both the indirect and symbolic nature of the revelation through the words of Scripture and suggests that such indirect communication is of immense value for human beings. As will be seen, these are aspects which are also central in Augustine's use of the term *figura,* which, moreover, unlocks still other features of the bishop's figurative exegesis.

In *On Christian Teaching,* Augustine's theory of signs presents a schema of communication entailing two things: *signa* (signs) and *res* (things). His statement introducing the subject, however, leads to more complex matters.

> All teaching [*doctrina*] concerns either signs or things, but things are learned through signs. Strictly speaking, I have here called a "thing" that which is not used to signify something else, such as wood, stone, cattle, etc., but not that wood, which we read Moses cast into the bitter waters to rid them of bitterness, nor that stone, which Jacob placed at

5. This is the central theme of the article by Ulrich Duchrow, "*Signum* und *Superbia* beim jungen Augustin," *REAug* 7 (1961): 369-72.

his head, nor that beast [ram] which Abraham sacrificed in place of his son. These are things in such a way that they are also signs of other things. (1.2.2)

Augustine thus states that "things" in the strict sense of that term are those realities which are not used to signify something else. "Signs," however, are used to signify; the most common signs in use among human beings are words. Here, however, he is also saying that there are certain "things" which can act as "signs," i.e., to point beyond themselves to something else. He has, therefore, expanded his concept of "thing" to include entities that we might call "symbols" or *figurae.* The literal meanings of such words as "wood, stone, head of cattle" are thus transferred to something else; in the instances proffered by Augustine in the passage from *On Christian Teaching,* they are symbolic of Christ.

Indirect language, through riddles, therefore, may be understood in the context of Augustine's theory of signs. Such language uses "things" as "signs" — it turns the literal meaning of a word into a symbol which points beyond itself to something else. One can discover, moreover, through careful analysis of the text, symbolic meanings. One may find, for example, that the rock which Jacob placed at his head at Bethel is the "Rock," or Christ. Furthermore, Augustine argues that such exegesis brings greater joy to the exegete than if the truths expressed symbolically were to be literally stated. In *On Christian Teaching* 2.6.7-8, Augustine demonstrates in a long figurative exegesis from the Song of Songs how he learns about the truths of the faith with greater pleasure when they result from figurative exegesis![6] In that same passage, he argues that such

6. The translation of this text is as follows:

Why indeed is it, I ask you, that, if someone should say that those are holy and perfect people, by whose life and conduct the church of Christ cuts off from all sorts of superstitions those who come to her, and, in imitation of the saints, incorporate themselves in some manner within her; who, as good, faithful, and true servants of God, putting aside worldly burdens, have come to the holy font of baptism and, ascending from it, by the conception of the Holy Spirit give forth the fruit of twofold love, i.e., of God and neighbor — why is it, then, that, if anyone should say these things, one delights one's listener less than if one should expound, with the same understanding, that verse from the Song of Songs [4:2], where it is said to the church, as if she were being praised like some beautiful woman, "Your teeth are like a flock of shorn sheep, coming up from the washing bin, which all bring forth twins, and there is not a sterile one among them"? Surely, a person does not learn anything else, does one, than if one heard this in plain language without the help of this similitude? Nevertheless, in some way, I see the saints more pleasurably when I see them like the teeth of the church, cutting them off from their errors, and bringing them, as if they were chewed and thereby tamed by the softening of the hardness of their hearts,

language helps to curb pride and prevent boredom. Figurative language, furthermore, can serve as a means for us to search for God with greater diligence and delight. In *Epistle* 55.11.21, Augustine states that figurative expressions in Scripture are meant to excite love for God, which draws us upward to him.[7] Though obscure, therefore, the verbal revelation of God enables us to "seek his face."

There is, however, another point that needs to be emphasized in the passage quoted above from *On Christian Teaching* before turning to *figura* itself. The symbols referred to in the text are not words, properly speaking; they are spatiotemporal realities. It seems clear that Augustine has taken the Stoic doctrine of the σημεῖον or "sign" and used it as the basis for his own linguistic theory; furthermore, the bishop has taken a Stoic term linked to language and has applied it to nonlinguistic items as well.[8] If there are spatiotemporal realities that may also serve as signs, one may argue that, in Augustine's figurative exegesis, events may function as words.[9] Here is another foundation for understanding his use of the term *figura* in figurative exegesis.

V. The *Figurae,* or Symbolic Events, of Scripture

In order to begin to examine the role of *figura* itself in such exegesis, the following passage is presented from *Commentary on the Psalms (Enarratio in Psalmos)* 39.2: "The ancient people of the Old Testament celebrated

---

into her body. I also recognize with the greatest delight the sheep as those who are shorn of worldly burdens as if they had laid aside their fleece, and, "coming up from the washing bin," i.e., from baptism, bring forth "all twins," the two precepts of love; and I see none of them unable to bring forth that holy fruit.

Why, however, I should see all of this with greater pleasure than if no such similitude were brought forth from the divine books — since both the thing and thought are the same — is difficult to say and quite another question. There is, nevertheless, no doubt that all things are recognized with more delight through similitudes and are found much more joyfully when they are sought out with some difficulty. (2.6.7-8)

7. The text from this epistle is as follows: "Ad ipsum autem ignem amoris nutriendum et flatandum . . . omnia ista pertinent, quae figurate nobis insinuantur." (For the nourishment and renewal of the very flame of love . . . all of these things pertain, which are made known figuratively to us.)

8. The Stoic origin of the theory of signs is demonstrated by B. D. Jackson, "Semantics and Hermeneutics in Saint Augustine's De Doctrina Christiana" (Ph.D. diss., Yale University, 1967).

9. See Strauss, *Schriftgebrauch,* 104-13, who notes in particular the transformation of events into words for Augustine *(facta = signa = verba).* See also below, n.12.

symbols of a thing to come [*figuras futurae rei*], when the true sacrifice, which the faithful know, was being announced beforehand in symbols [*in figuris*] . . . all of these things were like words [*verba*] of one making a promise. . . . The promise was made by certain signs. . . . Now the signs of promise have been removed, because the truth has been made manifest." Here we see events which function as signs, and, by extension, as words. The event as a signifying element operates analogously to a word; God is seen as making a promise, a very verbal exercise, through those events. Here also, we see *figura;* of interest here, among other aspects of its use, is its appearance in a verbal context ("announced beforehand in symbols"). A closer examination of this word is now needed to determine both its origin and its use in Augustine's figurative exegesis.

VI. *Figura*'s Background in Pagan and Christian Latin

The term is used by earlier Christian Latin writers as a rubric for symbols; such usage probably finds its origin in the Latin translations of 1 Cor. 10. There, Paul gives an interpretation of the events of the Exodus and tells the Corinthians that those events are τύποι ("types") and have occurred τυπικῶς ("as types") — terms rendered by *figura* in the Latin translation of this text.[10] The term thus has a long history by the time it comes to Augustine; what he does with it, however, is striking. He, too, uses it as a name for "symbols," but, as in the passage quoted above, he places it in the context of speech. In *Commentary on Psalm* 98.10, for example, concerning the events of the Exodus, Augustine states that God "was speaking through figures" — *loquebatur per figuras.* Its close connection with the verbal nature of God's revelation to human beings is thus made clear.

What we may see emerging is as follows. Augustine uses *signum,* a term derived ultimately from Stoicism, to describe the means of communication. Within the more general theory of signs, which encompasses all expressions, both literal and figurative, one finds *figura,* the general term for both words and events understood figuratively. In his use of the word, Augustine suggests the indirect nature of God's revelation; in this,

10. The relevant portions of 1 Cor. 10 are as follows: "Now these things are types of us [*Haec autem figurae nostrae fuerunt*], lest we become desirous of evil, as they were. . . . All of these events occurred among them as types [*omnia autem ista in figura contingebant illis*]." This is the Old Latin version of the Corinthians text, as it is quoted in Augustine's *De utilitate credendi (On the Usefulness of Belief),* written in 391/392. Despite the appearance of the Vulgate in Augustine's own lifetime, he continued to quote the Old Latin version of this portion of Scripture.

he is clearly using *figura* as a synonym for "thing used as a sign." Yet, by implication, the term *figura* and Latin words derived from it also carry with them another aspect of figurative exegesis already noted above: its aesthetic nature. It is in this aesthetic aspect that one may see the other major source for Augustine in his use of the term, for it appears that Augustine has united both the Christian idea of "type" or "symbol" expressed in terms of *figura* with something else — the notion of *figura* as "figure of speech," a translation of the Greek σχῆμα and in evidence in Latin from the time of Quintilian (ca. A.D. 30/35–100), who is apparently the first to use the term in this way.[11] It would be reasonable to assume that Augustine the rhetorician was aware of this usage; one finds such evidence in his exegesis, an example of which is now presented.

VII. The Rhetoric of God by Means of *Figurae*

One may see Augustine's use of *figura* as a "figure of speech" as well as a symbol in *Epistle* 102.6, in which he argues for the importance of the historicity of Jonah.

> It is surely neither an absurd nor an inopportune enquiry about the meaning of these things, so that, in their exposition, they are believed not only to have occurred but also to have been written down in order to signify something. . . . If things that are only said, but not done, figuratively [*figurate*] move us to faith, how much more should those which are not only said but also done figuratively [*figurate*]. For just as humans customarily use words, so too does divine power use events; likewise, just as new or less frequently used words add luster to human speech, when they are scattered about in moderation and in suitable fashion, divine eloquence is rendered more lustrous in a certain way by marvelous events that harmoniously signify something else.

There is thus a divine eloquence,[12] which is a function of divine power. It uses events the same way a human rhetorician uses words — to catch our

11. Paul Keseling, in "Augustin und Quintilian," *Augustinus Magister* 1 (1954): 201-4, states that Augustine may have had direct contact with Quintilian, but that this is not clear; other possible sources for Augustine's knowledge of Quintilian may be indirect, such as from Fortunatianus and C. Julius Victor (4th century A.D.).

12. Strauss, *Schriftgebrauch,* has dealt ably with the concept of God's revelation as *eloquentia;* in particular, he presents a very lengthy and illustrative analysis of the concept of God's revelation as speech. It is here that one finds Strauss's insightful analysis of God's activity in history seen as *signum* or *signa* by Augustine; a historical event or *factum* may thus be seen as a *signum* and, further, *verbum.* To elucidate this point, he also uses the passage from *Epistula* 102 that I quote here; see *Schriftgebrauch,* esp. 104-13.

attention, to persuade us to faith. God is thus the master rhetorician in history; by means of events as his words, he catches our attention and moves us to a goal. We are in the realm of the art of persuasion, the goal of classical rhetoric; but it is nevertheless a Christian world. For Augustine, the goal is persuasion to truth, the truth that is embodied in Christ, the Word of God, the Mediator between God and human beings.

Through the term *figura,* therefore, one may see the full ramifications of God's verbal revelation in Augustine's theory of figurative exegesis. God uses words to communicate his will, but he also uses events. Such events are *signa* or signs as "symbols," in which the literal event becomes a means of communicating still another reality. There is, moreover, yet another aspect to God's revelation; not only does God "speak" through events, but he does so as a master rhetorician! We are thus indeed able to speak of a "divine eloquence." Though God must speak indirectly, he does so with art. The exegete who knows that God is a master rhetorician may delight in the art of his Master. The focus of the Master's message, however, is seen in God's Word, both in the Scripture and in the Incarnation.

VIII. The Human Authors of Scripture

Event as word has several other important results as well. It was noted earlier that Augustine mentioned Christ's communication of truth through the human authors of Scripture. One should note especially the reference to the writing down of the event as Augustine states it in the case of Jonah. The human author of Scripture has an important role to play. In 1 Cor. 10, Paul makes the same point: "they were written down for our instruction." The written word, memorializing the event, can thus enable the exegetes of Scripture to use the event as their own word to their congregation, for God has charged the event with life and meaning. The words of Scripture witness to an eternal purpose, founded on the Son of God; they do not grow old, nor are they ever out of date for Augustine. The exegetes are free to remove the event from its original context, as long as they are guided by the truth of the faith that is exemplified most fully by the love demonstrated by Christ on the cross.[13] There God's purposes are made visible;

13. In *On Christian Teaching* 2.41.62, Augustine emphasizes the priority of love as a foundation for biblical hermeneutics and equates that love with the sacrifice made by Christ on the cross: "Sed hoc modo instructus divinarum Scripturarum studiosus, cum ad eas perscrutandas accedere coeperit, illud apostolicum cogitare non cesset: 'Scientia inflat, caritas aedificat' [1 Cor. 8:1] . . . ut 'in caritate radicati et fundati' possimus 'comprehendere cum omnibus sanctis quae sit latitudo et longitudo et altitudo et profundum,' id est, crucem Domini." (But after having been instructed in this way [i.e., in the various branches of

there his eternal purposes are made manifest in time, just as they are made manifest in the temporal words of Holy Scripture.

IX. The Figurative Exegesis of the Revelation of God

Another important factor in understanding Augustine's figurative exegesis — indeed, understanding why such a term is appropriate for his "nonliteral" exegesis — comes to the fore when one tries to define the nature of such exegesis. After a careful examination of Augustine's nonliteral exegesis, one comes to a surprising conclusion — it is not often easy or fruitful to speak of Augustine's nonliteral exegesis only in terms of "allegorical" or "typological." Indeed, it is difficult to come to a consensus about the meaning of those terms themselves. One may attempt to understand allegory as simply a fictitious narrative meant to underscore a moral truth or some other form of general truth. The choice of Herakles, the Cave of Plato, *Pilgrim's Progress* — all are allegories. They are not to be taken as historical or real. In typology, however, one interprets a text that is seen as historical, one takes its historicity quite seriously, and one sees the events, etc., mentioned in it as foreshadowings of other historical events, personages, etc. Thus, the raising of the bronze serpent by Moses to heal the people is seen in the Gospel of John as a type of the Crucifixion.[14]

Augustine, however, has a point of view that often is neither typological nor allegorical. While clearly allegorical or typological exegeses may be found in his works, those categories are not adequate for all of his nonliteral exegesis. For example, he speaks of an eternal Jerusalem, the Kingdom of God, of which the earthly Jerusalem is a symbol. The earthly kingdom is, in one sense, a foreshadowing; yet it also announces a reality already present.[15] It thus points upward as well as forward. We have thus

knowledge commended in book 2 of *De doctrina Christiana*], as the student of the divine Scriptures begins to approach their careful study, let that student not forget this statement by the Apostle, "Knowledge puffs up; love builds up" . . . so that, "having been rooted and established in love," we may be able "to understand with all the saints what is the breadth and length and height and depth," that is, the cross of the Lord.)

14. In John 3:14, the incident of the bronze serpent raised for the healing of the people of Israel bitten by poisonous snakes in the wilderness (Num. 21:4-9) is interpreted as a symbol of the crucifixion of Christ.

15. One example may be seen in *City of God* 15.2, in which Augustine discusses the manner in which the heavenly city is represented by an earthly city, the latter having itself been foreshadowed by Hagar, the concubine of Abraham (Gal. 4:21–5:1). Augustine speaks in terms of "a prophetic image" *(imago prophetica)* and "prefiguration" *(praefigurare)*, as well as truth to be expressed in the future *(expressae, sicut futura est, veritatis)*. Nevertheless,

a perspective that sees a basically ahistorical reality — for it is eternal — being manifested in time.[16] This is Augustine's perspective. It cannot be divided neatly into "allegorical" and "typological"; the most appropriate term to sum up the complex fabric of Augustine's nonliteral exegesis of Scripture is, indeed, "figurative." By means of *figurae* or symbols, God can speak his eternal purposes in the course of history. "Figurative" thus goes to the heart of the verbal nature of God's revelation of his purposes to human beings. As has been seen, the angels see those purposes directly by "reading" God's eternal reality without the syllables of time; we, however, are not so privileged. Augustine's "blessed hope," if one may use that term, is to look forward to the time when faith will give way to sight, and the indirect word, expressed through verbal and spatiotemporal symbols, will give way to direct contact with God. "Then we shall see him." Yet even now we can gain some knowledge of him, "for he speaks to us."

Conclusion

This, then, is the rhetoric of God, the One who speaks his eternal purposes to the angelic host without syllables marked by time, and to us through the course of history. By turning the realities of space and time into *figurae* or symbols which are also *signa* or signs, which accommodate God's revelation to human understanding, and which are memorialized in the written words of the human authors of Scripture, God addresses human beings by means of verbal "signs" that sum up with power and art his eternal purposes and reality. While "we see now in a mirror, through a riddle" in this life, that reality, and those purposes, are made manifest ultimately in the Word, his Son.

---

quoting Paul, the bishop states, "The Jerusalem which *is* above, which *is* our mother, is free" *(Quae autem sursum est Hierusalem libera est, quae est mater nostra)* (emphasis in English translation is mine). The symbolic representations of the heavenly Jerusalem, therefore, point both upward and forward, and represent the complex relationship between symbol and reality that can at times be found in figurative exegesis.

16. In this matter, I come to the same conclusion as Strauss, *Schriftgebrauch,* chap. 3, who sees in the rhetorical distinction of *finitas-infinitas* the manner in which the rhetoric of Scripture blends together the eternal message of God with temporal, human words.

6. *The Myth of the Augustinian Synthesis*

David W. Johnson

The centrality of Augustine of Hippo in the development of Christian doctrine in the West is so remarkable that it seems almost impossible to be overstated. Indeed, it sometimes seems as if historians of doctrine apply a variant of the Franciscan Mariological principle to Augustine: "Every conceivable excellence is to be applied." In particular, it is often stated that Western theology became Augustinian theology, or more explicitly, that the thought of Augustine became the basis of the doctrine of the church: a so-called Augustinian synthesis was bequeathed to the Middle Ages, which then proceeded to modify, adjust, misunderstand, confuse, or simply ignore the basic principles of Augustinian doctrine in order to justify a cultus based on merit. One thus sees in the theology of the Middle Ages a fall from Augustinianism analogous to the fall of the church after the age of the Apostles, or indeed to the fall of humanity itself.[1] Individual historians recast this picture in accordance with various confessional and personal idiosyncracies, of course, but the general picture of a triumph of Augustinianism at the transition between the patristic and medieval eras remains virtually undisputed.[2]

1. To be followed, in most Protestant accounts at least, by the Reformation, seen as a resurrection of the pristine gospel. Thus the history of doctrine is a reprise of the *Heilsgeschichte* itself.

2. So Adolph von Harnack (*History of Dogma,* trans. Neil Buchanan [New York: Dover, 1961, repr. from the Eng. trans. of 1900], 7 vols. in 4, 6:275-317) describes a revision of the Augustinian doctrine of grace in the direction of merit; Jaroslav Pelikan (*The Growth of Medieval Theology (600-1300),* vol. 3 of *The Christian Tradition* [Chicago: University of Chicago Press, 1978], pp. 50-105) speaks of the church as being pressed "beyond the Augustinian synthesis"; and Harry McSorley (*Luther: Right or Wrong?* [New York: Newman; Minneapolis: Augsburg, 1969], 212 et passim) documents the rise of "Neo-Semipelagianism" in the late Middle Ages, attributable to the loss of knowledge of Orange II.

Either to validate or to disprove this general picture, one must consider two questions. The first investigates the formal authority of Augustinianism: At what point and by what process did the individual theology of Augustine of Hippo become the doctrinal consensus of the church? The second question deals with the material content of that consensus: Did the doctrinal consensus of the church really represent an Augustinian viewpoint? The answer to the first question revolves by historical fiat around the nature and influence of the Second Council of Orange as a triumph of Augustinianism. The second question can be approached through the existence of a unique biblical commentary — an attempt by Cassiodorus to rewrite Pelagius's commentary on the Pauline epistles along Augustinian lines. Both of these fields of inquiry suggest that the "Augustinian synthesis" may be a myth — an artifact constructed by historians of doctrine rather than a reflection of what actually was the case. Each of these questions will be taken up in turn.

I. The Status and Influence of the Second Council of Orange

"Augustinianism" as a theological position is somewhat difficult to characterize. There is almost no topic in theology that Augustine did not consider at one point or another, but he never produced an overarching theological system.[3] There is no doubt, however, that during his mature years Augustine was consumed by soteriological matters. He was working out the issues of election and transformation long before he encountered the thought of Pelagius, but the Pelagian controversy gave those issues polemical sharpness and urgency. Almost by default, then, "Augustinianism" usually refers to the doctrine of grace that was worked out in the course of the Pelagian and Semi-Pelagian controversies.

If one investigates the question of when and how Augustine's doctrine of grace became the general position of the church, one finds an immediate difficulty: the issues of the Pelagian and Semi-Pelagian controversies were never considered at an ecumenical council.[4] Doctrines of Pelagius's friend

3. Indeed, one could hardly expect him to do so on the grand scale of an Aquinas. But one scarcely finds any of the smaller systematic expositions, either, similar to Origen's *On First Principles* or Gregory of Nyssa's *Catechetical Orations.* Perhaps *On Faith and the Creed* comes closest to that sort of enterprise in the Augustinian corpus, but that little work cannot really contain all that is implied by "Augustinianism."

4. The history of the condemnation of Pelagianism is contained in most of the standard histories of doctrine, but perhaps most fully in John Ferguson, *Pelagius: A Historical and Theological Study* (Cambridge: W. Heffer & Sons, 1956).

and (perhaps) disciple Callistus were condemned at Carthage in 412. Pelagius himself was declared free of heresy by a council in Jerusalem in 415, in part because he was willing to repudiate Callistus. Africa promptly recondemned Pelagius in 416. He was excommunicated by Pope Innocent, restored by Pope Zosimus, condemned again in Africa in 417 and 418. This condemnation was upheld, with reluctance and under imperial pressure, by Pope Zosimus. In any case, the councils which dealt with the issues raised by both the Pelagian and Semi-Pelagian controversies were local synods. The extent to which they were representative of the whole church is problematic at best.

The most prominent candidate for a conciliar triumph of Augustinianism is the Second Council of Orange in 529. At this council, twenty-five canons were approved that stress the absolute priority of grace and the intrinsic sinfulness of the human person. However, the question of predestination was only touched upon to the extent that predestination to evil was rejected.[5]

The difficulty with appealing to Orange II as the conciliar triumph of Augustinianism is that during most of the Middle Ages it was either not understood or not known at all. Henri Bouillard has demonstrated that medieval theologians relied on compilations of extracts and quotations rather than original sources, and that Orange II was not included in many of the major compilations or the collections of canon law. Even when one does find the acts of Orange II in such a compilation, the historical context necessary to make them intelligible is not apparent. Accordingly, the knowledge that there was a Semi-Pelagian controversy was by and large lost to the Middle Ages, until it was rediscovered by Thomas Aquinas himself through a reading of the pertinent texts of Augustine.[6] The acts of Orange II

5. The most succinct statement of the doctrine of Orange II is contained in its Confession of Faith: "We ought to preach and believe, that the free will has been so inclined and weakened by the sin of the first man, that no one since would be able either to love God as he ought, or to believe on God, or to work what is good before God, unless the grace of the divine mercy had preceded him. We believe that, grace having been received through baptism, all the baptized are able and under obligation to perform by the assistance and co-operation of Christ the things which pertain to the salvation of the soul, if they have resolved to labor faithfully. But that some have by the divine power been predestinated to evil, we not only do not believe, but even if there are any who are willing to believe such an evil thing, we with all detestation pronounce an anathema upon them. He, no good merits preceding, inspires in us faith and love of himself, so that we may both seek in faith the sacraments of baptism, and may be able after baptism, by his assistance, to perform those things which are pleasing to him." From R. Seeberg, *Textbook of the History of Doctrines,* 2 vols. in 1 (repr. Grand Rapids: Baker, 1964), 1:382.

6. Henri Bouillard, *Conversion et grâce chez Saint Thomas d'Aquin* (Paris: Aubier, 1944), 92-122.

itself were not generally available until their publication just before the Council of Trent.

It is then simply untrue that there was a triumph of Augustinian doctrine over that of Pelagius or the Semi-Pelagians on a conciliar level, in the way that there was a triumph over Arianism at Nicea and Constantinople. Orange II was the most forthright statement of an Augustinian doctrine of grace, but Orange II tended to be either misunderstood or simply unknown. After the generation immediately involved in the controversy had passed away, it had little appreciable theological effect until the Reformation era.

One may argue, however, that Orange II, whether remembered or not, was at least representative of the prevailing theological climate, and that it represented a broad Augustinian consensus in Western theology. This hypothesis can be tested through examination of the previously mentioned commentary produced by Cassiodorus. To this commentary we now turn.

II. Cassiodorus's Rewrite of Pelagius's Pauline Commentaries

After having been a Prime Minister to Ostrogothic kings and then a war refugee (and possibly a political prisoner) in Byzantium, Cassiodorus Senator returned to his family estates to direct a monastic and scholarly enterprise known as Vivarium.[7] He dedicated himself and his monks to a life of prayer and study. One of his most famous works, the *Institutiones Divinarum Litterarum,*[8] is simultaneously a handbook of Christian theological literature, a compendium of secular arts, and a rule for the direction of his monks. Cassiodorus was less than "the savior of Western civilization," as some have styled him.[9] He was, however, a key figure in the transition from the ancient world to the Middle Ages.[10]

At Vivarium, Cassiodorus had in his possession a commentary on the letters of Paul. This commentary came to him with a high reputation, and some attributed it to Pope Gelasius. Cassiodorus, however, detected in it

7. Cassiodorus's dates are uncertain. His birth is variously placed between 480 and 490. He was ninety-three when his last major work was completed. His return to Vivarium from Byzantium was sometime after 551.

8. Critical edition by R. A. B. Mynors, *Cassiodori Senatoris Institutiones* (Oxford, 1937). Eng. trans. by L. W. Jones, *An Introduction to Divine and Human Readings* (New York: Octagon, 1966).

9. So Jacob Hammer, "Cassiodorus, the Saviour of Western Civilization," *Bulletin of the Polish Institute of Arts and Sciences in America* 3 (1944-45): 369-84.

10. Cf. Gustav Bardy, "Cassiodore et la fin du mode ancienne," *Année théologique* 6 (1945): 383-425.

"the poison of the Pelagian heresy."[11] In fact, the commentary was that of Pelagius himself, although that was not established until the twentieth century.[12] Cassiodorus revised the Romans section, inserting in the process extensive quotations from the works of Augustine and various other sources. He then assigned his students to expurgate the rest of the commentary.

Thus, ironically, Cassiodorus attempted to produce an Augustinian Pauline commentary from the work of Pelagius himself. This revision can serve as a kind of laboratory in which to investigate how well the issues of the Pelagian controversy were understood in the sixth century. Did Cassiodorus and his students really succeed in their attempt to purge the Pelagian poison? Or did elements of Pelagius's theology remain unrecognized in the revised commentary?

The doctrine of predestination provides a convenient theological locus to examine the editorial revisions of Pelagius and his students.[13] There is a clear and consistent divergence between Pelagius and Augustine on this issue, as Pelagius equates predestination with foreknowledge, and Augustine with a primordial divine decree.

III. The Doctrine of Predestination in the Cassiodorus Revision

Raising the question of grace in the way that it was raised in the Pelagian controversy leads almost inevitably to the question of predestination. If grace is understood as transforming power, as it was on the Augustinian side, one must wonder why this power is given to some and not to others, or at least why it is effectual in some and not in others. Augustine had taken up this question even before the Pelagian controversy began, in the treatises *De diversibus quaestionibus* 83 and *Ad simplicianum,* and he was to return to it in *De praedestinatione sanctorum* and *De dono perseveran-*

11. *Institutiones* 1.8.1 (Jones, *Introduction,* 90).

12. This was decisively proven by Alexander Souter, *Pelagius's Expositions of the Thirteen Epistles of St. Paul,* 1: *Introduction,* Texts and Studies 9 (Cambridge: Cambridge University Press, 1922-31), 319, following a suggestion by C. H. Turner, "Pelagius' Commentary on the Pauline Epistles and its History," *JTS* 4 (1902-3): 132-41. The work by Souter is in three parts. Part II is the text of the Pelagius commentary. Part III contains later interpolations into the commentary, made when the commentary circulated under Jerome's name. I will cite this work as Souter I, Souter II, or Souter III, with the appropriate page number.

13. For a more extended comparison of Pelagius and the Cassiodorian commentary see David W. Johnson, "Purging the Poison: The Revision of Pelagius' Pauline Commentaries by Cassiodorus and his Students" (Ph.D. diss., Princeton Theological Seminary, 1989).

tiae, written ten years after Pelagius had disappeared from the scene and was very likely dead.[14] His ultimate response was that grace-as-transformation is given individually to some and not to others. The rationale for this individual selection lay hidden in the will of God and was not accessible to human reason.

Pelagius equated predestination with foreknowledge, a view which he could find in Ambrosiaster,[15] Origen-Rufinus,[16] and even in the early works of Augustine himself.[17] Pelagius thus could feel with some confidence that he was expressing the theological consensus of the church in the following reading of Rom. 8:29.

> *Those who according to his purpose were called as saints. For those he foreknew.* According to which he planned to save by faith alone those he had foreknown were going to believe, and whom he called gratuitously to salvation; how much more greatly will he glorify those who work for salvation. *And predestined them to be conformed to the image of the glory of his son.* To predestine is the same as to foreknow. Therefore He foresaw those who were going to conform in life, and willed that they be conformed in glory, because "he will transform our lowly body, conforming it to his glorious body." *In order that he be the firstborn of many brethren.* "The firstborn from the dead" in glory.[18]

Pelagius's use of the terminology "by faith alone" has been seen as an alien element in his theology, an accommodation to Pauline thought rather than his own system.[19] Pelagius, however, is quite careful and

14. See J. Patout Burns, "The Interpretation of Romans in the Pelagian Controversy," *Augustinian Studies* 10 (1979): 43-54, for a history of the development of Augustine's doctrine of predestination.

15. Pelagius's "those he had foreknown were going to believe" *(quos praescierat credituros)* is almost a direct echo of Ambrosiaster's "those God knows are going to believe." Cf. Alfred J. Smith, "The Latin Sources of the Commentary of Pelagius on the Epistle of S. Paul to the Romans," *JTS* 19 (1918): 201-2, and Souter I, 179.

16. "A comparison of the comm[entary] of P[elagius] on these verses [Rom. 8:28-30] with the corresponding exposition of O[rigen]-R[ufinus] — VII 7 on vv. 28, 29, VII 8 on v. 30 — suggests that while P shews no trace of anything approaching to language-dependence on O-R, he must have found much in the older commentator which accorded with, and no doubt helped to determine, his own particular point of view. . . . God's purpose is determined by His foreknowledge of the characters and merits of men" (Smith, *JTS* 20 [1919]: 160-61).

17. In *Expositio Quarundam Propositionum ex Epistula ad Romanos,* Augustine had written: "He did not predestine anyone, except those whom he foreknew were going to believe and follow His call." Quoted in Smith, *JTS* 20 (1919): 59, along with other, similar texts. See also Smith, *JTS* 31 (1929-30): 21-35.

18. Quotations from Pelagius are my own translations of the text contained in Souter II. Bible verses are in italics; the commentary is in normal type.

19. Georges de Plinval, "Points de vues récents sur la théologie de Pélage," *RSR* 46

consistent in his use of the term: he refers to the forgiveness Christ obtained for others through his death on the cross. We appropriate this forgiveness only by believing.[20] Beyond this appropriation, however, there is still the necessity of living out the Christian life. Herein lies the characteristic Pelagian emphasis on grace as the teaching and example of Christ: "The grace by which we conquer has offered us teaching and example."[21]

For Pelagius, then, predestination is simply God's knowledge of those who will respond to grace by meeting forgiveness with belief, precept with obedience, and example with imitation. Since there is no question of an infusion of grace or a transformation of human capacities, grace for Pelagius has a very public character about it. It is openly offered and may be grasped by whoever will grasp it.[22] Those who do grasp it will be rewarded by heavenly glorification and eternal life, even more so than those who were called only because God foreknew they would believe.[23] Such foreknowledge neither grants nor removes the ability to respond to grace. It only guarantees that God knows from the beginning who will be saved.

Cassiodorus, then, found in the Pelagian commentary the doctrine that predestination really is only God's foreknowledge of merit. One would expect him to replace that doctrine with an Augustinian one in revising the

---

(1958): 229. See R. F. Evans, *Pelagius: Inquiries and Reappraisals* (New York, 1968), 163 n. 109.

20. Pelagius posits a duplex scheme of justification. Referring to Rom. 10:5 he writes, "Moses himself distinguished between two forms of justification, of faith of course, and also of works, because the one will justify by means of works, the other only through believing. [*Ipse Moses distinxit inter utramque iustitiam, fidei scilicet atque factorum, quod altera operibus, altera sola credulitate iustificet accedentem.*]" See Souter II, 81-82. Pelagius can thus maintain that there *is* justification by faith alone without having to say that there is *only* justification by faith alone. Pelagius ties the appropriation of the forgiveness of sins *sola fide* firmly to baptism, as in the comment on Rom. 5:17: "Justification is given through baptism, not possessed from merit. [*ipsa iustitia donatur per baptismum, non ex merito possidetur.*]" See Souter II, 47. To say this, however, does not require the sort of transformation upon which Augustine insisted in his own doctrine of grace.

21. *Four Letters of Pelagius*, trans. Robert F. Evans (New York: Seabury, 1968), 111. Pelagius: "Gratia[m] uincendi et doctrinam praebuit [et] exemplum." See Souter II, 52.

22. Evans summarizes Pelagius's conception of grace under five points. Grace is (1) human rationality, through which comes the ability to be without sin, (2) the law of the OT, (3) the forgiveness of sins due to the death of Christ, (4) Christ as our example, and (5) the teaching of Christ, both as a new moral law and as information about the process of salvation. "Pelagius has no doctrine of grace other than this" (Evans, *Four Letters*, 111).

23. At this point perhaps we see Pelagius going beyond anything that anyone had said before. Doubtless his purpose is hortatory, but the implication is that salvation on account of works not only exists, but is superior to salvation because of faith, even though both were presumably foreknown.

commentary. And in fact, Cassiodorus incorporated large extracts from Augustine's treatise *Ad simplicianum* into the commentary, which regarded predestination as God's primordial decision to bestow transforming grace without regard to merit. But whether Cassiodorus followed this doctrine in his own additions to the commentary has been questioned by Julian Gross.[24]

Gross first points to Cassiodorus's comment on Rom. 8:29-30:

> *Those who according to.* Just as it says we also were elected before the foundation of the world. *His purpose were called as saints.* The purpose of God is to justify the ungodly by faith alone without works of the law or any other possible merits. Such faith is not from nature, but is the gift of God: the fruit of the spirit is faith, among other things. For not all are called, but according to his purpose they are called; since many are called but few are chosen. Therefore they are called according to his purpose who also were elected before the foundation of the world. *For those whom he foreknew he also predestined to become conformed to the image of his son.* He predestined, in order that he who through his gift was conformed in life was also conformed in glory: who transformed our earthly body to be conformed to the body of his glory. Whence also John: we shall be like him.

Gross argues that this passage shows Cassiodorus is actually very close to the thinking of Pelagius. To demonstrate this thesis, Gross quotes a portion of the comment on Rom. 8:29 which we have just seen, along with a portion of the comment on 8:30, as follows: "He predestined, in order that he who through his gift was conformed in life was also conformed in glory . . . he foreknew, he predestined, he called and he justified. Because all indeed were foreknown and predestined, and many called and justified." Gross comments: "Although not so clearly as in the Pelagian text [on Rom. 8:29, above, plus the following sentence from the comment on v. 30: 'He called those he foreknew were going to believe' (Quos praesciit credituros, hos vocavit)], so also in the reviser the subordination of election to divine foreknowledge unmistakenly manifests itself."[25]

It is not at all clear that Cassiodorus's comment on Rom. 8:29-30 contains either explicitly or implicitly the doctrine that predestination is identical to or dependent on foreknowledge. Certainly there is nothing as flat as Pelagius's "To predestine is the same as to foreknow."[26] Cassiodorus

24. J. Gross, "Cassiodorus und die augustinische Erbsundenlehre," *ZKG* 69 (1958): 299-308.

25. Ibid., 307.

26. "Praedestinare idem est quod praescire." Comment on Rom. 8:29.

does keep to the structure of one sentence in Pelagius's comment on Rom. 8:29,[27] but he alters the wording:

PELAGIUS	CASSIODORUS
He foresaw those who were going to conform in life, and willed that they be conformed in glory	He predestined, in order that he who through his gift was conformed in life was also conformed in glory

Cassiodorus changes the key verb in the clause, "foresaw" *(praeuidit),* to "predestined" *(praedestinavit).* That certainly suggests a theological correction, as does the insertion of "through his gift" *(dono ejus).* The gift is that of faith, as Cassiodorus's comment on the preceding verse, Rom. 8:28b, indicates:

> *[According to his] purpose are called saints:* The purpose of God is, that without works of the law, or whatever other merits, he justified the unrighteous by faith alone, which faith is not from nature, but is the gift of God: the fruit of the spirit is also faith, among other things. For not all are called, they are called according to his purpose: since many are called, but few are chosen. Therefore those are called according to his purpose who also are elected before the foundation of the world.

These two comments, taken together, really tend to emphasize that predestination has to do with the free gift of faith and God's activity of calling, rather than having to do with foreknowledge. Cassiodorus is at pains to show that faith is not a natural capacity or activity, but is a gift of God and a fruit of the Spirit. It does not seem possible at all to read the priority of foreknowledge over election in Cassiodorus on the basis of Rom. 8:29.

Gross finds a second instance of this theme in Cassiodorus in Rom. 11:2a:

PELAGIUS	CASSIODORUS
God has not cast off his people whom he foreknew. He has not cast off that people whom he foreknew were going to believe.	*God has not cast off his people whom he foreknew.* Whom he foreknew: that is, he predestined to be saved: because from that people many believed because of the gift of the grace of Christ:

27. All the quotations from Cassiodorus and his students are my own translations from the text in PL 68, under the name of Primasius. This is not a modern critical edition, and the text is occasionally garbled or contains grammatical errors. I have tried to reproduce this text as literally as possible in the translation, and have not attempted to correct such errors.

> because in him the future is already accomplished: without doubt therefore he foreknew: and because he foreknew, he predestined: but to have predestined is to have arranged what he himself was going to do.

This passage is much more disturbing. "Without doubt therefore he foreknew: and because he foreknew, he predestined [sine dubio ergo praescivit: et quia praescivit, praedestinavit]" really does seem to give some priority to foreknowing over predestining. In the face of Cassiodorus's extensive quotations from *Ad simplicianum* in the commentary and his statements in the commentary on Rom. 8, this is really astonishing. There may be some pressure from the sequence of terms in the text of Rom. 8:29: "Those he foreknew he also predestined" (Quos praesciit et predestinauit). However, there is no indication that Cassiodorus has perceived or is trying to resolve any inconsistency between Augustine and Paul. This seems to be simply an incoherency: What Cassiodorus says in relation to Rom. 11:2 is directly contrary to what he has quoted in Augustine, and the tenor of his own remarks.

It is hard to account for this incoherence. The purpose of Pelagius's own equation of predestination with foreknowledge is clear: he wants to avoid any doctrine which might imply that a person's ultimate destiny is fated or decreed by God, so that that person's willing to do the good would be without effect. Cassiodorus, on the other hand, is consistent in maintaining that grace is necessary in order to do good works, and without grace good works are impossible, as in the following passage commenting on Rom. 11:6:

> *And if by grace, then not through works.* This distinguishes between grace and predestination, because predestination is the preparation for grace: but grace itself is already a gift. . . . But whoever says that God's grace is preceded by men through the merit of their good works, and the grace of God is given to the merits, is a Pelagian: for it is not grace if it is not gratuitously given: if it is rendered as something owed to those who deserve it: let it not be so! For God anticipates and precedes us, not we God. In many places Paul often declares this, placing the grace of faith before works; not to reduce works, but in order to show that works are not the predecessors of grace, but the consequences: so that of course someone will not think himself to have seized hold of grace on account of his works being good: he cannot do good works unless he will have received grace through faith.

Is it really possible to hold such sentiments as, "it is not grace if it is not gratuitously given: if it is rendered as something owed to those who deserve it," alongside "Whom he foreknew: that is, he predestined to be saved: because from that people many believed because of the gift of the grace of Christ: because in him the future is already accomplished: without doubt therefore he foreknew: and because he foreknew, he predestined"? The only likely conclusion is that Cassiodorus at times follows Augustine's doctrine, which gives the priority to predestination, and at times follows another doctrine entirely, found in the words of Pelagius, which gives priority to foreknowledge, and that his theological acumen is not acute enough for him to maintain consistency.

Thus Cassiodorus displays some incoherency in the doctrine of predestination, sometimes quoting or reproducing an Augustinian position, and sometimes following Pelagius in reducing predestination to foreknowledge. The student commentary also shows such incoherency, as can be seen in the following examples:

On Gal. 1:15

PELAGIUS	**STUDENTS**
But when it [well] pleased him who from my mother's womb set me apart.	*But when it pleased him who from my mother's womb set me apart.*
He who had set me apart already in the womb in foreknowledge, when he wished, he accomplished what he knew was going to happen.	He who had set me apart already in the womb in foreknowledge, when he wished, he accomplished what he knew was going to happen. "His mother's womb" can also be understood as the synagogue.
And called me through his grace.	*And called me through his grace.*
Not on account of my merits.	Not on account of my merits.

This comment is interesting first of all because it demonstrates the divided mind of Pelagius himself. On the one hand, in the second half of the verse, he definitely distinguishes between grace and merit. But the preceding comment attributes Paul's election to foreknowledge, which is entirely consistent with Pelagius's reduction of predestination to foreknowledge in the Romans commentary. It is possible to maintain that the foreknowledge of merit is not merit as such, and so one called through foreknowledge of future merit is not necessarily called on account of merit itself. This would enable one to reconcile the comments on the two halves of the verse. There is no doubt, however, that the call is due to foreknowledge and God's anticipation of what will be. The student commentary retains this reading of Pelagius in its entirety, adding the possibility of a figurative interpretation equating "mother's womb" with "synagogue," but otherwise leaving the comment intact. Thus the students follow Pelagius in equating predestination with foreknowledge.

In one of the classic loci of the doctrine of predestination, Eph. 1:4, we see almost complete equivocation on the part of the students:

PELAGIUS	**STUDENTS**
Even as he chose us in him before the foundation of the world, that we should be holy and without blemish.	*Even as he chose us in him.* He predestined in Christ. *Before the foundation of the world, that we should be holy and spotless.*
Because nothing is new to God, with whom were all things before they were made, not as certain heretics dream, that souls have been segregated beforehand in heaven.	Because nothing is new to God, with whom were all things before they were made: not as certain people dream, that souls have been elected in heaven before the world: but His church is predestined through foreknowledge, and elected, without spot or wrinkle on them, because He Himself knows who are His. Not as the Pelagians believe concerning this passage, that they can be unstained by accepting the commandments using free will alone. They say, "Since God foreknew what we were going to be, he elected us before the foundation of the world, and predestined us in Christ." But it is not so, not because he did foreknow what we were going to be, but in order that we should be such, through that same election of his grace he made us so himself: by this grace he made us welcome to his beloved son. When therefore he predestined us, he foreknew his own work, which makes us holy and spotless.

The students' rewrite of this passage is contradictory. On the one hand, it correctly identifies the Pelagian equating of predestination with foreknowledge and provides a refutation, which includes an unacknowledged quotation from Augustine.[28] On the other hand, most of the substance of Pelagius's own comment is retained which denies a primordial segregation — or election, to use the students' substitute term. The result is an incoherency, such as we saw in the work of Cassiodorus himself. Souls may not have been segregated in heaven on account of God's foreknowing their good works, but if in fact through the election of grace God was to make some acceptable to his beloved Son and others not similarly acceptable, there had to be a primordial segregation of some sort. Otherwise, the separation must have been the result of previsioned merit — the very point the student commentary is at such pains to deny. Thus, this comment contains both a Pelagian and an Augustinian account of election, and the two are in flat contradiction.

The rewrite of Eph. 1:11 shows the same inconsistency:

PELAGIUS	STUDENTS
In whom we [ourselves] have also been called.	*In that we ourselves have also been called by a special choice.*
We who, from out of the Jews, believe[d] [in] Christ.	We who, from out of the Jews, believed.
Having been predestined	*Having been predestined*
Marked beforehand by way of faith. Or: preknown.	Marked out beforehand, or preknown and foreknown: not because of the fact that we were, but because through his agency we evil ones were going to be good.
According to the purpose of God	*According to the purpose of God*
By which he indeed made it a plan to restore all things, but first the lost sheep of the house of Israel.	As he announced, to restore the Jews at first, and afterward the Gentiles: even though only a part of the Jews believed.
Who accomplishes all things	*Who works all things*
The cause of all these things is the will of God, which is without doubt rational.	The cause of all things is the will of God, good without doubt, which every person of faith knows to be reasonable. If he himself is the cause of all things, what comes of the Pelagian arrogance? He who accomplishes all

28. "Sed non ita est . . . immaculatos facit." This is taken from *De praedestinatione sanctorum* 18.36, and 19.38.

	things, therefore, works also in order that we begin to believe.
According to the counsel of his will.	*According to the counsel of his will.*
Not according to our merits.	Not according to our merits. Those who say: My good will made me a Christian? When he heard "according to the counsel of his will," they should hush concerning merits.

Again, in this passage, we see the divided mind of Pelagius. On the one hand, he equates predestination and foreknowledge. But he is also willing to say, "Not according to our merits" (Non secundum merita nostra). Certainly Pelagius is at pains to say that foreknowledge is knowledge of faith, and — presumably — not of works of the law, but we have seen that Pelagius considers faith itself to be a meritorious human act on the part of the believer. God's foreknowledge anticipates our belief, but does not produce it.[29] One wonders whether controversy had simply not yet pressed Pelagius into consistency, or whether he might say he was talking about God's general governance *(qui omnia operatur)* and not our specific salvation, in which merit does come into play.

In any case, the student commentary follows Pelagius in identifying predestination and foreknowledge, and even adds its own synonym. It then attributes the causality to God, saying it is his power that brings us to the good. Presumably, then, what God foreknows is his own work in us.[30] The Pelagian identification of predestination and foreknowledge is at least qualified, but the passage remains somewhat confused.

In the case of both Cassiodorus and his students, then, we find an intermixture of Augustinian and Pelagian doctrines on predestination. However much Augustine was regarded as a formal authority, materially his doctrine stood side by side with that of Pelagius. There are, of course, always limits to a case study, and one hesitates to extrapolate too far. But there was nothing really extraordinary about Vivarium except the personality of Cassiodorus himself. One can argue that at Vivarium we see what was possible at that time with those resources, and it appears that a full, consistent assimilation of Augustine, even by people who had every intention of doing so, was not possible.

29. See, e.g., Pelagius on 1 Tim. 2:4: "*Who wants all men to be saved.* Hence it is proven that God does not put the power of believing into anyone, nor does he take away freedom of will" (*Qui omnes homines uult saluos fieri.* Hinc probatur deum nemini ad credendum uim inferre nec tollere arbitrii libertatem). See Souter II, 480.

30. This is similar to the line Augustine takes in *De corruptione et gratia* 12.

IV. Conclusions

An Augustinian synthesis in the theology of the early Middle Ages, or a triumph of the Augustinian doctrine of grace, is difficult to document on either the formal or the material level. There is no doubt that Orange II produced a somewhat moderated Augustinian doctrine of grace, but Orange II had little discernible historical effect during this time — and indeed, throughout the medieval period. On the material side, we see in Cassiodorus an unintegrated and in fact incoherent mixture of Augustinian and Pelagian themes.

Cassiodorus and his students sat amidst the ruins of great systems. They attempted to construct a livable edifice out of used bricks. The result was, as we have seen, inconsistent and incoherent, but at least it was a place to dwell for a time. The thought of Augustine remained as a resource, even if it was shoulder to shoulder with the anonymous (in the case of the Cassiodorus revision) Pelagius.[31] Conversely, however, the thought of the misnamed or anonymous Pelagius was constantly present to provide an alternative to Augustinianism, or perhaps more strongly, to subvert it. It was as if some of the old bricks in the new house were explosive, and it was only a matter of time before they went off. One might argue that they kept going off all the way to the Reformation. One might indeed argue that they are going off even yet.

31. The difficulty is compounded by the fact that another edition of the Pelagius Pauline commentaries was circulating under Jerome's name throughout the Middle Ages. Thus, alongside the anonymous Pelagius of Cassiodorus, we have Pelagius in fancy dress in what current scholarship calls Pseudo-Jerome.

III. LATE MEDIEVAL EXEGESIS

7. *Meister Eckhart and a Millennium with Mary and Martha*

Blake R. Heffner

Prologue

Since the rise of the historical-critical method, interpreters of the Bible have taken the search for meaning beyond the received text. The horizon for investigation has widened to include the historical situation behind the text and the author/editor's peculiar rendition of it (redaction criticism), the way a passage functions within its literary context (form criticism), and the variations which accrued during its scribal transmission (textual criticism).

More recently, the reader/hearer's own context has become a significant focus of our search for meaning (witness the new hermeneutic). In this way, the horizon for interpretation has also become more refined as the received text is scrutinized through specific contextual lenses (e.g., liberation and feminist perspectives).

This paper is grounded upon the principle that the meaning of the received text of the Bible is not exhausted by either the original intention of the author or the contemporary questions which we may bring to the text. To ask what a text means should also involve asking what it has meant. Every text has its own history of interpretation: a story which can itself be revelatory.[1]

1. For contemporary literature suggesting this perspective see Donald K. McKim, ed., *A Guide to Contemporary Hermeneutics: Major Trends in Biblical Interpretation* (Grand Rapids: Eerdmans, 1986), esp. the following articles: Karlfried Froehlich, "Biblical Hermeneutics on the Move," 175-91 (esp. 188-89); David C. Steinmetz, "Theology and Exegesis: Ten Theses," 27; idem, "The Superiority of Precritical Exegesis," 65-77.

To illustrate this, we will trace the interpretive history of a familiar gospel narrative — viz., Jesus' visit to the house of Mary and Martha at Bethany, found in Luke 10:38-42:

> Now as they went on their way, he entered a village; and a woman named Martha received him into her house. And she had a sister called Mary, who sat at the Lord's feet and listened to his teaching. But Martha was distracted with much serving; and she went to him and said, "Lord, do you not care that my sister has left me to serve alone? Tell her then to help me." But the Lord answered her, "Martha, Martha, you are anxious and troubled about many things; one thing is needful. Mary has chosen the good portion, which shall not be taken away from her."

Luke alone tells this story — situating it between Jesus' teaching about the Good Samaritan and the Lord's Prayer.[2]

Traditionally, this passage is the locus classicus in Christian spirituality for comparing the ways of action and contemplation.[3] Such a typology would seem quite simple to apply: Mary is the pious, prayerful contemplative; while Martha is the less spiritual, active one. Yet, by the late Middle Ages, Meister Eckhart, the famous Dominican preacher, actually cast Martha, not Mary, as the more mature and fruitful disciple. Quite contrary to the literal sense of the text, he depicted Martha as the happier, freer, and more fulfilled of the two sisters![4] We hope to show how this interpretation

2. Scholars have filled reams of paper discussing just the textual and redactional questions spawned by this pericope. G. B. Caird suggests that "few stories in the Gospels have been as consistently mishandled as this one" (*Saint Luke,* Pelican Commentary [Philadelphia: Westminster, 1963], 149), cited by Robert W. Wall in "Martha and Mary (Luke 10.38-44) in the Context of a Christian Deuteronomy," *JSNT* 35 [1989]: 29 n. 2.

Other recent studies include: Jutta Brutscheck, *Die Maria-Martha-Erzählung: Eine redaktions-kritische Untersuchung zu Lk. 10.38-42* (Frankfurt/Bonn: Hanstein, 1986); and Gordon D. Fee, " 'One Thing Needful'?, Luke 10:42," in *New Testament Textual Criticism: Its Significance for Exegesis: Essays in Honour of Bruce M. Metzger,* ed. E. J. Epp and G. D. Fee (Oxford: Clarendon, 1984), 61-75.

For a stimulating theological discussion see Elisabeth Schüssler Fiorenza, "Theological Criteria and Historical Reconstruction: Martha and Mary, Luke 10:38-42," Center for Hermeneutical Studies in Hellenistic and Modern Culture, Colloquy 53, ed. Herman Waetjen (Berkeley: Graduate Theological Union and University of California at Berkeley, 1986), 63 pp.

3. For the early exegetical history of this text, see D. Csanyi, "Optima Pars: Die Auslegungsgeschichte von Lukas 10,38-42 bei den Kirchenvätern der ersten vier Jahrhunderte," *Studia Monastica* 2 (1960): 5-78. For the medieval period, see Dietmar Mieth, *Die Einheit von vita activa und vita contemplativa in den deutschen Predigten und Traktaten Meister Eckharts und bei Johannes Tauler* (Regensburg: F. Pustet, 1969), as well as other works cited below. For a study in English, see M. E. Mason, *Active Life and Contemplative Life: A Study of the Concepts from Plato to the Present* (Milwaukee, 1961), 68ff.

4. Meister Eckhart, "Intravit Jesus in quoddam castellum . . ." (Sermon 86). See

may not be as outrageous as one might think, but actually fits creatively within a rich and variegated hermeneutical history.[5]

We will trace the path of this history over roughly the millennium between Origen of Alexandria (d. ca. 254) and Meister Eckhart (d. 1328). Picture the following as a Dantean excursion through the school of exegetical tradition.

Scene One

Peering into the room, we see a panel discussion in progress. Clement and Origen of Alexandria are engaged in a lively dialogue with some of the pagan philosophers — Plato, Aristotle, and Plotinus. The classroom is filled with auditors listening intently as Origen speaks.

Origen is the father of the allegorical or "mystical" interpretation of this pericope.[6] Like Plato, who taught that "the world is not our home,"[7] Origen believes we have a destiny which cannot be fully achieved here: "We are on a journey; we have come into this world that we may pass from virtue to virtue, not to remain on earth for earthly things."[8]

Origen interprets Luke's Bethany narrative as an allegory of the classic Aristotelian distinction between the civic or "practical" life (βίος πράκτικος) and the spiritual or "theoretical" life (βίος θεωρέτικος), which became better known as the "active" and "contemplative" ways.[9] Martha, being troubled about the demands of hospitality, represents the way of action; while Mary, sitting at the feet of Jesus and waiting upon his every word, is the epitome of contemplation. In rebuking Martha for her labors, and praising Mary for choosing the best part and the one thing necessary, Origen hears Jesus sanctioning his Gnostic intuition that the active life is

---

Bernard McGinn, ed., with Frank Tobin and Elvira Borgstadt, *Meister Eckhart: Teacher and Preacher* (New York: Paulist, 1986), 338-45. Original text in *Meister Eckhart: Die deutschen und lateinischen Werke* (Stuttgart/Berlin: W. Kohlhammer, 1936-), *Deutsche Werke* III (hereafter, DW), 481-92.

5. One burden of this paper is to show that Eckhart's interpretation is not "so original and antitraditional" as is commonly thought. Cf. Frank Tobin's comment appended to his Eng. trans. in *Meister Eckhart,* 345 n. 1.

6. Mieth, *Einheit,* 76.

7. Diogenes Allen's phrase, in *Philosophy for Understanding Theology* (Atlanta: John Knox, 1985), 39ff.

8. Origen, "Homily XXVII on Numbers," in *Origen,* trans. Rowan A. Greer (Toronto: Paulist, 1979), 254.

9. Alois M. Haas, "Die Beurteilung der *Vita contemplativa* und *activa* in der Dominikanermystik des 14. Jahrhunderts," in *Arbeit Musse Meditation: Betrachtungen zur* Vita activa *und* Vita contemplativa, ed. B. Vickers (Zürich, 1985), 109ff.

subordinate to the contemplative. They are not exclusive options, but two stages on the single Christian path toward perfection. The active, ascetic life is ordered toward temporal things, "passing from virtue to virtue"; but only the contemplative life, ordered toward God alone, leads one beyond earthly things toward our eternal Home.[10]

The large group of auditors surrounding Origen and his partners consists of the theologians Evagrius Ponticus (d. 399), Jerome (d. 419), John Cassian (d. 432), and others — who laid the foundation for monastic spirituality in the medieval West.

On our way out, we are met by an odd, gaunt gentleman standing by the door distributing leaflets. He is John Chrysostom (d. 407) from the School of Antioch, who is filing a minority report. Like his namesake, John the Baptist, Chrysostom appeared as a voice crying in the wilderness, rejecting the "allegorical" interpretation of this story. He contends that Jesus' counsel to Martha implies neither wholesale reproof of work nor a categorical approval of leisure. Everything hinges, rather, on the significance of the moment. Christ does not praise Mary for her "contemplative life" but rather for her knowledge of "the time" (καιρός). Likewise, he does not reprove Martha for her active hospitality; rather, it is her concern for peripheral matters (μέριμνα) that is awry.[11] When the Lord comes to one's house declaring the in-breaking of the Kingdom, then it is time to drop everything and be attentive.

Scene Two

Turning into the next room, we perceive the sanctuary of Hippo Cathedral, with the unmistakable form of Augustine preaching on the story of Martha and Mary with all his rhetorical genius. The bishop was himself steeped in Hellenistic philosophy and generally thought to adopt the Neoplatonic view that subordinates action to contemplation.[12] In his preaching, however, we get a more balanced picture: Augustine lauds both women and views them as complementing each other.[13]

10. Ibid., 111.

11. Mieth, *Einheit,* 45-46, esp. n. 65.

12. Paul Kuntz is correct that this view (shared by Etienne Gilson among others) must be qualified; see "Practice and Theory: Civic and Spiritual Virtues in Plotinus and Augustine," in *Arbeit Musse Meditation,* 65-86 (esp. p. 85 n. 27).

13. Two sermons are of particular importance here: nos. 103 and 104. See PL 38:613-18. (Hereafter these sermons will be cited by sermon number, with chapter, section, and PL column number.)

To begin with, Augustine declares, there are notable similarities between Martha and Mary: they "were two sisters, both siblings in the flesh but also in religious observance; both cling to the Lord; both served the Lord present in the flesh harmoniously."[14] Even as they prefigure two forms of life, "both were pleasing to the Lord, both amiable, both disciples [giving shape to] two types of life: present and future, laborious and quiet, calamitous and blessed, temporal and eternal . . . two lives — both innocent, both laudable — two lives in the same house and just one fountain of life."[15]

Martha is not considered a second-rate disciple. On the contrary, she "received him as pilgrims are customarily received; indeed, as a handmaid received her master [*Dominum*], as a sick person her healer [*Salvatorem*], as a creature her Creator."[16] Indeed, Martha complements her sister Mary: "this one is disturbed [with feeding], so that one may [simply] feast; this one orders many things, so the other may [simply] behold one."[17] If these sisters are headed in different directions, they are for that very reason indispensably connected. And this connection is not so much hierarchical as dialectical. "Martha has to set sail in order that Mary can remain quietly in port."[18]

Why would Augustine give so much esteem to Martha and the active way? It is probably due to the course of his personal life. From the sheltered life of a contemplative philosopher in Thagaste, Augustine was thrust into an exceedingly active (and practical!) life as a priest and later bishop in Hippo.[19] He preached with the heart of a pastor who knows and loves his sheep. Unlike the idyllic "flight from the world" which one finds in the Gnostically oriented writings of Origen and other monastic theologians, Augustine's incarnational balance led him to depict the Christian journey as a being "otherworldly in the world."[20]

This incarnational view continued to develop throughout the Middle Ages. Augustine's voice is still audible in the preaching of John Tauler (d. 1364), a notable disciple of Eckhart, who declared: "Amen! Our Lord did not scold Martha for her works, for they were holy and good; rather,

14. Sermon 103, I, 2; PL 613.
15. Sermon 104, III, 4; PL 617-18.
16. Sermon 103; PL 613.
17. Sermon 103, II, 3; PL 614.
18. Sermon 104, II, 3; PL 617.
19. Peter Brown gives insight into the "intensely personal" nature of this change, far deeper than the superficial differences between the quiet and leisure of Thagaste and the obvious strain and demands of his duties in Hippo (P. Brown, *Augustine of Hippo* [Berkeley: University of California, 1969], 204-5).
20. Ibid., 324.

he rebuked her for her 'fretting and fussing about so many things'" (NEB).[21]

Scene Three

In the next room we encounter a colloquy of Cistercians discussing the ideal of a "mixed life," including both active charity and contemplative prayer. By the eleventh century, Luke 10:38-42 had become the Gospel lesson for the Feast of Mary's Assumption (August 15).[22] When Bernard of Clairvaux (d. 1153), the most renowned Cistercian, preached on this occasion, he likened the village of Bethany to the world and the sisters' house to Mary's womb. Both sisters dwell therein: Martha, the elder, has the privilege of receiving the Savior on earth in her womb; while Mary, the younger, prepares herself to receive the heavenly Christ. "Martha decorates the house; Mary fills it. The busyness [*negotium*] of Martha and the 'not idle leisure' [*non otiosum otium*] of Mary are both united in the Blessed Mother Mary. The 'best part' belongs to her, who is simultaneously a mother and a virgin."[23] Bernard views the contemplative life as only the "better part." The best would comprehend both Martha's and Mary's portions.

Although Bernard had doubts as to whether such a goal is achievable in this life, his confrere Aelred of Rievaulx (d. 1167) was convinced that Martha and Mary must be united in a soul. Their tasks dare not be divided among different people. Just as Jesus did not come to Mary only spiritually but also bodily, likewise, the individual who, in imitating Mary, would prepare to receive Jesus must receive him in this life both physically and spiritually. "As surely as Christ is poor and walks by foot on the earth, and gets hungry and thirsty, it is necessary that both these women are in the same house and both these actions are in the same soul."[24]

Later, Caesarius of Heisterbach (d. ca. 1245) began extolling the life of St. Elizabeth of Thuringia as a perfect illustration of the "mixed life." She

21. Tauler's word is *sorgvaltikeit.* See Johannes Tauler, "Divisiones ministracionum sunt," in *Die Predigten Taulers aus der Engelberger und der Freiburger Handschrift . . .,* ed. Ferdinand Vetter (Berlin: Weidmannsche, 1910), 178, l. 23.

22. This feast was instituted as early as the 9th century, according to Martina Wehrli-Johns, "Maria und Martha in der religiösen Frauenbewegung," in *Abendländische Mystik im Mittelalter:* Symposion Kloster Engelberg 1984, ed. Kurt Ruh (Stuttgart: J. B. Metzlersche, 1986), 355 and 363 n. 7.

23. Ibid., 355.

24. PL 195, 303-16; cited in ibid., 356.

conceived her vocation as reflecting both Bethany sisters. Like Martha, she busied herself in caring for the sick and the poor. At the same time, like Mary, she surrendered herself deeply in contemplation. She wanted to combine a daily love of neighbors with the love of God through inner prayer.[25]

Caesarius goes on: "She satisfied Christ through works of mercy, like Martha, and was satisfied, like Mary, through his divine Word." He praises her as the embodiment of both Bethlehem and Jerusalem. Bethlehem, meaning "house of bread," signifies the active life; while Jerusalem, meaning "vision of peace," symbolizes the contemplative way.[26]

This sphere of Cistercian mysticism was like a womb within which important themes of later medieval piety were nurtured: veneration of the Blessed Virgin Mary, a focus on the incarnate life of Jesus, and the spread of this "mixed ideal." In addition, Cistercians have been connected with the nascent cult of the Bethany sisters themselves, typified by the hagiographical *Life of Saint Mary Magdalene and of her Sister Saint Martha.*[27] Finally, one sees an unmistakably Cistercian influence upon later spiritual movements: including the mendicants (particularly the Franciscans), the religious "women's movement" (notably the lay Beguines), and the hospital movement or "Revolution of Charity." Many of the early Beguines and other communal groups situated themselves near a hospital; for it was deemed the house of Mary and Martha, Christ's earthly quarters.[28]

Scene Four

The next room is a scriptorium, where we find Franciscan and Dominican friars copying manuscripts from their spiritual masters. These mendicant (or begging) orders emerged in the early thirteenth century out of the fertile spiritual soil of the itinerant lay preachers, canons regular, and Cistercians of the twelfth. With the friars, apostolic life moved directly into the world.

25. Ibid., 354. Cf. A. Huyskens, ed., *Die Schriften des Casarius von Heisterbach über die heilige Elisabeth von Thüringen . . .* (Bonn, 1937), 329-90.

26. Ibid., 354-55.

27. Paralleling the rise of Marian veneration and the spread of this "mixed" ideal, there developed a cult of the Bethany sisters. Veneration of Mary Magdalene began as early as the middle of the 11th century and peaked in the late 12th. Even a cult of Martha arose in Tarascon ca. 1187. See ibid., 356ff. See also the recent Eng. trans. and excellent annotations by David Mycoff, *The Life of Saint Mary Magdalene and of her Sister Saint Martha,* Cistercian Studies Series 108 (Kalamazoo: Cistercian Publications, 1989), 166 pp.

28. Wehrli-Johns, "Maria und Martha," 356. Cf. Michel Mollat, *The Poor in the Middle Ages: An Essay in Social History,* trans. Arthur Goldhammer (New Haven: Yale University Press, 1986), 98-102.

In direct contrast to the early church ascetics who fled cities to seek God in the desert, the Franciscans and Dominicans were led into the streets of cities and towns to preach the gospel and to beg for alms. Surely, this prompted a fresh hearing of the Martha/Mary pericope.

Francis of Assisi is renowned for his engagement with the world and fraternity with his brothers. He also had zeal for contemplative prayer and periods of solitude. He encouraged those friars who desired to pursue a life of prayerful seclusion. In designing a "Rule for Hermitages," Francis employed the story of Martha and Mary as his blueprint. Every hermitage should be limited to three or four brothers. Two of them are to serve as "mothers" and follow the life of Martha, while the two "sons" should follow the life of Mary. The mothers are to provide the climate wherein contemplation may flourish, "[protecting] their sons from everyone, so that no one can talk with them." The sons, in turn, "should sometimes assume the role of the mothers, as from time to time it may seem good to them to exchange roles."[29] Francis saw that the two ways are complementary and interdependent. The idea that those roles can and should be exchanged reflects his profound spiritual insight: that humility ranks with poverty among the "few" things needful.

Thomas Aquinas, the most illustrious Dominican friar, turned to the Bethany pericope in order to develop a systematic treatment of action and contemplation. He takes every advantage the pericope affords to exalt the superiority of contemplation: "Mary has chosen the best part and that will not be taken from her" (Luke 10:42).[30] Unlike Francis's idea that those who are active Marthas should serve as "mothers," Thomas holds that the active life is "more the servant than the mistress of the contemplative."[31] Nevertheless, Thomas allows that the very "best" part is *not* contemplation alone, but the active teaching and preaching which flow from the fullness of contemplation. "It is a greater thing to give light than simply to have light, and in the same way it is a greater thing to pass on to others what you have contemplated than just to contemplate."[32] This captures the very essence of Dominic's founding vision for an Order of Preachers. Hence,

29. Francis of Assisi, "The Rule for Hermitages," in Regis J. Armstrong, OFM Cap., and Ignatius C. Brady, OFM, *Francis and Clare: The Complete Works* (New York: Paulist, 1982), 147-48.

30. Paul Kuntz rightly notes, however, that one cannot glibly summarize Thomas's position (as Hannah Arendt has) by saying, "The contemplative life is simply better than the active life" (Kuntz, "Practice and Theory," 77). As usual Thomas's view is much more synthesized and nuanced than that; see below. For Thomas's analysis, see *Summa Theologiae* (hereafter *ST*) 2.2 qq. 179-82, in *Albert & Thomas: Selected Writings*, ed. Simon Tugwell (New York: Paulist, 1988), 534-85.

31. *ST* 2.2 q. 182, a. 1; Tugwell, 577.

32. *ST* 2.2 q. 188, a. 6; Tugwell, 630.

at the summit of perfection, Thomas falls in with the increasing tendency to fuse Mary and Martha.

Scene Five

Just down from the mendicants, we enter a convent where religious women and Beguines are excitedly discussing a poem entitled "Life of the Blessed Virgin and Teaching Savior."[33] This poem presents an intriguing image of Mary the virgin mother of Jesus which plays upon the traits of both Bethany sisters: "a contemplative/active Mary who, after the resurrection of Christ put herself completely into the service of preaching."[34] Mary is remarkably depicted as if she lived in such a Beguinage.

> Until her wedding, Mary lives together with other virgins near the temple. She is never idle, but always occupied in good works. Her principal occupation is weaving; however, she also exercises the other works of mercy. It is in Martha's house at Bethany where Mary learns of her son's imprisonment. Both women betake themselves to Golgotha. After Christ's resurrection Mary devotes herself (in the house of John the theologian) to Bible study and preaching. Later she entrusts John with the preaching and leads a retired life in the house of holy Zion, in community with other brothers and sisters "who spent their faculties and resources on the necessities of the apostles."[35]

Now we are not far removed from that remarkable scene wherein Martha is cast as the more mature and fulfilled sister.

Scene Six

The next chamber is a magnificent courtroom. Meister Eckhart is standing before a panel of judges commissioned to examine his works for heresy. As we enter, he is confidently summarizing his message:

> When I preach, I am careful to speak about detachment and that a person should become free of self and of all things. Secondly, that one should be re-formed in the simple good that is God. Thirdly, that one should

33. A rough translation of "Vita beata virginis et salvatoris rhythmica"; Wehrli-Johns, "Maria und Martha," 360.

34. Ibid.

35. Ibid., 360-61.

> think of the great nobility which God has placed in the soul, so that a person may thereby come to God in a wonderful way. Fourthly, concerning the purity of divine nature — there is such brilliance in it that it is inexpressible.[36]

Eckhart's most radical claims regarding detachment and spiritual freedom were deemed by his inquisitors to be "quite evil sounding, very rash, and suspect of heresy."[37] Historically many have considered him a quietist. This makes it all the more fascinating to watch him work with Luke 10:38-42.[38] If anyone were seeking a basis for purely passive devotion, Jesus' counsel to Martha would open the door: "Martha, Martha, you are careful, you are worried about many things. One thing is necessary. Mary [who is just sitting and listening] has chosen the best part, which can never be taken away from her." Yet, on at least two occasions, Eckhart chose this very passage to uphold the active life and condemn false patterns of freedom and inactivity.

Once (on the Feast of Mary's Assumption?), beginning with a passing reference to Martha receiving the Lord at her house, he developed the theme of Mary as both "a virgin and a wife."[39] As a virgin, she represents one who

36. Meister Eckhart, DW II, 528.5–529.2; cited by A. M. Haas, "Schools of Late Medieval Mysticism," in *Christian Spirituality: High Middle Ages and Reformation,* ed. Jill Raitt (New York: Crossroad, 1989), 147.

37. This is the official language of the papal bull "In agro dominico" (March 27, 1329) issued by Pope John XXII. See Edmund Colledge, OSA, and Bernard McGinn, trans., *Meister Eckhart: The Essential Sermons, Commentaries, Treatises, and Defense* (New York: Paulist, 1981), 77-81.

38. Eckhart dealt with this text quite often. In addition to the two sermons to be discussed below, he gives a fairly traditional interpretation to the passage in his *Commentary on John;* see ibid., 165-77, passim.

There is an additional anti-quietistic interpretation in a sermon attributed to Eckhart by Franz Pfeiffer: "In his, quae patris mei sunt, oportet me esse" (Luke 2:49), *Deutsche Mystiker des vieraehnten Jahrhunderts,* 2: *Meister Eckhart* (Leipzig, 1857; repr. Göttingen, 1906), no. 33, pp. 607-8. Here we have a complementary view of Martha and Mary which falls squarely within Eckhart's received tradition:

> The one [contemplation] is good. The other [virtuous activity] is necessary. Mary was praised for having chose the better part but Martha's life was useful, for she waited on Christ and his disciples. St. Thomas says that the active life is better than the contemplative, for in it one pours out the love he has received in contemplation [see above, n. 32]. Yet it is all one; for what we plant in the soil of contemplation we shall reap in the harvest of action and thus the purpose of contemplation is achieved. There is a transition from one to the other, but *it is all a single process with one end in view* —that is God. . . . In the unity [one beholds] in contemplation, God foreshadows [the variety of] the harvest of action. (*Late Medieval Mysticism,* ed. Ray C. Petry, LCC XIII [Philadelphia: Westminster, 1957], 179.)

39. Meister Eckhart, "Intravit Jesus in quoddam castellum" (Sermon 2), DW I, 24-45; see Colledge/McGinn, *Meister Eckhart,* 177-81.

is truly detached — free of all intellectual images and empty of self-will. She is perfectly receptive to God. However, receptivity alone can remain barren and unproductive. The gifts of God spoil and perish if they are not "born back" to God. In order to be fruitful, the virgin must also be a wife, free and renewed in every present moment to wait upon God and follow him wherever he would guide. Eckhart contrasts this freedom and fruitfulness with the relatively barren sort of "flight from the world" which he found prevalent among many religious.[40] They get so caught up in their own austere mortifications that they are no longer free to wait upon God and follow him spontaneously, or respond to the needs of those around them. They are like a "spouse," so committed to their regimen of "prayer, fasting, vigils, and all kinds of exercises and penances" that they bear very little fruit.[41]

It is in another sermon, however, that we find Eckhart at his inimitably daring best, turning the literal sense of Luke's Bethany story inside out.[42] Martha, who is chronologically the older, can be perceived as more mature spiritually as well. She has learned through experience how to be active and still in essential *(weselich)* communion with Christ. Mary, the younger one, feels her soul embraced by God's goodness, an ineffable longing for "she knew not what," and the sweet consolation which comes from the eternal Word flowing from the mouth of Christ.[43]

At this point Eckhart invites listeners to indulge in some conjecture. Suppose Mary was caught up in religious fervor. When Martha asks the Lord to have Mary come assist her, he queries, could it not be out of endearment, rather than frustration? "We might call it affection or playful chiding. Why? She realized that Mary had been overwhelmed by a desire for the complete fulfillment of her soul. Martha knew Mary better than Mary Martha, for Martha had lived long and well."[44] Maybe Martha's plea was for her sister's progress and maturation. "It was as though she were saying: 'My sister thinks she can do what she pleases while she sits by you filled with consolation. Let her find out whether this is true, and tell her to get up and leave you.' "[45] Eckhart urges that this last remark was said with a tenderness that the literal dialogue could not convey. Thus, the

40. On the piety of nuns with whom Eckhart appears to be dealing, see Otto Langer, "Zur dominikanischen Frauenmystik im spätmittelalterlichen Deutschland," in *Frauenmystik im Mittelalter,* ed. Peter Dinzelbacher and Dieter R. Bauer (Stuttgart: Schwaben, 1985), 341-46.

41. Colledge/McGinn, *Meister Eckhart,* 178.

42. Meister Eckhart, "Intravit aesus in quoddam castellum" (Sermon 86), DW III, 481-92. See McGinn/Tobin/Borgstadt, *Meister Eckhart,* 338-45.

43. Ibid., 338.

44. Ibid.

45. Ibid., 339.

preacher throws another jab at certain super-contemplative nuns: "We harbor the suspicion that dear Mary was sitting there more for enjoyment than for spiritual profit. Therefore Martha said, 'Lord, tell her to get up,' because she feared that [Mary] might remain stuck in this pleasant feeling and would progress no further."[46] Perhaps Jesus' reply was not to chasten Martha but merely to assure her that her sister would reach her full potential.

Martha, on the other hand, is the picture of perfect detachment and spiritual freedom in that her work does not hinder her. (This too requires significant conjecture!) Her detachment is not some sort of Stoicism:

> Some people maintain that one should become so perfect that nothing pleasant can move us and that one be untouched by pleasure or suffering. They are wrong in this. I say that a saint never became so great that he could not be moved. I declare, on the other hand, that it certainly does happen in this life that absolutely nothing can cause the saints to move away from God. Do you think that you are imperfect so long as words can move you to joy and sorrow? This is not so. Christ was not like that. He made that clear when he said, "My soul is sorrowful unto death." Words caused Christ pain. . . . And so I say that a saint never reached nor can reach the state where suffering does not hurt him and pleasure not please him. . . . But it certainly happens to saints that nothing can move them away from God. Even if their hearts are made to suffer, their will remains utterly steadfast in God. . . . Whatever then happens does not conflict with eternal happiness, as long as it does not spill into the highest part of the spirit, up there where it remains in unity with God's dearest will.[47]

So, Martha was moved — but not moved from God. Thus, Meister Eckhart sought to resolve the apparent contradiction between what Jesus says about Martha's being "full of care" and his conviction that she "stood in lordly, well-founded virtue with a free spirit, unimpeded by anything."[48]

But what of Mary and the promising words that the Lord utters regarding her? "This is why Christ said, 'She has chosen the best part,' as if to say, 'Cheer up, Martha; this will leave her. The most sublime thing that can happen to a creature shall happen to her: She will become as happy as you.' "[49] How is that? Here Eckhart climaxes his sermon with a masterful gleaning of his exegetical tradition: driving home his message about the "activity" of true spiritual freedom and still accounting for the fulfillment of "contemplative" Mary. Echoing earlier scenes, he declares:

46. Ibid.
47. Ibid., 343.
48. Ibid., 342.
49. Ibid.

> Now some people want to go so far as to achieve freedom from works. I say this cannot be done. It was not until after the disciples received the Holy Spirit that they began to perform virtuous deeds. "Mary sat at the feet of the Lord and listened to his words," and learned, for she had just been put in school and was learning to live. But afterward, when she had learned and Christ had ascended into heaven and she received the Holy Spirit, then she really for the first time began to serve. Then she crossed the sea, preached, taught, and became the servant and washerwoman of the disciples. Thus do saints become saints; not until then do they really begin to practice virtue. For it is then that they gather the treasure of true happiness.[50]

Epilogue

This brings our millennial tour to a close. How diverse the times and situations; how unique the interpretations we encountered; and yet, there is a surprising coherence, a flow to it all. John Chrysostom, ironically, seems to have signaled its direction when he refused to accept any hierarchical structure between Martha and Mary. Augustine tempered the dualism of the Neoplatonic ideal through his balanced pastoral style — eager to praise both sisters and draw out their complementarity. The Cistercians served as creative channels of the tradition as, through the lectionary, they began to conceive connections between Mary the mother of Jesus and both Bethany sisters. They anticipated Meister Eckhart's view of the "best" as being a "virgin and a wife," virtually a combination of Martha and Mary. They also played a significant role in guiding the burgeoning "women's movement" toward a "mixed" ideal. The mendicants were both bearers and transformers of the tradition too. Francis saw not only the practical wisdom of having both "contemplatives" and "actives" live together; he perceived the spiritual value of having them actually exchange roles. Thomas, for all his intellectualism, realized that Mary could not have the "best" portion and still remain seated at the feet of the Lord. Better still, she should rise and share the fruits of her contemplation.

By this time, it should be clear that Meister Eckhart's interpretation is not so outlandish after all. Nor is it as original or "anti-traditional" as has been suggested.[51] Indeed, when the Marian image developed among the Beguines is considered, Eckhart seems to be gleaning his interpretation from the very fresh-flowing fountain of his received tradition.

50. Ibid., 344.
51. Frank Tobin, *Meister Eckhart*, 345 n. 1. See n. 5 above.

Following the exegetical path of this single pericope offers a fruitful yield. First, it serves to debunk a common caricature of medieval life as bifurcated into two mutually exclusive realms, the sacred and the profane, with those who are heavenly minded being no earthly good. We have illustrated how, throughout the High Middle Ages, the course of Western spirituality was directed toward constantly bringing the sacred and the secular together. Meister Eckhart represents the epitome and finest fruits of this tradition. Second, for those of us who live in a period characterized by radical secularization, Eckhart's exegetical legacy addresses our need to sense the sacred within the secular itself and supports our efforts to develop a spirituality that is both in and for the world.

You may still wonder whether all this has anything to do with the meaning of the gospel narrative. Surely, it has had a history all its own, quite apart from the context in which the evangelist composed it. But is this what it "means"?

Our answer must be yes, at least in part. We acknowledge the need to go beyond a text itself to encounter its meaning, with its original context and our contemporary situation as vital horizons for investigation. We ought then to acknowledge the exegetical tradition itself as a channel of revelation. This is particularly true from the standpoint of a hermeneutics for preaching. Insofar as we may believe that the Holy Spirit inspired Luke to write the narrative — made it become flesh, so to speak, through his pen — and expect the Spirit to speak through the text to our own day, then we must reckon that the selfsame Spirit has been at work "enfleshing" this Word in other generations. Their interpretive legacy is of more than antiquarian interest: it should be seen as part and parcel of the text's fullest meaning. Indeed, with David Steinmetz we can affirm that "knowledge of the exegetical tradition of the church is an indispensable aid for the interpretation of Scripture."[52]

52. David C. Steinmetz, "Theology and Exegesis: Ten Theses," in *Guide to Contemporary Hermeneutics,* 27.

8. *The Fusion of Papal Ideology and Biblical Exegesis in the Fourteenth Century*

Christopher Ocker

Ardent publicists of the absolute rule of Peter's successors in the fourteenth century rested their case on the Bible, where Peter, acknowledged first bishop of Christendom in the West, received the keys of heaven and an extraordinary power over the people who aspired to be its citizens.[1] One text was axiomatic — Christ's declaration, "you are Peter [Πέτρος], and on this rock [πέτρα] I will build my church" (Matt. 16:18). Surprisingly, a papalist interpretation of this passage was new to biblical exegetes as late as the thirteenth century, even though popes had tirelessly used it to support

1. Consider Michael Wilks, *The Problem of Sovereignty in the Later Middle Ages. The Papal Monarchy with Augustinus Triumphus and the Publicists* (Cambridge: Cambridge University Press, 1963), 40, 43, 169-70, 238, 307, 339, 346-48; see also Brian Tierney in nn. 11 and 12 below. Wilks's exhaustive book includes some misleading assumptions, most notably, insofar as this essay is concerned, the assumption that a "Thomist" view of the Petrine commission is not papalist. See ibid., 346-48; contrast Karlfried Froehlich, "Saint Peter, Papal Primacy, and the Exegetical Tradition, 1150-1300," in *The Religious Role of the Papacy: Ideals and Realities, 1150-1300,* ed. Christopher Ryan, Papers in Mediaeval Studies 8 (Toronto: Pontifical Institute of Mediaeval Studies, 1989), 18-19 (Professor Froehlich kindly provided me with a prepublication copy of the essay, for which I am grateful). For what follows on Augustine's interpretation, see ibid., 8-12.

I wish to thank the Master and Fellows of Trinity College, Cambridge, for permission to use John Baconthorpe's Postilla, *and the Bayerische Staatsbibliothek, Eichstätt, the Universitätsbibliothek, Würzburg, the Universitätsbibliothek, Frankfurt am Main, the Staatsbibliothek, Mainz, and the Biblioteca Nacional de Catalunya, Barcelona, for permission to use their manuscript collections during research that has contributed to this paper.*

their claims to power since late antiquity. The favored interpretation came from Augustine and dominated exegesis at least until the thirteenth century: the foundation of the Church is Christ alone (following 1 Cor. 3:11 and 10:4), and when Christ commissioned Peter, he did not commission him alone or necessarily place him above the other apostles, but commissioned all the apostles with him, as well as all their episcopal successors and not just popes (following Matt. 18:18).

Professor Froehlich is the first to have examined this exegetical surprise in a meticulous study of patristic and medieval interpretations of Matt. 16:18-19 and other relevant passages.[2] His results shed new light on the tenacity of traditional exegesis and on the transformation of interpretation and theological thinking in the two centuries following the Gregorian Reforms. By the 12th century, the attraction of the bishop of Rome as an antidote to a monstrous, polycephalous Church would increasingly affect the minds of theologians, who began to accept a new vocabulary of Peter's commission and Petrine authority, even though they generally maintained the old tradition on Matt. 16:18-19.[3] Innocent III (1198-1216) knitted a papalist interpretation of Christ's commission of Peter to his intricately persuasive arguments for the absolute power of the papal office, and his personal success as a sovereign ruler and as a Church reformer assured the prevalence of a papal status based upon the commission of Peter as "vicar of Christ" and the availability of a new syntax by which to pick apart the punctual exchange between Jesus and his fisherman.[4] All of this was

2. K. Froehlich, *Formen der Auslegung von Matthäus 16,13-18 im lateinischen Mittelalter* (Ph.D. diss., University of Basel, 1961; published in part, Tübingen, 1963), which added important corrections to the only previous work on the exegetical history of the passage, Joseph Ludwig, *Die Primatworte Mt. 16,18.19 in der altkirchlichen Exegese,* Neutestamentliche Abhandlungen 19/4 (Münster/Westfalen: Aschendorff, 1952). See also Froehlich, "Saint Peter."

3. For the exegesis, see Froehlich, *Formen,* 146-60. For the new vocabulary, adapting the title, *vicarius Christi,* which had been used in previous centuries as a name for bishops (as well as for emperors), see Michele Maccarrone, *Vicarius Christi. Storia del titolo Papale,* Lateranum n.s. 18/1-4 (Rome: Facultas Theologia Pontificii Athenarii Lateranensis, 1952), 75-78, 92-93, 109ff. Maccarrone overthrew the old view of Harnack, that popes appropriated the title from the imperial tradition. Cf. Adolf von Harnack, SPAW (Berlin: Preussische Akademie der Wissenschaften, 1927). For the relation of developments in the use of the title to exegetical developments, see Froehlich, "Saint Peter," 41.

4. For "vicar of Christ," see n. 3 above. The *Petrus/petra* pun was avoided by making Christ the referent of the metaphor, *petra.* For the history of this, see Froehlich, *Formen,* 88-93, 126-60; idem, "Saint Peter." Innocent III used the traditional interpretation to develop an intricate view of the papacy profoundly informed by Christology. See Wilhelm Imkamp, *Das Kirchenbild Innocenz' III (1198-1216),* Päpste und Papstum 22 (Stuttgart: Anton Hiersemann, 1983), 159, 280-89. Prof. Froehlich sees this as a fusion of exegetical tradition and papal theory.

conveniently publicized in Innocent's decretals and well represented in theological and canonistic glosses and commentaries of the thirteenth century. There existed a stocked arsenal of papal arguments loaded with Scripture, and thus, ardent publicists and protagonists of the total and absolute rule of Peter's successors in the fourteenth century could persistently thump their Bibles, along with many other codices.

Some recent scholarship touches on the uses of the Bible in polemical literature of the fourteenth century, and it permits, at least, a crude reconstruction of papalist uses of Scripture among the most important theorists.[5] Both traditional and papalist readings of Matt. 16:18-19 (as well as other relevant verses that cannot occupy us here) were used. Many Bible readers who were sympathetic to episcopal interests — hoping to limit papal sovereignty with conciliar power — remembered and applied the old exegetical tradition.[6] The exegesis that informed such a use of the text was not necessarily anti-papal in the extreme, because most polemicists would allow popes some juridical supremacy while limiting papal claims to uniquely carry out the rule of Christ on earth, a mission most bishops wished to share as rulers with some independent measure of sovereignty and not as papal bailiffs.[7] Their interpretation could advocate a mild, juridical primacy. Papal publicists could also demonstrate considerable inconsistency in the exegesis of particular passages, even though they all sought to advocate the absolute claims of the Petrine see. Giles of Rome adapted the traditional interpretation of Matt. 16:18 (according to which the "rock" is Christ, not Peter) and argued for Peter's unique proximity to the "rock," "as if Christ would say, 'I am the rock, and you are called Peter [the stone] from this rock, and upon this rock, that is, me myself, I shall build my Church. Therefore you, Peter, who got your name from me, the rock, you are to rule and govern the entire Church that is built upon me; you feed my sheep, not only these or those, but all of them universally.' "[8] To Giles, the following verse of the Gospel, where Peter is given power

5. Three of the more important works on fourteenth-century discussions of the papacy include considerable references to the Bible, but without the kind of systematic attention to the relation of Bible and political theory that Ullmann or Kantorowicz had sometimes undertaken. See Wilks, *Sovereignty;* Brian Tierney, *Foundations of the Conciliar Theory* (Cambridge: Cambridge University Press, 1968); idem, *Origins of Papal Infallibility, 1150-1350,* Studies in the History of Christian Thought 6 (Leiden: Brill, 1972).

6. Tierney, *Foundations,* passim; Wilks, *Sovereignty,* 339, 342, 347, 355, 534-35.

7. Tierney, *Origins,* 161-62.

8. Aegidius Romanus, *De ecclesiastica potestae,* ed. Richard Scholz (Leipzig: Hermann Böhlaus Nachfolger, 1929; repr. Aalen: Scientia Verlag, 1961), 50. This exegesis is also good legal doctrine: D.xxi, Gratianus; Emil Friedberg, ed., *Corpus Iuris Canonici,* 2 vols. (Leipzig: Bernhardt Tauchnitz, 1879, 1891), 1:66-67.

to bind and to loose "upon the earth," clarifies the nature of his ruling and governing. The power seems obviously spiritual (the penitential power of bishops, which Giles will grant as an endowment only to Peter and his successors, who distribute it to bishops, who in turn distribute it to priests). But the power is exercised "upon the earth," where souls are united to bodies, and to Giles this unmistakably implies that Peter and his successors have dominion over souls and bodies and everything associated with them — that is, over the entire world.[9] Augustinus Triumphus, true to his colors, used the passage in a similar way.[10]

But other papalists were less free with the traditional interpretation of the passage, so they found ways to circumvent its pro-episcopal nuances. Hervaeus Natalis denied that the commission actually involved the conferral of any authority, because the authority could only be conferred after Christ had risen from the dead (and it was conferred, at John 21:15-17, on Peter alone).[11] Guido Terreni conceded that bishops receive their power directly from Christ, assuming the traditional interpretation, but he denied that this could compromise the supremacy of the papal will.[12] We witness a theologian's irresistible affection for diversity and syncretism in the decades before the papal schism. Recent commentaries and canonistic texts furnished papalist uses of a variety of biblical passages, and these provided some interpreters new alternatives, even though the recent options could not cause a particular interpretation of a single passage to become universally accepted — hence diversity among the papalists.

This is an important point, for it suggests that the biblical foundations of fourteenth-century papalism did not rest on the interpretation of any single passage of the Bible, but more abstractly and evasively in a kind of mental synthesis of papal interests and the act of interpreting — or in what has been much better described as "the imaginative fusion of exegesis and papal ideology."[13] The fusion of papalism and biblical studies answered a

9. *De eccl. pot.* 58-59, 78-79, 103, 108.

10. Wilks, *Sovereignty,* pp. 43, 355, 356-57. Both Giles and Augustinus were Augustinian friars; the color of their habits was black.

11. He was referring to the bestowal of the power of jurisdiction. See Tierney, *Origins,* 160-64. Peter's unique acquisition of the power of jurisdiction was traditional theological and canon law doctrine until the mid-thirteenth century. See ibid., 31-32, 84-85, 155-58, 160, 161-62, 263.

12. Guido, rather eccentrically, had the sacramental power of orders and the power of jurisdiction in mind. The traditional view considered the former to be given by Christ directly to all bishops upon ordination and the latter to be given by Christ directly to popes, who distributed juridical power to bishops. See ibid., 262-63.

13. Froehlich, "Saint Peter," 43, with reference to Innocent III and suggesting his influence on thirteenth-century commentators.

persistent need in late medieval exegesis and theology: the need to acquire a means to determine reliably a true interpretation of an authoritative source. It was only one of several ways in which commentators tried to satisfy their longing for univocal truth.[14] But it was also one of the more reliable and one of the safest options they had. In the following pages, I wish to take a somewhat tentative stab at this synthetic way of thinking by looking briefly at the availability of authoritative interpretation and at papalist exegesis itself.

I. Canonistic Authority

No commentator doubted that the meaning of the Bible is always true, a fact far less trivial than one might suspect, for if it is true, the meaning of a passage should be as unitary as truth itself.[15] In reality, commentators found that their sources and their contemporaries frequently disagreed over the interpretation of the text, even when treating the literal meaning (the "plain sense," which simply explained what events or ideas are directly represented in the language of a passage).[16] Every student of theology knew

14. For univocity, consider Henri de Lubac, *Exégèse medievale, les quatre sens de l'Écriture,* 2 vols. (Paris: Aubier, 1964), 2/2:282, 308. The desire for univocal meaning was exacerbated by the conceptual dependence of theology on Scripture; no one contested the presupposition that all theological conclusions must be consistent with (or based upon, depending upon the angle from which one looks at the problem) the Bible, most contending that the scriptural basis must be the literal meaning. See Hermann Schüssler, *Der Primat der Heiligen Schrift als theologisches und kanonisistisches Problem im Spätmittelalter,* Veröffentlichungen des Instituts für Europäische Geschichte Mainz 86 (Wiesbaden: Franz Steiner, 1977), 73-78; Albert Lang, *Die theologische Prinzipienlehre der mittelalterlichen Scholastik* (Freiburg, 1964), passim. The assumption beneath this is that the literal meaning will simply tell the plain truth. Had we the occasion, we could examine this assumption in exegesis by looking at two issues that frequently arise in fourteenth-century commentaries to the letters of Jerome that served as prologues to the Bible — the simplicity of "rustic" biblical language and the truth of statements that are intended to be false (i.e., when the Bible reports a deceit perpetrated by someone). It would be interesting to compare the reflections of authors on biblical language and meaning to the intense discussions of the unity of theological science (e.g., Gregorius Ariminensis, *Lectura super primum et secundum Sententiarum,* ed. W. Eckermann, Spätmittelalter und Reformation, TU, 6 vols. [Berlin/New York: de Gruyter, 1981ff.], 1:92-120).

15. Consider Albert the Great, Thomas Aquinas, and Henry of Ghent, in de Lubac, *Exégèse,* 2/2:282, 308.

16. Fourteenth-century exegetes seem to have stressed grammatical and rhetorical study of language more than the immediate correspondence between literal speech and things. The latter approach could serve as the basis for the separation of literal and nonliteral interpretations (Gillian Evans, *The Language and Logic of the Bible,* 2 vols. [Cambridge: Cambridge University Press, 1984, 1985], 1:78-79). The former could minimize the distinc-

that this was a theoretical impossibility, for Scripture could not reveal conflicting doctrines.[17] Conflicting literal interpretations, one exegete wrote, must be decided by religious authority.[18] But, another noted, the authoritative interpretations of the fathers and of the glosses often disagree. Exegesis should, he concluded, reconcile conflicting interpretations by deliberately following the model of canon law.[19] Good instincts informed such attitudes. The canon law, ideally conceived, was really the law of Christ applied.[20] It provided structure to ecclesiastical society, a society whose stringent hierarchical order, its tensions notwithstanding, provided fourteenth-century clerics the surety of unity and catholicity in the world.[21] Some commentators will formally submit themselves to the lord of the Church in dedicatory letters to popes, offering advance recantations of whatever their sovereign might find objectionable.[22] The commentaries are,

---

tion between literal and nonliteral, and this may account for the prominence of theological analysis in the commentaries.

17. Consider Hugolinus de Urbe Veteri, *Commentarius in quattor libros Sententiarum,* ed. W. Eckermann, 4 vols. (Würzburg: Augustinus-Verlag, 1980-1988), 1:136, 2:348, for a typical reaction to speculation over the possibility of revealed falsehoods in the Bible.

18. Required, e.g., in a prologue to the Bible attributed to Nicolaus de Gorran (Würzburg, Universitätsbibliothek), M.p.th. 151, f. 17rb.

19. Jacques Fournier, *Postilla super Mattheum* (Barcelona, Biblioteca Nacional de Catalunya, Ms. 550), f. 1va-1vb.

20. Not that all law in the Church is divine law, since the statutes that regulate life in the Church were legitimately far more mutable. D.i, Gratianus and c. 1; D.v, Gratianus. *Corpus Iuris Canonici* 1:1, 7. Theologians, as we shall see, were inclined to stress the role of legislative authority established by Christ with the apostles, which interprets law and regulates practices not clearly defined there. Consider also Peter Cramer, "Ernulf of Rochester and Early Anglo-Norman Canon Law," *JEH* 40 (1989): 500, for early canonistic conceptions of the relation of precept to divine law and Bible; Leonard Boyle in n. 26 and Brian Tierney in n. 23, below, for the fusion of theology and canon law; and contrast Michele Maccarrone, "Teologia e Diritto Canonico nella *Monarchia,* III, 3," *Rivista di storia della Chiesa in Italia* 5 (1951): 7-42, for views of the animosity between canon law (particularly the decretals) and theology.

21. Gabriel Le Bras, *Institutions ecclésiastiques de la Chrétienté médiévale,* Histoire de l'Église 12/1-2 (Paris: Blough et Gay, 1959), 2:206-13.

22. For example, Hermann Schildesche in a now lost preface dedicated to Clement VI that was attached to his commentary on the Song of Songs (Adolar Zumkeller, "Wiedergefundene exegetische Werke Hermanns von Schildesche," *Augustinianum* 1 [1961]: 241-42, 245). Nicolaus Eymerich similarly declared his fealty in a prologue to his Matthew commentary (Barcelona, Biblioteca Nacional de Catalunya, Ms. 1280), vol. 1 [of 3], f. 2r), and Nicolaus de Lyra declared that ecclesiastical authority is more definitive than the conclusions drawn from Hebrew exegesis in his commentary to the Prologue to the Bible (*Postilla super Bibliam,* prologus secundus [ad Bibliam totam], 4 vols. [Strassburg, 1492; repr. Frankfurt am Main: Minerva, 1971], vol. 1, f. 4ra [counting from the title page]). Richard FitzRalph also offered advance recantations to Clement IV in the preface to his *Summa de questionibus Armenorum* (Katherine Walsh, *Richard FitzRalph at Oxford, Avignon and Armagh: A Four-*

in fact, as orthodox as their dedications, a fact the authors had known better than anyone. Very unmindful of the fate of Galileo, they confess that interpretation is relative to the government of Christian society. Theologians did not agree on the norms by which the community might determine true interpretations or decide how an interpretation could serve as a critical norm over against the official doctrine of the Church. The papacy, a general council, the consensus of the fathers, or the exegete were all proposed as final judges of the true interpretation of the Bible.[23] Some exegetes, however, would have us believe that no rational comprehension of the text could supercede the judgment of Peter's successor.

So they culled the opinions of popes from the canon law and stuck them in their lectures and writings.[24] The use of law in intellectual activity became so prevalent that both canon and civil laws could rank, beside the liberal arts, as one of theology's two handmaids.[25] A burgeoning literature of popular law for priests lent easy access to authoritative judgments on all the relevant issues facing fourteenth-century clergy.[26] Some legal ama-

---

teenth-Century Scholar and Prelate [Oxford: Clarendon, 1981], 131). It is instructive to remember that the occasion of a scholastic heresy trial was normally a quodlibet or a lecture on the *Sentences,* not biblical exegesis per se (or an attempt, like FitzRalph's, to convince papal enemies). Consider William J. Courtenay, "Inquiry and Inquisition: Academic Freedom in Medieval Universities," *ChH* 58 (1989): 178. The advance recantations are expressions of orthodoxy rather than expressions of paranoia.

23. See Schüssler, *Primat,* 294ff.; see also B. Tierney, "Canon Law and Church Institutions in the Late Middle Ages," *Proceedings of the Seventh International Congress of Medieval Canon Law,* series C: subsidia, Monumenta Iuris Canonici 8 (Vatican City: Biblioteca Apostolica Vaticana, 1988), 61-62.

24. For a very fine description of the attempt to bring canon law and theology together in a coherent view of Christian society and the "fusion" of the two in discussions of social issues, see Tierney, "Canon Law," 51-52, 63-65. For the continued place of canon law in theology since the 16th century, see Pierre Legendre, "L'inscription du droit canon dans la théologie: Remarques sur la Seconde Scolastique," *Proceedings of the Fifth International Congress of Medieval Canon Law,* series C: subsidia, Monumenta Iuris Canonici 6 (Vatican City: Biblioteca Apostolic Vaticana, 1980), 443-54. Consider also Ulrich Bubenheimer, *Consonantia Theologiae et Iurisprudentiae. Andreas Bodenstein von Karlstadt als Theologe und Jurist zwischen Scholastik und Reformation,* Jus Ecclesiasticum 24 (Tübingen: Mohr [Paul Siebeck], 1977).

25. E.g., Robert Holcot, sharply criticizing those who consider law higher than theology. Beryl Smalley, "Wyclif's *Postilla* on the Old Testament and His Principium," in *Studies Presented to Daniel Callus,* Oxford Historical Society Publications n.s. 16 (Oxford, 1964), 271-72. Even opponents of papal power used canon law in their lectures and writings as a kind of ethical norm. See Jirí Kejr, "Das Hussitentum und das kanonistische Recht," *Proceedings of the Third International Congress of Medieval Canon Law,* series C: subsidia, Monumenta Iuris Canonici 4 (Vatican City: Biblioteca Apostolica Vaticana, 1971), 191-204.

26. Some of the most prevalent were vocabularies of law, stuffed with entries on procedural matters and legal rights pertaining to aspects of clerical work and the Church courts (e.g., "accusation," "condemnation," "judges," "inheritance," "question of posses-

teurs proved proficient; the literature was competent.[27] Friars rehashed the material for convent lectures, making the collections even more relevant to the ecclesiastical laborer.[28] Handbooks often treated practical issues with

---

sion," "oath," "testator"). The most extensive study of this literature is Emil Seckel, *Zur Geschichte der populären Literatur des römisch-kanonisches Recht*, Beiträge zur Geschichte beider Rechte im Mittelalter 1 (Tübingen: Mohr, 1858; repr. Hildesheim: Georg Olm, 1967). Seckel thought this literature was more prevalent in Germany (ibid., 473). Legal historians have almost entirely overlooked this literature; a notable exception is Walter Ullmann, who pointed out its availability in fourteenth-century England (Walter Ullmann, "John Baconthorpe as Canonist," in *Church and Government in the Middle Ages: Essays Presented to C. R. Cheney on His Seventieth Birthday* [Cambridge: Cambridge University Press, 1976], 223-46; repr. in Ullmann, *Scholarship in the Middle Ages* [London: Variorum Reprints, 1978], no. 10). Leonard Boyle pointed out that Baconthorpe used confessional handbooks (Johann of Freiburg and Guillelmo of Pagula) for his citations of theologians (L. E. Boyle, "The *Summa confessorum* of John of Freiburg and the Popularization of the Moral Teaching of St. Thomas and of Some of His Contemporaries," *St. Thomas Aquinas, 1274-1974: Commemorative Studies*, ed. A. A. Maurer, et al., vol. 2 [Toronto: Pontifical Institute of Mediaeval Studies, 1974], 245-68; repr. in Boyle, *Pastoral Care, Clerical Education, and Canon Law* [London: Variorum Reprints, 1981], no. 3, pp. 263-64). Consider also Bertrand Kurtscheid, "Die Tabula utriusque iuris des Johannes von Erfurt," *Franziskanische Studien* 1 (1914): 269-90; Valens Heynck, "Studien zu Johannes von Erfurt," *Franziskanische Studien* 40 (1958): 229-60 (for his theological work). These made canon law accessible to amateur jurists engaged in pastoral care or teaching theology, a group far more diverse and fluid than professional clerical lawyers (for which, see Erich Genzmer, "Kleriker als Berufsjuristen im Späten Mittelalter," in *Études d'histoire du droit canonique dédíees à Gabriel Le Bras,* 2 vols. [Paris: Siery, 1965], 2:1207-36). For the prevalence of the literature, consider the "abbreviations," breviaries, concordances, and alphabetical registers of the *Decretum* and the *Decretales* in medieval libraries (e.g., Paul Lehmann, ed., *Bistum Mainz, Erfurt,* Mittelalterliche Bibliothekskataloge Deutschlands und der Schweiz 2 [Munich: Beck, 1928], 668-69).

27. Ullmann, "Baconthorpe," 226-27. For Baconthorpe, consider also B. Smalley, "John Baconthorpe's Postill on St. Matthew," *Medieval and Renaissance Studies* 4 (1958): 91-115, repr. in idem, *Studies in Medieval Thought and Learning* (London: Hambleton, 1981), 289-43; Ernst Borchert, *Die quaestiones speculativae et canonicae des Johannes Baconthorpe über den Sakramentalen Character,* Veröffentlichungen des Grabmann-Instituts n.s. 9 (Munich: Schönigh, 1974).

28. Consider Seckel, *Beiträge,* 121-25, for marginal additions. A *Glossa super poeniteas* written in a neat, small gothic hand of the 14th century ends: "explicit summus penitencie cum reportatis lectis bonis, lecta per Meinhardum sublectorem in Erfordia." A late fourteenth-century hand identifies the treatise as property of the Carthusians of Mainz (Stadtbibliothek Mainz, Hs. I. 166, ff. 90v-98r). It is a somewhat disjointed work. A manuscript of the early 15th century (a marginal note at the explicit is dated 1402; the almost total lack of typical scribal corrections could suggest that it is an autograph) provides nice evidence of the process of revision and alteration to which such texts were submitted. The text was to be the *Summula juris canonici* of the thirteenth-century Franciscan, Heinrich of Merseburg, a text frequently supplied with apparatuses and used in one of the more important vocabularies of canon law in the late Middle Ages, that of Astenasius. See Seckel, *Beiträge,* 199 n. 171, pp. 262-63 and n. 119, pp. 332, 334. A brief preface explains that priests must have knowledge. A rubric announces that the commentary begins ("accedatur ad litteram") and a convent lecturer mentions the occasion of his revisions (Stadtbibliothek Mainz, Hs.

a more pronounced doctrinal aspect, like mendicancy or papalism[29] — subjects in which the convergence of biblical truth and authoritative judgment were emphatically expected. Legal "vocabularies" — alphabetically arranged lists of terms with brief comments and references to canons, decretals, and glosses — were an efficient vehicle for the transmission of papalist thought, when they included entries on terms like "apostle," "authority," and "pope." For example, one vocabulary leads the reader to Gratian's *Decretum* and sharp statements of the superiority of papal power to that of the emperor, the necessity of papal power in defining the faith and putting penitential judgment into effect, the immunity of popes from all human judgment (excepting the case of a heretical pope), the freedom of a pope to create laws that supercede those of his predecessors (although cautiously noting a contrary canon), the inviolability of papal judgment, and the jurisdiction of the papacy over any and all religious affairs.[30]

Another vocabulary leads the reader to decretals and their sometimes logorrheic explanations of papal absolutism.[31] The entry on "pope" begins

---

II.330, ff. 1r-59v, here 3r): "Cum summa Heinrici fratribus legerem, et quosdam casus lectioni interserere, quos textus eiusdem summule non habebat, fratres multimodis precibus ac importunis instancijs me rogauerunt, ut eosdem casus uerbis breuibus [ms. del.: et] ac simplicibus annodarem, ad quos fratres simplices pro expediendis pluribus prolexitatibus uerterent, qui non possent se ad confitentes sibi in lacebrosa silua de iure canonico aliquid expedire. . ." He continues to explain that he is hindered by failing eyesight (and would rather not entertain questions), and he explains his predilection for the more famous authors. The result is a text that has no resemblance to that of Heinrich of Merseburg.

29. Seckel's vocabularies are all rather nondoctrinal, but a cursory look at some other manuscripts shows that his texts are not entirely representative. Consider entries on "auctoritas" and "papa" in an anonymous *Auctoritates Decreti Gratiani* (Frankfurt am Main, Stadt- und Universitätsbibliothek, Praed. 17, ff. 70va-109vb, here ff. 72r-v, 95v); an extensive entry on "Papa" in an anonymous *Auctoritates ex decretalibus, Decreto, legibus, poetis interdum mixtim* (ibid., ff. 137vb-216va, here 190vb-191rb); a brief entry stressing limitations on papal authority, under the term "papalicus," in another anonymous collection of the same volume (ibid., f. 292ra-rb); and entries on "apostolus," "mendicantes," and "papa" in a *Repertorium iuris ordine alphabetice* wrongly attributed to Johannes Calderinus (Stadtbibliothek Mainz, Hs. I.446, ff. 1r-361v, here ff. 30ra-rb, 210vb, 246ra-247va) (for the real Calderinus, see Friedrich Stegmüller, *Repertorium Biblicum Medii Aevi,* 11 vols. [Madrid: Consejo Superior de Investigaciones Cientifiques, 1940-1980], 3:263, no. 4280).

30. I am referring to the references to D.xcvi, c.10; D.xx, Gratianus; D.xxi, Gratianus; C.ix, q.3, c.13; D.xl, c.6; C.xxv, q.1, c.6; C.xxv, q.2, c.4; C.xvii, q.4, c.19; D.xii, c.2. One reference, C.xxiv, q.3, c.32, is misrepresented as a text for the immunity of the pope from human judgment (it actually condemns a hypothetically heretical pope as an arch heretic; *Auctoritates* [see n. 29 above], ff. 72r-72v, 95va).

31. *Auctoritates ex decretalibus, Decreto, legibus, poetis interdum mixtim,* on "Papa" (Frankfurt am Main, Stadt- und Universitätsbibliothek, Ms. Praed. 17, ff. 137vb-216va, here 190vb-191rb). I am referring specifically to the references to *Sexti* 1.2.1; *Clem.* 2.11.2; *Sexti* 1.6.3; 2.14.2; *Dec. Greg.* 3.8.4; 1.6.4; 1.33.6.

with a pungent line: "the pope is considered to have all law in the cavity of his chest," which means that his laws supercede any others that they might contradict, according to the decretal which is cited. The entry then furnishes texts which promote the localization of Christ's rule of the earth in the person of Peter's successor, the identity of the pope as the "universal pastor," the power of a pope to depose an emperor, the right of the papacy to grant exceptions "above the law," the necessity of episcopal submission to the apostolic see, the superiority of the papal office to the emperor, and a variety of administrative stipulations for the proper performance of papal jurisdiction. Allusions to and quotations of Matt. 16:18 or 16:19 (often used separately) are frequent; several cited decretals furnish punctilious interpretations of biblical texts that stress Peter's role in carrying out the rule of Christ on earth, the witness of two martyred apostles — Peter and Paul — to the steadfast orthodoxy of the Roman church, the power of the keys as a foundation of universal rule, and the union of imperial and priestly (Mosaic and Aaronic) powers in Christ, who invested the same authority in Peter and his successors.[32] The expert will recognize a fair representation of papalist doctrines of sovereignty, doctrinal authority, and spiritual and temporal jurisdictions. Everyone will be gratified to see the champions, not least of whom is Innocent III, as well as some of the less known.[33]

A clever reader could find much by following his or her fingers from references to sources. The sources themselves are better than many other dialectically superb treatises on papal authority, for they are self-authenticating, not only because, in them, popes declare their own authority, but the Bible also declares it with them.[34] This, in itself, might imply that canon

32. Ibid., references to *Sexti* 1.6.17; 2.14.2; *Dec. Greg.* 1.33.6; 2.1.13.

33. The union of priestly and imperial powers is found in the last two decretals mentioned in n. 32 above, both of Innocent III, which also provide interpretations of several biblical images and passages (Moses and Aaron, the two swords, Christ and Peter, the two lights in the firmament; Matt. 16:19; John 21:17, et al.). The entry also includes decretals of Boniface VIII (*Sexti* 1.2.1) and Nicolaus III (*Sexti* 1.6.17).

34. The inviolability of a pope's claim to exercise inviolable judgment is, of course, strikingly tautological. A canon lawyer might think of the ancient formula, "nullus potest iudex in sua causa," which was derived from Ulpian in Justinian's *Digest* (*Digesta* 2.1.10: "Qui iurisdicioni praeest, neque sibi ius dicere debet neque uxori vel liberis suis neque libertis vel ceteris, quos secum habet"; see Theodore Mommsen, ed., *Corpus Iuris Civilis,* 3 vols. [Berlin: Weidmann, 1877, 1880, 1883], 1/2:18). The issue arose, however, in a special context: the resignation of Coelestius V and the ability of a pope to exercise judgment over himself. Johannes Andreae raised the subject in his comment on *Sexti* I.vii.1 (*Corp. Iur. Can.,* 2:971), where Boniface VIII briefly defends the legitimacy of Coelestine's resignation (I have the commentary from a fourteenth-century manuscript of *Sexti libri cum apparatu Johannis Andree* [Stadtbibliothek Mainz, Hs. I.496, f. 39v, left margin]). Johannes examines

law — indeed, papalist decretals and doctrine — are a kind of trenchant biblicism. Other handbooks would make the implication inescapable. These were concordances of the Bible and the canon law, a body of literature which scholars have noticed only with displeasure and have hardly studied.[35] One "concordance of the authorities of the Bible and the canons" circulated under the name of the fourteenth-century abbot of Joucels, Jean of Nivelles. It provides references to the *Decretum* of Gratian, the thirteenth-century gloss on it, and later decretals.[36] The concordance is arranged according to the books of the Bible, adducing something for as many chapters as possible (an unlikely success; chapters are often skipped). A relatively long list of canons follows Matt. 16:18.[37] The reader is led to a wealth of papalist biblicism: the history of the papacy from Aaron to Peter, the role of the martyrdoms of Peter and Paul as witness to the immovable faith of the Roman see and as confirmation of its primacy, Peter

---

the problem first in conjunction with stipulations of seniority derived from inheritance law (*Dig.* XXVIII.iv.3, *Corp Iur. Civ.,* 1/2:379) and then in conjunction with the concession of absolute power (*Inst.* I.ii.6; ibid., 1/1:3). His conclusion: "Si Papa, qui habet plenitudinem potestatis, ii. q. vj. Decreto [C.ii, q.6; *Corp. Iur. Can.,* 1:466-83] [et] ix. q. iii. [c.ix, q.3, c.13-21; *Corp. Iur. Can.* 1:610-12], cuncta per mundum istam legem datam potuit cedere honori in honori, ut hic et ubi non est senior, accipiendum est quod est uerisimilis ut data lege 'proxime' redigendum" [*Dig.* XXVIII.iv.3, namely, that there be no higher judge, leaving him judge of himself]. Thus, a pope did exercise authority over himself. This issue seems never to have arisen in conjunction with the papal defense of papal authority, per se, and we could speculate that this was partly due to the function of the Bible in papal rhetoric: popes were not asserting themselves, as it were, out of the blue, but maintaining the "steadfast faith" of the Roman Church promised by Christ to Peter and bearing witness to the Petrine commission. Papalist interpretations serve as the objective basis of papal claims.

35. For example, Johann Friedrich von Schulte, *Die Geschichte der Quellen und Literatur des canonischen Rechts,* 3 vols. (Stuttgart, 1875, repr. Graz: Akademische Druck und Verlagsanstalt, 1956), 2:250. The texts must have a history of adaptation and emendation like that of the vocabularies (see n. 28 above), but to my knowledge, there has been no attempt at a textual history comparable to Seckel's study of the other handbooks (see n. 26 above). Obviously, I can do little more here than point to their existence and note some interesting content.

36. H. Gilles, "Un canoniste oublié: l'abbé de Joucels," *Revue historique de droit française et étranger,* 4th series, 38 (1960): 578-602. Stegmüller, *Repertorium Biblicum,* 3:400, no. 4834, promises to be a very incomplete list of manuscripts, but also notes four early editions. I have examined two manuscripts: Würzburg, Universitätsbibliothek, M.ch.q.3, ff. 2ra-40ra (of the late 14th century), and Stadtbibliothek Mainz, Hs. I.23, ff. 140r-187v (late 14th–early 15th centuries; both manuscripts are written on paper). The concordance is one part of Jean's *Memoriale Decreti* and circulated apart from it, it seems, widely. See Gilles for manuscripts in France. Stegmüller wrongly believed that Jean flourished in the 11th century. Except where noted, I use the Mainz manuscript.

37. They are C.xxiv, q.1, c.10; C.xxiv, q.1, c.17; D.xix.7; D.xxi, Gratianus; D.xxi.2; D.xxi, 3; D.xxiii, 1, 2; C.ix, q.3, c.14; C.ix, q.3, c.18; C.xxiv, q.1, c.22; *De pen.* D.iii, c.10; D.x, 6; C.xi, q.3, c.14; *Dec. Greg.* I.xxxiii.6; *Sexti* II.xiv.2; *Clem.* II.xi.2. Mainz, Hs. I.23, f. 167v.

as the distributor of sacramental power to the other apostles and to all priests, the immunity of popes from all human judgment, the sovereignty of papal jurisdiction over all ecclesiastical courts, the superiority of the priestly office to the imperial office, the necessity of episcopal obedience, and the papacy's right to the imperium during an imperial vacancy.

Of course, Matt. 16:18-19 also pertains to penance. Accordingly, some penitential references only presuppose primacy or have nothing to do with it at all,[38] but these are few, and the reader comes to them with a very papalist *tu es Petrus* and *tibi dabo claues* ringing in the ears. An exegete careful to toe the canonistic line could refer to this concordance while interpreting any book of the Bible and would, thereby, come across papalist readings of other passages, as well.[39] Brian Tierney showed long ago that canonistic doctrine is not always cut-and-dried papalism. Likewise, a handbook might better represent episcopal interests, like the sparse, if not paltry, *Table Containing Authorities and Sentences of the Bible,* by the Bologna canon lawyer, Johannes Calderinus (d. 1365).[40] But even here, a

38. Peter is frequently presented as an example of the possibility or necessity of penance and as proof that repentant clerics retain their ecclesiastical grade (ibid., references to D.1, c.14; D.1, 25; C.xxiv, q.3, c.1; C.xxiv, q.3, c.1; *De pen.* D.ii, c.40; D.i, c.44; D.xcvi, 9; D.vi, 1; C.xi, q.3, c.48; C.xxiii, q.4, c.24; C.xxxiii, q.2, c.8). Another nonpapalist canon uses Matt. 16:19 as the basis for the penitential power of all priests (*De pen.* D.i, c.88). One reference leads to two possible decretals that defend the immunity of the Dominican and Franciscan Orders granted by popes (strongly suggesting that the addition of the reference was made by a friar; *Dec. Greg.* V.xxxi, 16 or 17).

39. Two examples suggest that a number of papalist readings may be hidden in other references of the Concordance. Mainz, Hs. I.23, f. 173r, on Luke 22:31-32: "Ait autem dominus, 'Symoni ecce Sathanas,' et circa usque 'non deficiat fides tua, et tu aliquando conuersus confirma fratres tuos.' xxij. d. Gratianus i [D.xxi, Gratianus; 1:66-67], iii. q. i., 'nulli' in versu 'quere' [C.iii, q.1, c.5; 1:506], de penitencia, d. ii., 'si enim' uersu 'Petrus' [*De pen.* D.ii, c.40; 1:1202-6], de baptismo, 'maiores' [*Dec. Greg.* III.xlii.3; 2:644]." The first passage is overtly papalist: Gratian's summary description of papal primacy. The second example is from the entry for Exod. 4, Würzburg, Universitätsbibliothek, M.ch.q.3, f. 4rb (I happen to have it in my notes from this manuscript): " 'Ipse,' scilicet Aaron, 'loquetur parte ad populum et erit os tuum,' de penitencia, d. ii., paragraphus 'opponitur' [*De pen.* D.ii, c.39, Gratianus; 1:1200-1202]; in Christo os eius, viii. q. i., c. 'in scriptis' [C.viii, q.1, c.9; 1:592]." The second reference uses Heb. 5:4; 2 Cor. 5:14, 15; and John 21:17 to argue that whoever turns away the one appointed to feed the sheep shows that he or she has little love of the *summus pastor* (i.e., Christ), which could easily be taken as a strong allusion to the Petrine see.

40. Schulte, *Geschichte,* 2:247-53. Johannes Calderinus, *Tabula continens auctoritates et sententias Biblie* (Würzburg, Universitätsbibliothek, M.ch.f. 10), ff. 2ra-51vb (see also Stegmüller, *Repertorium Biblicum,* 3:263, no. 4280, which notes some early printed editions). The entry for "apostolus" is found on f. 4rb in a garbled form. The references are mostly nonprimatial (D.xciii, 25, *Corp. Iur. Can.* 1:329-30; C.xxiv, q.3, c.39, ibid., 1:1001-6; C.xxiii, q.4, c.43, ibid., 1:923; C.xxiii, q.6, c.1; ibid., 1:947-48), but one canon stresses the superiority of the Roman see as the see of Peter and Paul (D.xxiii, 1; ibid., 1:77-79).

reader can encounter a primatial canon in the entry for "apostle" (see n. 40). Perhaps more important is the reinforcement a "harmony" of the canon law and the Bible gives to the assumption that the constitution of the Church and the regulation of the common life is, at once, legal and biblical. Viewed from the perspective of intellectual activity itself, it nourishes the expectation that truth is one — in the Bible and in the organization of Christian society.

The handbooks raise rudimentary questions about their own convoluted textual histories (there is not even a poor catalogue of manuscripts and editions of their various forms) and myriad possibilities for the transmission of papal (and some patristic and conciliar) judgment to all kinds of situations that require clergy to interpret authoritative sources, like the preparation of lectures, treatises, and sermons, or nearly any religious conflict in the parish and diocese. I call attention to them to draw two minimal conclusions: they facilitate the convergence of authoritative judgment and biblical interpretation, and they pass on papalist interpretations themselves.

II. Papalist Exegesis

Both the fusion of authority with interpretation and papalist interpretations themselves were delightfully contemporary, as anyone who has ever heard that there were popes, bishops, a council, and critics in the fourteenth century will immediately recognize. Few of us, preoccupied with conciliarism or nominalism (before the papal schism assured the Conciliar Movement a role beyond France and when nominalism was frequently a mixture of philosophical currents and traditional doctrines), have appreciated how these things affected intellectual activity in pedestrian but consequential ways.[41] The fusion of papal ideology and biblical exegesis appears in theological texts and biblical commentaries, as well as in the polemical treatises that emerged from the grand debates of the century.[42]

41. For the complexity of the origins of nominalism and the complexity of its character in the 14th century, a very good summary treatment is in William Courtenay, *Schools and Scholars in Fourteenth-Century England* (Princeton: Princeton University Press, 1987), 193-218. I mean to suggest that papalism may sometimes have affected intellectual activity more concretely than either conciliar theory or nominalism, at least during the Avignon papacy, especially during its last two decades when there was little reason to doubt the reality of papal power.

42. Guido Terreni included a discussion of papal teaching authority in his harmony

Like so much of late medieval exegesis, the present state of scholarship is such that it is not yet possible to conclude how prevalent papalist exegesis was among fourteenth-century commentators, but two good examples of it have been known for some time: John Baconthorpe's *Postilla* on Matthew (written at Oxford or Cambridge in the late 1330s) and Johannes Klenkok's *Postilla* on Acts (written at Erfurt in the late 1360s).[43] I have occasion to examine the latter in another context;[44] I shall therefore only refer to some features of its exegesis, in due course. Beryl Smalley wrote a detailed essay on Baconthorpe's *Postilla,* and it includes a thorough study of his use of canon law (see n. 27). Nevertheless, its attention to papal ideology is somewhat peripheral, and its treatment of Matt. 16:18-19, very cursory; with some justification, therefore, we may reconsider Baconthorpe's exegesis of the Petrine commission, without retreading the broader features and context of the commentary itself, except insofar as is necessary.

Baconthorpe's commentary is structured theologically, considering the subject matter of each chapter as the fulfillment of OT prophecies, so that the Gospel becomes a long and detailed proof that Jesus is the Messiah. This might satisfy the missionizing instincts of a Carmelite (which Baconthorpe was), but it was also typical of the age for commentators to use the

---

of the Gospels and in his commentary on the *Decretum* (Guido Terreni, *Quaestio de magisterio infallibili Romani Pontificis,* ed. B. Xiberta, Opuscula et Textus, fascicle 2 [Münster: Aschendorff, 1926], 6). See B. Smalley, "Problems of Exegesis in the Fourteenth Century," in *Antike und Orient im Mittelalter,* ed. P. Wilpert, Miscellanea Mediaevalia 1 (Berlin: Walter de Gruyter, 1962), 266-74. Baconthorpe used canon law extensively in his *Sentences* commentary and in his exegesis (Smalley, "Problems"; and idem, "John"; Ullmann, "Baconthorpe"); so too did Johannes Klenkok (an extensive study of this will be found in my dissertation for Princeton Theological Seminary, "Interpretation, Authority, and Religious Community in Fourteenth-Century Germany: Johannes Klenkok's *Postilla* on the Acts of the Apostles in Its Intellectual and Cultural Contexts"). Consider also Hans Bütow, "Johannes Merkelin, Augustinerlesemeister zu Friedberg/Neumark," *Jahrbuch für Brandenburgische Kirchengeschichte* 29 (1934): 3-35, esp. 11. The use of canon law in theology and exegesis would contribute much to the condition lamented by some authors: unreflectively amassed authorities (e.g., Heinrich Langenstein of Hessen, in his commentary on the prologue to the Bible, Stadtbibliothek Mainz, Hs. I.449, f. 58vb, and Jean Gerson [cited in B. Smalley, "Jean de Hesdin, O.Hosp.S.Ioh.," in *Studies in Medieval Thought,* 380]). But Gerson, like at least one other earlier critic of canon law, Robert Holcot (see n. 25 above), also used practical legal literature. See Boyle, *"Summa,"* 265-66.

43. See references in the previous note. Smalley called it "canonistic exegesis," although she overlooked Klenkok's use of the method ("Problems"). See idem, *English Friars and Antiquity in the Early Fourteenth Century* (Oxford: Basil Blackwell, 1960), 299-300. In fact, they not only used canon law but employed a papalist reading of it.

44. See my dissertation, mentioned in n. 42 above.

scheme of prophecy and fulfillment in some way to define the literary form of a Gospel and the demands it makes of the interpreter.[45] The scheme applies to chapter 16, where Baconthorpe uses it to summarize the chapter's contents, introducing a finely nuanced and sensitive analysis of traditional and Petrine interpretations of the passage.[46] The subject of the chapter is the foundation of the Church upon the rock; the crucial prophecy is the story of the rock from which Moses drew water and from which the Israelites and their livestock *(iumenta)* drank. Augustine, commenting on 1 Cor. 10:4, interpreted the rock as Christ and the water as spiritual drinking, says Baconthorpe (Paul actually said that).[47] Baconthorpe adds that there are two kinds of people in the Bible: Jews (who live rationally, *per iumenta*) and Gentiles (who are irrational, "like beasts").[48] The prophetic event in the ancient desert means that the Church, which the Messiah will build, will be upon the rock and from the flowing waters of grace from which the people and their beasts shall drink, i.e., the Jews and the Gentiles who constitute a Church built upon Christ and who drink the spiritual waters of the sacraments of grace. This unexceptional allegory is then given a papalist slant in a paraphrase of Matt. 16:18-19, in which Baconthorpe stresses the role of Peter in building the Church upon Christ, as if Jesus had said, "so shall I build the Church upon my rock: . . . you [Peter] will lay the stones upon me, that is, the firm authority by which you will receive the pure and turn aside the unclean," which is precisely why the following verse grants Peter the power of binding and loosing.[49] The rock may be

45. See Cambridge, Trinity College, James Ms. 348, ff. 99ra-191ra; ff. 99ra-102vb for the prologue, which lays out the theological structure of the commentary by discussing the unwillingness of the Jews to believe the message of the apostles and by summarizing what is "proved" in each chapter of the Gospel. Beryl Smalley pointed out that Baconthorpe's apologetic is aimed at friars who filled their commentaries with classical illustrations ("John," 306-12). She might have pointed out, in addition, that the scheme of prophecy and fulfillment goes hand in hand with this polemical aim by emphasizing biblical history as an interpretive context. There is no evidence that Baconthorpe was engaged in active debate with contemporary Jews. For the use of the scheme of prophecy and fulfillment in definitions of the genre of a Gospel, especially Matthew, consider Pertrus Aureolus, *Compendium sensus litteralis totius divinae Scripturae,* ed. Philibert Seeboeck (Quarrachi: Collegia s. Bonaventurae, 1896), 193-94; Nicolaus de Lyra's prologue to Matthew, *Postilla* (see n. 22 above), vol. 4, ff. 4ra-vb (counting from the title page); Jacques Fournier, *Postilla super Mattheum* (see n.19 above), f. 126ra-rb. The same subject matter was sometimes treated in commentaries to the fourth book of Peter Lombard's *Sentences,* at distinctions 1 and 2.

46. The commentary to Matt. 16 is on ff. 156rb-158ra.

47. For Augustine, see Froehlich, "Saint Peter," 8-9.

48. He attributes this interpretation to Gregory the Great on Matt. 2 and to the Gloss.

49. At f. 156va: "Et intelligas hic, quod cum dicitur 'super hanc petram edificabo ecclesiam meam,' intelligitur principaliter de Christo. Est enim sensus: tu es Petrus, Petrus a me petra dictus super qua petra, a qua Petrus es dictus, principaliter edificabo ecclesiam

Christ, but Peter is the principal recipient of his authority — a typical adaptation of the traditional interpretation to papalist ends.

The exegesis proper is literal, peppered with two allegories, beginning with v. 13 and continuing line by line. The commission took place at Caesarea, located in a region settled by the tribe of Dan but later inhabited by Gentiles: Jesus and the apostles came to Caesarea because Christ wished to make the Church of Jews and Gentiles. Jesus raises his question, "who do people say that I am," and the first answer — "John the Baptist," according to some — invites a brief digression to Herod and the Baptist. Brief and uneventful comments follow Jesus posing the question again to his disciples and Peter answering with his confession, a confession that admits, following the *Glossa ordinaria,* that Jesus is not only the Christ, but also the one true God. Jesus says, "Blessed are you, Simon Bar-Jona," and Baconthorpe gives a quick definition of "Bar-Jona." "And I say to you" (v. 18) is the "general commission," and Baconthorpe immediately turns to Marsilius of Padua and Jean de Jandun and their defense of episcopal authority, and the comments become lengthier.[50] Marsilius and Jean think that Peter is no more head of the Church than the other apostles (and the commentator's listeners and readers will immediately recognize

---

meam et super hanc petram, per quam tu es Petrus, edificabo ecclesiam meam ministerialiter. Et hoc dicit ministerialiter. Sic edificabo super hanc petram ecclesiam meam, quia tu super me ordinabis lapides, id est firmam auctoritatem qua mundos recipies et leprosos abicies, de quibus sequitur 'et quodcunque ligaueris' et cetera, 'et quodcunque solueris' et cetera. Et sic patet quod euangelium hic loquitur de fundacione ecclesie super Christum petram."

50. At f. 156vb: "Ubi [Matt. 16:18, 'et ego dico tibi'] notandum est primo quod una heresis nouiter fuit orta que dicebat quod beatus Petrus apostolus non fuit plus caput ecclesie quam quilibet aliorum apostolorum, et fuit Marcili de Padua et Iohannis de Ianduna, et hanc condempnat dominus Iohannes xxii. in constitucione que incipit 'certum processum' [actually 'Licet iuxta doctrinam'; see Smalley, "John," 323], et probat Petrum esse uerum caput et uicarium singularem Christi, quia hic in singulari dicitur, 'tu es Petrus, et super' et cetera, et in Iohanni singulariter dicitur, 'pasce agnos meos,' et iterum, 'tu uocaberis Cephas, quod interpretatur caput,' et iterum, hic dicitur, 'tibi dabo claues regni,' et omnia que secuntur dicuntur in singulari. Ex hijs in ista constitucione format Papa racionem sic: 'maior auctoritas non limitata quam limitata,' id est maior est que non solum est communis cum alijs sed personalis et singularis que est limitata ut sit generales. Tamen sed 'omnes alij apostoli ceperunt hoc modo potestatem limitatam,' id est in communi tantum sic 'supra uerum corpus Christi conficiendum, sumendum et alij ministrandum, que quidem auctoritas seu potestas fuit in cena domini omnibus apostolis attributa, siue illa quam post resurrectionem dominus supra corpus misticum dedit illis, dicens "quorum remisseritis peccata, remissa sunt, et quorum retinneritis, retenta sunt," siue eciam in ascensione quando dixit eis, "euntes ergo docete omnes gentes baptizantes eos in nomine patris," et cetera. Petro autem hanc potestatem illuminatam [*lege:* sine limitatione]' non cum alijs concessit et in singulari cum dixit, 'pasce agnos meos,' et sic de alijs auctoritatibus allegatis, ergo et cetera" (for the constitution, Charles du Plessis d'Argentre, *Collectio judiciorum de nouis erroribus* [Paris: Andreas Caillean, 1728], 1:306).

the implication — all bishops have equal authority). John XXII condemned them and proved that Peter is the only vicar of Christ in his bull, *Licet iuxta doctrinam,* the crux of the matter resting in the number of a subject and verb: "you [singular] are Peter," or "you [singular] feed my sheep" (John 21:15-17), or "you [singular] are 'Cephas,' which means 'head' " (John 1:42). Baconthorpe is summarizing John XXII's definition of the heresy and response to it. He reproduces the pope's distinction between the common power of all priests to consecrate and administer the sacraments and the "general" power given to Peter alone. Next, he defends the antiquity of the papalist position — perhaps recognizing that "the Bavarian's henchmen" *(fautores bauari)* had some claim to episcopal traditions — by digging into the canons.[51] Canons support a brief list of assertions: the heresy is ancient; as a heresy, it amounts to dissent from the Roman Church; all ecclesiastical authority resides principally in Peter; no one is bound or freed by the power of the keys without being bound or freed by Peter; and heretics challenge the validity of Peter's judgment. A brief comment added to the end of v. 18, "and the gates of hell shall not prevail against [the Church]," explains that the threat comes from heresy on two fronts, infiltration and tyrannical persecution, an allusion to spiritual Franciscans and Ludwig of Bavaria.

All of this serves as background to Baconthorpe's interpretation of the power that Christ gave Peter in v. 19, which quickly devolves to two controversial subjects of the early fourteenth century: papal freedom in creating laws and the "key of knowledge."[52] The exegesis is simple. Baconthorpe explains, using an allegorical interpretation of the building of the tower of Babel drawn from the *Historia scholastica,* that Christ promised to build his Church upon a firm foundation, because he intends it to overcome the flood of heresies. Hence, he gave his own authority to Peter when he invested him with the power of the keys, so he could let in pure people and throw out the dirty ones. The interpretation merely adapts, to papalist ends, the *Glossa ordinaria*'s stress on the power of the keys as the instrument by which the Church remains pure.[53] This simple interpretation would suffice, had the exercise and meaning of the keys been uncontested.

The remainder of the discussion of v. 19 is a doctrinal digression, very

51. References to D.xxii.1, *Corp. Iur. Can.* 1:73; C.xxiv, q.1, c.5, ibid.; 1:968; C.xxiv, q.1, c.14, ibid., 1:970.

52. James Ms. 348, f. 157ra-157rb.

53. PL 114:142. The *Glossa ordinaria* ascribes this power to all the apostles. Cf. Peter John Olivi's interpretation, quoted in Tierney, *Origins,* p. 184 n. 1, for the background to the issues that Baconthorpe raises here.

closely related to the interpretation of the passage itself, even though apologetics may not sound like good and proper exegesis. John XXII condemned those (unnamed Franciscans) who tried to limit papal sovereignty by binding a pope to the decrees of his predecessors. The commentator does not explain that the argument was an attempt to prevent the pope from tampering with thirteenth-century decrees protecting their observance of poverty; rather, he stresses the infringement of a pope's power to change the law.[54] With such matters in the air, the author is compelled to provide a more precise explanation of the "keys." There are three kinds, he says, in a somewhat eccentric description of episcopal powers: a penitential key, conferred by Holy Orders; a juridical key, which includes the authority to settle doctrinal disputes; and a key of excommunication and absolution.[55] All three make up the authority given by Christ to Peter; they constitute the Roman Pontifex's "capital and universal power."

Again, without directly addressing his opponents' position, he turns to the device by which they elevated papal decrees to inviolable status: the doctrine of the key of knowledge (derived from Luke 11:52).[56] Baconthorpe appears, at first, to ignore the new interpretation that regards the key of knowledge as the basis of infallible papal judgments, and reviews, instead, the issue raised by the *Decretum* and Peter Lombard's *Sentences* — whether the knowledge required to administer penance is separate from the power conferred at ordination (i.e., whether the key of knowledge is distinct from the key of power). A short review of theological opinion leads him to a somewhat reductionistic conclusion: the "knowledge" in question is actually the *authority* to exercise knowledge. As such, the power of the keys, i.e., absolute sovereignty, cannot be limited by a "key of knowledge," because the latter is just another expression of sovereignty. The point is verified by the canons, which ascribe to the papacy the absolute power of God upon the earth and require of popes only enough knowledge of the faith to assure that they not be heretics.

At the first blush, the presence of apologetic arguments in the exegesis of the passage might seem a weird intrusion of doctrinal and polemical concerns that would better be treated in their own contexts and not obstruct the noble work of literal interpretation. To Baconthorpe, as to most fourteenth-century exegetes, the discussion of notes and questions — and with

54. See Tierney, *Origins,* passim, for the controversy; for Baconthorpe, see Ullmann, "Baconthorpe."

55. The traditional division of episcopal powers distinguishes sacramental, juridical (which includes excommunication), and teaching powers. See Le Bras, *Institutions,* 2:366-68.

56. It was developed by Peter John Olivi and added by Franciscans to Ludwig of Bavaria's "Sachsenhausen Appeal" of 24 May 1324; see Tierney, *Origins,* 182-83.

them, a variety of theological sources, including the canon law — contributed to interpretation.[57] The inclusion of papal judgments, in particular, helps establish the meaning of the passage, partly because the commentator believes that the papacy has always interpreted it properly, even though he works with only fragments of the papal tradition derived from the *Decretum.* Papal judgment makes a decisive contribution to the meaning of the text by defining the nature and implications of papal authority. The power conferred on Peter and his successors is, thereby, determined to be a sovereignty without limits. This coheres with the interpretation of other related subjects in the Gospel. For example, Baconthorpe sees the commission of the apostles in Matt. 10 as the creation of the episcopal office; he sets this in the context of the ecclesiastical hierarchy, in which Peter comes first, which is why he is mentioned first in Matt. 10:2.[58] The tribute money of Matt. 17:23-26 demands a description of the superiority of papal power to that of the emperor.[59] The Gospel, in this Carmelite's hands, likewise defends the conventual practice of mendicant poverty, which is also determined by papal authority.[60] In all of this, canon law, theological exposition, and exegesis coalesce in a friar's comprehensive view of biblical truth and social reality, in which the papacy plays a leading role.

The fusion of papal ideology and exegesis was not restricted to the common stock of Petrine texts. An eloquent witness is Johannes Klenkok's commentary on the Acts of the Apostles. Klenkok introduced his commentary with a detailed discussion of a doctrine intended to discredit popes: the power conferred in the commission of Peter requires the practice of apostolic poverty; "successors of the apostles" who do not observe it do not have the power to administer penance.[61] The vast majority of popes, bishops, friars, and priests stand disqualified. Spiritual Franciscans, some Beguines, some Beghards, and the opponents of friars like this doctrine. Klenkok attacks it on all fronts, twisting conventual views of mendicant poverty, papalism, and a papalist view of the penitential office into twenty-

57. It seems to me that Lyra's *Postilla* is an exception to the fourteenth-century norm of treating questions and "notes" in conjunction with the interpretation of the text. An analysis of the development of the form, exceptional in its appreciation of the exegetical role of theological digressions, is Karlfried Froehlich, "Bibelkommentare — Zur Krise einer Gattung," *ZTK* 84 (1987): 465-92.

58. Following a discussion of clerical grades, f. 143va: " 'Nomina sunt hic primus Symon,' quia tamquam principali apostolo Christus dimisit sibi ecclesiam regendam."

59. Text and analysis in Smalley, "John," 324-34.

60. Also treated in the commentary on Matt. 10, at ff. 144rb-145vb.

61. Eichstätt, Staatsbibliothek, Ms. 204, ff. 117ra-122va treat 28 arguments pertaining to apostolic power and apostolic poverty, which involve not only papal power but also the penitential power of mendicant friars.

eight propositions and counterarguments, before moving to Acts 1:1.[62] The commentary itself repeatedly returns to the apostolic life, mostly in defense of the ministry of the mendicant orders. The exegete does not convert the biblical text into a treatise on papal authority, although he finds occasion to defend the superiority of the pope to the emperor while commenting on Acts 25.[63] Nevertheless, papalism informs much of his interpretation, partly because it supports the mendicant ministry that is so much on Klenkok's mind, and partly because he methodically applies the canon law to the language and ideas of the text.[64] That is, papalism affects exegesis not only by making interpretations into papal arguments, but also by providing a very concrete framework within which to practice exegesis and exercise theological judgment. This pertains, then, not merely to a kind of polemical exegesis, but to a way of attaining understanding relative to an authority.

The hermeneutical implications of the fusion of papal ideology and exegesis are obscured by common assumptions about the Bible and papalist theory and by rigid attention to the fourfold meaning or hopeful obsession with literary exegesis. The exegetical tradition on "papalist" passages, like Matt. 16:18-19, assured that the biblical foundations of papalist theory would remain complex, because fourteenth-century commentators who were committed to the papal party were prone to adapt traditional (non-papalist) interpretations to their own ends, as, e.g., Innocent III had done. They did not simply grab the old interpretation of the popes, that the "rock" is Peter. Moreover, the opinions of the popes that were at their fingertips, in the canons and decretals, included a colorful variety of literal and nonliteral interpretation, and not surprisingly an interpreter could — as Baconthorpe sometimes did (Klenkok, as well) — move easily between literal and nonliteral meanings, without consigning them to different parts of the page (or of the mind; Lyra gives us a wrong impression of the fourteenth century). There were profound conceptual reasons for this mish-mash in fourteenth-century exegesis that have been scarcely understood.[65] A careful analysis of the rhetorical functions of arguments drawn from a variety of exegetical sources, among them the canon law, could shed much

62. At the conclusion of the response to the twenty-eighth argument, Klenkok promises, "omnia tacta hic plenius tangentur in postilla sequenti Actus apostolorum" (f. 122va), which he does, in fact, do.

63. Ibid., ff. 187vb-188ra.

64. A detailed analysis will be found in my dissertation (see n. 42 above).

65. Contrast the assumption that papalist argument was generally founded on the literal sense, Diana Wood, "Clement VI and the Political Use of the Bible," in *The Bible in the Medieval World: Essays in Memory of Beryl Smalley,* ed. Katherine Walsh and Diana Wood, Studies in Christian History, Subsidia 4 (Oxford: Basil Blackwell, 1985), 238. Clement VI's interpretations are more typical of the variety in papalist exegesis.

light on the fourteenth-century discovery of meaning in the Bible. In short, I have only pointed to the existence of the material, where it might be found, and what its context might be.

This much should be granted: fourteenth-century commentators increasingly used their lectures as an opportunity to hammer on the heads of opponents, whether the enemies be recent critics of papal power (or of related aspects of clerical authority) or more idealized, "classical" heresies.[66] It would be naive to dismiss this as contentious opportunism at the expense of exegetical science, and it would be foolish to try to bowdlerize the interpretation of the text of its pregnant digressions. Interpreters could assume an incredible degree of coherence in their universe; the cords between biblical meaning, ecclesiastical authority, and religious and social problems were wound dense. The free movement that we witness in some commentaries between Bible and law (but also theology, philosophy, and natural science) was largely taken for granted, even though not always pursued systematically. They saw no tautology in a pope declaring that the truth of interpretation is on his side. Controversies have intellectual reflexes; papalist exegesis is a case in point.

66. Jacques Fournier used exegesis to answer "classical" heresies (commentary in n. 19 above). The defense of the faith was frequently noted as a tangential aim of interpreting the Gospels (e.g., Baconthorpe, Fournier, and Nicolaus Eymerich [see n. 22 above; but Eymerich, *Postilla*, vol. 1, f. 3v]).

9. *Jean Gerson on the "Traditioned Sense" of Scripture as an Argument for an Ecclesial Hermeneutic*

Mark S. Burrows

Within the polemical arena of sixteenth-century biblical scholarship, Protestant voices routinely announced their abrupt departure from the fundamental exegetical methods of the medieval schools, above all in rejecting the use of tradition in the theological task. In a characteristic outburst in the *Table Talk*, for example, Luther insisted that "the text of Holy Scripture alone endures; Augustine and Ambrose offer us nothing."[1] Again, and in

1. *Tischreden*, WA 2, 1745. The claim that Scripture *alone* should be the theological norm is a rhetorical claim that Luther often expressed, but one which his actual exegetical practice and even his advice regarding theological education did not always support. Thus, for example, in *To the Christian Nobility*, Luther challenges the honor given to the study of the *Sentences* which he argues had come to "dominate the situation in such a way that we find among the theologians more heathenish and humanistic darkness than we find the holy and certain doctrine of Scripture." Later in the same treatise, however, he concedes that "the Sentences ought to be the first study of young students in theology. . . . Indeed, the writings of all the holy fathers should be read only for a time, in order that through them we may be led to the Holy Scriptures. As it is, however, we read them only to be absorbed in them and never come to the Scriptures. We are like people who study the signposts and never travel the road. The dear fathers wished, by their writings, to lead us to the Scriptures, but we use them as to be led away from the Scriptures, though the Scriptures alone are our vineyard in which we ought all to work and toil." *To the Christian Nobility of the German Nation Concerning the Reform of the Christian Estate*, trans. C. M. Jacobs, rev. James Atkinson (St. Louis, 1966), 204-5; WA 6, 461. In other words, the fathers are to serve as prolegomenon to the study of Scripture itself, precisely in order to lead us properly into Scripture. This understanding seems to be the rationale which inspired among Protestants a renewed attentiveness to catechetical instruction and the formulation of new "evangelical" creeds. This concern also led Melanchthon to write his *Loci communes*, and John Calvin his *Institutes of*

much the same mood, he rejected in one of his treatises against Emser the validity of a "spiritual" exegesis, contending that "it is much more certain and much safer to stay with the words and the simple meaning [of Scripture], for this is the true pasture and home of all the spirits."[2] But should we accept such protestations at face value as an accurate assessment of the state of biblical study at this juncture? Or are they not rather an index of the turbulent currents of sixteenth-century *Kontroverstheologie?* The latter is certainly true; the former, we must now recognize, is doubtful. Luther's sweeping opposition to the supposed excesses of medieval allegory should be read in basic continuity rather than conflict with developments in later medieval exegesis. Indeed, his critique aligns his position firmly within this historical trajectory when he concedes, in his *Lectures on Genesis,* that "grammar should not rule the meaning [*res*], but ought to be guided by the meaning."[3] The question which Luther faced — along with earlier medieval

---

the Christian Religion. Calvin, in fact, instructs his reader in the preface to the French edition of 1560 that "I can at least promise that [this work] can be a key to open a way for all children of God into a good and right understanding of Holy Scripture" (*Institutes of the Christian Religion,* 2 vols., ed. John T. McNeill, trans. F. L. Battles, LCC [Philadelphia, 1960], 1:7). With regard to Luther, Gerhard Ebeling rightly notes that alongside the Reformer's strongly worded aversion to any "books" other than "die blosse lautter schrifft oder Biblie," is his insistence that catechetical instruction provides the essential perspective for the study of Scripture: "Doch sieht Luther nüchtern die Notwendigkeit einer den Bibelleser leitenden Norm im Sinn eines Bekenntnisses. Es ist ratsam, bei jeder Auslegung sich an den Grundregeln des Katechismus auszurichten, eventuell auch Melanchthons Loci communes heranzuziehen, dessen Kommentare er im übrigen noch am ehesten empfehlen kann, da sie sich die klassischen Kommentare, den Römer-, Galater- und Hebräerbrief zum Vorbild genommen haben. Diese Leitung der Auslegung vom Bekenntnis her will sachlich nichts anderes sein als eine Anleitung, der Selbstauslegung der Schrift nachzugehen" (*Evangelische Evangelienauslegung: Eine Untersuchung zu Luthers Hermeneutik* [Darmstadt, 1962], 406; see also ibid., 402-9). On this point see also Jaroslav Pelikan, *Luther the Expositor* (St. Louis, 1959), 71-88; John M. Headley, *Luther's View of Church History* (New Haven/London, 1963), 69-94. More recently, and with reference to the Reformers more broadly, G. R. Evans has rightly noted that "the habit of looking to the Fathers was not broken in the changes of the Reformation. On the contrary, it seemed to many of the reformers that it was only since the patristic age that things had begun to go wrong, and that it was therefore necessary to go back to the Fathers for help in interpretation" (*The Language and Logic of the Bible: The Road to Reformation* [Cambridge, 1985], 21).

2. Martin Luther, *Answer to the Hyperchristian, Hyperspiritual, and Hyperlearned Book by Goat Emser in Leipzig, Including Some Thoughts Regarding His Companion, the Fool Murner,* in LW 39 (St. Louis, 1970), 179.

3. Martin Luther, *Lectures on Genesis,* 16.12, in LW 3 (St. Louis, 1961), 70-71. Elsewhere in this lecture Luther goes on to say that "knowledge is of two kinds: (1) what the words mean; (2) what the subject matter is. To one who has no knowledge of the subject matter the knowledge of the meaning of words will be of no help. . . . It is not grammar that gives us this meaning; it is the knowledge of sacred matters. . . . See to it that you are thoroughly familiar with the subject matter; after that it will be easy to learn the grammar.

exegetes — was not *whether* but *how* the meaning *(res)* of the text was to be discerned; grammatical analysis alone could not fulfill this demand, because "the letter [τὸ γράμμα] kills, but the spirit [τὸ πνεῦμα] gives life" (2 Cor. 3:6).[4] This is the problematic confronting theologians during the later Middle Ages, who increasingly turned away from the fourfold exegesis[5] practiced in the earlier monastic tradition in order to concentrate their attention on the *sensus litteralis.*[6] We must thus locate Luther as an heir to

---

He who sins in the matter of grammar commits a venial sin, but to sin in the subject matter is a mortal sin" (ibid., 67, 72).

4. For a thorough discussion of the use of this passage in late medieval exegesis, with specific attention given to Jean Gerson and the Petit affair, see Karlfried Froehlich, " 'Always to Keep the Literal Sense in Holy Scripture Means to Kill One's Soul': The State of Biblical Hermeneutics at the Beginning of the Fifteenth Century," in *Literary Uses of Typology from the Late Middle Ages to the Present,* ed. Earl Miner (Princeton, 1977), 20-48. This biblical passage (i.e., 2 Cor. 3:6) had provided patristic biblical commentators with one of their central arguments in defense of allegorical or spiritual exegesis. Cf., e.g., Origen *On First Principles* 1.1 (2), PG 11:122B; Gregory of Nyssa, "Prologue" to *Homilies on the Song of Songs,* PG 6:757 (*In Canticum Canticorum,* ed. H. Langerbeck [Leiden, 1960], 6); Augustine *On Christian Doctrine* 3.5.9, CCSL 32:82-83.

5. In the opening remarks to his important study of fifteenth-century exegesis, Karlfried Froehlich noted that the origins of the fourfold exegetical method — itself an elaboration of the fundamental Pauline "letter/spirit" dialectic — seem to be found in John Cassian and Eucher of Lyons, while a cursory explanation of this schema is already present in Philo's exegesis of Ezekiel's vision; see "Biblical Hermeneutics," 21-24. In the later Middle Ages, we find a marvelous metaphorical application of this exegetical approach in the *Didascalicon* of Hugh of St. Victor, who described the threefold meanings of Scripture — i.e., history, allegory, tropology — by means of the image of a building. This metaphor, which came to have an enduring legacy in the High Middle Ages, portrayed history as the foundation of exegesis, allegory as its main structure consisting of stones of different sizes carefully set into place by the master mason, and morality (or tropology) as the color which conveys "the meaning of things" rather than "the meaning of words" alone. See *Didascalicon* 6.2-5; cf. also Hugh, *De arca Noe morali* 1.1, PL 176:513C, where he describes how God resides in the soul through knowledge and love such that "knowledge constructs the building of faith, while love on the basis of virtue paints the building in the form of color spread upon the entire surface." The analogy can be traced to Gregory the Great's *De universo* 14.23, PL 111:400. Bernard of Clairvaux offers a different metaphor to describe the various "senses" of Scripture, interpreting the "storeroom," "garden," and "bedroom" mentioned in the Song of Songs to refer to three levels of exegesis: "The man who thirsts for God eagerly studies and meditates on the inspired word, knowing that there he is certain to find the one for whom he thirsts. Let the garden . . . represent the plain, unadorned, historical sense of scripture, the storeroom its moral sense, and the bedroom the mystery of divine contemplation" (*On the Song of Songs,* serm. 23.2.3, trans. Kilian Walsh [Kalamazoo, MI, 1976], 28; *Sermones super Cantica Canticorum,* vol. 1, *S. Bernardi Opera,* ed. J. Leclercq, C. H. Talbot, H. M. Rochais [Rome, 1957], 140). Nicholas of Lyra returns to the fourfold schema and summarizes it with the memorable lines: "Littera gesta docet/Quid credas allegoria/Moralis quid agas/Quid speres anagogia." For a discussion of this verse, see Beryl Smalley, *Studies in Mediaeval Thought and Learning* (Oxford, 1979), 285.

6. The pioneering work of Beryl Smalley on this question has accentuated the in-

his predecessors, and this despite his most vehement denunciations to the contrary.[7]

Yet to identify the "literal sense," as late medieval theologians often did, as both the primary domain of exegesis and the foundation of the theological task was not yet to settle the hermeneutical question. In an age wracked with conflicts theological and ecclesiastical, both church leaders and their critics frequently found themselves embroiled in disputes concerning the exact nature of that elusive sense. Such debates often took shape as efforts to defend, or dismiss, an authoritative reading of the meaning *(res)* "behind" Scripture's grammatical sense. As Thomas Aquinas had framed this task, anticipating Luther at least on a theoretical plane, "the duty of every good interpreter is to consider not the words, but the [proper] sense" of the words *(non considerare verba sed sensum).*[8] The question facing Luther along with Gerson and other late scholastic predecessors, therefore, was: How does one apprehend the *res* which underlies the *verbum* (or *signum,* to follow Thomas)? How is one to grasp — and medieval exegetes, unlike recent deconstructionist critics, were not yet brash enough to question this possibility — the authentic *sensus* of the

---

creasing interest from the 12th century in the literal sense and a "natural" or historical rather than spiritual exegesis; see her *The Study of the Bible in the Middle Ages* (Oxford, 1941; repr. Notre Dame, 1964). In this study Smalley argued that the decline of spiritual exegesis corresponds to the rise of what she considered to be a more scientifically defensible approach; indeed, she offers a strident caveat in her concluding chapter in which she laments that the renewed interest in mysticism, "even though . . . confined to a small circle, . . . provides a fascinating though alarming example of the way in which the history of exegesis prolongs itself in that of its historians. . . . Conditions today are giving rise to a certain sympathy with the allegorists. We have a spate of studies on medieval 'spirituality.' The scholars who tried to counteract its effect on exegesis are still too little appreciated" (p. 360). One of the products of this sympathy, which attempts to trace the demise of modern theology at the hands of the Enlightenment and its successors, is Andrew Louth's study, *Discerning the Mystery: An Essay on the Nature of Theology* (Oxford, 1981). Cf. also David Steinmetz, "The Superiority of Pre-Critical Exegesis," *TToday* 37 (1980): 27-38.

7. G. R. Evans has made the same point, arguing that the exegetical approaches of the sixteenth-century Reformers exhibit continuities alongside challenges to earlier practice: "There was, undoubtedly, much in the outcome that was new and revolutionary and a sense of making a fresh start. But the extent to which mediaeval scholarship led the way has often been underestimated, and the condemnation of the scholastics has tended to sink with them a proper recognition of what they achieved as students of the Bible. Sixteenth-century writers were themselves not always quite clear what it was they were putting behind them. They were less clear still perhaps how much they were taking with them" (*The Road to Reformation,* 2). Her conclusion, however, that in the late Middle Ages "questions of logic gave way to questions of language" (p. 3), is puzzling, since already in the 12th century the question of the nature of language in general, and biblical language in particular, had become a dominant concern of theologians.

8. *In Matth.* 27.1, n.2321, ed. R. Cai (Turin, Rome, 1951), 358.

"bare" letter? There is surprising agreement among university theologians of early fifteenth-century Paris that the literal sense alone should occupy the exegete's attention. But how was one to grasp its true sense, to recover its proper meaning in the midst of apparent ambiguity and confusion, particularly when theologians argued for widely differing "literal" readings of the same biblical texts?[9]

On this point of exegetical *practice* the general agreement on basic *principle* faltered. No longer could theologians suppose, as had Thomas Aquinas in a characteristically confident mood, that "Holy Scripture sets up no confusion, since all meanings are based on one, namely, the literal sense."[10] Such an assertion seemed wildly naive in the polemical atmosphere of the early fifteenth-century church, an arena of theological controversy in which the coherence of biblical language splintered under competing readings. At this juncture it had become increasingly clear that while "many meanings" *(plures sensus)* might be present in the literal sense, as Augustine and later Aquinas had argued, it did not follow that such "multiplicity of meanings" would not lead to "ambiguity or any other kind of mixture of meanings," as Aquinas had concluded.[11] In the heated forum

9. Froehlich argues, with penetrating insight, that late medieval exegesis joined together Aquinas's earlier conviction that God's intention stood as the definition of the true literal sense with an anti-Thomist distrust of words to the point of a "free-for-any-guess" approach: "Because words were no longer regarded as invested with some kind of unambiguous truth but rather can be deceptive, they might be related to truth in different ways, and biblical words were no exception. . . . When the theological virtues had become part of a system of ambiguous words and could be given meanings based on differing goals, then the door was open (to put it positively) for a new kind of creative playing with different meanings of equal claim to truth" ("Biblical Hermeneutics," 46-47). One might add here that this development anticipates the recent assault of deconstructionist criticism, which has been aptly characterized recently as "nihilist hermeneutics"; see Robert W. Jensen, "Can a Text Defend Itself? An Essay *De inspiratione scripturae*," *Dialog* 28/4 (1989): 251-53.

10. Thomas Aquinas *ST* Ia q. 1, a 10 ad 1. Aquinas's theoretical discussion of biblical interpretation in the opening question of this treatise — and his practical application of that theory in terms of his biblical commentaries and theological treatises — demonstrates a remarkable confidence in the retrievability of meaning based upon an assumed clarity of biblical language; thus, e.g., he here argues for a multiplicity of meanings rooted in language which he refuses to consider as in any sense ambiguous. Luther would later return to this conviction, arguing against Emser that "the Holy Spirit is the simplest writer and adviser in heaven and on earth. That is why his words could have no more than one simplest meaning which we call the written one, or the literal meaning of the tongue. . . . One should not therefore say that the Scripture or God's word has more than one meaning" (*Answer to . . . Emser,* 178-79). Of course, Aquinas meant that the single "sense" might yet legitimately bear a multiplicity of meanings, though these had to be in essential agreement and did not set up any "ambiguity" *(aequivocatio)*.

11. *ST* Ia q. 1, resp. and ad 1; here I follow the translation from the Blackfriars' edition, *Summa theologiae,* vol. I (London/New York, 1963), 39. See also above, n.10. The

of late fourteenth- and early fifteenth-century ecclesiastical debates, such a conviction no longer seemed tenable. To the contrary, theological arguments grounded in conflicting interpretations of Scripture — not only in its multiple senses, but in its foundational *sensus litteralis* — had lapsed into such "confusion" that theologians found themselves thrust into the vexing arena of a Babel *redivivus:* the polemic arena of discourse had led to conflicting grammars of interpretation. Thrown upon the horns of the exegete's dilemma, theologians of the later Middle Ages increasingly found themselves pierced either by an arbitrary exposition rooted in an unbounded individualism, on the one side, or by an equally capricious application of magisterial authority, on the other. In both cases the realist confidence in the perspicacity of biblical language had broken apart, setting a course toward a nihilistic hermeneutic which the Protestant Reformers could only temporarily divert.

This paper examines a chapter in the still dimly understood story of late medieval exegesis,[12] in this case by exploring one solution to the quest for the literal sense amid the increasing exegetical confusion and theological polemic during the early fifteenth century: namely, the defense of a "traditioned sense" as the interpretive norm governing biblical exegesis which we find in the later works of Jean Gerson (d. 1429). The first section surveys Gerson's proposal of this ecclesial norm as the appropriate means of resolving the ambiguities of biblical language; here we trace his construction in treatises written during the Council of Constance (1414-1418) of a "hermeneutic of tradition." In the concluding section, this historical discussion broadens to consider the continued applicability of such a hermeneutical theory; here we explore from a contemporary vantage point the role which tradition plays in exegesis, drawing upon Hans-Georg Gadamer's philosophical arguments and the "canonical approach" of Brevard Childs.

---

reference to Augustine, cited here by Thomas, is from *Conf.* 12.31, PL 32:844. Augustine had earlier allowed for the ambiguity of biblical language, pointing specifically to texts in which "what he who wrote the passage intended remains hidden" (*On Christian Doctrine,* 3.27.38, CCSL 32:99-100). He based this conclusion, however, upon the premise that "Scripture teaches nothing but charity" (non autem praecipit scriptura nisi caritatem; ibid., 3.10.55, CCSL 32:87); in instances of varying interpretations Augustine lays down three rules: he argues that one must ask whether a reading accords with truth taught clearly elsewhere in Scripture (context), whether it agrees with "right faith" (doctrine), and whether it encourages us to love (practice).

12. This is a conclusion also shared by G. R. Evans, who in a study of medieval exegesis remarks that "we are particularly ill-informed about the fifteenth century" commentaries and exegetical work. See *The Road to Reformation,* 2.

I

Gerson, chancellor at the University of Paris and leading figure in the conciliar proceedings at Constance, defended what he called the "sense handed on by the holy Fathers" as the key to avoiding the exegetical confusion which lay at the heart of theological debates, first at Paris, of course, but with even greater force at the council.[13] In tracing the development of this idea in his thought, we shall confine our attention to texts written during this period, since it is at this juncture that Gerson found himself confronted with a series of theological crises which either evolved out of or involved differing exegetical readings. During the council these crises reached a climax in the trial of John Hus, though the essential outlines of this confrontation are already discernible in Gerson's writings from the period immediately preceding the council, and his response to Hus's theological position extends into the treatises written after Hus's execution.[14] Indeed, this response involves not only matters of theological detail but the broader theoretical framework for exegesis; it is this aspect of his theological thought which will occupy our attention in this study.

Within this context we see that Gerson defined the hermeneutical task in startling anticipation of Luther: in similar style to the later Protestant, Gerson argued for a distinction of "meaning" and "grammar," insisting that "Scripture has its own logic and grammar" and thus must be interpreted differently than one might approach the "speculative sciences."[15] But he

13. See Jean Gerson, *De consolatione theologiae,* in *Oeuvres complètes,* ed. P. Glorieux, vol. 9, *L'oeuvre doctrinale* (Paris, 1973), 237. All citations from Gerson's works are henceforth cited from this edition, with "G" (= Glorieux) followed by appropriate volume and page numbers.

14. Indeed, Gerson's encounters with Hus, whom he considered as a representative of the Wycliffite position, were not "news" when he arrived in Constance early in 1415; the Paris faculty had already addressed this confrontation in a series of condemned propositions from Hus's *De ecclesia,* pronounced in the spring of 1414, and Gerson had carried on a lengthy correspondence during the summer months to instruct the Archbishop of Prague, Conrad de Vechte, regarding the appropriate response to this problem. Yet this condemnation concerned itself with specific theses — theological and ecclesiological — and did not address the deeper problem of exegetical method by which Hus had arrived at these conclusions.

15. We shall return to this point later in the essay; see below, p. 166. For the origin of this citation, see "Réponse à la consultation des maîtres," in G 10, 241. In his study of Gerson and the Petit affair, Froehlich admits that while he has not "fully investigated this statement, [it] sounds very much like Reformation hermeneutics" ("Biblical Hermeneutics," 42-43). My essay intends to clarify this statement, set within the broader framework of Gerson's writings during the Council of Constance; I explore this point more fully in *Jean Gerson and "De Consolatione Theologiae" (1418): The Consolation of a Biblical and Reforming Theology for a Disordered Age* (Tübingen, 1991); see esp. pp. 103-25, "The Construction of a *Theologia Biblica.*"

parts paths with Luther in how he conceived that this sense might be recovered, arguing vigorously in favor of the Church's historical tradition as the proper guide in locating the *res* embedded within the *verbum.* And here we come to the constructive solution to the interpreter's dilemma posed earlier: during the proceedings at Constance Gerson turned with increasing insistence to the early Church — the *sensus a sanctis patribus traditus* — as the norm governing how the *sensus litteralis* might be faithfully recovered and preserved.[16] Against the competing exegetical arguments of Hus and his circle, Gerson defended this norm as the key to interpreting Scripture faithfully: that is, "not arbitrarily" but according to "its own proper meaning."[17] This "ecclesial hermeneutic" grounded, as we shall see, his response to conflicting theological voices of his day.

Yet such an approach did not imply a blanket allegiance to the Church's magisterial authority; Gerson never suggested that *any* theological statement from the Church's tradition — or from the "present" magisterium, however conceived — might identify Scripture's true literal sense. In clarifying this point he admits his dependence upon Henry Totting of Oyta,[18] who articulated in his *Quaestiones sententiarum* the governing thesis that the "truths which alone must be reputed as 'catholic' and thus necessarily believed for salvation" belong to one of two categories: they are matters "either asserted explicitly in the biblical canon or able to be inferred as a necessary and formal consequence from these."[19] Elsewhere

16. In his discussion of "the reformulation of the concept of tradition" in Luther's thought, John Headley calls this grasp of the Church as the active vehicle of "tradition" *traditio activa,* as contrasted with a constitutive norm (revelation) which he calls *traditio passiva* (*Luther's View of Church History* [New Haven/London, 1963], 69). Heiko Oberman coined his own terminology for the view which held for "the sufficiency of Holy Scripture as understood by the Fathers and doctors of the Church," calling it "Tradition I," though he supposed on the basis of the Gerson texts he had studied that the chancellor belonged in another category which he called "Tradition II" (*The Harvest of Medieval Theology: Gabriel Biel and Late Medieval Nominalism* [Cambridge, MA, 1963], 372). On this point see also below, n. 24.

17. See *De sensu litterali,* G 3, *L'oeuvre magistrale,* 335: "Sensus scripturae litteralis iudicandus est prout ecclesia spiritu sancto inspirata et gubernata determinavit, et non ad cuiuslibet arbitrium et interpretationem."

18. See, e.g., his remark in "Réponse à la consultation des maîtres," G 10, 241: "Rursus hanc materiam de sensu litterali sacrae scripturae declaravit pulchre magister H. de Hoyta in suo prologo super Sententias. Videatur illic si habeatur."

19. This thesis is a peculiar restatement, one might well argue, of the Augustinian "faith seeking understanding": in this case, in terms of an exegetical model according to which Scripture's own logic provides the foundation for interpretation. Oyta explains this in the "third article" of his *Quaestio de sacra scriptura:* "An iste veritates sole reputande sint catholice et de necessitate salutis credende, que vel explicite in canone biblie asseruntur vel ex eis in consequencia necessaria et formali inferri possunt." See Henrici Totting de Oyta,

in the same treatise Oyta adds an important caveat to this thesis which is critical in understanding his approach, insisting that while "all the truths from the writings of the holy Fathers" which are also "approved by the Church" are to be counted as "catholic truths," not all "judgments" *(sententia)* emanating from these writings deserve such distinction.[20] The writings of the "doctors" must first receive the Church's approbation to be included among "catholic truths" which it was necessary to believe: Theologians formulated their own "judgments," but only the Church had the authority to declare those judgments as binding on the faithful. They were thus heirs rather than arbiters of "catholic truth." Gerson had embraced this methodological premise before he arrived at Constance, though his controversial encounters during the council apparently confirmed this conviction; but we must note that for Oyta as for Gerson after him, this truth was itself conceived as inextricably related to Scripture, either as part of its intended literal sense (revelation received) or as a logical consequence of this (revelation interpreted or explained).[21]

How, then, did Gerson locate the "literal sense" in the midst of competing theological arguments, disputes which exposed what appeared to be an irresolvable ambiguity lodged within biblical language itself? For Gerson, as for Oyta before him, this was anything but a theoretical question. Faced with a variety of controversial disputes — e.g., Matthew Grabow's assault upon the Brethren of the Common Life; Jean Petit's argument for tyrannicide; the Hussite insistence on communion for the laity "in both kinds"[22] — Gerson found himself faced with conflicting interpretations not only of "catholic truth" but of Scripture itself in its "literal sense." In a cluster of treatises and letters written during the Council of Constance (1414-1418) which address a variety of unresolved controversies, the nature of biblical exegesis became a primary point of debate. I shall focus upon

---

Quaestio de sacra scriptura et de veritatibus catholicis, ed. Albert Lang, in *Opuscula et Textus: Historiam ecclesiae eiusque vitam atque doctrinam illustrantia, Series Scholastica,* ed. J. Koch, Fr. Pelster, SJ (Münster, 1953), 61. For further discussion of Oyta's theology, which has been aptly characterized as a "mediating" theological position, see Albert Lang, *Heinrich Totting von Oyta: Ein Beitrag zur Entstehungsgeschichte der ersten deutschen Universitäten und zur Problemgeschichte der Spätscholastik* (Münster i. W., 1937), 161, 177; see also Heiko Oberman, "Some Notes on the Theology of Nominalism with Attention to Its Relation to the Renaissance," *HTR* 53 (1960): 55.

20. "Licet omnes veritates librorum sanctorum doctorum per ecclesiam approbate sint inter veritates catholicas numerande, non tamen omnibus sentenciis, que inveniuntur in sanctorum opusculis iam per ecclesiam divulgatis est de necessitate salutis adherendum" (Oyta, *Quaestio,* 66).

21. For a more detailed discussion of this point, see my *Jean Gerson and "De Consolatione Theologiae,"* esp. pp. 114-20, "On the Sufficiency of Scripture."

22. Again, I explore these disputes in detail in ibid., chaps. 4-6.

several of these in which the challenge to the Church's authority, in specific points of doctrine and ecclesiastical practice, pressed Gerson and his critics toward the problem of biblical authority and its authentic interpretation. Gerson's concern in answering these assaults, as we shall see, led him not to a simple defense of ecclesiastical prerogative nor to a capricious defense of authority but to articulate a "hermeneutic of tradition," a defense of the "holy Fathers" and above all of the primitive Church as the normative guide for discerning Scripture's *sensus litteralis*.

Recent studies of Gerson dispute this point, pointing to texts from his writings which seem to suggest that Gerson identified exegetical authority with the contemporary rather than historical Church. G. H. M. Posthumus Meyjes argues that Gerson so emphasized the role of the Spirit over the Church, and Church over Scripture, that we must speak of a "two source" theory of revelation: i.e., Scripture and the (present) Church.[23] Heiko Oberman agrees, identifying Gerson as advocate of the "spirit-guided Church" which grants to the Church what he calls both a practical and an "ontological" priority over Scripture to the point that through the Church's interpretation "the canonical boundaries are enlarged and Holy Scripture is materially extended."[24] Steven Ozment also accepts this view, pointing to the Spirit once again as the modus operandi through which the magisterium derives its authority.[25] Finally, J. Samuel Preus goes even further to describe Gerson as the proponent of a "spirit-governed Church" which became the unquestioned arbiter in determining Scripture's proper literal sense.[26]

All of these studies see Gerson — against Oyta, strangely, whom Gerson himself explicitly calls upon as his guide in such matters — as accentuating the Church's present magisterial authority to interpret Scrip-

23. G. H. M. Posthumus Meyjes, *Jean Gerson: Zijn Kerkpolitiek en Ecclesiologie* ('s-Gravenhage, 1963), 259ff.

24. See Oberman, *Harvest,* 385-90. As I shall argue, on the basis of the treatises written during Constance, Gerson apparently moved into the position which Oberman characterizes as "Tradition I," which argued for "the sufficiency of Holy Scripture as understood by the Fathers and doctors of the Church" (ibid., 372; cf. also n.16 above). While Gerson did not completely reject his earlier acceptance of canon law as one means of interpreting Scripture, his later writings demonstrate a marked preference to underscore the primary authority of the early Fathers in determining questions of biblical interpretation.

25. See his "The University and the Church: Patterns of Reform in Jean Gerson," in *Mediaevalia et humanistica* n.s. 1 (London/Cleveland, 1970), 111-26.

26. J. Samuel Preus, *From Shadow to Promise: Old Testament Interpretation from Augustine to the Young Luther* (Cambridge, MA, 1969), 79-82. Preus here argues that "the *fundamentum* rests in the church *alone*" because only the "spirit-governed Church" is able "to judge and declare what the *literal* sense of Scripture is."

ture and thereby resolve ecclesiastical disputes. Of course, this conclusion would align Gerson with the later Tridentine affirmation of the sources of revelation in Scripture *and* tradition,[27] setting him at the same time in proximity to both papalist and enthusiast extremes since both depended in different ways upon an immediate interpretation of the biblical text. Yet these discussions misread or ignore Gerson's later exegetical strategy, in which he carefully defends the "sufficiency" of Scripture as the revelation of those things necessarily to be believed for salvation, while defending the *historical* and above all *primitive* Church as the final arbiter of the *sensus litteralis.* The question of the difficulty which such a presumption raises — viz., the task of delineating this voice, and the admittedly naive presumption that the early Fathers spoke with one voice — must be at least acknowledged at this juncture; we shall return to this point, with further comments, in the final section of this paper.

To reconstruct Gerson's position we must turn to a range of texts from the period of the council (1414-1418). First, his *On the Necessity of Communion for the Laity in Both Kinds* (1417) is crucial to this question, since Gerson prefaces this argument against the "utraquists" with ten "rules" guiding biblical exegesis. Second, we turn to his *On the Consolation of Theology,* written at the close of Constance (1418), in which Gerson refutes a cluster of Hussite positions (e.g., the definition of simony; the opposition to "judicial correction" in matters of heterodox teaching; the ecclesiology of the "predestined"; the vigorous defense of "zeal" in effecting reform; etc.). But in turning to these arguments Gerson defends his position not by invoking magisterial authority but through a careful treatment of Scripture — in direct answer, apparently, to Hus's plea, repeated at numerous junctures during his trial, to be instructed by "better and more relevant Scripture than those that I have written or taught"[28] — and its authoritative interpretation (i.e., *sensus a sanctis patribus traditus*). He does not simply counter one theological argument with another, nor does he oppose one scriptural text against another, since this would ignore the problem of ambiguity lodged in that language itself. Rather, he defends an interpretive method by which the proper *sensus litteralis* might be re-

27. This subject appeared finally during the fourth session at Trent (April 1546), in the "Decree Concerning the Canonical Scriptures": "all saving truth and rules of conduct . . . are contained in the written books and in the unwritten traditions, which, received by the apostles from the mouth of Christ himself, or from the apostles themselves, have come down to us, transmitted as it were from hand to hand." See *The Canons and Decrees of Trent,* ed. and trans. H. J. Schroeder (St. Louis/London, 1941), 17, 296.

28. For an account of this trial by Peter Mldanovice, see *John Hus at the Council,* trans. and ed. Matthew Spinka (New York, 1965); see esp., e.g., pp. 194, 209, 214, 229.

covered, turning principally to the guiding norm of patristic exegesis.[29] In other words, exegesis is set within an ecclesiological horizon — *not* of the Church's present authority, Spirit-governed or otherwise, but of the Church's *historical* tradition. Finally, we will examine his *Response to the Consultation of Masters* (1418), in which Gerson offers an extended discussion of the nature of the literal sense and the proper manner by which it might be recovered.

The question which these various treatises address, in differing ways, is how one was to answer the controversial theological/exegetical arguments offered by Hus and his circle without simply countering one opinion with another. Gerson is wary of simply endorsing the exercise of ecclesiastical discipline in such cases, particularly since Hus had requested again and again to be corrected by "better and more relevant" Scripture. Rather, he articulates a careful defense of the locus of the Church's authority, one based not upon the present magisterium but upon the Church's historical tradition. In his treatise on *Communion in Both Kinds,* he contends that "Sacred Scripture in its authentic reception and interpretation [*in sui receptione et expositione authentica*] is ultimately resolved by the authority, reception, and approbation of the universal Church, and above all [*praesertim*] by the early Church [*ecclesia primitiva*] which received these Scriptures and its understanding of them directly from Christ through the revelation by the Holy Spirit, at the day of Pentecost and at many others."[30] This claim echoes his earlier assertion in *On the Literal Sense of Sacred Scripture* (1414) that the "literal sense" was revealed *per Christum et apostolos* in such a manner that later theologians *(sacri doctores ecclesiae)* merely "have drawn forth" *(elicuerunt)* this "sense" — i.e., by discerning the "catholic truth" lodged within the biblical language — through further reasoning, prompted by the need to oppose heresy and articulate a clearer grasp of this sense. The text *(verbum)* and its meaning or interpretation *(sensus),* in other words, are given together in *one* revelation to the early Church *(ecclesia primitiva)*. This assertion of the Church as the context of the reception and proper interpretation of Scripture defines "tradition" as an interpretive authority, not in contemporary but in historical terms; this appears to be the case despite the proviso he adds that the Church received an "understanding" of the scriptural revelation "at the day of Pentecost *and*

29. The question of how Gerson construes "tradition" calls for a more detailed exploration which the limitations of this paper do not allow. It appears that the theologians he most favors among the early fathers are Augustine, Pseudo-Dionysius, and Gregory the Great, though he also supplements these with an eclectic selection of medieval fathers whom he considers as expositors of this early tradition.

30. G 10, 58.

at many others," a phrase which he apparently intends as a reference to *ecclesia primitiva,* or the church of the early Fathers, and not to the "modern" magisterium. This is borne out by his interpretation of Augustine's dictum, a commonplace in medieval theological arguments in this context,[31] that "I would not have believed the gospel if the authority of the Church had not compelled me": in a much earlier treatise, he had interpreted the language of this passage, explaining that Augustine's use of *ecclesia* referred to the "primitive" Church because of its proximity to Christ.[32]

Looking at the second text of this group, *On the Consolation of Theology,* we find Gerson returning to the question of exegetical method once again. Defining *theologus* as "a good man learned in sacred scripture" — itself a variation upon the Ciceronian definition of a philosopher — he argues that what he calls "biblical erudition" depends upon two conditions: first, the holiness of the interpreter; and second, the reader's faithfulness to the interpretive norms of the Church's historical tradition. As he puts it, we must not be like those who "impudently force the Holy Scriptures to serve their own corrupt habits and desires, distorting the sense [of the text] passed down by the holy Fathers if they are not indeed ignorant of it."[33] This is an argument interesting to us for two reasons.

31. On this point, Oberman has remarked that this passage stands "invariably [as] the medieval authority" on this question (*Harvest,* 385). For the original citation see Augustine, *Contra epistolam Manichaei quam vocant fundamenti,* in PL 42, 176; Gerson applies this term on numerous occasions in his writings, one of which is to be found in *Communion in Both Kinds;* G 10, 58.

32. See *De vita spirituali animae,* G 3, 139: "Ibidem enim ecclesiam sumit pro primitiva congregatione fidelium eorum qui Christum viderunt, audierunt et sui testes exstiterunt." This agrees with his affirmation, in a much later treatise, that Scripture must be interpreted in harmony with the early Church, "since it received [the Scriptures] along with its understanding of them directly from Christ" (*De necessaria communione laicorum sub utraque specie,* G 10, 58). See above, n. 30.

33. G 9, 237: "sacras denique litteras impudenter suis inquinatis moribus et desideriis subservire compellunt sensum a sanctis Patribus traditum distorquentes, imo saepe nescientes." The phraseology which Gerson here uses is remarkably close to the Tridentine claim, in the "decree concerning the canonical Scriptures" (i.e., from the fourth session; April 1546) which addresses the problem of "private" interpretation of Scripture: no person "shall, in matters of faith and morals pertaining to the edification of Christian doctrine, *distorting the Holy Scriptures in accordance with his own conceptions, presume to interpret them contrary to that sense which holy mother Church, to whom it belongs to judge of their true sense and interpretation, has held and holds,* or even contrary to the unanimous teaching of the Fathers, even though such interpretations should never at any time be published" (praeterea ad coercenda petulantia ingenia decernit, ut nemo suae prudentiae innixus, in rebus fidei et morum ad aedificationem doctrinae Christianae pertinentium, *sacram scripturam ad suos sensus contorquens, contra eum sensum quem tenuit et tenet sancta mater ecclesia,* cujus est judicare de vero sensu et interpretatione scripturarum sanctarum, aut etiam contra unanimem consensum patrum ipsam scripturam sacram interpretari audeat, etiamsi hujus-

First, this expresses Gerson's longstanding conviction that one of the professional "tools" required of theologians was "a pious life and moral character."[34] Text and reader stand in a mutually influential relationship, defined by Gerson — and, one might add, by the early Fathers and medieval doctors in general — primarily in moral terms: the character of the reader influences the manner of reading, an insight into the prejudicial role of the observer which in the post-Newtonian world has gained a fresh hearing. Second, the interpreter must submit to the *sensus a sanctis patribus traditus* rather than manipulating texts to confirm one's own preconceptions — again, an argument including a moral dimension. In broader context we now recognize the "Fathers" whom Gerson here identifies not as those of the "Spirit-filled" Church of his own day, but as those of the early Church who received the Scripture together with an understanding of it directly from Christ *(ecclesia . . . recepit eam* [i.e., *scripturam*] *et ejus intellectum immediate a Christo)*.[35] Discerning the proper "sense" of the text depends upon one's perspective, both moral and historical (or "traditional").

Finally, in his *Response to the Consultation of Masters,*[36] Gerson aligns his understanding of the exegetical task with Augustine,[37] Nicholas

---

modi interpretationes per ordinarios declarentur et poenis a jure statutis puniantur); see *Canons and Decrees,* 18-19, 298. Agreeing with Gerson's formulation, the conciliar fathers at Trent affirmed that the proper interpretation of Scripture was the responsibility not of private judgment, but of the church's historical tradition; they added, in contrast to Gerson, an equal emphasis upon tradition understood in terms of the *present* magisterium (i.e., "eum sensum quem tenuit et tenet sancta mater ecclesia").

34. See Froehlich, "Biblical Hermeneutics," 40; also, see Gerson's discussion of what he called "rule four," in his response to the "utraquists," *Communion in Both Kinds,* G 10, 56. Such an approach should not be confused with the difficulties raised by the Donatists, about whom Gerson had much to say elsewhere and repeatedly in his writings; in contrast to such a position, which had become a "rising tide" during this period, Gerson's concern is not with the efficacy of the Church's sacraments in the hands of "unworthy" priests or bishops, but with the interpretive perspective necessary for a proper reception of the meaning of Scripture. On this general point, and with specific reference to Gerson's anti-Donatist polemic against Hus and his circle, see Jaroslav Pelikan, *Reformation of Church and Dogma (1300-1700),* vol. 4, *The Christian Tradition: A History of the Development of Doctrine* (Chicago, 1984), 92ff.; see also Oberman, *Harvest,* 220ff. It is also interesting to note that Luther adhered to a similar principle; one example of this conviction is his assertion, against the excesses of papalist loyalties, that "the Holy Spirit can be possessed only by pious hearts"; in context this is an affirmation of the necessary role which the "pious life" played in biblical interpretation. See *To the Christian Nobility,* 134.

35. G 10, 58.

36. See ibid., 241.

37. He here specifically cites Augustine's *De doctrina christiana,* referring to it as a general reference for this question.

of Lyra (d. 1340),[38] and, more recently, Henry Totting of Oyta (d. 1397),[39] to argue that the biblical interpreter must follow three rules: first, the wider biblical context; second, the *modus loquendi* through "figures, tropes, and rhetorical expressions"; and third, the *usus loquendi* established by the "holy doctors and expositors of sacred scripture." This final argument establishes the "sense" of the text, since Scripture must not be explored "according to a power of logic or dialectic applied in speculative sciences. . . . Sacred Scripture has its own proper logic and grammar."[40] It should be clear at this juncture that Gerson not only intended this claim to separate, in nominalist fashion, Scripture (revelation) from secular texts (literature),[41] but also meant this as the defense of the necessity vis-à-vis the former for an authoritative exegesis: this had to be so, since Scripture operated according to its own peculiar "logic" and "grammar." The historical tradition, or so he argued, provided Gerson with the key to grasping the intended meaning of the text beyond the ambiguity and confusion of the bare words, a "sense" which was "handed down by the holy Fathers" — above all in the early Church.

This "hermeneutic of tradition" is the theory which stabilizes what we might call Gerson's ecclesial exegesis; in this manner he emphasizes the need to ground theological arguments not merely in "scripture alone" but in the proper understanding of Scripture which is to be discerned within the historical Church (i.e., tradition). Indeed, Gerson recognized the danger — clearly articulated by Hus and his circle — of invoking the principle *sola scriptura,* which he reckoned would ultimately legitimate "any interpretation" and devolve into a principle characterized with contempt in a later age as "private judgment" (i.e., "et non ad cuiuslibet arbitrium vel interpretationem").[42] Scripture alone provides the foundation for theological argument, but it must be read in line with the historical tradition rather

38. Here he cites a text which he often alludes to elsewhere in his writings, the "Prologue" to Nicholas of Lyra's *Postillae super Bibliam.*

39. Here as elsewhere Gerson cites his "Prologue" to the *Sentences,* lectures which Oyta delivered in Paris during the years of Gerson's training in the arts. It is this text, as I argue elsewhere, which provides Gerson with his view of biblical sufficiency; for further discussion of this point, see my *Jean Gerson and "De Consolatione Theologiae,"* esp. pp. 114-20, "On the Sufficiency of Scripture."

40. G 10, 241.

41. On this point, note Froehlich's suggestive argument in "Biblical Hermeneutics," 43-47: "In his nominalist tendency toward separating the Bible from other literature, Gerson was against extending to any other writing the positive privilege of biblical 'truthfulness' " (ibid., 44).

42. See G 3, 335. For a provocative discussion of the "Use . . . [and] Abuse of Private Judgment," see John Henry Newman, *The Via Media of the Anglican Church,* 3d ed. (London, 1877; repr. Westminster, MD, 1978), 128-88.

than according to "private" judgment. To borrow the apt terminology of Albert Lang, the Church according to this position functions in a "normative" rather than "constitutive" role in mediating the one revelation in Scripture; it is the interpreter and not supplier of revelation, and thus establishes the general boundaries within which that revelation is to be received.[43]

Gerson's approach to biblical interpretation, which is for him the foundation of the theological discipline and the norm for church life, thus depends upon the vantage point by which one approaches Scripture. Of course, the biblical text is the "sufficient" authority for theology and ecclesiastical life just as the literal sense was its foundation; this is to state a commonplace among those churchmen — both the conciliar fathers and their critics — gathered at Constance during the second decade of the fifteenth century. The issue that consumed the attention of both Hus and Gerson during this council was not *whether* but *how* Scripture's authority was to be applied, and this involved distinctively different applications of "tradition" in the exegetical project. On this point Gerson committed himself to recovering the proper (authoritative) *sensus litteralis* by invoking not the Church's present magisterium but the "traditioned sense" — *sensus a sanctis patribus traditus* — as a normative and formal interpretive principle.

II

Gerson's defense of a "traditioned sense" anticipates, in a curious fashion, recent developments in the field of hermeneutics, both philosophical and biblical. Regarding the former, the parallel to the hermeneutic principle of Hans-Georg Gadamer, explored in his *Truth and Method,* is striking: tradition functions for Gadamer, against the grain of Enlightenment rationalism and its more recent heirs, as a "legitimate prejudice" by which one might recover the "authentic" meaning of a literary text. He assumes that the meaning of narrative emerges from and continues to sustain a historical community of discourse.[44] Of course, Gadamer does not suggest that one

43. See Albert Lang, *Die theologische Prinzipienlehre der mittelalterlichen Scholastik* (Freiburg i. B., 1963), 200ff.

44. See Hans-Georg Gadamer, *Truth and Method* (New York, 1986), 272-73. Here Gadamer articulates his notion of a "fusion of horizons" as the interpretive structure by which one gains a *historical* prejudice toward a given text. Indeed, this is the heart of Gadamer's argument with Enlightenment methods of interpretation: he opposes the assumption that one might grasp a text through the application of reason alone, suggesting rather that one must "rehabilitate" an adequate concept of prejudice vis-à-vis the text. Thus, he

might somehow substitute a new dogmatism of historical tradition for that of rationalism; rather, he defends, against all forms of positivist or reductivist reading, the attempt to recover the "sense" of a text that is mediated in historical communities. On this score, one might well ask of Gerson, as modern historical critics have effectively done in opposing a dogmatic reading of Scripture, whether this "traditioned" sense can retain its authentic message in the midst of contextual changes — linguistic, cultural, ecclesiastical, etc. That is, if we receive texts *only* as mediated in historical communities, does this allow for the distortion which tradition itself can introduce into the "original" message of a text?[45] Tradition as such cannot become an absolute dogmatic norm, at least not with a presumption of its own unquestionable hermeneutical "innocence." And, of course, the variations and even vagaries within the early tradition(s) should warn us against assuming that the Vincentian canon might be applied as a descriptive norm by which one might recover a supposedly univocal chorus of the early Fathers.

But such caveats should not obscure the fundamental question which this point does raise, one which literary critics have begun to recognize but which has been too often ignored among biblical critics: viz., whether an authentic meaning (or, variously, authorial "intention") can be recovered within communities, past and present, out of which texts arose and within which they continue to speak. One of the voices to recognize this possibility within the field of biblical hermeneutics is Brevard Childs, whose "canonical approach" seeks to read scriptural texts, against the logic of form criticism, according to the canonical context by which such texts are shaped and subsequently transmitted.[46]

---

prefaces the section from this work entitled "The Extension of the Question of Truth to Understanding in the Human Sciences" with a citation from Luther: "Qui non intelligit res, non potest ex verbis sensum elicere" (p. 151), a text which is strikingly similar to the citation earlier noted from his Genesis lectures (see above, n. 3). Gadamer insists that by reading a text within the historical trajectory of its reception — the tradition which bears the "sense" of a text — we find one means to "acquire a horizon," and in this manner we "inhibit the overhasty assimilation of the past to our own expectations of meaning" so that we might "listen to the past in a way that enables it to make its own meaning heard" (p. 272). At the same time, of course, Gadamer is adamant in resisting any temptation to collapse interpretation solely into a retreat into tradition, as if one might speak exclusively of one normative horizon "whose bounds are set in the depths of tradition" (p. 273).

45. This is the point where the questions raised by reader response criticism do offer a constructive word of caution to those who engage in the task of reading texts. For further discussion of this hermeneutical approach, see, for example, Bart Ehrman, "The Text of Mark in the Hands of the Orthodox," esp. pp. 20-21, herein.

46. Childs has consistently attempted to speak of the "canonical shape" of biblical literature; see, e.g., his *Introduction to the Old Testament as Scripture* (Philadelphia, 1979),

According to Childs, one must learn to read Scripture within the arena of tradition which he describes as "the confessional stance of the Christian faith,"[47] a method whereby the reading of biblical texts proceeds with a logic which might be described as an "ecclesial reception."[48] This is no absolute allegiance to tradition over against the text, nor the positing of a theological or even homiletical reading which violates historical faithfulness.[49] Rather, Childs's adherence to a canonical approach intends to avoid both a reductionism which would ignore the "received tradition,"[50] at one extreme, as well as an interpretation based strictly on "extrinsic, dogmatic categories" imported from outside the text,[51] at the other. He seeks through this method to discern in Scripture an "interpretative structure" which the canonical text "received from those who have used it as sacred scripture" — a contemporary variation, it would appear, on Gerson's thesis that the early Church received and conveyed the text together with its "authentic" sense. Canonical *texts* must be read within a canonical *context*, a horizon of interpretation which Gerson defined in terms of a "traditioned sense."

Within the guild of Protestant biblical criticism, such a reevaluation of tradition is often still held in suspicion, attacked as a betrayal of the

---

73: "It is a misunderstanding of the canonical method to characterize it as an attempt to bring extrinsic, dogmatic categories to bear on the biblical text by which to stifle the genuine exegetical endeavour. Rather, the approach seeks to work within that interpretative structure which the biblical text has received from those who formed and used it as sacred scripture." This canonical approach defined in this manner has to do not only with the formation of the text, but with the re-reception of Scripture within the communal context which is itself formed by that text. The text shapes the community, and in turn the community shapes the reading of the text.

47. See Brevard Childs, *The New Testament as Canon: An Introduction* (Philadelphia, 1984), 37.

48. Childs does not use such terminology, though his argument points in this direction when he suggests that "it belongs to the exegetical task that the modern reader takes his point of standing within the authoritative tradition by which to establish his identity with the Christian church. . . . The canonical approach to the New Testament begins with those historical communities who received and heard the gospel in ways congruent with portions of the New Testament canon. . . . In spite of the constant emphasis on the diversity within the New Testament by modern scholars, historically by the end of the second century, if not before, the gospels were being read holistically as a unity within the circumference proscribed by a rule-of-faith" (*New Testament as Canon,* 42-43).

49. At the same time, however, this approach does guard against a reductivist criticism which poses as an exclusively "historical" method. Childs answers this criticism in vigorous terms; see *New Testament as Canon,* 38-39, and his response to a series of reviews of his *Introduction to the Old Testament* in *HBT* 2 (1980): 199-211.

50. Thus, e.g., see Childs, *New Testament as Canon,* 40.

51. On this point see Childs, *Introduction to the Old Testament,* 73; idem, *New Testament as Canon,* 37-40; see also above, n. 46.

"proven results" of higher criticism or dismissed as an invitation to an arbitrary dogmatism. Both critiques, as we have here suggested, depend upon an insufficient grasp of the historical demands facing the reader of literary texts, insisting as they do upon an artificially rigid distinction or even polarization of Scripture and tradition. Gerson's approach to the hermeneutical problem facing the Church of his day, although not a direct solution to such contemporary suspicions, nonetheless anticipates the basic challenge lodged in this critique: his defense of a "traditioned" sense upholds the coherence of positing an interpretive authority within a community out of which texts arise and within which they are transmitted. This is a theoretical argument which finds an echo in Childs's canonical approach as in Gadamer's attempt to speak of legitimate prejudices as conditions of understanding: these approaches join in the attempt to "rehabilitate" against the forces of Enlightenment rationalism the role of communal authority, or tradition, in recovering a text's "voice."

What, then, can we say of Gerson's hermeneutical method? What is the contribution of his argument for a "legitimate prejudice" which answers the apparent equivocation of biblical language with an argument from the "traditioned sense" of Scripture? First, we must recognize that Gerson's contribution to later medieval hermeneutics lay not in delineating ambiguities in biblical texts; his critics were the voices who pressed this point to the center of ecclesiastical life. Nor does his originality (rarely a virtue among medieval scholars, in any event) lie in his reliance upon an authoritative reading. His contribution should rather be located in his advocacy of an ecclesial hermeneutic, an interpretive approach necessitated because of the practical ambiguities of language and the potential by which the reader might "distort" its sense as a means of moral self-justification. As we have noted, he grounds this method upon two foundational principles: first, historical context, since faithful interpretation demanded a reception of the text in accord with *ecclesia primitiva;* and second, moral context, since all reading depends upon the character of one's own judgments.[52] *What* one reads depends upon *how* one reads, and Gerson insists that one must first acquire the proper "grammar" of interpretation based on ecclesial tradition and moral perspective.

Surely Gerson would have agreed with Luther's later claim that

52. Hans Frei has noted this as one of the distinctive features of what he called "the traditional realistic interpretation of biblical stories," arguing that precritical readers of Scripture sought to "fit" themselves into the biblical narrative by recourse to figural exegesis, on the one hand, and on the basis of their "mode of life," on the other. See *The Eclipse of Biblical Narrative: A Study in Eighteenth and Nineteenth Century Hermeneutics* (New Haven/London, 1974), 3.

"grammar should not rule the meaning, but ought to be guided by the meaning," since he argued that Scripture had its own peculiar "logic." The question he faced was not *whether* but *how* this meaning should guide our reading of the text's "grammar," particularly since he faced critics for whom Scripture and tradition, as one historian has suggested, "began to seem not colleagues but rivals."[53] But is it possible that we might recover such a "grammar," one guided by the "meaning" *(res)* inherent within the text, in a situation in which this rivalry has become even more intense — with a host of Protestant theologians dismissing "tradition" not only on dogmatic but also on sociopolitical grounds and with deconstructionists rejecting altogether the feasibility of recovering an authentic meaning of texts? How are we to undertake the task of biblical exegesis in a world which defines itself as "postmodern," an age in which exegesis of all sorts seems besieged with conflicting voices, and one in which, to recall the thrust of George Steiner's penetrating cultural analysis, the modes of "hermeneutic encounter" have been reduced to barren "archaeologies"?[54] In the midst of such a crisis, Gerson's confident hermeneutic seems unabashedly anti-modern, and perhaps this is both its strength and its weakness: its strength, in reminding us that the grammar of scriptural language testifies to a hope which exceeds the diminishing forms of cultural rationality; its weakness, in presuming that "tradition" offers a univocal, transparent reading of texts whose proclaimed realities are distant from us and whose inherent sensibilities are alien to our own. But in either case his presumption warns us that we must become and remain critical of any reductivism which would measure a text's meaning according to the "cultural grammar" of a later age. As Childs has argued in similar style, the reader of Scripture must take a "point of standing" within "the authoritative tradition by which to establish his identity with the Christian church"[55] — and, we might add, to locate the *res* without which its "grammar" remains "non-sense."

All of this poses afresh the question with which we began: namely, the relation of Scripture and tradition. Gerson viewed Scripture as embedded within tradition, and vice versa, such that the task of exegesis depended upon a "reading with the Church." One reaches the meaning of biblical texts only through tradition — and, more specifically, the early community because of its proximity to the original "sense" of Scripture. With this approach Gerson parts paths not only with Aquinas's trust in the unequivocal character of biblical language but also with the later Re-

53. See Evans, *The Road to Reformation,* 27.
54. See George Steiner, *Real Presences* (Chicago, 1989), 230-31.
55. See Childs, *New Testament as Canon,* 40.

formers' ideal[56] of a self-authenticating or Spirit-authenticated text: Gerson confronted the ambiguity of Scripture in practice, and sought to retrieve its authentic "sense" through the mediation of the "legitimate prejudice" (Gadamer) of the early Christian community (i.e., "the holy Fathers"). In an age which had not yet jettisoned the normative authority of Scripture for the theological task, and which had not yet had to confront later confessional attacks upon tradition, this approach sought to hear the authentic "voice" of the text *(res)* embedded within the community of its origin as the antidote to linguistic ambiguity or interpretive discord. By establishing a continuity between the formation and reading of biblical texts as the proper grounding of a "traditioned sense," this ecclesial hermeneutic offers an at least viable alternative to the hermeneutical impasse of deconstructionism into which our "postmodern" age has fallen as well. For as Aquinas reminds us, and Gerson's method demonstrates, we who would encounter *verbum Dei* in Scripture — and thus accept both the privileges and duties of Christian readers — must consider "not the words but the proper sense of the words." And, as we have argued, we recover this sense by following the Reformers' call *ad fontes:* not only to Scripture but to tradition as well.

56. On this point, as we have earlier suggested, theory and practice did not always agree; the Protestant Reformers' rhetoric against the corruptions of medieval "tradition" did not jettison the authority of earlier theologians altogether, but sought to return "to the source" of Scripture — if often through the mediation of what they considered foundational doctrines, either as conveyed through the creeds (early and "modern") or as clarified by patristic theology. Cf. above, n. 1. In a later generation, Lancelot Andrewes (d. 1626) spoke eloquently to this point when he argued that God's truth is to be discerned through "this Booke [Scripture] chiefly, but in a good part also by the bookes of the Ancient Fathers, and Lights of the Church, in whom the scent of this ointment was fresh, and the temper true; on whose writings it lieth thick, and we thence strike it off and gather it safely"; see his *Ninety-Six Sermons* (Oxford, 1841), III, 291, cited in John Coulson, *Religion and Imagination in Aid of a Grammar of Assent* (Oxford, 1981), 21. The distance between Protestant rhetorical claims against "tradition" and the actual interpretive practice — an approach which might best be called "creedal" exegesis — bears further study.

10. *Christopher Columbus as a Scriptural Exegete*

John V. Fleming

It is well known that in the final years of his life Christopher Columbus, the Admiral of the Ocean Sea, was occupied with a major project — the unripe fruit of which has come down to us as the Book of Prophecies *(Libro de las profecías)* —designed to provide a spiritual context for what he increasingly came to regard as the charismatic nature of his voyages of discovery and the prophetic nature of his own nautical vocation. Though it is unlikely that the Admiral's prophetical pretensions were entirely posterior to his voyages to the New World, they were unquestionably encouraged by the dramatic nature of his discoveries and of the European reaction to them, and by the Boethian vicissitudes of his own political fortunes. It is accordingly extremely difficult to demonstrate that he embraced a coherent and definable set of interpretive principles as opposed to a kind of middlebrow exegetical opportunism with which he attempted to aggrandize the significance of his experience. Yet for a context which has in large measure concerned itself with erudite troglodytes, learned doctors of divinity, and Parisian professors, this Mediterranean sailor — *non professor, sed piscator!* —may offer a certain change of tempo, as well as suggest how certain learned exegetical habits had penetrated the sphere of popular culture in the late Middle Ages. Though Columbus's biblical knowledge has not been entirely neglected by scholars, there is, so far as I know, no study of his exegesis.[1] I hope this essay may serve as a beginning.

1. See Francisco Alvarez, "Cristóbal Colón y el estudio de la Sagrada Escritura," *Archivo Hispalense* 17 (1952): 129-40.

In 1501, in Cadiz or Seville, Columbus wrote a remarkable letter to his royal patrons, the Reyes Católicos, in which he explained the genesis of his program of exploration.[2] It is in effect a brief essay "De arte exegetica." I call it that not merely because in it the Admiral explicates several specific scriptural texts, but because it reveals a number of semiotic attitudes necessarily of interest to any student of the history of biblical exegesis. The letter is, indeed, a kind of anthology of "scenes" from exegetical history. It was once said of Henry James that he had a mind so fine that it could not be penetrated by an idea. Columbus's mind was by contrast as porous and fissured as a sponge; it caught ideas the way a collander catches spaghetti. His mind was absolutely full to overflowing with ideas, very few of them his own and a great many of them middlebrow clichés of the kind propogated in our own time by *Reader's Digest* and in the late Middle Ages by the propaedeutic handbooks, guides, précis, anthologies, cribs, and trots prepared by the evangelists of the mendicant orders.

Among the large and fundamental questions that this brief essay necessarily eschews but which cannot go entirely unmentioned are the two related issues of Franciscanism and Joachimism. Several recent studies have sought to demonstrate a more or less specific Joachimism in Columbus's thought.[3] My own conclusion is that his Joachimism, if it existed at all, was largely a stylistic manifestation of his Franciscanism. The latter — his personal and knowledgeable involvement in Franciscan spiritual circles — was a highly significant feature of his intellectual personality. The testimony of the Dominican missionary Bartolomé de Las Casas to the Admiral's special Franciscan devotion and to the fact that he was seen in the streets of Seville in Franciscan habit is entirely credible.[4] I think he probably was a member of the Third Order, as were so many other prominent members of the Sevillan circle of merchant bankers and maritime entrepreneurs. It may not be so easy, however, to distinguish between the two issues. There was probably not a Franciscan in Europe in the year 1500

2. I shall cite the edition of Consuelo Varela: Cristóbal Colón, *Textos y documentos completos*, vol. 1, *Relaciones de viajes, cartas y memoriales,* 2d ed. (Madrid, 1984), 277-81.

3. See, among other recent studies, the following: Juan Perez de Tudela y Bueso, *Mirabilis in altis: Estudio crítico sobre el origen y significado del proyecto desubridor de Cristóbal Cólon* (Madrid, 1983); Alain Milhou, *Colón y su mentalidad messianica en el ambiente franciscanista español* (Valladolid, 1983); and Pauline Moffit Watts, "Prophecy and Discovery: On the Spiritual Origins of Christopher Columbus's 'Enterprise of the Indies,'" *AHR* 90 (1985): 73-102. There is a classic study of millennialism among the Franciscan missionaries of Mexico: John Leddy Phelan, *The Millennial Kingdom of the Franciscans in the New World,* 2d ed. (Berkeley/Los Angeles, 1970).

4. Bartolomé de Las Casas, *Historia de las Indias,* ed. André Saint-Lu (Caracas, n.d.), 1:29-32.

who was not a "Joachimist" in some casual sense of the word — rather as there was not a Socialist in Europe in 1950 who was not a "Marxist."

One recurrent theme of the letter, and of the personal image projected by Columbus in the last decade of his life, is that of the exaltation of the humble. He, Columbus, this ugly duckling, had achieved what none of the great ones of the world could achieve; and, of the wide range of potential benefactors who might have shared his glory, only their Catholic Majesties had confidence in him. They, no less than he himself, were clearly inspired by the Holy Ghost. "Only in your highnesses did faith and constancy remain. Who doubts that this illumination was from the Holy Spirit as well as from me? The same [Spirit] with his marvellous rays of clarity consoled with his holy and sacred Scripture in voice loud and clear with forty-four books of the Old Testament, and four Gospels, and with twenty-three epistles of those blessed apostles."[5]

The claim implicit in this passage is rather astounding. Columbus suggests he achieved the westward passage to the Orient through the Spirit-filled reading of the Scriptures, and that Ferdinand and Isabella backed his project through the same agency. But quite apart from *what* he says, the manner of saying it is most curious. For surely this is a bizarre mode of scriptural citation. First of all we have the curious pleonasm of the phrase "sacred and holy Scripture" [*santa y sacra Escritura*]. The explanation of this awkward form probably relates to an idea in Columbus's mind of the fundamental Latinity of Scripture. It is common enough in medieval vernacular works for passages of Scripture to be cited in Latin, as though they would not be the same passages in the vulgar tongue. In fact, Columbus's own citations are mainly in Castillian; only one, the beginning of the prologue to the Gospel of John, seems too holy, or rather sacral, for such reduction. Here, the classicism *sacra* invokes the Latin aura.

More notable yet is the curiously mathematical enumeration of the books of the Bible. The casual reader of the passage might be forgiven for thinking that the numbers are the most important thing about it. There are, the Admiral says, forty-four books in the Old Testament. The Clementine Vulgate has forty-six, but the manuscript evidence of the medieval prologues is so complicated that it would be easy enough to arrive at other numbers. For example, Jerome clearly regarded 1 and 2 Samuel, 1 and 2 Kings, 1 and 2 Chronicles, and Ezra-Nehemiah as single books. By this reckoning there

5. "En sólo Vuestras Altezas quedó la fee y costaçia. ¿Quién dubda que esta lumbre no fuese del Espírito Santo, así como de mí? El cual con rayos de claridad maravillosos consoló con su santa y sacra Escritura a vos muy alta y clara con cuarenta y cuatro libros del Viejo Testamento, y cuatro Hevangelios con veinte y tres Hepístolas de aquellos bienaventurados Apóstoles" (ed. Varela, 278).

are forty-*two* books, a number regarded with mystical favor by various medieval exegetes because it corresponded with (among other things) the number of the stations of the Exodus, with the number of generations between Abraham and Christ in the prologue to the Gospel of Matthew, and with the number of bad boys eaten up by bears for calling Elisha "Baldy" (2 Kgs. 2:24). Forty-two becomes one "number of completeness," and we see its structural involvement in an astonishingly wide range of medieval Latin and vernacular texts, such as, e.g., Dante's *Vita nuova*.

However, Columbus does not say forty-two any more than he says forty-six. He says forty-four. Why? Since one of the points of his letter to the Spanish monarchs is to advance the claim that he knows the Bible inside out, it would be slightly anticlimactic to conclude that, as a matter of fact, he could not even properly count the number of books in the Bible he owned; but I fear this is a possibility we must at least entertain. He was not incapable of computational error. After all this man did miscalculate the distance between Andalucia and the coast of continental Asia by a factor of well over one hundred percent, insisting to his dying day that he was in suburban Kyoto when in fact he was in downtown Havana. By this standard an error of a mere ten percent or so may be regarded as astonishing accuracy. Still, the answer probably lies elsewhere. Columbus did have one powerful authority for the number forty-four: Augustine, in *De doctrina christiana.* In the eighth chapter of the second book Augustine, in a fashion almost as peculiar as that of Columbus, enumerates the canon he recognizes as authoritative, concluding that there are forty-four authoritative books in the Old Testament.[6] To this peculiar division I shall return in a moment.

But it is not possible to conclude that Columbus follows Augustine in any uncomplicated way, for his account of the books of the New Testament differs from Augustine. When we turn to Columbus's characterization of the New Testament, we encounter a difficulty of a slightly different sort. According to Columbus the New Testament is composed of "four Gospels with twenty-three epistles of those blessed apostles." Here the difficulty is not with the number of the books — which agrees with the later medieval consensus as opposed to Augustine, who excluded the Catholic epistle of Jude — but with their generic distribution. The four Gospels are simple enough; but the next book, the Acts of the Apostles, neither is nor so far as I know was ever in medieval characterization an "epistle." The standard medieval catalogue of the epistles identified twenty-one, divided between fourteen Pauline, three Johannine, two Petrine, and two Catholic epistles.

6. His "quadraginta quatuor libris Testamenti Veteris terminatur auctoritas" (*De doc. chris.* 2.8.13).

The final book was, of course, the Apocalypse. The form of the Apocalypse is at least technically epistolary — the letter of John to the seven churches which are in Asia — though I do not find its exegetical treatment as an "epistle" among medieval biblical scholars.

It is possible, of course, that in making a duplex division of the books of the New Testament, Columbus is simply reflecting a liturgical convention as he would have experienced it as an assistant at Mass: scriptural readings distributed between "Gospels" and "epistles."[7] Yet it seems also likely that Columbus has reorganized the traditional distribution of the biblical books for *numerological* reasons. In the same exegetical primer in which he has established a canon of forty-four Old Testament books, after all, Augustine had written a lengthy passage on the numerological skills needed by the exegete (*De doc. chris.* 2.16.25). Any good Franciscan of Columbus's day of course knew that the total number of books in the New Testament, twenty-seven, was inevitable; it is the trinity of trinity, the cube of three. Columbus, not satisfied with mere patristic commonplace, goes further; he fudges things in order to come up with the number twenty-three, but he does that only because of his investment in the number *twenty-two.* That seems to be the number that is in Columbus's mind, and it seems likely that in concluding that there are forty-four books in the Old Testament, he follows not merely the authority of Augustine's number but what he perceives as the numerological spirit in which Augustine advances it. For Augustine's enumeration of the canon of the Old Testament in the second book of *De doctrina christiana* is actually the enumeration of two groups of twenty-two.[8] It seems likely that the final number of forty-four is in part determined by the desirability of a double twenty-two. There is a fragment of an equation in Columbus's mind:

$$\frac{2x}{x + 1},$$

in which x has the value of twenty-two.

But what does it all add up to, or divide out as, or perhaps multiply into? What is on the other side of the imaginary "equals" sign following mathematical notation? The answer is, perhaps, that it all adds up to a certain conception of apocalyptic fruition. By 1501, when he wrote his exegetical essay to the king and queen, Columbus had long since concluded

7. This possibility was suggested by Dr. Elsie McKee in discussion following the oral presentation from which this essay derives.

8. Augustine has the following two groups of books: (a) Pentateuch; Joshua, Judges, and Ruth; 4 King[dom]s; 2 Paralipomenon; Job, Toby, Esther, and Judith; 2 Maccabees; 2 Esdras — twenty-two in all. (b) Psalms, 3 Solomonic books, Wisdom, Ecclesiasticus; 12 minor prophets; 4 major prophets — twenty-two in all.

that he was a prophet of Yahweh and that his life's enterprise, the westward passage to the Indies, was a clearly identifiable episode in prophetical history. His hermeneutics accommodated that belief. Things almost always look clearer in retrospect, and as Doctor Johnson reminds us, precept is generally posterior to performance. Looking back over his own life viewed as a special chapter of salvation history, and in the context of a letter in which he claimed that he learned how to sail to Cipango through the Spirit-directed reading of Holy Writ, it made pellucid sense to him to enumerate the canon in two divisions of twenty-two, or rather $2x + (x + 1)$.

For there are twenty-two letters in the Hebrew alphabet, a fact that determined a number of poetical and structural features of the Hebrew Scriptures. This is unavoidably obvious in the acrostic of certain well-known texts, such as Ps. 119, the so-called Great Psalm, or the book of the Lamentations of Jeremiah. Lamentations has five chapters, four of which have twenty-two verses. The first four chapters are genuine acrostics, with each verse beginning with the appropriate Hebrew letter in the appropriate order (chap. 3 has 66 verses, with three verses for every Hebrew letter).

None of this had been wasted on the rabbis nor, of course, on their platonizing Christian successors. The first of these in terms of importance and influence was the apocalyptic exegete we call St. John the Divine, the author of the final book in the canonical Christian Scriptures. Only recently, comparatively speaking, has the author of the Apocalypse been taken to be someone different from John the Evangelist, whose words, according to Columbus, exceed the power of any intellect to grasp in their full sublimity.[9] The Apocalypse has twenty-two chapters. To speak in "Franciscan" terms, one should say that *of course* it has twenty-two chapters, for it is really quite inconceivable that the Spirit would, in the apocalyptic circumstance, have used any other number. The first thing that the apocalyptic Christ of this book says — which is naturally and appropriately also the last thing he says — is that he is the alphabet of divine history. ἐγὼ τὸ ἄλφα καὶ τὸ ὦ, ὁ πρῶτος καὶ ὁ ἔσχατος, ἡ ἀρχὴ καὶ τὸ τέλος: "I am Alpha and Omega, the first and the last, the beginning and the end." This Christ speaks in Greek, for his scribe John writes in Greek, a language whose alphabet has twenty-*four* letters. Never mind; he is thinking in allegorical Hebrew, and in a metaphoric pattern from the Hebrew Scriptures that imposes itself on most of the major images of his vision. So for that matter was Augustine, when he structured his definitive history of history in Latin in twenty-two books against the pagans.

9. "En espeçial San Juan: *In prinçipio erat Verbum, et Verbum erat apud Deum,* etc., palabras tan altas de presonas que nunca deprehendieron letras" (ed. Varela, 279).

Columbus believed that the wisdom of the Scriptures was plenary, complete, definitive. It taught all things, including the path to Cipango over the western sea. The Scriptures "end" in apocalyptic revelation both in a structural and a teleological sense. But if the number of "completion" is twenty-two, how does Columbus arrive at twenty-three? Such a problem was child's play for an Ambrose or a Gregory. If twenty-two is the completeness of the Old Dispensation, the completeness of the New Dispensation will be twenty-two plus one. There is an analogy to this kind of thinking in the exegetical history of a biblical figure that I have studied elsewhere — namely, the *centuplum* or hundredfold increase ("whosoever gives up house or brothers or sisters or father or mother or wife or children or land for my sake . . . shall receive an hundredfold" [Matt. 19:29, AV]).[10] The perfect completion of the *centuplum* was computed exegetically to be one hundred and one, the stipend of ascetical reward, and it is for this reason that there are one hundred and one stanzas, lines, or metrical units in numerous medieval works bearing on an ascetical theme: e.g., *Sir Gawain and the Green Knight* and *Pearl.* Earlier medieval numerologists handled the catalogue of New Testament books in a slightly different way. Since Acts was in a certain sense the extension of Luke, which in its very incipit it refers to as "the former treatise," it made sense to classify it with the Gospels. Then followed the twenty-one epistles, which a twenty-second book — the Revelation of John, with its twenty-two chapters — crowned with completeness.

Such, in broad outline, is my speculation concerning Columbus's curiously numerical reference to the Scriptures, a reference that is, in my opinion, sufficiently eccentric and self-advertising to demand an explanation of some sort. If we grant the speculation the tentative allegiance that a hypothesis can command, we may see features of Columbus's exegetical temper that are, in the context of a symposium on exegetical history, highly suggestive. The Admiral was, so far as we know, a man without any sort of advanced formal schooling. Yet he was both a reader and writer of Latin, and he displays a surprisingly informed command both of the classical texts in his fields of special interest and of the latest treatises to issue from the newly invented printing press. In Columbus we have the example of an "amateur" exegete, a kind of hermeneutical auto-didact. I should point to five particular aspects of Columbus's exegetical thought.

In the first place, the silent clichés in Columbus's mind are of learned origin. Their possible genealogies are too numerous and too complex to

10. See John V. Fleming, "The Centuple Structure of the *Pearl,*" in *The Alliterative Tradition in the Fourteenth Century,* ed. B. S. Levy and P. E. Szarmach (Kent, OH, 1982), 81-98.

trace in this brief essay, but they derive from the fathers and from the rich tradition of Apocalypse commentary in which Iberian exegetes — including Isidore, Beatus, Arnold of Villanova, and Nicholas of Lyra — played so important a role.

In the second place, the apocalyptic pattern of thought is quasi-Joachite. I earlier denied that Columbus was a Joachimist, but following the lead of Maurice de Gandillac — who aptly calls Dante a "pseudo-Thomist" — I could agree to call Columbus a "pseudo-Joachite." By this I mean that there is at least the stylistic attempt to link a reading of the Scriptures with an implicit macro-historical scheme. The final sentence of his letter, which I take to be an editorial revision, reads thus: "Abbot Joachim the Calabrian said that he who must rebuild the house of Mount Zion must come forth from Spain."[11] This sentiment is found in no authentic work of Joachim of Fiore, but it does feature in the wild and wildly popular Catalonian prophecy *Ve mundo* ("Woe to the world in a hundred years!"). In Columbus's mind, the westward passage to the East was closely related to various schemes of contemporary millenarian vogue, such as the repulsion of the Turkish menace and the recapture of Jerusalem.

A third point is that the exegetical impulse is highly personal. Columbus seeks a way to read himself and his own project into exegetical history. In an allegorical and tropological reading that has many antecedents in Franciscan thought, he identifies himself quite personally with the "children" who cried out "Hosanna to the Son of David!" These "children" are the humble and the "marginalized," folks held of little account by the wisdom of the world, yet righteous in their innocence in the eye of God.

We may next note that the process involves what from the viewpoint of "scientific" scriptural criticism must necessarily seem some unsubtle use of a coercive "finagle factor." The exegete fudges his materials. If one needs forty-four books of the Old Testament, one will find a way of getting forty-four books of the Old Testament. Like many other medieval autobiographers, including Augustine, the most famous of them all, Columbus's commitment is to the *spiritual* truth and data and events, not to mere surface "reality."

Finally, we may note the essential and fundamental inconsequentiality of the mode of thought. It is decorative rather than discursive. It does not lead anywhere in particular; instead it sets a kind of intellectual mood. Columbus knows that an exegetical and prophetical vocabulary is important, but he shows no particular need to demonstrate *why* it is important.

Columbus's exegetical letter was written at a time when the Admiral's

11. "El abad Joahachin Calabrés diso que había de salir de España quien havía de redificar las casa del monte Sión" (ed. Varela, 281).

mind was fully engaged with the topic of prophecy and with his project of a book of prophecies. The sources of inspiration which he invokes — apart from the inspiration of the Holy Spirit, that is — range from the maddeningly general ("many holy doctors and sacred theologians," *santos* and *sacros,* again) to the impressively current and precise, such as Pierre d'Ailly's *De concordia Astronomie veritatis et narrationis historice.* By this time in his life, quite clearly, he had developed a sweeping if imprecise hermeneutical field theory in which the "signs" of the quotidian semiotics of the nautical life — the meaning of cloud formations, flights of birds, the declination of the compass needle, or the presence of floating seaweed in the brine — took their place alongside the meaning of the book of Daniel or the prologue to John's Gospel in some private, coherent, indeed seamless ecology of knowledge.

This was an attitude to which the Admiral had been drawn, gradually, by his life's experience, and it would be risky to suggest that it characterized the largely undocumented dreamer and schemer of the 1480s. Still, I do find considerable evidence even in the journal of the first voyage that Columbus, in a fashion more characteristic of medieval spiritual writers than of Renaissance merchant bankers, presents the details of his own biography as refracted through the prism of a certain kind of scriptural understanding. Columbus did not come to *write* exegesis until about 1500, but he was clearly *living* exegesis a good deal earlier. That is, I fully realize, a large and somewhat puzzling claim. While it cannot be fully explored in an essay of this character, it can perhaps be suggested by the invocation of a single biographical incident from Columbus's first American voyage, the voyage of 1492.

On Christmas Eve in 1492, on a warm and untroubled Caribbean night, the ship called *Santa Maria* slid aground on an effluvial sandbar from which she could not be dislodged. At the moment of disaster the Admiral slept below, exhausted, we are told, from two days and nights without rest. Juan de la Cosa, master mariner and fiduciary partner in the limited corporation, was in command of the ship; but he too had gone to bed, since the night was so fair and patently unthreatening. Thus it was that the tiller, and the destiny, of the flagship of a great maritime enterprise was turned over to a nameless cabin boy. Bartolomé de Las Casas, the Dominican missionary whose *Historia de las Indias* preserves a curiously reformatted edition of Columbus's journal of the first voyage, makes sure that we know that the Admiral had strictly forbidden that children should ever guard the tiller, whether in wind or in calm, at any time during the journey.

That necessary word of exculpation, probably of self-exculpation, since the words are likely those of Columbus himself, is one of the relatively few negative or pessimistic elements in what should be a tale of unqualified disaster. Instead, Columbus gives a brief and irenic account of the foundation of the first Christian settlement in the "New World," a city called Nativity, since its birth was effected from the bowels of the ship called Mary at the moment of midnight on Christmas. There was neither room nor provender on the other two ships for the crew of the *Santa Maria,* so that a certain number of the ships' company must be left behind. Yet this shipwreck was, says the Admiral, a great mercy of Providence, for the Christians found themselves on a paradisal island among a race of humankind beautiful in body and soul alike. "They are a people of love without venality," write Columbus-Bartolomé. "They love their neighbors as themselves; they have a language that is the sweetest in the world; they are meek, and always smiling."[12]

Nearly every element in this story, with the possible exception of the islanders' disconcerting lack of cupidity for the trinkets and garbanzo beans rescued from the shipwrecked stores of the *Santa Maria,* seems more or less wildly improbable. Many scholars have been unwilling to take it naively, but there is little agreement concerning the truth that its apparent disingenuousness might mask. One recent theory maintains that the episode was a staged accident, an act of benevolent sabotage. Columbus, a *converso* or even in fact a crypto-Jew, devised this means of saving a certain number of his relatives and coreligionists from the more uncertain fate of the general population of Castillian Jewry.[13] The voyage of the *Santa Maria,* like that of the *Mayflower* in a later century, was a forced pilgrimage of religious persecution.

I confess that I find this explanation dubious, yet in the same breath I must add that it is hardly more dubious than what I find in the pages of Columbus's log. I have come to believe that what Columbus's log often reveals was what was in his mind's eye rather than what he saw. And what was in his mind's eye as he wrote this entry, or rather in his mind's ear, was Isaiah's messianic prophecy of the peaceable Kingdom as chanted in the first Christmas Mass at the now far-distant Franciscan house of La Rábida: "The calf and the lion and the sheep shall abide together: and a little child shall lead them" (Isa. 11:6). Christopher Columbus, the "outsider," the Franciscan *idiota,* was one kind of child. The nameless cabin boy at the tiller was another.

12. "Dize el Almirante . . . 'Ellos aman a sus próximos como a sí mismos, y tienen una habla la más dulçe del mundo, y mansa y siempre con risa' " (from the journal of the first voyage, ed. Varela, 98).

13. Sarah Leibovici, *Cristophe Colomb juif* (Paris, 1986), 92-100.

We may put the question somewhat crudely and ask whether this account of the founding of the first, doomed European settlement in America is "history." Did all this happen *in reality,* as our typical vocabulary rather pretentiously might put it? Was there in fact a village named Navidad, and did it find its strange birth in the manner described? The answer to the first question — did Navidad exist? — is almost certainly yes; but the answer to the second question will depend, as so much in medieval exegesis depended, upon whether one speaks *literaliter* or *spiritualiter.* Let me invoke a historically distant but intellectually proximate analogy. Did Saint Augustine, whose passionate commitment to truth no sane reader of good will could for a moment question, "really" sit beneath a *fig tree* in a *garden* and "really" hear the singsong voice of *children* chant "Tolle, lege"? On this question the greatest Augustinian authorities are divided. No doubt the greatest Columbian authorities, should they ever turn their attention to the unlikely topic of the Admiral's hermeneutics, will prove to be divided too. My own view must be that Columbus has presented us with an episode in his personal history that, if it is to be understood, must be read through the same scriptural prism which refracted its elements in the writing.

IV. REFORMATION EXEGESIS

11. Luther's Humor as a Tool for Interpreting Scripture

Eric W. Gritsch

I. Faith and Humor

"He who sits in the heavens laughs; the Lord has them in derision" (Ps. 2:4). Reinhold Niebuhr preached on this text in 1946, alerting his audience to the fact that humor and faith "deal with the incongruities of our existence."

> Humor is concerned with the immediate incongruities of life and faith with the ultimate ones. . . . Laughter is our reaction to immediate incongruities and those which do not affect us essentially. Faith is the only possible response to the ultimate incongruities of existence which threaten the very meaning of life. . . . Humor is, in fact, a prelude to faith; and laughter is the beginning of prayer. In the holy of holies, laughter is swallowed up in prayer and humor is fulfilled by faith.[1]

1. Reinhold Niebuhr, *Discerning the Signs of the Times: Sermons for Today and Tomorrow* (New York: Scribner's, 1946), 111, 112.

This essay also commemorates the collegial learning and jesting at the court of the U.S. Lutheran-Catholic Dialogue in which Karlfried Froehlich and I represent a Lutheran Saxon-Habsburg coalition. Moreover, I shared with Karlfried Froehlich the experience of theological education in the Basel Alumneum under the direction of Oscar Cullmann, whose eightieth birthday in 1982 united us once again in literary form. See Eric W. Gritsch, "Sharing of Teaching Authority: An Offering of Unity," in Testimonia Oecumenica in Honorem Oscar Cullmann Octogenarii, *ed. Karlfried Froehlich (Tübingen: Hans Vogler, 1982), 114-15.*

When Luther lectured on the same passage in 1532, he viewed God's laughter as his way of hiding his wrath from the follies of humankind. "He laughs because He grants time for repentance."[2] This divine attitude ought to teach us how to laugh at our enemies, because before God they are insignificant. Just as God laughs at vain human attempts to drive him out of heaven, so believers can laugh at their enemies in the name of Christ, who said, "Be of good cheer, I have overcome the world" (John 16:33). The thought of God deriding idolaters ought to give believers some relief during the interim between Christ's first and second coming, this meantime that is quite mean.

> We should, then, become accustomed to these storms in which a Christian must live and dwell continuously, and we should withdraw to the shadows and lay hold of the invisible. Then it will come about that we shall laugh at the fury of the Turk, the popes, tyrants, sects, heretics, and all the adversaries of Christ's kingdom, as a comical spectacle. He who is able to do this everywhere and always is a true doctor of theology. But neither Peter nor Paul nor the other Apostles could always do this. Therefore we must confess that we are also only students and not doctors in this art, although we do not deserve the name of students, since we are either angry or vexed when God laughs.[3]

In the face of such a situation, Luther saw himself as a court jester, in accordance with Paul's insight that the one who wishes to be wise must become a fool (1 Cor. 3:18). In 1520, Luther told the German nobility that he was a jester in the garb of a monk, but added, "Since I am not only a fool but also a sworn doctor of holy Scripture, I am glad for the opportunity to fulfill my doctor's oath, even in the guise of a fool."[4]

Luther could laugh about the incongruities of human life demonstrated in marriage, politics, and other temporal relationships. With the author of Ecclesiastes he could say that "all is vanity." Yet he echoed Paul's conviction that neither life nor death can separate believers from the love of God in Christ (Rom. 8:38-39). Thus humor discloses a glimpse of eternal joy beyond death, as well as a sense of paradise, something of God's image within human life.

2. "Commentary on Psalm 2," 1532, LW, 55 vols., ed. Jaroslav Pelikan and Helmut Lehmann (Philadelphia: Fortress; St. Louis: Concordia, 1955-1986), 12:23. Since the edition of the first thirty volumes cites the original text in the Weimar edition of Luther's works on every page, I need not refer to it here. See WA, 57 vols., ed. J. F. K. Knaake et al. (Weimar: Böhlau, 1883ff.).

3. LW 12:28.

4. "To the Christian Nobility of the German Nation," 1520, WA 6:404.31-405.3; LW 44:124.

Being grounded in the conviction that the God of wrath is simultaneously the God of mercy, the God of the law that reveals sin and the God of the gospel that promises salvation, Luther became the master of a humorous style. His faith in God's majesty cradled in the man Jesus is the primary source of what has been called his abundant imagination and his creative humor.[5]

How Luther used this humor to interpret Scripture is the focus of this presentation. Only Roland H. Bainton has made a similar attempt, in his translation and editing of Luther's Christmas sermons.[6] Thus the exploration of Luther's humor as a tool of biblical exegesis, as well as theological reflection, is still one of the tasks to be undertaken by Luther researchers.

I shall use Luther's lectures on Genesis and Galatians to depict the relationship between humor and biblical witness. Luther labored for a whole decade to interpret Genesis to his students (1535-1545). The result was a gigantic commentary on salvation history from the creation of the world to the death of Joseph.[7] In 1535 he also lectured on Galatians, his favorite epistle, which he called "My Katie von Bora."[8] Both commentaries provide illustrative examples of the relationship between Luther's theology and his humor, which the new Webster dictionary has defined as "that quality in speech, writing, or action which tends to excite laughter, the capacity for perceiving the amusing or ludicrous." Luther also used wit, "the keen perception and apt expression of surprising, incongruous, subtle, or ludicrous relations between phenomena, ideas, and words."[9]

5. Fritz Blanke, *Luthers Humor. Scherz und Schalk in Luthers Seelsorge* (Hamburg: Furche, 1957), 42. Blanke, however, did not focus on the relationship between humor and incarnational theology.

6. Roland H. Bainton, *The Martin Luther Christmas Book* (Philadelphia: Fortress, 1948). Focusing on homiletical wit, Bainton lets Luther speak in a very Baintonian manner. For samples of this wit in a variety of contexts, see Eric W. Gritsch, "Luther's Humor: Instrument of Witness," *Dialog* 22 (1983): 176-81; idem, *Martin — God's Court Jester: Luther in Retrospect* (Philadelphia: Fortress, 1983), 197-202. See also Nathan Söderblom, *Humor och Melankoli och andra Lutherstudier* (Uppsala: Sveriges kristilige Studentrörelses Skriftserie, 1919), chaps. 1-3. Summary in German in *Luther* 5 (1923): 63-65.

7. Luther had begun work on Genesis in March 1535 and completed it on Nov. 17, 1545. See *Lectures on Genesis,* LW 1-8. On their history and publication, see Peter Meinhold, *Die Genesisvorlesung Luthers und ihre Herausgeber* (Stuttgart: Kohlhammer, 1936). Luther had preached on Genesis texts occasionally since 1519. See Heinrich Bornkamm, *Luther and the Old Testament,* tr. Eric W. and Ruth C. Gritsch (Philadelphia: Fortress, 1969), 269-70.

8. "Table Talk," Dec. 14, 1531, to Jan. 22, 1532, no. 146; WA.TR 1:69.18-19; LW 54:20. See also *Lectures on Galatians,* LW 26-27. Luther had offered some lectures on Galatians as early as 1519. I am using the 1535 series.

9. *New Webster's Dictionary of the English Language* (Delair Publishing Company, 1984).

II. Lectures on Genesis

Although Luther used traditional medieval hermeneutical principles in his exegesis, especially those of Nicholas of Lyra (ca. 1270-1349), there is much that is sui generis. Like God in the Psalms (2:4), Luther was more often than not "above" the interpreters. Commenting on the creation of the world in six days, he warned his readers of the existing exegetical confusion particularly regarding what Gen. 1:6 calls "heaven." "Ambrose and Augustine have rather childish ideas. Therefore I recommend Jerome, who maintains complete silence on these topics."[10] Medieval commentators, using Aristotle's view of science, contended that dung beetles were brought into being from the impact of the sun on horse manure. Luther had doubts: "The sun warms, but it would bring nothing into being unless God said by His divine power: 'Let a mouse come out of the decay.'"[11]

On the other hand, Adam, according to Luther, was a kind of superman before the Fall — tall, extremely intelligent, and handsome, surpassing all other living creatures. "I am fully convinced that before Adam's sin his eyes were so sharp and clear that they surpassed those of the lynx and the eagle."[12] He mused that these gifts made Satan jealous, and so the jealous Satan tempted Eve — "perhaps at about noon" — to desire even more than God had already provided for her and Adam in paradise. "So it is wont to be to this day. Where the Word of God is, there Satan also makes it his business to spread falsehood and false teaching; for it grieves him that through the Word we, like Adam in Paradise, become citizens of heaven. And so he successfully incites Eve to sin."[13] In Luther's mind, Adam and Eve were the first members of the Church who had ignored God's first admonition about the tree of knowledge (2:16). "If they had not fallen into sin," he lamented, "Adam would later have transmitted this single command to all his descendants. From it would have come the best theologians, the most learned lawyers, and the most expert physicians."[14] When he commented on Adam's long life of 930 years, he was nevertheless convinced that theirs was a "golden age," for people back then lived a healthy life, were moderate in their diets, responsible to other family members, and happy with each other. "Thus that age was truly a golden one. In comparison with it our age hardly deserves to be called an age of mud."[15]

10. LW 1:28.
11. LW 1:52.
12. LW 1:62.
13. LW 1:82.
14. LW 1:105.
15. LW 1:341-42. Quotation from 342.

His imagination and humor moved into high gear when commenting on the story of Noah and the flood. Other exegetes had been particularly concerned about the ark's size, the number of animals it accommodated, and the space provided for them on the three decks (6:15). According to Luther: "It is likely that Noah and the birds occupied the uppermost deck, the clean animals the middle one, and the unclean animals the lowest, although the rabbis would maintain that the lowest was used for putting away the manure. I myself believe that the manure was thrown out, perhaps through the window. . . . We shall put aside countless other questions. [But] what was the nature of the air in the ark, since that mass of water, especially when it went down, gave off a great and pestilential stench?"[16]

The rainbow as a sign of God's covenant with Noah (9:12-16) prompted Luther to comment on the speculation of philosophers regarding the nature of rainbows. "A philosopher, I am sure, will figure out something, for he will regard it as a disgrace not to be able to give reasons for everything. But he certainly will never persuade me to believe that he is speaking the truth."[17] He himself was quite willing to call such "phenomena" as rainbows, flying dragons, leaping goats, "antics of demons in the air" obeying God's will.[18]

Luther declared that allegorical exegesis is of little, if any, help because allegories are generally fabrications of a confused intellect, and sometimes analogies of faith to pacify terrified consciences.[19] He added that the pope uses allegories to substantiate his tyrannical power, claiming that the papal office is the sun and secular authority is the moon deriving its light from the sun (as Pope Innocent III had claimed in 1198).[20]

The stories of Abraham and Lot led him to think of the relationship between law and love and how this relationship can become confused. "Hence the German proverb about the young doctor of medicine who needs a new cemetery, the jurist who recently took over a public office and starts wars all over the place, and the young theologian who fills hell with souls."[21] Just a little expertise can be dangerous: "If someone is able to write four Greek words to explain one Psalm, he is puffed up with his knowledge as if by yeast."[22] Luther also offered his own judgment on polygamy in the Old Testament: it was not instituted just to curb sexual lust among the Jews but

16. LW 2:67, 69.
17. LW 2:147.
18. Ibid.
19. LW 2:151.
20. LW 2:152.
21. LW 2:340.
22. LW 3:5.

also to keep women in check, since they are by nature weak, quarrelsome, and proud. Polygamy keeps them out of trouble,[23] Luther contended, for marriage — monogamous or polygamous — is a remedy for lust, "and through marriage God permits sexual intercourse."[24]

The description of Abraham's faith became an occasion for Luther to expound his theology of the hidden and revealed God: when one reflects about God one should know that the best way to do so is from his lap, that is, with childlike trust. "If you fall out of it [the lap], that is, if you presume to know anything beyond what has been revealed in the Word, you plunge into the depths of hell."[25]

Sodom's sin (19:1-28) was to Luther an example of the smugness of evil and the swiftness of divine punishment: the most respectable citizens of Sodom violated the law of hospitality with their demand for sexual relations with their male guests. "They not only showed no courtesy towards the guests, they did not allow the tired men to rest even for an hour in someone else's house."[26] Luther once again related Scripture to contemporary life by using Lot's announcement of divine judgment on Sodom and the conviction of his sons-in-law that he was joking (19:14): Lot's family behaves like Pope Leo X, who once invited two philosophers to dinner to discuss the immortality of the soul. One philosopher was for it, the other against it. Luther reported: "When, after a long, hot debate, the pope had to decide which of the two had spoken more correctly, he said to the one who had defended the immortality of souls: 'To be sure, you seem to be stating facts; but your opponent's discourse creates a cheerful countenance.' Epicureans are in the habit of doing this; over against the clear truth they draw conclusions that suit flesh and reason."[27] This tale, like that of Lot's family, illustrated to Luther how smug some people are when they think they have power. They claim the power to judge right and wrong, but their judgments disclose only their own self-righteousness. They reminded Luther of a certain nun who took delight in her own devotions and stayed away from the other nuns. She imagined she had been rewarded with a crown of gold. The other nuns saw only cow dung instead of a crown.[28]

Lot's sexual sins with his two daughters (19:31-33) impelled Luther to muse, "Why does Moses state that Lot was not aware of it?" He an-

23. LW 3:47.
24. LW 3:48.
25. LW 3:139.
26. LW 3:252.
27. LW 3:268.
28. LW 3:277.

swered, "Lot had been absorbed in the height of excitement, and for this reason does not remember afterwards what he did."[29] Moreover, he was drunk. What about the motives of Lot's daughters? "They devised this plan not because they are stirred by lust but because of their extraordinary compassion for the entire human race."[30] Luther explained that there were no more men on earth to preserve the human race, and so the daughters made their father drunk in order to suppress his moral judgment regarding this unusual deed. "Why does God permit His own to fall in this manner?" Luther asked, and answered, "God wants us all to humble ourselves and to glory solely in His mercy, because, so far as we are concerned, no one is better or saintlier than the other, and no one sins so gravely."[31] He insisted that he did not want to excuse Lot and his daughters, but just to set forth the clear reasons for "their great disturbance" which was God-willed. "This awful fall teaches two lessons: (1) that you should humble yourself before God, and (2) that you should continually pray to God for the guidance of the Holy Spirit."[32] When even the biblical saints become too smug, as the story of Lot suggests, God moves in to teach these lessons.

Luther regretted that Abraham was willing to sacrifice Isaac (22:9) without even any conversation with him, and therefore suggested a conversation that Moses should have recorded. "I do not know why Moses omitted it, but I have no doubt that the father's address to his son was extraordinary, and I think that its main topic was the command of God and the resurrection of the dead."[33] Moses should have included many more details than are now contained in the text, he told his readers. He was convinced that Abraham delivered a beautiful funeral sermon at the grave of Sarah, "for in Holy Scripture no other matron is so distinguished."[34]

Rebecca is for Luther an example of obedience without procrastination, because she did not yield to the temptation to stay home (24:55-61). "Procrastination is a hidden evil, but it is horribly injurious. The Holy Spirit does not bestow His gifts on procrastinators; He bestows them on those who are prompt, ready, and alert."[35]

Keturah, Abraham's second wife (25:1), prompted Luther to utter his opinion of spouses. He suggested four classes of them: (1) those who marry to have children; (2) those who marry for the sake of avoiding fornication

29. LW 3:308.
30. LW 3:310.
31. LW 3:311-12.
32. LW 3:312.
33. LW 4:113.
34. LW 4:189.
35. LW 4:297.

and to be chaste; (3) those who desire wives solely for pleasure; and (4) those who marry old ladies for their wealth. "May God give them the cup of suffering," he commented.[36] He insisted that one should enjoy marriage for what it is, namely, God's institution as an order of creation, never so sacred as not to be seen with humor. "We are permitted to laugh and have fun with and to embrace our wives, whether they are naked or clothed,"[37] just as Isaac fondled his wife Rebecca (26:8).

The quarrels in Reuben's family and Reuben finding mandrakes (30:14-24) reminded Luther that the Holy Spirit glories in such "puerile and domestic matters." These small matters reminded him of the Christian essentials like the Word, baptism, and absolution. "We are certain that God is with us and for us. I would rather be in hell with God present than in heaven with God absent."[38]

When Luther read the story of Rachel's devious theft of household gods (31:33-35), he told his listeners, "here Satan is aiming at Rachel's throat."[39] Luther saw God *and* Satan playing with people — exemplified in the story of Jacob wrestling with God (32:24). Jacob could have had all kinds of ideas about it, but he did not, Luther said. He then told the story of a young man confessing his lust for women to a hermit. "You cannot prevent the birds from flying over your head," said the hermit, "but just let them fly and do not let them build nests in the hair of your head. Let them be thoughts and remain such; but do not let them become conclusions."[40]

III. Lectures on Galatians

Luther lectured on Galatians because he thought that "there is a clear and present danger that the devil may take away from us the pure doctrine of faith and may substitute for it the doctrines of works and of human traditions."[41] He declared that those who try to obtain God's favor by doing "good works" are like the dry earth that tries to produce rain.[42] Thus for Luther justification by faith alone is the theme of Galatians. "Once this has been established, namely that God alone justifies us solely by His grace through Christ, we are willing not only to bear the pope aloft on our hands but also to kiss his feet."[43]

36. LW 4:304-5.
37. LW 5:37.
38. LW 5:355.
39. LW 6:59.
40. LW 6:133.
41. LW 26:3.
42. LW 26:6.
43. LW 26:99.

When speaking of human reason as a source of self-righteousness, Luther employed an analogy: "As soon as reason and the Law are joined, faith immediately loses its virginity."[44] The distinction between law and gospel is presented in a monologue on what Luther calls "the terrified conscience":

> When your conscience is completely terrified by a sense of sin, you will think of yourself, "At the moment you are busy on earth. Here let the ass work, let him serve and carry the burden that has been laid upon him; that is, let the body and its members be subject to the Law. But when you ascend into heaven, leave the ass with its burdens on earth, for the conscience has no relation to the Law or to works or to earthly righteousness. Thus the ass remains in the valley; but the conscience ascends the mountain with Isaac, knowing absolutely nothing about the Law or its works but looking only to the forgiveness of sins and the pure righteousness offered and given in Christ."[45]

According to Luther, living by faith alone means being like a bride who is alone with Christ, her bridegroom. "But later on, when the Bridegroom opens the door and comes out, then let the servants return to take care of them and serve them food and drink. Then let works and love begin."[46]

Luther praised Paul for using "most delicious language" in telling the Galatians that he died to the Law through the Law in order to live with God (Gal. 2:19). "Here Paul is the most heretical of heretics"[47] — because he refused to live by the Law. So one can say to the devil, Luther wrote, "Mr. Devil, do not rage so. Just take it easy! For there is one who is called Christ. . . . He is your devil, you devil, because he has captured and conquered you, so that you cannot harm me any longer."[48] According to Luther, the truly faithful can never love the Law; those who say they do are like insane thieves and robbers claiming to love their prison and shackles.[49]

Luther's agreement with Paul on Gal. 4:6 ("And because you are sons, God has sent the Spirit of his Son into our hearts") is summed up by the comment: "He [God] says: 'I am giving My own Son into death, so that by His blood He might redeem you from sin and death.' Here I cannot have any doubts, unless I want to deny God altogether. And this is the reason why our theology is certain: it snatches us away from ourselves and places us outside ourselves, so that we do not depend on our own strength,

44. LW 26:113.
45. LW 26:116.
46. LW 26:137-38.
47. LW 26:156.
48. LW 26:162.
49. LW 26:340.

conscience, experience, person, or works but depend on that which is outside ourselves, that is, on the promise and truth of God, which cannot deceive."[50]

IV. Conclusion

Luther's humor is best displayed in his interpretation of Scripture because he was, above all, a biblical theologian. He often pitted Scripture against tradition, using satire and imagination in his polemics against the defenders of the tradition in Rome.[51] Although he used the traditional methods of interpretation summed up in the fourfold sense of Scripture made popular by Nicholas of Lyra (1270-1349), he amplified the literal and tropological senses rather than the analogical or allegorical ones.

Since Scripture had literally saved his life — his breakthrough to the gospel known as the "tower experience" sometime between 1513 and 1518 — Luther contracted the literal and tropological senses of Scripture into a kind of existentialist interpretation: Scripture becomes the Word of God when it pertains and applies to the turmoil *(Anfechtung)* in the interpreter's life. "The word in Scripture is of two kinds. The first does not pertain or apply to me, the other kind does. And upon that word which does pertain to me I can boldly trust and rely, as upon a strong rock."[52] He could even joke about that in a "table talk," applying it to the story of Noah's drinking (Gen. 9:20-21): "Tomorrow I have to lecture on the drunkenness of Noah, so I should drink enough this evening to be able to talk about that wickedness as one who knows by experience."[53] Yet his commentary on Noah's sin reveals the sober judgment that Noah's behavior is cause for great offense.[54]

Luther saw his whole being interwoven with Scripture, the book that disclosed God's radical love for the sinner. As a result, nothing in his life could scare him anymore — be it devil, death, or sin — because the just live by faith in that God alone. He could laugh at himself and at others whenever he or they began to slide back into a self-righteousness that no longer allowed God to be God. Scripture merely illustrated how easy it

50. LW 26:387.

51. For an analysis of the problem of Scripture and tradition in Luther's work see Gritsch, *Martin — God's Court Jester,* chap. 5.

52. "How Christians Regard Moses," 1525; WA 16:385.13-15; LW 35:170.

53. "Table Talk," between Oct. 27 and Dec. 4, 1536, no. 3476; WA.TR 3:344.19-20; LW 54:207.

54. LW 2:167.

was to commit the sin of pride and desire to be like God, described in Gen. 3:5. So, when all was said and done that could be said and done about a biblical text by existing hermeneutical methods, Luther crowned the efforts with perceptive expressions of the surprising, incongruous, and even ludicrous relationship between God and his creatures.

Luther was able to overcome his depressions and melancholy by exercising a sense of humor grounded in the biblical truth that God, no one else, is in charge of the world and, through Christ, justifies the ungodly. As he grew older, he increased his use of humor in commentaries, treatises, sermons, and letters. He used more satire, more self-deprecation, and more foul language in order to scare the devil away. This was his way of alerting himself and others to the proper distinction between the human and the divine. Once this distinction is understood one can break out into laughter and indeed acquire an apocalyptic gallows humor with regard to the aches and pains of a world destined to end soon. This kind of humor creates an emotional distance between oneself and circumstances that would otherwise depress one very much. Thus wit becomes a witness to the God who sits in heaven and laughs.

It would be counterproductive to try to offer a scholarly, systematic exposition of Luther's humor as a tool for interpreting Scripture. Luther himself once tried to write a scholastic exposition of the article of justification, but his effort failed when Luther called "the cheerful exchange" *(fröhlicher Wechsel)* of human sin for divine righteousness through Christ a "rhapsody" — not a scholarly term.[55] In other words, it is better to be poetic or musical about justification than to be scholastic. According to Luther, there is a link between laughter and poetry, between the sound of humor and the sound of music which, "next to the Word of God, deserves the highest praise."[56]

Scripture is the cradle for the rhapsody of God's love for his creatures. True students of Scripture should be able to detect how God laughs and winks at the world, which, in Luther's view, is but one mask of God.[57] "We are sad by nature, and Satan is the spirit of sadness. But God is the spirit of gladness and preserves us."[58]

55. See the fragmentary outline of a treatise on justification, "De iustificatione," 1530, WA 30/2:657-76. Also "The Freedom of the Christian," 1520, WA 7:25.34; LW 31:351.

56. *Martinus Luther Musicae Studiosis,* 1538, WA 50:371.1-2; LW 53:323.

57. *Lectures on Galatians*, 1535, LW 26:95. Luther spoke of "masquerade" *(mummenschantz)* and a "face mask" *(larva).*

58. "Table Talk," Dec. 28, 1531, to Jan. 2, 1532, no. 2342b; WA.TR 2:425.5-6.

12. *Calvin among the Thomists*

David C. Steinmetz

Among the three Protestant commentators John Calvin mentions favorably in the preface to his 1540 commentary on Romans was an ex-Dominican, Martin Bucer (1491-1551). Bucer had entered the Dominican Order in 1506 at the age of fifteen. In 1516 he transferred to the Blackfriars cloister in Heidelberg, where in April, 1518, he heard Martin Luther preside at a theological disputation sponsored by Luther's own order, the Hermits of St. Augustine. Bucer was so captivated by Luther's thought that he applied for release from the Dominican Order and in 1521 became a simple parish priest in Landstuhl. After brief parochial duty in Landstuhl and Weissenburg, Bucer fled for refuge to the imperial city of Strasbourg, where he became the pastor in turn of the churches of St. Aurelia (1524-1531) and St. Thomas (1531-1540). From Strasbourg he swiftly rose to prominence as one of the principal leaders of the Reformation in the Holy Roman Empire.

In 1538 Calvin, who had been expelled from Geneva, arrived in Strasbourg to become the pastor of the congregation of French refugees. From 1538 until his return to Geneva in 1541, Calvin and Bucer were frequently in each other's company. Two years earlier, in 1536, while serving as the pastor of the Church of St. Thomas, Bucer had written a lengthy commentary on Romans called the *Metaphrases et Enarrationes Perpetuae in Epistolam ad Romanos,* which he published through the Strasbourg printer, Wendelin Rihil.[1] Four years later, in 1540, using the same

1. Martin Bucer, *Metaphrases et Enarrationes Perpetuae Epistolarum d. Pauli Apos-*

This essay was written with the aid of a grant from the Herzog August Bibliothek in Wolfenbüttel, West Germany.

Strasbourg printer, Calvin published his own much shorter *Commentarii in Epistolam Pauli ad Romanos,* and included in his dedication high praise for Bucer's 1536 commentary: "Finally there comes Bucer, who spoke the last word on the subject with the publication of his writings. In addition to his profound learning, abundant knowledge, keenness of intellect, wide reading, and many other varied excellences in which he is surpassed by hardly anyone at the present day, this scholar, as we know, is equalled by few and is superior to very many. It is to his especial credit that no one in our time has been more precise or diligent in interpreting Scripture than he."[2]

The question has frequently been asked whether Bucer as a former Dominican brought with him to the Reformation theological and exegetical insights shaped by the teaching of the preeminent theologian of his old order, Thomas Aquinas.[3] If so, did Bucer in turn influence the thinking of John Calvin in a Thomistic direction? The issue is, of course, far too broad to be resolved in a single essay. Yet it is possible to pursue in one essay a limited case study that may provide a partial answer to a long and complicated question. What I propose to do in this essay is to examine the exegesis of Rom. 9 by Thomas Aquinas, Martin Bucer, and John Calvin, in order to isolate the agreements and disagreements between them and to determine whether those agreements and disagreements argue for or against the presence of a common school tradition.[4] In order to provide a contemporary context for Bucer's exegesis, I will compare Bucer's interpretation of Paul at several points with the exegesis of two Dominican theologians who did not become Protestant: Thomas de Vio, known as Cajetan (1468-1534), and Ambrosius Catherinus Politus (1484-1553).

---

toli. Tomus Primus continens Metaphrasim et Enarrationem in Epistolam ad Romanos (Strasbourg: Wendelin Rihil, 1536).

2. T. H. L. Parker, ed., *Iohannis Calvini Commentarius in Epistolam Pauli ad Romanos* (Leiden: Brill, 1981), 2 [hereafter cited as Calvin, *Commentarius*]. English translation by Ross Mackenzie, in *Calvin's Commentaries: The Epistles of Paul the Apostle to the Romans and to the Thessalonians,* ed. David W. and Thomas F. Torrance (Grand Rapids: Eerdmans, 1961), 2 [hereafter cited as Calvin, *Romans*].

3. W. P. Stephens is not inclined to think that Thomism is an important factor in Bucer's development. See, e.g., his comment in *The Holy Spirit in the Theology of Martin Bucer* (Cambridge: University Press, 1970), 18: "It is not clear how far the influence of Thomism is more than superficial, affecting Bucer's language rather than his fundamental understanding of the Christian faith." See also Karl Koch, *Studium Pietatis: Martin Bucer als Ethiker* (Neukirchen, 1962), 9, 12-13, 19, 70, 80.

4. The commentaries on Paul by Thomas Aquinas were available in printed editions in the early 16th century and reprinted three times between 1522 and 1532. On this and related questions see Denis R. Janz, *Luther on Thomas Aquinas: The Angelic Doctor in the Thought of the Reformer* (Stuttgart: Franz Steiner, 1989), 105.

I

Thomas Aquinas probably delivered his commentary on Romans as a series of lectures during his second regency at Paris (1270-72).[5] The exposition is divided into five *lectiones,* covering respectively 9:1-5, 6-13, 14-18, 19-23, and 24- 33.[6] The central theme that ties the various sections together for Thomas is the question of the origin of grace. Does grace spring from divine election alone or is it based on human merit?[7] Interwoven with this theme is the question of the place of Jews and Gentiles in the history of salvation.

The first *lectio* struggles to explain Paul's astonishing wish to be "accursed and cut off from Christ for the sake of [his] brethren," the unconverted Jews. Such a wish appears to some medieval critics of Paul to contradict the order of charity by which Christians are bound to love God supremely and their own salvation more than the salvation of any other human being. Paul could mean that he hoped to be anathema (i.e., separated from final salvation), at least for a time, if it would contribute to the conversion of the Jews and thus to Christ's honor. At any event, what Thomas is careful to show is that Paul's seemingly exaggerated sorrow is not irrational. The people whom Paul loves so intensely are a great people. They alone have descended from Jacob and the patriarchs; they alone have been graced with certain spiritual benefits; they alone have provided the stock from which Christ descended according to the flesh (a point, Thomas notes, that undercuts the Manichean, Valentinian, Nestorian, and Arian heresies).[8]

The second *lectio* follows the sudden turn in Paul's argument from a consideration of the greatness of the Jews as a nation descended from Jacob to a narrower consideration of a remnant among the Jews who form a spiritual seed elected by God. Paul contends that not all the natural descendants of Abraham are his spiritual descendants. Abraham's spiritual children are the children of promise. By the grace of God's promise they have been made Abraham's children through faith. Jews who thought they were worthy of the grace of God because of the merit of their ancestors

5. For a discussion of the problems surrounding the dating of Thomas's commentary on Romans, see James A. Weisheipl, O.P., *Friar Thomas D'Aquino: His Life, Thought and Works* (Washington: Catholic University of America Press, 1974, 1983), 246-49.

6. For the text of Thomas's exposition, see the "Expositio in Omnes Sancti Pauli Epistolas," in *Sancti Thomae Aquinatis Doctoris Angelici Ordinis Praedicatorum Opera Omnia,* 13 (Parma: Typis Petri Fiaccadori, 1872), 91-102.

7. Ibid., 91.

8. Ibid., 92-94.

could always get around the example of Abraham. After all, while both Isaac and Ishmael were children of Abraham, they were children by different mothers. Sarah was free; Hagar was a slave. Furthermore, Ishmael was conceived while Abraham was uncircumcised and therefore still a Gentile; Isaac was conceived after Abraham's circumcision. Ishmael as the descendant of a Gentile father and an enslaved mother was naturally excluded from the blessings offered only to the Jews.[9]

In order to counteract this kind of subterfuge, Paul appeals to the example of Rebecca. Rebecca's son, Jacob, was elect; her twin son, Esau, was reprobate. Unlike Isaac and Ishmael, Jacob and Esau came not only from the same father but also from the same mother. They were conceived through the same sexual act and born on the same day at the same time through an identical act of labor. In spite of the identity of their natural circumstances, God nevertheless chose Jacob as the child of his promise and rejected Esau.[10]

On what grounds, however, was God's choice based, if not natural descent from Abraham? Certainly not a difference in astrological charts, as the Manicheans falsely argued, or in foreseen merit, as the Pelagians incorrectly thought! God's choice was made before Jacob and Esau had been born and therefore before they had made any moral choices. Paul also excludes from consideration Origen's fantasy of a pretemporal fall. Neither preexisting works in this life (Pelagius) nor preexisting works in another life (Origen) form the basis for God's choice of Jacob over Esau. According to his own spontaneous will God elects one twin over the other, not because Jacob was already holy but in order to make him so.[11]

Paul's argument has raised for Thomas important theological questions that need to be clarified before he can proceed further with his exposition. To explain what Paul means by election, Thomas distinguishes three important terms (that are, of course, indistinguishable in God): namely, love *(dilectio)*, election *(electio)*, and predestination *(praedestinatio)*. Love wills the good for someone absolutely. Election wills some good for one person rather than another. Predestination directs the preferred object of love to the good willed by the electing agent. Love therefore precedes predestination as the will concerning an end naturally precedes the direction of someone to it.[12]

In other words, the election of Jacob over Esau is rooted in an absolute

9. Ibid., 94.
10. Ibid.
11. Ibid.
12. Ibid., 94-95.

and mysterious love that cannot be rationalized. God predestines Jacob, i.e., directs him to final salvation, because he has loved and chosen him. The choice and direction are based on God's absolute love and on no other cause, however plausible. Whatever good there is in Jacob is the result of God's electing love and not its cause. The notion, therefore, that election is based on foreknowledge, even in part, is rejected by Thomas as absurd. God predestines the elect to merit glory, but merit remains the effect and not the cause of predestination.[13]

The same cannot be said with respect to Esau. The choice of Jacob over Esau can be described as the nonelection, though not reprobation, of Esau. Esau is not reprobated simply because he was not chosen (though the nonchoice of Esau is almost as mysterious as the choice of Jacob). Reprobation is based, at least in part, on God's foreknowledge of Esau's demerits. Esau is reprobated, i.e., destined for punishment, because he richly deserves it. The wicked deeds that Esau commits during the course of his life provide the partial ground for his reprobation. In short, the election and predestination of Jacob demonstrate God's mercy; the reprobation of Esau, his justice. The relationship to God of Jacob and Esau (and of all the elect and reprobate) is asymmetrical. Works are not the basis for election; they are, however, an incomplete cause of reprobation.[14]

Paul's discussion of predestination, however, poses for Thomas a further question in *lectio* three: what about distributive justice? If God is just, then surely God must distribute benefits to equals equally. Paul had gone to great lengths in Rom. 9:10-13 to show that at the moment of their birth there was no difference between Jacob and Esau, save for the difference interjected by God through the mysterious election of Jacob. If God is just and if Jacob and Esau were, as Paul himself had demonstrated, equal in a way Isaac and Ishmael could never be, then surely the election of Jacob over Esau flies in the face of God's distributive justice. According to distributive justice, God ought to have chosen both or neither as objects of his mercy. *Tertium non datur.*[15]

Paul proposes a solution from Exod. 33:19. He cites a translation of the Septuagint that ascribes all human goods to the mercy of God. Thomas reads this verse to mean that every benefit tending to salvation is an effect of predestination. He therefore rejects the solution found in the Gloss that the distributive justice of God can be preserved by appealing to a foreseen good use of grace by Jacob. According to this solution, God chose Jacob

13. Ibid., 95.
14. Ibid.
15. Ibid.

over Esau because he foresaw that Jacob would make a better use of God's grace if grace were offered to him. Thomas finds this solution inadmissible because God is the source both of the infused grace by which sinners are justified and of every subsequent good use of grace. To illustrate his point Thomas draws an analogy between the realms of nature and supernature. Just as in nature God causes not only the forms of things but also their motions and operations, so too in redemption the will of God is the sole origin of the habit of grace and every gracious action that flows from it. Jacob's good use of grace is God's gift to Jacob and not Jacob's gift to God.[16]

Distributive justice has a place in *ex debito* relations, i.e., in arrangements in which one party is obligated to another because of contractual agreements or overriding moral claims. But no such obligations govern the realm of mercy. It is not a violation of distributive justice to forgive one of two debtors. Since all human beings are sinners, God can mercifully forgive some and justly punish others.[17]

In view of Thomas's heavy emphasis on the causality of God, the question naturally arises whether sinners make any contribution toward their own salvation. As Thomas reads Paul, the primary causality in redemption must always be assigned to divine grace. However, the human will as a secondary agent is moved by God to embrace the good. God moves all things according to the mode of their nature. Therefore human beings are moved by God to will and to run through the mode of free choice. Human beings act freely when they will and run, but they do so only because God as the principal agent moves them toward ends he has chosen.[18]

The example of Pharaoh offers Thomas an opportunity to explain what he has in mind. While God moves human beings toward good and evil by a certain interior instinct, he does not move human beings toward what is good in the same way he moves them toward what is evil. As a principal agent God directly inclines the human will toward what is good. God's relationship to evil, however, is more occasional and indirect. God proposes to the human will something that is good in itself, but which human malice perversely abuses and turns toward evil ends. Pharaoh was aroused by God to defend his realm; he abused this legitimate impulse from God when he repressed the Israelites through gratuitous acts of cruelty.[19]

16. Ibid., 96.
17. Ibid.
18. Ibid., 97.
19. Ibid.

In his relationship to Pharaoh, God partly ordained and partly permitted what transpired. God ordained that the wickedness of Pharaoh should demonstrate God's glory. But while God ordained such wickedness, he did not cause it. Pharaoh, taking the occasion of sin from the various goods God proposed to him, merited the punishment God's justice imposed. God hardened Pharaoh, not by prompting him to sin but by interposing no grace. To say anything else would make God the author of evil in a direct and unqualified sense.[20]

The fourth *lectio* begins with Paul's objection to his own solution: why does God show pity to Jacob and not to Pharaoh? Can any reason be found except the will of God alone? Is the will of God simply irresistible? If so, why does God hold human beings responsible? As Thomas understands Rom. 9, Paul wants to assert both that there is no explanation for the electing activity of God except God's will and that the electing will of God can, to a certain limited extent, be explained and defended.[21]

Thomas provides two examples to defend God from the charge of arbitrary injustice. The first example is teleological and appeals from specific cases to the overall plan that directs the whole. A builder who constructs a house out of stone may place some stones in a place of prominence, while relegating other stones, equally durable and attractive, to the lowly task of buttressing the foundation. The artisan is guided by his vision of the end, the perfection of the house he intends to build. So, too, God in his providential care of the universe exercises both mercy and justice, election and reprobation, to achieve the ends his wisdom has ordained.[22]

The second example is anthropological and is built on Paul's image of the potter and the clay. The image seems particularly apt to Thomas because human beings are descendants of Adam, who was created by God from the dust of the earth. Like clay, human beings are vile in their origin. Their natural vileness was made even viler by Adam's fall into sin. If God leaves some human beings in their weakness and sin, he undoubtedly appoints them to ignoble use, but does them no injury about which they could justly complain. God has the free power to make from the corrupt matter of humankind, as from clay, men and women prepared for glory. He has the same freedom to abandon others to the misery they have merited.[23]

20. Ibid., 97-98.
21. Ibid., 98.
22. Ibid.
23. Ibid., 99.

The fifth and final *lectio* returns to the second main theme of Rom. 9, the relationship of Jews and Gentiles. After Paul shows that the grace of God is given by divine election, he demonstrates that election pertains to Gentiles as well as to Jews. Although the Jews received privileges denied the Gentiles, salvation is nevertheless offered to each on the same terms. The true children of the covenant are the children of Abraham by faith. The people of God are constituted, not by circumcision and law keeping, but by the electing grace of God. The mysterious love and justice that distinguished Ishmael from Isaac, Esau from Jacob, broke down the wall of separation that divided Jew from Greek, Isaac and Jacob from Ampliatus and Urban. While such a message is offensive to unbelieving Jews, it repeats themes that run throughout the whole Bible, OT as well as NT. Thomas ends his lecture by amplifying the catena of quotations Paul provides to demonstrate this point.[24]

II

Bucer, like Thomas, divides Rom. 9 into five sections, breaking the first two sections at vv. 5 and 13.[25] However, unlike Thomas, who divides the chapter at vv. 18 and 23, Bucer breaks sections three to five at vv. 21 and 29. Furthermore, whereas Thomas separates Rom. 9 into five *lectiones* without further subdivisions, Bucer subdivides each of his five *enarrationes* into an *expositio,* an *interpretatio,* and a series of concluding *observationes*.

Bucer uses the word *enarratio* to mark the major subdivisions of his commentary. The *expositio* is a running commentary that summarizes and clarifies the passage as a whole. The *interpretatio* explains individual words and phrases, while the concluding *observationes* repeat theological or devotional themes important for the life of faith. The *enarratio* of section four has five *observationes,* while *enarrationes* of the other sections have four each. In addition there is one *conciliatio,* in which Bucer tries to harmonize that statement of Paul that God hardens some sinners with the statement that God wills the salvation of every person, and one *quaestio,* in which Bucer explores the role of human free choice.

Aside from differences in form, three things strike the reader of Bucer's commentary: (1) that Bucer is concerned with several questions and themes posed by his contemporaries that do not occur, or do not occur in the same way, in the earlier *lectiones* of Thomas Aquinas; (2) that Bucer

24. Ibid., 100-102.
25. Bucer, *Metaphrases,* 381-412.

is nevertheless in general agreement with the Augustinian exposition of election by Thomas, if only in the sense that both appeal in similar ways to a common Augustinian source; and (3) that at least on one question, the limited freedom of second causes, Bucer is specifically indebted to Thomas.

For example, Erasmus had raised the question whether v. 5, "of their race, according to the flesh, is the Christ. God who is over all be blessed forever. Amen," is, as traditionally understood, an anti-Arian confession that Christ is both God and man; or whether it is simply an ascription of praise to God the Father that follows immediately upon the confession that Christ is descended from the patriarchs. Erasmus inclines toward the latter view without prejudicing the claim that Christ is both divine and human.[26] The Dominican commentators, Cajetan and Politus, disagree with Erasmus. Cajetan simply repeats the traditional view that 9:5 is the first place in Romans where Paul calls Christ God,[27] while Catherinus Politus hints darkly that Erasmus is an enemy of the doctrine of Christ's divinity.[28] Calvin agrees with Cajetan and Politus, deploring the "audacious attempt" of Erasmus and others "to create darkness where there is full light."[29] Bucer, on the other hand, is sympathetic to Erasmus's view. Scripture clearly teaches that Christ is God in so many places that it is not necessary (and probably counterproductive) to try to elicit that teaching from such an ambiguous passage as 9:5.[30] Thomas, who is much less concerned with philological matters than sixteenth-century commentators, finds the passage unproblematic and uses it as a confession of the true humanity and divinity of Christ in order to refute Manichean, Valentinian, Nestorian, and Arian heresies.[31] While Cajetan, Calvin, and Politus agree with Thomas Aquinas against Bucer, who agrees with Erasmus, their disagreement is historically insignificant, since the debate centers on a question that had not been raised in Thomas's own day.

More significant is the agreement of Thomas and Bucer over the doctrine of election. Unlike Thomas, Bucer does not distinguish between love, election, and predestination. Like Thomas, however, he rejects the notion that election is based on foreknowledge, an idea he associates with

26. Desiderius Erasmus, *In Novum Testamentum Annotationes* (Basel: Froben, 1535), 391.

27. Thomas de Vio Cajetan, *Epistolae Pauli et Aliorum Apostolorum* (Paris: Carola Guillard et Jean de Roigny, 1540), 64.

28. Ambrosius Catherinus Politus, *Commentaria in Omnes divi Pauli et alias septem canonicas Epistolas* (Venice: Vincent Valgrisius, 1551), 90.

29. Calvin, *Commentarius,* 198; idem, *Romans,* 196.

30. Bucer, *Metaphrases,* 285.

31. Thomas Aquinas, "Expositio," 92-93.

Origen, Chrysostom, and Ambrosiaster.[32] Against the argument that equates election with prevision of the future, Bucer appeals to the authority of Augustine.[33] Everything concerning human salvation depends on the mysterious mercy of God. The faithful remnant in Israel and the Church is constituted by God's free election.[34] Bucer discourages speculation concerning God's electing activity or faithless questioning concerning his justice. "The mere will of God," he writes, "is the cause of everything and that will is itself justice."[35]

There is, in other words, no cause for what God does beyond God's will. It is impious for human beings to inquire into it, since everyone knows that God always works for the best. At any rate, sinful human beings, who are caught in the web of their own wickedness and deceit, have no right to call God to account, who always wills what is just and good. Rather than question the justice of God, human beings ought to entrust themselves to his Spirit and cling to the self-revelation of God in his Word.[36]

Cajetan is also willing to argue that election and reprobation hang from the mere will of God.[37] However, to avoid the alarming notion that a good and just God wills evil against the reprobate apart from any consideration of their works, Cajetan observes that one must distinguish between reprobation and the execution of reprobation. Apart from any consideration of their works, God withholds his grace from the reprobate and leaves them to cope with temptation without the assistance of grace. In that sense they are reprobated *non ex operibus,* without reference to their moral achievements and failures.[38] But judgment on the reprobate is never executed before the reprobate actually sin.[39] God can therefore never be accused of partiality or injustice, since reprobation involves the punishment

32. Bucer, *Metaphrases,* 391-92.

33. Ibid., 392.

34. Ibid., 410.

35. Ibid., 395: "Caussam vero horum ne inquiramus, multo minus inesse aliquid iniquitatis in iudiciis Dei suspicemur. Ipsa Dei voluntas Deo caussa est omnium et ea ipsa est iustitia."

36. Ibid., 399, 404.

37. Cajetan, *Epistolae Pauli,* 65: "Nihil enim aliud ex authoritate Paulus intendit, nisi quod hinc apparet, quod non ex operibus nostris, sed ex voluntate Dei eligentis, et vocantis unus eligitur et alter reprobatur."

38. Ibid., 65: "Solutio est quod deus ab aeterno vere quosdam eligit et quosdam odio habet: pro quanto quibusdam ab aeterno vult conferre opem gratiae suae et adiuvare illos usque ad gloriam aeternam, quosdam autem ab aeterno quoque vult permittere sibiipsis, nec adiuvare eos gratuito auxilio quod electis decrevit conferre. Et hoc est deum illos odio habere, hoc est deum reprobare illos non ex operibus."

39. Ibid., 65: "Cum quo tamen stat quod nullus damnatur nisi ex propriis operibus. Nec sententia siquidem nec executio damnationis fit antequam huiusmodi reprobi peccent."

of real guilt. Election and reprobation are truths on the part of God that are always associated with human free will and responsibility.[40]

Ambrosius Catherinus Politus approaches the problem of reprobation from a slightly different angle. He notes that there are theologians who correctly and, perhaps, too easily confess that predestination rests on grace, while insisting that reprobation rests on human demerits.[41] Unfortunately, their carefully balanced view of election and reprobation does not respond to the passage in Rom. 9 which affirms that Esau was reprobated by God before he had done anything worthy of divine hatred.[42] Perhaps, Politus suggests, the word "hatred" *(odium)* may be a gentler word in the Bible than it seems to us in our common usage.[43] At any rate, Esau demonstrated by his evil works that he was a type of the reprobate and worthy of divine judgment.[44]

In the *conciliatio* that deals with the apparent contradiction between God's universal will of salvation and his act of hardening sinners, Bucer appeals to the distinction in Augustine between the *vocatio congrua* and *incongrua* or what later Calvinism calls the distinction between effectual and ineffectual calling. The *vocatio congrua* is the preaching of the gospel to the elect, who are moved by God to embrace it. The *vocatio incongrua* is the preaching of the gospel to the nonelect, who are not assisted by the mercy of God and so are left in their sins. The Church is commanded to preach the gospel to all creatures, knowing full well that only the elect will profit from it.[45]

In the *quaestio de libero arbitrio* that is included in the *enarratio* of section three (9:14-21), Bucer cites Thomas's definition of free choice as "the will by which we choose what reason through mature deliberation perceives and judges to be more advantageous."[46] Agents exercise free

40. Ibid., 67v: "Quocirca ad curiositatem dico illa esse vera ex parte divinae electionis seu reprobationis, sed non esse vera sola, sed associata aliis veritatibus ex parte nostri, scilicet quod sumus liberi arbitrii, quod faciendo quod ex nobis est erimus per divinam gratiam salvi, et quod nostris meritis salvamur aut damnamur nos adulti."

41. Politus, *Commentaria,* 96: "Sunt enim qui recte quidem sentiunt de re ipsa, et facile confitentur praedestinationem non esse ex meritis bonis, sed a gratia. Reprobationem autem non posse esse nisi ex meritis malis."

42. Ibid., 96: "Sed ipsi interim ad hunc locum non respondent, ubi sicut de Iacob dicitur, illum non quia fecerit aliquid boni, electum fuisse: Ita de Esau, non quia fecerit ipse aliquid mali, esse odio habitum, ac per hoc reprobatum."

43. Ibid, 97: "Hic certe odium non accipitur pro odio vero, nisi ut postponatur pater et mater Deo."

44. Ibid, 97: "Non me latet alia de causa Esau tenuisse reprobatorum typum: non quidem ex nativitate, sed ex improbitate sua, et pravitate."

45. Bucer, *Metaphrases*, 397-99, 407.

46. Ibid., 400: "Recte itaque Thomas Aquinas liberum arbitrium, voluntatem intelligit qua eligimus, quod ratio consultatione conducibilius esse deprehendit et arbitrata est."

choice when they act according to their own best judgment. Free choice to be truly free must be in the power of the acting agent.[47] Bucer raises this point in order to make two others.

First, the action of a first cause does not exclude the action of second causes.[48] While God is the primary agent who is at work in all human willing and doing, God works in such a way as to make human beings the agents of their own acts. "Through God's act we know things, choose them, embrace them, flee them, [and] direct our bodily energies."[49] What Bucer seems to have in mind is the point also made by Thomas that human beings are moved by God to will and run through the mode of free choice.

Even more important for Bucer is his second point: namely, that human willing and acting can accomplish nothing unless perfected by the mercy of God.[50] In its present condition the human will is so debilitated by sin that it is incapable of doing anything pleasing to God without the assistance of Christ's Spirit.[51] The notion that the action of God as first cause does not exclude the action of human free choice as a second cause is a disquieting rather than comforting thought if it means that human free choice can only elect what displeases God. Unless human free will is redeemed by God's grace, it merits eternal death.[52]

The good news, of course, is that God uses human wickedness as an instrument to achieve his own ends and to illuminate the honor of his own name. While believers should imitate God's great leniency in their dealings with other human beings, they should also realize that God's power is commended to them through the punishment of the wicked.[53] Furthermore, they should understand that God's chastisement of his people (as exemplified by God's punishment of unbelieving Israel) always bears fruit for them in the end.[54]

While Bucer is indebted, at least to some extent, to Thomas for his understanding of free choice and the role of second causes, his discussion

47. Ibid., 400.

48. Ibid.: "Atqui caussa prima non excludit actionem caussarum secundarum."

49. Ibid.: "Qui utique eius actu res cognoscimus, eligimus, amplectimur, fugimus, corporis vires admovemus."

50. Ibid., 404. I am in agreement with W. P. Stephens, *Holy Spirit,* 261, when he observes concerning Bucer's discussion of free choice: "Similarly, the use of the term will, considered as free, when one speaks of man's psychological co-operation in his salvation, should be distinguished from its use as bound or enslaved, when one speaks of man's inability to do anything for his salvation theologically."

51. Bucer, *Metaphrases*, 401.

52. Ibid., 410.

53. Ibid., 409.

54. Ibid., 410.

of election shows little direct dependence on Thomas's exegesis. Unlike Thomas, Bucer does not distinguish between election and predestination or attempt to offer a theodicy based on an argument from design. Whereas Thomas emphasizes the justice of God that permits and then punishes the wickedness of the reprobate, Bucer appeals to the wisdom and goodness of God that merits unwavering confidence and trust. Although Bucer sounds some specifically Thomistic themes in his exposition of Paul, it is probably more accurate to say that Bucer, like Thomas, embraces a strongly Augustinian view of election than to say he embraces it in a distinctively Thomistic way.

III

Calvin breaks Rom. 9 into eight sections (vv. 1-5, 6-9, 10-13, 14-18, 19-21, 22-23, 24-29, and 30-33), agreeing with Thomas in two divisions (vv. 1-5, 14-18) and with Bucer in only one (vv. 1-5). Unlike Bucer, who separated his commentary into *expositio, interpretatio,* and *observatio,* Calvin combines running commentary, discussion of individual words and phrases, and the elucidation of theological and devotional themes into one continuous, verse-by-verse exposition.

The list of agreements among Thomas, Bucer, and Calvin is impressive: all three reject predestination based on foreknowledge, insist that human salvation is dependent on God's election alone, confess that there is no reason higher than God's own will for the election of some over others, and affirm the justice of God in the punishment of the reprobate. Furthermore, Calvin shares with Bucer a horror of speculative theology that attempts to probe the mystery of predestination beyond the limits set by God's self-revelation in Scripture.[55] Yet there are differences among the three, some substantial, some simply a matter of nuance.

For example, Calvin distinguishes between two elections: the election of all the descendants of Abraham, Ishmael as well as Isaac, to be God's favored people, the natural children of his covenant; and the second or secret election of a remnant among Abraham's descendants in whom the power and efficacy of God's promise is found.[56] Ishmael and Esau are children of the promise only in the first sense; Isaac and Jacob are elect

55. Calvin, *Commentarius,* 204-5. See esp. 205: "Haec ergo sit nobis sancta observatio, nequid de ipsa scire appetamus, nisi quod Scriptura docet: ubi Dominus sacrum os suum claudit, viam quoque ultra pergendi mentibus nostris praecludamus."

56. Ibid., 199.

children in the second sense as well. Moreover, the second election is not restricted to the natural descendants of Abraham but overrules the boundaries established by the first or general election.[57]

Because it could be objected that the differences between Ishmael and Isaac were natural differences explainable under the terms of the first or general covenant with Abraham, Paul offers the example of Jacob and Esau, who were twins born of the same father (Isaac) and mother (Rebecca).[58] Calvin agrees with Thomas and Bucer that this example undercuts any view of election based on the foreknowledge of human good works. Indeed, God could see nothing in the corrupt nature of Jacob and Esau that would induce him to show favor to either. Neither Jacob nor Esau was "possessed of a single particle of righteousness."[59] The favor God shows to Jacob rests on God's "bare and simple good pleasure."[60] "God has a sufficiently just cause for election and reprobation," writes Calvin, "in his own will."[61]

When the question of God's justice is raised by Paul, Calvin responds by adopting a severely anti-apologetic stance. Whereas Thomas offers a limited theodicy and Bucer appeals to God's goodness, Calvin takes the position that to mount a spirited defense of God's justice is to detract from God's honor.[62] God has the rightful power of life and death over his creatures.[63] His authority is not the absolute justice of which the sophists (read: scholastics) teach, who distinguish between God's absolute and ordained power. Such theologians separate God's power from his justice and so turn him into a tyrant.[64] God's power is always united with his justice, even in decisions that seem most offensive to human reason.[65]

Nevertheless, in spite of the fact that Calvin declines to offer more than a sketchy apologetic for God's justice, he does make some attempt to explain how God's electing and reprobating activity should be viewed. The apologetic has three elements: (1) God is debtor to no human being and so may confer his kindness on whomever he will.[66] This argument is

57. Ibid., 200.
58. Ibid., 201.
59. Ibid., 202.
60. Ibid.
61. Ibid., 203: "Deum in suo arbitrio satis iustam eligendi et reprobandi habere causam." Cf. Calvin, *Romans,* p. 201.
62. Calvin, *Commentarius,* 209.
63. Ibid., 210.
64. Ibid., 208.
65. Ibid., 212: "Secunda responsio, qua breviter demonstrat, etiamsi incomprehensibile sit hac parte Dei consilium, elucere tamen inculpatum eius aequitatem, non minus in reproborum interitu, quam salute electorum."
66. Ibid., 206: "Hoc autem oraculo declaravit Dominus, se nemini mortalium esse

strikingly similar to Thomas's contention that distributive justice has no place outside *ex debito* relations. (2) The reprobate are in fact wicked and are therefore justly punished by God. Indeed, the godly praise God all the more when they contemplate the wretchedness of the ungodly, who do not escape God's wrath.[67] (3) Finally, the power which God exercises over his creatures is not an inordinate but an equitable right, similar in every respect to the power of a potter over his clay.[68] Therefore, both the salvation of the elect and the punishment of the reprobate demonstrate God's "unimpeachable equity," even though there is no reason why God elects except his purpose alone.[69]

Calvin breaks most sharply with Thomas (and, to a more limited extent, with Bucer) over the question of the hardening of Pharaoh. Calvin complains that many interpreters attempt to mitigate the harshness of 9:17-18 by appealing to God's permissive will, which leaves the nonelect to their own devices, or by positing a general impulse from God that is abused by the wicked.[70] The notion that Pharaoh had been aroused by God to defend his realm but abused this impulse when he repressed the Israelites or that equates hardening with the noninterposition of grace is flatly rejected by Calvin. God did not merely move or permit Pharaoh to be hardened; God hardened Pharaoh in order to destroy him. The ruin of the ungodly is not merely foreseen or permitted by God but ordained.[71] The asymmetrical relationship between election and reprobation so carefully worked out by Thomas is flattened into a harsher symmetry by Calvin.

The good news for Gentiles is that election, since it rests on God's good pleasure alone, "exists wherever God has willed it to be."[72] There is no difference of nationality in election. God has put Gentiles on a level with Jews and now extends his mercy to both. If one asks why Jews, who sought righteousness from God, were rejected, while Gentiles, who did not, were shown mercy, Calvin replies that there is no real answer except the secret predestination of God. Perhaps, Calvin suggests, God may have wanted to show that trust in good works (as exemplified

---

debitorem: gratuitae esse beneficentiae quicquid illis [tribuerit]: deinde hanc beneficentiam liberam esse, ut eam erogaret, cui placeret."

67. Ibid., 212-13.

68. Ibid., 211-12.

69. Ibid., 212.

70. Ibid., 208-9. See, e.g., p. 209: "Porro nequis imaginetur, quodam universali et confuso motu Divinitus actum fuisse Pharaonem, ut in illum furorem rueret, notatur specialis causa, vel finis."

71. Ibid., 209.

72. Ibid., 214; idem, *Romans*, 212.

by the Jews) is the chief obstacle to attaining a righteousness that is only given to faith.[73]

IV

If the question of reprobation is set aside, it would be difficult to find three more vigorous exponents of an Augustinian reading of Rom. 9 than Thomas Aquinas, Martin Bucer, and John Calvin. All three reject predestination based on God's foreknowledge of human merit, insist that human salvation is grounded in divine election alone, acknowledge that there is no reason higher than God's will for the election of Isaac and Jacob over Ishmael and Esau, and assert that God is just in the punishment of the reprobate. While there are differences between them in matters of detail, there are no significant differences between them in matters of substance.

However, to say that Thomas, Bucer, and Calvin are strongly Augustinian in their understanding of Rom. 9 is not to say that they are Augustinian in exactly the same way. Neither Bucer nor Calvin repeats Thomas's important distinction between love, election, and predestination, or attempts to justify reprobation by appealing to a grand design in which places of honor must be offset by places of dishonor. Indeed, several of Thomas's most characteristic modifications of the Augustinian tradition find no corresponding echo in the expositions of Bucer and Calvin.

Bucer, who accepts the important role of second causes, is clearly more receptive to Thomas's ideas than Calvin is, who rejects Thomas's notion of a general impulse toward the good and finds no place in his theology for divine permission. This difference between Bucer and Calvin becomes evident when the question on the table is the reprobation of the nonelect. Thomas, Bucer, and Calvin all agree that the final explanation for reprobation, as for election itself, lies in the mystery of the divine will. The nonelection of Esau like the election of Jacob rests on God's free decision and therefore remains a mystery that cannot be rationalized. Yet the response of Thomas and Bucer to this mystery differs from Calvin's response. Thomas defends God's justice, while Bucer recommends God's goodness. Against both, Calvin understands himself to be maintaining God's honor.

The question whether Thomas, Bucer, and Calvin share a common school tradition can be answered in the affirmative only if one means by a common tradition the tradition of the Augustinian exegesis of Rom. 9.

73. Calvin, *Commentarius,* 220.

To be sure, Bucer repeats Thomas's definition of free will and his contention that the motion of a first cause enables rather than excludes the motion of second causes. But even Bucer is far less keen than Thomas to develop an apologetic for God's justice. Bucer urges his readers to trust the kindness and goodness of God and to set aside their doubts concerning God's justice. Only Calvin seems to revel in the affront to human conceptions of justice posed by the doctrine of election. To defend what requires no defense detracts from God's honor.

The thesis that Calvin is the beneficiary of a Thomistic school tradition mediated to him by Martin Bucer finds no support in the admittedly limited context of the interpretation of Rom. 9. Although it is true that Calvin agrees with Thomas and Bucer on most exegetical issues and that Bucer adopts some themes from Thomas in his interpretation of Paul, their agreement may be better explained by appealing to a common Augustinian heritage than to a common school tradition. Indeed, on the issue of the justice of God's action, Calvin shows himself unfriendly to what he regards as the misguided attempt of Thomas and others to mitigate the harshness of God's decree. Calvin wants to fix the unwavering attention of all theologians, including Thomas and Bucer, on the "eternal and inexplicable counsel of God, whose righteousness is worthy of our worship rather than our scrutiny."[74]

74. Ibid., 213; idem, *Romans,* 211.

13. *Some Reflections on Relating Calvin's Exegesis and Theology*

Elsie Anne McKee

Like many of the long cast of characters who have influenced Christian history in a significant way, John Calvin has been analyzed, praised, and damned. Though William Bouwsma's recent portrait suggests that Calvin the man may have been more complex than is often thought,[1] it is Calvin the thinker who has been the chief focus of argument. Quite frequently, widely divergent and sometimes even contradictory ideas have been traced to Calvin. As John Leith's new book makes clear, many of the opposing developments may well have roots in Calvin's theology.[2] Others, however, may have been imported into the treatment of the Reformer by later interpreters whose conclusions are not fully satisfying because their perspective is anachronistic: questions *mal-posées,* or one-sided answers which do not take into account the historical context in which Calvin wrote.

The object of this presentation is to name and briefly discuss a few of the problems in Calvin scholarship connected with the relationship of theology and exegesis in the Genevan Reformer's thought. In view of the limited space, only three of the major issues will be sketched.

1. William Bouwsma, *John Calvin: A Sixteenth-Century Portrait* (Oxford: Oxford University Press, 1988).

2. John H. Leith, *John Calvin's Doctrine of the Christian Life* (Louisville: Westminster/John Knox, 1989).

I. The Order of Teaching

The first question to be considered is the persistent separation of Calvin the theologian from Calvin the exegete. Calvin has been known as a "systematic" theologian because he organized his teaching so carefully. When Calvin ordered his theology according to the right pattern of teaching, he did not thereby mean to denigrate, much less eliminate, that which came later in the order. As some twentieth-century scholars have pointed out, Calvin made a conscious effort to provide cross references to clarify the conceptual framework. This pattern of cross references has been traced within the *Institutes,* illuminating in new ways the relationship of such topics as Creator and Redeemer, Scripture and faith, regeneration and justification.[3] Until recently, though, there has been very little attention to the possibility that Calvin might have provided cross references beyond the *Institutes,* or what these interconnections might mean in understanding the Genevan Reformer's thought as a whole. Here I would like to suggest how the *ordo docendi* principle may cast light on the relationship of theology and exegesis.

It is clearly recognized that Calvin was one of the great theologians of the Western church, and his *Institutes of the Christian Religion* is usually seen as the single most important theological textbook to come out of the Protestant Reformation. Calvin is also often cited as a remarkable exegete, whose biblical commentaries continue to be reprinted — and even sometimes read! — in the late twentieth century. These two facets of the Reformer's work are rarely treated together, however, and indeed the *Institutes* has overshadowed everything else for so long that many people practically forget the commentaries.

This split between Calvin's theology and his exegesis, which has handicapped or even prevented a fair assessment of the rest of the Reformer's thought, owes something to Calvin himself and something to the inattention of his modern interpreters. From Calvin's side, the split derives from the "order of teaching" by which he elected to separate theology from exegesis. Calvin understood his chief task to be the faithful exposition of Scripture. For him this had two main parts: the *Institutes,* conceived as a catechism or an introduction to Scripture organized according to the

3. Calvin, *Institutio Christianae Religionis 1559,* in *Opera Selecta* (Monachii in Aedibus, 1926-52), ed. P. Barth, G. Niesel et al. (Hereafter cited as OS.) Here see 1.2.1; 1.6.1; 1.7.4; 1.7.5; and also 3.3.1. Cross references are pointed out in notes in the McNeill-Battles English translation, *Calvin: Institutes of the Christian Religion,* 2 vols., LCC (Philadelphia: Westminster, 1960), 1:40 n. 3, 71 n. 3, 78 n. 12, 81 n. 18. (Hereafter cited as *Institutes.*) Several of Calvin's references are to *ordo docendi,* 1.1.3, 3.3.1.

humanist *loci communes* principle, and the individual commentaries and sermons which explained particular biblical texts. Having observed the limitations in the practices of a number of outstanding contemporaries, Calvin decided that the order of teaching would be best served by separating his introductory text, his commonplace book, from his commentaries.[4] So much has always been obvious. What has not usually been seen is that Calvin also put clear cross references between the *Institutes* and the exegetical works, not only in the prefatory materials, but also in the body of each text. In the commentaries, these cross references are occasional and explicit;[5] in the *Institutes* they are frequent and implicit, and have usually been overlooked or misconstrued as "mere proof texts."

One major reason that scholars have missed the cross references between Calvin's theological textbook and his exegetical works is the changing theological climate of the post-Enlightenment period. In an age when historical-critical studies have altered the ways the Bible is interpreted, and the hermeneutics of suspicion has challenged every writer's motivations, Calvin's biblical citations in the *Institutes* are frequently seen as "proof texts" for views arrived at on other grounds. Thus it has sometimes been difficult for modern readers to take seriously the Reformer's claim to have based his theology on Scripture, and the biblical references which are scattered broadcast through Calvin's writings are usually accorded close attention only when they seem to the twentieth century extremely farfetched.[6]

One way of dealing with the problem of separation between Calvin's theology and his exegesis, therefore, is to suspend disbelief and examine with an open mind exactly how the *Institutes* and the commentaries are related. To do this one must also challenge the often repeated notion that Calvin never changed his mind. This latter view is partly the result of the fact that the *Institutes* is almost always read in the 1559 version, as a "flat"

4. Comments on method and division: dedication to Romans commentary, *Iohannis Calvini Commentarius in Epistolam Pauli ad Romanos,* ed. T. H. L. Parker (Leiden: Brill, 1981), 1-3. "Preface to the Reader" in the *Institutes,* OS 3:6-7.

5. A rapid survey of the explicit cross references in the NT commentaries gives fourteen: Acts 6:3; Rom. 3:21; 3:28; 1 Cor. 1:1; 3:9; 3:14; 5:5; 9:5-6; 2 Cor. 4:17; 5:10; Eph. 3:18-19; 1 Tim. 2:6; 3:8; 1 Pet. 1:20. Note that two of these are related to the diaconate.

6. Instances of farfetched exegesis: on Rom. 12:8, see R. H. Henderson, "Sixteenth-Century Community Benevolence," *ChH* 37 (1969): 427; J. K. S. Reid, "Diakonia in the Thought of John Calvin," in *Service in Christ,* ed. J. I. McCord and T. H. L. Parker (London: Epworth; Grand Rapids, Eerdmans, 1966), 106; R. M. Kingdon, "Was the Protestant Reformation a Revolution? The Case of Geneva," in *Transition and Revolution,* ed. R. M. Kingdon (Minneapolis: Burgess, 1974), 73. On 1 Tim. 5:17, see T. F. Torrance, "The Eldership in the Reformed Church," *SJT* 36 (1984): 503 et passim.

text. If, however, one studies each edition of the book from 1536 through 1559, noting carefully how biblical references as well as substance develop over time in both the *Institutes* and parallel commentaries, one can begin to see the interplay between theology and exegesis in a new way.

What may be one of the clearest examples of the interrelationship between the *Institutes* and the commentaries, which illustrates both the mutual influences of the two and a form of development in Calvin's theology, is found in the teaching on the diaconate. In 1536 the brief passage on the diaconate is largely a typical Protestant reaction against Roman understanding of a sacramental diaconate as a step leading to the priesthood.

> The origin, ordination, and office of the deacons are described by Luke in The Acts [Acts 6:3]. . . . This was the office of deacons: to attend to the care of the poor and minister to them; . . . Then Luke added an account of their institution. Those they had chosen, he says, they ordained in the presence of the apostles: praying, they laid their hands upon them [Acts 6:6]. Would that the church today had such deacons, and appointed them by such a ceremony; namely, the laying of hands. . . . Paul also speaks of the deacons: [1 Tim. 3:8ff.] . . . But what likeness to this is there in the deacons which these men devise?[7]

Calvin refers to the traditional passages of Acts 6 and 1 Tim. 3, indicating that Acts 6 in particular has been misunderstood. Medieval exegetes had considerable difficulty with Acts because they could not reconcile laying on of hands (v. 6), the sign of ordination, with the temporal (profane) task of serving tables. Thus they emphasized Timothy, because the linking of bishops and deacons fitted a more sacramental view of holy orders. Ordination for a temporal task presented no problem for Protestants, who saw charity as a holy vocation, and thus made Acts the dominant voice in determining the nature of the diaconate.[8]

Calvin adds nothing to the treatment of the diaconate in the *Institutes* in 1539, though a double diaconate is introduced in the third edition in 1543. This is significant because some scholars have claimed that the Reformer instituted a twofold diaconate as a way to sacralize and control the bipartite organization of the civil welfare system in Geneva. Though Calvin knew the welfare reforms established in Geneva in 1535, he did

7. Calvin, *Institution of the Christian Religion . . . 1536,* ed. F. L. Battles (Atlanta: John Knox, 1975), 235. Chap. 5, OS 1:218-19.

8. For discussion of exegetical history of Acts 6:1-6, 1 Tim. 3:8-13, see Elsie Anne McKee, *John Calvin on the Diaconate and Liturgical Almsgiving* (Geneva: Librairie Droz, 1984), chaps. 6-7. (Hereafter cited as *John Calvin.*) For social welfare reform arguments, see chap. 4.

not develop a double diaconate until 1540. What happened in that year was the publication of his commentary on Romans, which included some exegetical problems which led to development in the teaching on the ministry, especially the diaconate.

In Rom. 16:1-2, Paul refers to a woman, Phoebe, as a "deacon." In attempting to explain what these verses could mean and how they could be fitted into the Protestant charitable diaconate based on Acts 6 and 1 Tim. 3, Calvin noted that Phoebe was praised for hospitality. Therefore he sought clarification from other passages of Scripture, most notably 1 Tim. 5:9-10, where Paul instructs Timothy to set apart hospitable elderly widows to serve the needy of the church. This Timothy pericope was in fact a problem in itself, because it was the key Roman Catholic proof text for women's vows of celibacy. Calvin believed that in both Romans and Timothy Paul was referring to women deacons who minister to the physical needs of the saints. It remained to see how these women were related to the men who served tables. Calvin knew the early modern tradition which interpreted Rom. 12:6-8 as a list of ecclesiastical offices, and he built on elements of v. 8 to explain how Phoebe and the widows were related to the deacons of Acts 6 and 1 Tim. 3. In Rom. 12:8, those who give liberally are the male administrators, while those who do mercy cheerfully are the women nurses.[9]

Thus, when Calvin revised and expanded his discussion of deacons in the *Institutes* of 1543, he incorporated the exegesis developed in his Romans commentary to explain that the early church had two sorts of deacons, men and women.

> The care of the poor was entrusted to the deacons. However, two kinds are mentioned in the letter to the Romans: "He that gives, let him do it with simplicity; . . . he that shows mercy, with cheerfulness" [Rom. 12:8; cf. Vulg.]. Since it is certain that Paul is speaking of the public office of the church, there must have been two distinct grades. Unless my judgment deceive me, in the first clause he designates the deacons who distribute the alms. But the second refers to those who had devoted themselves to the care of the poor and sick. Of this sort were the widows whom Paul mentions to Timothy [1 Tim. 5:9-10). . . . Their origin, institution, and office are described by Luke in The Acts [Acts 6:3]. . . . Here, then, is the kind of deacons the apostolic church had, and which we, after their example, should have.[10]

9. See ibid., chaps. 8-9, for discussion of exegetical history of Rom. 12:8 and Rom. 16:1-2 with 1 Tim. 5:3-10. The argument is traced most fully in E. A. McKee, "Calvin's Exegesis of Rom. 12:8 — Social, Accidental, or Theological?" *CTJ* 23 (1988): 6-18.

10. Calvin, *Institutes* 4.3.9; McNeill-Battles, 2:1061-62; OS 5:50-51.

Note the biblical references; Rom. 12:8 links the male administrators of Acts 6 and the widows of 1 Tim. 5. (Both 1 Tim. 3 and Phoebe are still in the system, though they are not mentioned here.) Note also the prescriptive character of the model in Acts. In his sermons on this passage, Calvin explains that Paul's words to Timothy were a general rule, which served to make the story related by Luke normative for right church order throughout time.[11]

Calvin's teaching on the diaconate thus provides one demonstration of the symbiotic relationship between his theology and his exegesis. The need to explain difficult texts such as those about Phoebe and the widows shows not only how Calvin could be led into eisegesis (Rom. 12:8) but also how he might feel impelled to develop a doctrine, in this case adding nuances to his earliest notion of the diaconate in ways none of his predecessors had done.

II. The Traditioning of Scripture

We turn now to a second topic of misunderstanding with regard to Calvin's theology and exegesis. The general idea might be described as a misunderstanding of what *sola scriptura* meant to Calvin, a misconception of what kinds of tradition Protestant Reformers valued and how they used tradition. Another, more pointed way of phrasing this is to say that because Calvin's context in the "traditioning of Scripture" is rarely recognized explicitly, the Reformer is sometimes accused of freely reading into texts what he wanted to find there.

One basis for the idea that Calvin must have invented interpretations of texts to fit his needs is the popular notion that because the Reformers rejected tradition for "Scripture alone," they must have been the authors of all the exegetical ideas they espoused. No responsible scholars equate the major Protestant Reformers' view of *sola scriptura* with a naive "me and my Bible" attitude. They know that to deny tradition an authority equal to Scripture was perfectly compatible with a judicious use of the widest possible range of human knowledge, including the writings of predecessors in the great calling of studying and expounding the Bible. However, many modern writers do not take seriously the implications of this knowledge.

Thus, a chief source of the confusion about Calvin's eisegesis is ignorance of the exegetical tradition on the part of modern readers. It is of course appropriate to note — as Calvin himself did in theory, if not always

11. See McKee, *John Calvin,* 155-56.

in practice! — that he was a sinful human being, and therefore that his biblical interpretation could be shaped by motives he did not consciously recognize. That said, however, the student of Calvin must take responsibility for knowing the Reformer's context, which in this case means knowing the exegetical tradition available to a sixteenth-century theologian. It is anachronistic to measure Calvin by the standards of post-Enlightenment historical-critical methods, but it is just as inappropriate to ignore the historical tradition of biblical exposition which was the "mental furniture" of a widely read Christian humanist like Calvin.

Most simply put, much, if not most, of what seems to modern eyes like eisegesis in Calvin's interpretation of Scripture, is in fact borrowed from the exegetical tradition. Calvin almost never invents anything new, although he uses tradition selectively, combining and occasionally developing themes or their applications. It is Calvin's perspective, the vision which guides his use of the material available, which is distinctive, a topic to be treated in part three of this presentation.

An examination, in the context of exegetical history, of the key text Calvin cites in his teaching on discipline, and the third text on the office of elder, may illustrate the traditional origin of some of Calvin's interpretations which modern scholars have found the most shocking. The first instance is Matt. 18:15-18, the pericope which says that if a sinner does not listen to several other Christians in private, he or she should be rebuked publicly by the church. Some modern Protestant writers are quite surprised that Calvin explains "church" in v. 17 as the council of elders (i.e., lay elders and pastors). In fact, almost the entire pre-Reformation tradition of Matt. 18:17 restricts the meaning of church to some kind of representative body. For Eastern as well as Western exegetes and for Roman Catholics in the sixteenth century, it is obvious that the "church" which rebukes is the clergy. Protestants expanded this definition to include laity, of course, but most Protestants (even many Anabaptists) assumed or stated that it is a select number of lay Christians (men, naturally!), not the whole congregation, who reprove the sinner. Anabaptists obviously chose their elders from their own separate communities. Most mainline Protestants, such as Lutherans, Zwinglians, and some members of the Church of England, believed that these lay elders should be Christian rulers.[12]

12. John Chrysostom is the key voice in the East, and his views are repeated frequently by many commentators, notably Johannes Eck in his *Enchiridion.* There are "congregationalizing" tendencies in William Tyndale and others (1520s), but G. H. Williams indicates that even many Anabaptists gave senior men in their community the leadership of discipline. One humorous touch is supplied by the controversy between Jean Morely and Antoine de

Calvin's definition of church in Matt. 18:17 as a representative body of lay and ordained men, which acts for the whole congregation, is therefore the Protestant norm for his day. The only unusual points in Calvin's teaching are the identity of these lay elders and the New Testament model for the council. Calvin denies that Christian rulers and elders are necessarily identical. He bases this on his view of the New Testament as the model of right church order, and ministers in the New Testament, as everyone acknowledges, were not civil rulers. Calvin discusses the historical context for Christ's words about discipline, and he concludes that Jesus was referring to the "custom of his people," i.e., the Jewish Sanhedrin, because the Christian church was not yet a separate body. Since he understood the Sanhedrin as a religious, not a civil, authority, Calvin concluded that Jesus intended discipline to be exercised by a representative council of religious elders which would include lay members.[13] It is clear, then, that in the case of Matt. 18:17, Calvin's interpretation was peculiar not for restricting discipline to a council of elders, but for insisting that these men were laity and not identical with civil rulers. This is not to say that Calvin's exegesis and theology were not influenced by non-exegetical motives. It does mean, however, that other factors, including the exegetical tradition as recast by Protestants, and a conscious effort to deal with the historical context of a biblical text, should not be forgotten.

The second example of an interpretation which Calvin borrows and applies and which shocks twentieth-century readers is the double presbyterate in 1 Tim. 5:17. This verse exhorts the people to give double honor to presbyters who rule well, especially those who preach and teach. Some scholars are persuaded that, when Calvin affirms that this verse speaks of two kinds of presbyters, those who rule and teach and those who only rule, he is inventing an interpretation to support his distinction between pastors and elders. Digging in the history of interpretation of 1 Tim. 5:17 reveals

Chandieu, in the arguments over church polity in the 1560s. Chandieu says that Morely is not as congregationalist as he claims, since in Morely's church women and boys are excluded from the "church" which exercises discipline. An outline of the exegetical history of Matt. 18:17 is sketched in Elsie Anne McKee, *Elders and the Plural Ministry: The Role of Exegetical History in Illuminating John Calvin's Theology* (Geneva: Librairie Droz, 1988), chap. 1, pp. 34-36. (Hereafter cited as *Elders.*) For a summary see idem, "Calvin, Exegesis, and Discipline: The Exegesis of Matt. 18:17 and I Cor. 5:1ff. in the Sixteenth Century," in *Théorie et pratique de l'exégèse,* ed. I. Backus and F. Higman (Geneva: Librairie Droz, 1990), 319-27.

13. Calvin, *Institutes,* 4.12.2, 4.11.4, 4.11.1; OS 5:213, 199-200, 195. The "custom of his people" is mentioned in 4.11.4 in 1543. Then the commentary on the harmony of the synoptic Gospels (1554) specifies this custom as the Sanhedrin (*Opera Calvini Quae Supersunt Omnia,* ed. Baum, Cunitz, Ruess [Brunsvigae: Schwetschke, 1863-1900], 45:514). The Sanhedrin reference is made explicit in *Institutes,* 4.11.1, in 1559.

that for a considerable time prior to Calvin's writing, exegetes had recognized an informal distinction between at least two kinds of presbyters. Roman Catholics assumed — and then insisted, in opposition to Protestants — that not all presbyters preach, but all presbyters are still clergy. Most Protestants agreed that all presbyters do not preach, but they denied that there could be any clerical presbyters, i.e., ministers of (Word and) sacraments, who did not preach. So early Protestants applied the traditional notion of two kinds of presbyters to two distinct offices, sometimes as Paul's bishops and deacons (1 Tim. 3:1-13; Phil. 1:1) who preach and serve the poor, sometimes as pastors and magistrates who care for the Word and administer discipline.[14]

Calvin took the double presbyterate found in the tradition of 1 Tim. 5:17 and used it to explain the presbyterial status of lay elders, and the distinction between presbyters who preach and rule (pastors) and lay presbyters who only rule (elders). This verse also reinforced the distinctively ecclesiastical character of the lay elders, because church leaders in 1 Timothy, as in the rest of the New Testament, did not have civil authority.[15] Calvin's adoption of the double presbyterate was thus not at all shocking to the sixteenth century. It was his *adaptation*, what he did with it, that horrified some of his contemporaries. To Rome, the idea of *lay* presbyters was unthinkable, while German-speaking Protestants objected vigorously to Calvin's insistence that these lay presbyters who rule should be distinct, if not necessarily separate, from Christian rulers. Thus again, the substance of Calvin's interpretation was not new, but the final product definitely was, for reasons that will be stated more clearly in part three below.

It is clear, then, that one cannot simply condemn Calvin's exegesis on the grounds that he read into the text whatever he wanted to find. In

14. For criticism, see Torrance, *SJT* 36 (1984): 503ff. For exegetical history of 1 Tim. 5:17 see McKee, *Elders,* chap. 4. The focus on the task of presbyters as governing may be found as early as Thomas Aquinas's commentary on 1 Timothy, though generally the idea that some priests or bishops do not preach does not become a matter of dispute until Protestants begin to insist that all priests, i.e., pastors, must be able to preach and must do so. Early Zwinglians and then Lutherans named bishops and deacons or bishops and public officials as presbyters, in accord with the idea that pastors preach and Christian princes administer discipline.

15. McKee, *Elders,* esp. 87-88, 99-103. The two key texts for the elder are Rom. 12:8 ("those who preside, let them do it with solicitude") and 1 Cor. 12:28, both present in the *Institutes* by 1539, in an aside on civil government, 4.20.4. Calvin had followed one part of the tradition in using 1 Tim. 5:17 as a proof text for the material support of the ministry from the beginning (1536), but in 1543 he develops the double presbyterate part of the exegetical tradition. The histories of Rom. 12:8 and 1 Cor. 12:28 may be found in *Elders,* chaps. 2-3. The central passages for the elders are 4.3.8 (definition) and 4.11.1 (biblical texts fitted together in a pattern).

fact, Calvin continued to study both the Bible and its commentators, and he borrowed selectively from the exegetical tradition, where many of even his most outrageous ideas had already been expressed.

III. A Vision of Practical Theology

We come now to the third issue regarding the relationship of Calvin's theology and exegesis. This one could be phrased as a question: What is distinctive about Calvin's way of relating Scripture and theology? The answer to this question may also shed light on some of the reasons that, over the centuries, Calvin has been both loved and hated, and scholars have interpreted the Reformer in such diametrically different ways. First a word about what is not unique to Calvin, followed by a brief summary of what has been learned from the two points discussed earlier in this paper, then a sketch and critique of what is distinctively Calvinist.

It is useful to note what is not unique. Calvin's idea of a biblical theology was not peculiar to him, at least as an ideal. For centuries Christian theology had been the study of the Bible *(Sacra Pagina),* and in the Renaissance this ideal was repristinated by biblical humanists, especially Protestants, even if not all carried it through in practice. Calvin's method was not new. Although some people sought a biblical theology through making scriptural catenae, others, like Philipp Melanchthon, had preceded Calvin in the collecting of commonplaces out of Scripture (the *loci communes* way of developing theology). Not even Calvin's individual interpretations of various texts were new. Like other commentators, the Genevan Reformer drew on the exegetical tradition, especially as it was recast by Protestants. Thus neither Calvin's source (Scripture alone) nor the general methodology (humanist *loci*) nor yet the basic material of interpretation was unique.

The first two parts of this paper may contribute in some ways to an understanding of Calvin's distinctive way of relating theology and exegesis. It has been seen that there is more basis than many have thought for a stereoscopic view of the relationship between the *Institutes* and the commentaries, along with a certain development in the course of the mutual influences. This suggests that one factor in Calvin's uniqueness was a combination of orderliness and a drive toward comprehensiveness. He had a vision of theology and exegesis as two parts of one whole, with every exegete a theologian and every theologian an exegete, although the right order of teaching dictates separate treatment of doctrine and interpretation. It has also been observed that at least some of the Genevan Reformer's most peculiar interpretations had a firm foundation in exegetical tradition. This intense interaction with the "traditioning of Scripture" illustrates that a right, orderly, and comprehensive understanding of scriptural theology requires that the exegete-theologian be a person of faith who lives within the heritage of the church and takes that inheritance very seriously, even while always remembering that it can never have the last word.

What distinguishes Calvin, and gives his theology its impression of novelty, is the combination of a theological vision of the unity and authority and practical applicability of Scripture, with unusual architectonic gifts. Calvin attempted to present a coherent picture of revelation by building theology out of exegesis and guiding exegesis by theology. Nothing in Scripture might be omitted without a reason, everything must fit together in a way that honors God and edifies the church. In this process exegesis could shape theology and interpretation. Examples are the awkward passages on Phoebe and the widows which led to a twofold diaconate and a new use of Rom. 12:8, or the way the historical context of Matt. 18:17 could explain why the "church" was identified with the Sanhedrin.

More often, perhaps, theology molded exegesis. This might free some biblical texts to be heard anew. For example, the focus on justification by faith and the priesthood of believers led to the acceptance of ordination for the temporal office of serving tables in Acts 6 and the inclusion of laity in the government of the church in Matt. 18. Theology might also constrain exegesis, as when Calvin interpreted the widows of 1 Tim. 5 as deacons in order to deny the Catholic claim for vows of celibacy. Most notable, however, is the theological conviction of unity guiding the consistent way that Calvin fitted biblical texts together to make a coherent picture. The organizing of Acts 6:1-6; 1 Tim. 3:8-13; 5:9-10; Rom. 12:8; 16:1-2 into a single doctrine of the diaconate is the best example I know. The work on discipline and the elder, which links Matt. 18:17 with Rom. 12:8; 1 Cor. 12:28; and 1 Tim. 5:17, is another instance in Calvin's doctrine of the church.

What does all this add up to? Calvin's view of theology is the articulation of the whole biblical message for the edification and practice of God's people. Scripture is not obviously clear on every point; that is why the church needs theologian-exegetes to ferret out the meaning in the Bible so that Christians can live by this one authority. Calvin's ideas of biblical authority and Scripture as the source of Christian life were not unique, but his genius was to create one of the most coherent and comprehensive pictures of Scripture known to Christian theology. This is almost certainly the reason for the enormous impact of the *Institutes* in the Protestant Reformation and since.

Calvin's execution of his vision was not without faults, however. Sometimes the desired unity was achieved by rationalizing Scripture into an *apparently* "systematic" theology which forced texts onto a grid or failed to do justice to contradictory notes. Not everything in the Bible can be made to fit perfectly together, and Calvin's work has been interpreted in different ways in part because of dissonances in his own writings.

Thus one comes full circle to recognize that some of the difficulties of relating Calvin's exegesis and theology are inherent in the Reformer himself. Perhaps, though, it is possible now to distinguish more clearly the real problems from those that are imported. The separation of his theology and his exegesis is more our problem than Calvin's. The quarrels about Calvin's eisegesis are a shared problem. On our side the latter are owed in good measure to an ignorance of the exegetical tradition which would enable us to understand Calvin in context without anachronism. It is amusing to realize, and salutary to be reminded, that what shocked the sixteenth century is often taken for granted in the twentieth, while what we find outrageous was old hat to Calvin's contemporaries.

On Calvin's side, at least some of the problems of eisegesis are related to the presuppositions of his biblical theology, to the fundamental vision of how theology and exegesis are related. Most important is the conviction that all of Scripture is the authoritative revelation of one God and therefore in a real sense unified. The corollary of this is that scriptural teaching must be practiced as far as it is applicable to our time and place, and for Calvin its applicability was extensive, including not only doctrine but also the "right ordering" of the church, though not a rigid blueprint for everything. Logically enough, Calvin reasoned that all the pieces of scriptural teaching which are permanently applicable can and must fit together so that they can be practiced. Modern notions of biblical unity are not formulated in the same way as in the sixteenth century, and thus Calvin's determination to make all exegesis fit into theology can seem farfetched or rationalistic to the twentieth century.

Yet whatever its faults, Calvin's attempt to be a faithful interpreter of all of Scripture is an impressive achievement. One need not agree with him in toto to find Calvin's genius in relating theology and exegesis a fascinating and sometimes compelling creation by a gifted and dedicated Christian.

14. Marie Dentière's Use of Scripture in Her Theology of History

Jane Dempsey Douglass

The power of the "pure Word of God" to liberate the oppressed is a central theme of the theology of history of Marie Dentière, a sixteenth-century pastor's wife and mother of five children, who reflects on the political transformation of Geneva in the mid-1530s. So eager is she to tell her story of faith that her reader feels obliged to try to overcome the forces of history which have very nearly silenced her voice. She steps out from rather shadowy wings onto the stage in Geneva where she plays a fascinating role. Then again she fades into the wings, leaving us with many unanswered questions.

Marie Dentière had been the abbess of a convent in Picardy until she came to believe that the new evangelical faith was the true one. She left the convent and married a former priest. After the death of her first husband, she married Antoine Froment, a young evangelical pastor from France who was associated with William Farel and others coming out of the humanist reforming tradition of French Catholicism.[1] Froment began his work in Geneva by becoming a schoolteacher, offering to teach any boy or girl, man or woman to read. If in a month they had not learned, there would be

1. For a summary of the biographical sources for Marie Dentière, see Thomas Head, "Marie Dentière, A Propagandist for the Reform," in *Women Writers of the Renaissance and Reformation,* ed. Katharina M. Wilson (Athens, GA: University of Georgia Press, 1987), 260-67. Two brief excerpts from her writings follow in English translation, pp. 270-80. See also Jane D. Douglass, *Women, Freedom, and Calvin* (Philadelphia: Westminster, 1985), chap. 5, esp. pp. 100-104.

An earlier version of this article was included in one of the Taylor Lectures given at the Yale Divinity School in February 1990.

no charge for his services. Naturally, the reading materials were from the Bible, and great enthusiasm for his teaching arose. Soon, according to his own account, he was boldly preaching to crowds of Genevans in the public squares, at some risk to his life from citizens who were offended at the new doctrine.[2] Dentière, we know from the journal of a nun, Jeanne de Jussie, went to the convent of the sisters of St. Clare to preach in order to convert the sisters to the new faith.[3]

Dentière also wrote about the turmoil of reform the city was experiencing. In 1536, just after the city had declared itself for the Reformation, in the same year when Calvin published his first edition of the *Institutes* and, while passing through Geneva, was persuaded to stay and teach, Dentière published in Geneva a small book entitled *The War and Deliverance of the City of Geneva.*[4] This is claimed by a Genevan historian to be "the oldest literary production issuing from Geneva from a Protestant pen," "the first historical writing published in Geneva since the Reformation."[5] It was published anonymously, attributed simply to a merchant living in Geneva, certainly because female authorship would not have been regarded as acceptable.[6] Though the book follows the events leading up to the Reformation,[7] it is in character much more a theological reflection on those events than a chronicle.

Three years later, after Calvin and Farel had been expelled from Geneva by leaders hostile to their style of reformation, Dentière published in Geneva another little book entitled, *A Very Useful Letter Prepared and Composed by a Christian Woman of Tornay, Sent to the Queen of Navarre, Sister of the King of France, Against the Turks, Jews, Infidels, False*

2. Anthoine Fromment, *Les Actes et gestes merveillevx de la cité de Geneve, nouuellement conuertie à l'Euangille faictz du temps de leur Reformation et comment ils l'ont receue redigez par escript en fourme de Chroniques Annales ou Hystoyres commençant l'an MDXXXII,* ed. Gustave Revilliod (Geneva: Jules G. Fick, 1854), 12ff.

3. Jeanne de Jussie, *Le Levain du Caluinisme, ov commencement de l'heresie de Geneve, Faict par Reuerende Soeur Ieanne de Iussie, lors Religieuse à Saincte Claire de Geneue, & apres sa sortie Abbesse au Conuent d'Anyssi,* ed. Ad-.C. Grivel (Geneva: Fick, 1865, repr. Geneva: Les Frères Jullien, n.d.), 173-74.

4. Text found in Albert Rilliet, ed., "Restitution de l'écrit intitulé: *La guerre et deslivrance de la ville de Genesve* (1536)," *Mémoires et documents publiés par la Société d'histoire et d'archéologie de Genève* 20 (1881): 309-84.

5. Rilliet, "Restitution," 312, 314.

6. Rilliet, "Restitution," 309-35, makes a carefully documented and persuasive case for Dentière's authorship for the book; his argument appears to have been generally accepted.

7. Rilliet, "Restitution," 376 n. 87, argues that Dentière must have completed her work no later than the period between Easter and Pentecost of 1536. Calvin's *Institutes* was published in Basel in March 1536; it is therefore unlikely that she could have known this work before completing her own. Geneva's assembly of citizens voted for Reform in May 1536.

Christians, Anabaptists, and Lutherans.[8] Such a furor ensued that 1,500 copies of the book were confiscated, and the printer was imprisoned. The author was no secret. Probably because a woman could not plead in court, Froment appeared, acknowledged that his wife was the author, and urged release of the books. Prepublication censorship was now imposed by the city. Froment appeared repeatedly in vain before city officials to request release of the books,[9] despite an opinion from Berne that the content was merely inopportune and subject to possible misunderstanding, not contrary to Scripture or faith.[10] Froment later produced his own history of the Genevan Reformation, much more detailed and much less theological in character; his work suffered a similar fate.[11]

Both Dentière and Froment were significant leaders in the early years of the Genevan Reformation who became sources of discomfort to Geneva after the establishment of the new order, often at odds with it. Though they had supported Calvin and Farel in the early controversies, these pastors refer to them[12] in unflattering terms in their correspondence, irritated, for example, by Dentière's criticism of the ministers and her influence over Froment, who is seen as imprudent and insufficiently concerned about the church.[13]

Why then would one choose to study Dentière? There are several good reasons. First, she has been known by her nineteenth-century Genevan

8. *Epistre très vtile faicte et composée par vne femme Chrestienne de Tornay, Enuoyée à la Royne de Nauarre seur du Roy de France. Contre Lés Turcz, Iuifz, Infideles, Faulx chrestiens, Anabaptistes, & Lutheriens.* The title page falsely shows the place of publication as Anuers; it was published in Geneva, 1539. I have worked from excerpts published in Rilliet, "Restitution," 377-84, and A.-L. Herminjard, *Correspondànce des réformateurs dans les pays de langue française* (Geneva, 1878), 5:295-304.

9. Herminjard, 5:296 n. 2; pp. 302-3 n. 18; p. 304 n. 23; p. 322 n. 6.

10. For the role of Berne as consultant about the book, see Herminjard, 5:321-23: Berne requests that the printer be released from prison while the book is being studied; Herminjard, 5:332-33: the Council of Berne reports that "it is not contrary to Holy Scripture nor contrary to our faith and religion." But some parts could be misinterpreted, and it is "not appropriate for the time where we are." Further Berne assumes that the book was suppressed because the title declares it was written by a woman, since women have no right to the office of prophecy in the church; but Berne believes the author was not a woman. One wonders whether the same judgment would have been made if the consultants had believed it was written by a woman.

11. Revilliod, "Preface" to Fromment, *Les actes et gestes,* iii-viii. Cf. Head, "Marie Dentière," 265-66.

12. Note that references are to Froment and "the wife of Froment." Though it seems clear that Froment remarried, the date of his remarriage is uncertain. Therefore one cannot be certain after 1540 when these references cease to apply to Dentière. See Head, "Marie Dentière," 265-66, 269 nn. 32-34.

13. For example, Calvin, 1546: CO 12, 378; Farel, 1538: Herminjard, 5:151.

editors and a few specialists as an important figure in the history of the Genevan Reformation, but her contribution has scarcely been more widely recognized. Second, Dentière offers an unusual opportunity for us to study the theological reflection of a layperson and a woman in sixteenth-century Geneva. She was apparently the first and for a long time the last woman to publish in Geneva,[14] and she is therefore exceptional. She must have acquired her literary skills and some of her fundamental theological knowledge during her years in the convent, but she had certainly become Protestant in her theology. Furthermore, the few historians who mention her writings have not analyzed their theological content, which is the focus of this study. Third, Dentière was active before Calvin's arrival in Geneva, communicating to us something of the flavor of theological reflection there before it was shaped by Calvin.

Let us begin by analyzing Dentière's first book, *The War and Deliverance of the City of Geneva* from 1536. Then we will draw upon some materials from the second book for comparison and contrast.

Dentière addresses her work to those who marvel or are amazed at the wars, divisions, and debates that have been going on for three years in Geneva.[15] Though she apologizes modestly for her lack of literary refinement and suggests that God may touch the heart of someone more capable to tell the story better, it is clear that she feels compelled to use the skills she has to declare what God has been doing in Geneva.[16] One has the impression that recounting the story is so important that if she were to be silent, the very stones would cry out. She wants to describe the events which were "manifest and public to each person of the city" so that everyone may know how the inhabitants of the city were led and how God protected and defended them against all their enemies. To hear, see, and recount these events brings great consolation to those who love God and his Word, but it brings great desolation, ignominy, and confusion to the enemies, traitors, and adversaries of God.[17]

Already we see basic elements of the style and content of the book. It is a witness to God's gracious care of the faithful and God's punishment of the enemies, the unbelievers, the traitors. Stylistically, one is struck by the constant reiteration of the contrasts between those who love God and those who betray God, the faithful and the unfaithful. It seems likely that behind this narrative lies some acquaintance by Dentière with Augustine's

14. E. William Monter, "Women in Calvinist Geneva (1550-1800)," *Signs: Journal of Women in Culture and Society* 6 (1980): 204-7.

15. *La guerre,* in Rilliet, 339.

16. Ibid., 343.

17. Ibid., 339.

City of God, for it stands in the Augustinian tradition of history as the conflict between the two cities, the earthly and the heavenly, where hardship and suffering are seen as chastisement due to the divine providence.[18] One is reminded of Augustine's characterization of wicked rulers as robbers when Dentière regularly describes tyrannous leaders of church and state as thieves, robbers, and brigands — as well as traitors.[19] But whereas Augustine is focused on the theological meaning of an event which he sees as a disastrous calamity in the history of his own day, the fall of Rome, where evil seems for the time to win, Dentière's attention is centered on the theological meaning of events which she perceives to be a magnificent triumph of God's justice in her own time, the deliverance of Geneva from tyranny to liberty.

Behind Augustine, of course, is the biblical vision of God's action in history. Dentière's narrative is suffused with biblical imagery and allusions to biblical accounts of God's activity. Characteristic of the work is the illustration which stood opposite the first page in the original edition of the book. On the left is Moses before the burning bush, receiving the tables of the Law from the hands of God. On the right in the background are the Israelites worshiping the golden calf.[20] Visualized here are the Exodus theme, a favorite of Dentière, with its understanding of God's intervention on behalf of God's people, to deliver them from slavery and to give them the Law; and also the contrast of the true and the false believers, the true worship and service of God over against idolatry.[21]

It is striking that the deliverance by God which Dentière describes is almost exclusively corporate. By the very nature of her topic it is the community which is delivered from its enemies. She gives very little attention to any individual or subjective appropriation of that salvation, except for the constant reiteration of the hope it engenders.

In view of the sixteenth-century context, it is also striking that the enemies God is battling in Dentière's account are very concrete, historical enemies. The devil, so prominent in the writing of Luther[22] and other contemporaries and certainly not absent in Calvin, plays no role in Den-

18. *De civitate dei* 1.1.

19. Ibid., 4.4. See *La guerre,* 343, 348, 352, 359, 360-61, 374-75.

20. *La guerre,* 338. The transcription of the text of the book by Rilliet contains only a verbal description of the illustration, not a copy.

21. For the importance of the theme of the struggle against idolatry, see Carlos M. N. Eire, *War Against the Idols: The Reformation of Worship from Erasmus to Calvin* (Cambridge: Cambridge University Press, 1986), esp. chap. 4 on iconoclasm in Bern and Geneva from 1527 to 1536. Dentière reflects this struggle.

22. See, e.g., Heiko A. Oberman, *Luther: Man between God and the Devil* (New Haven: Yale University Press, 1989).

tière's drama. The enemies are primarily "papists," priests, and feudal lords who worship false gods and cruelly exploit, murder, rob, and betray the people.

Though Dentière draws heavily from the Hebrew Scriptures for her examples of God's action, she usually explicitly introduces into those stories the theme of *sola gratia,* God's free and gracious gift of grace without any merit on our part.

In her introduction, Dentière explains that one should not marvel that God has so miraculously delivered the Genevans, without their having merited or deserved it. "For it is always the work of God, when things are desperate from a human point of view, to show his strength and power, in order that all honor and glory belonging to him be given him. . . . For God is as powerful or more in the weakness, smallness, disdain and contempt of his people as in the exaltedness, wisdom, and prudence of others, and [as able] to give a victory with a small number as with a large multitude. Just as he has done for us and for many others in times past."[23]

Here Dentière introduces a characteristic theme: the hope against all hope. God is "the God of hope, the God of powers, the God of battles and victories," who is not subject to human beings but must be obeyed by all, even kings and lords of the earth, "whose hearts he holds in his hand. All he does is to say the word and the thing is done."[24] He cares for his people as he wishes, even against all hope. Abraham and Sarah (Gen. 13, 15)[25] as well as Zachariah and Elizabeth (Luke 1) are examples of couples beyond any hope of having children; yet God against all hope was powerful to give what he had promised, and they received offspring in their old age.[26]

Jesus' birth is a prime example for Dentière of this hope against hope. As she recounts the event, the stories of the Old Testament and New Testament intertwine, the Old as the type of the New, with an unusual parallel of Goliath and David to Herod and Jesus.

> Even Jesus Christ, the true son of God, came and was born of the virgin Mary at the most difficult time, more full of tyranny than one would know how to say, when Herod reigned, the one who to destroy and wipe out the renown of Jesus had little children killed. Notwithstanding, it was necessary that all his [Christ's] enemies be placed under the sole of his feet. And thus, it was necessary that this great Goliath, arrogant, conceited, and proud, well armed and equipped, be brought low, ruined

23. *La guerre,* 339-40.
24. Ibid., 340.
25. One might have expected also a reference to Gen. 21.
26. *La guerre,* 340-41.

> and destroyed, killed and put to death with his own knife by this little David, kind and blessed. What shall we say, therefore, now about his [Herod's] strength, his power, so quickly overthrown? That he found the one [Jesus] who is stronger and more powerful than he. The multitude [of warriors], prudence, strength do not give the victory here, but faith alone and full assurance that one has in God.[27]

Other examples of the victorious work of God against all hope would be Joshua and the walls of Jericho (Josh. 5, 6) and the victories obtained by faith, of those strong in battle over the Assyrians and foreigners (1 Kgs. 17, 19; Judg. [or Judith] 12, 14).[28] "Their God, is he not also ours? Yes, certainly! Is he less than he has been? No! The God of Abraham, of Isaac, of Jacob (Exod. 3), and of the other patriarchs and prophets, is he not our own? Ha! He is not the God of the idolaters, made by a human hand, asleep or at the tavern, like the god Baal. But he is the living God, who consumes by fire the sacrifice of Elijah, showing himself to be the God of the children of Israel (1 Kgs. 18)."[29]

The children of Israel, suffering in Egypt under Pharaoh, were miraculously delivered against all hope (Exod. 1–2; Acts 7), even in the most despairing time. For Dentière, their deliverance becomes the historical model of the liberation of Geneva. Dentière tells the story of Moses, Pharaoh's hard-heartedness, and the Exodus, marveling at God's finding unexpected ways to accomplish the divine purpose. Finally, Pharaoh remained determined to murder the Hebrews and wipe out their name from memory, and those few Hebrews were in hopeless extremity, hemmed in on all sides, between the sea, a mountain, and a large enemy army. There seemed to be no way out, and there was nothing more to eat. At that moment God came to deliver them in a surprising way, dividing the sea so they could pass through with dry feet. "See well what deliverance this is, what grace, what mercy is shown them."[30] Dentière then turns to the Genevan situation, insisting that what God has done there is even greater: "For one enemy that they had, we had two; for one tyranny and cruelty, we had a

27. Ibid., 341.

28. Usually the biblical references are quite appropriate. Here, however, there is a puzzle. Dentière's text seems to refer only to victories of faith in battle. 1 Kgs. 17 is a victory of faith, but there is no battle. Her reference to "Judi." might refer to *Judicum liber* (Judges) where there are battles but no Assyrians. If it refers to the apocryphal book of Judith, which would itself be interesting, the references are to Judith's slaying of Holofernes, which is indeed in the context of the Assyrians and would fit her interest in bold biblical women. The comma in my text after "faith" is therefore an interpretation.

29. *La guerre,* 341.

30. Ibid., 341-42.

thousand; for one Pharaoh, one hundred; for one malice, envy, and obstinacy, one hundred thousand. In brief, it is impossible for a merchant like me to be able to know how to describe it adequately."[31] Geneva's deliverance is not by human action but by God "so that everyone may know that God is our God, powerful to do pardon, deliverance, and greater things, when and to whom God wills, without anyone having earned, merited, or deserved it. But if ever mercy was done to a people, it has been to us."[32]

What then is the tyranny suffered by Geneva which brought about the war of deliverance? Dentière sees the struggle fundamentally as an attempt by some to battle against God and God's Word; but as one learns from Isa. 33:1 and Ezek. 39, they in fact battled against themselves and were destroyed. As foolish as it would be to want to keep the sun from rising, it is even more foolish to want to impede the course of the Word of God. Tyrants, brigands, and murderers, "under cover of war, to maintain the faith and the law of the pope, exercised their brigandry to root out and destroy the true and lively Word of God, his holy gospel, the liberties and franchises of the city, a thing which is impossible for them."[33]

Dentière argues that the city of Geneva, since its founding, has had great liberty and freedom, without subjection to anyone, a freedom attested to by documents in the city hall. The city has the authority to elect syndics, as they do, to exercise justice and equity according to the Word of God. That means fair and impartial justice for everyone, punishing the evil and defending the good, punishing whatever is against God's law, like idolatry, blasphemy, debauchery, robbery, public drunkenness, while still giving all a kindly hearing. It also means listening to the voices of all who object to a particular way of living; if they can demonstrate by the Word of God that their viewpoint concerning belief and life is of God and according to the gospel of Jesus, then they will be welcome and heard. A good example of justice must also be set concerning the preachers.[34]

It is this justice that the Duke of Savoy, with his nobles, bishops, and priests, had been trying to usurp and take away by the force of tyranny for about thirty years, Dentière claims. Not only had they tried to take away justice but also all that belongs to it, life itself and personal safety. The wives and daughters of good merchants were no longer safe in their families but raped and carried away by force by the Savoyards without anyone

31. Ibid., 342-43.
32. Ibid., 342.
33. Ibid., 343-44; cf. 356.
34. Ibid., 344.

protesting, because those who did protest were persecuted. Since these things were unbearable to all people of honor and of heart, the Duke was asked to do justice, but he secretly permitted things to get worse. Some seeking to maintain the city's liberties and freedoms in good faith were killed, dismembered, and sent back in barrels, in derision and mockery. The Duke continued to persecute the city by famine — by forbidding his subjects to trade with the city, by war, and in other ways, seeking to destroy the city.[35]

God, however, inspired the Genevese to recognize this "good and venerable prince" (elsewhere she refers to him also satirically as "this good prince of peace")[36] for what he was and gave them courage to make an alliance with the cities of Berne and Fribourg to maintain their freedoms and liberties, in all justice and equity. Playing on the word *Duc,* which means both "Duke" and "owl," Dentière exults in the image of the Duke, the predator, who has now by 1536 been plucked naked, has lost all his feathers, i.e., his territories, including Savoy, to the King of France, and, with another play on words, can no longer fly. She urges women to brood their chicks boldly, for the owls will no longer eat them.[37]

We see that Dentière has cast the long-standing political tensions between the city and the Duke of Savoy into a religious context. With the recent arrival of evangelicals like Dentière and Froment in Geneva and the declaration of the city for the Reform, the struggles between Protestants in Geneva and Catholic Savoy come to be seen as religious in character. As a newcomer, she probably could not have realized that the exaggerated claims of Geneva's historical autonomy and appeals to Geneva's ancient charter of liberties, which she must have heard being made at that time, represented a polemical view of the city's history.[38]

It is in these hopeless circumstances, Dentière says, where the Duke like Pharaoh became more obstinate despite the wonders Moses performed in his presence, in the most difficult time when tyranny was at its worst, when one would not expect deliverance, that God took pity on the Genevese and willed to deliver God's people.[39]

35. Ibid., 344-45; cf. 345 n. 6.

36. Ibid., 345.

37. Ibid., 345-46. See nn. 8-11 concerning the wordplays.

38. See ibid., 345 n. 5, for some minor historical errors she makes. The assertion that the city had never been subject to any outside authority (p. 344) is inaccurate also, but such exaggerated claims were in fact being made at that time by the city as a strategy to repulse efforts by Berne and France to assume the sovereignty abandoned by the Bishop. See E. William Monter, *Calvin's Geneva* (New York: John Wiley & Sons, 1967), chap. 2, esp. pp. 30, 51, 55-58.

39. *La guerre,* 348-49.

How did God save the city from its enemies? By the power of the pure Word of God. As we have already seen, Dentière repeatedly stresses the efficacy of the Word of God. It cannot be destroyed by any enemy. But by its very power it stirs up opposition, just as it did when Paul was preaching (Acts 15, 19).[40] And so when real preaching began in the city, preaching of the pure Word of God, there was great turbulence, an armed standoff of the two camps for three days, and increased persecution of the evangelicals by the Bishop and his priests and nobles of the sort we have just described.[41]

Dentière's description of the first sermon of William Farel in Geneva in 1532 is a useful example of her style. She explains that Farel was passing through Geneva while visiting "Christian churches," presumably evangelical churches in the Bernese territories near Geneva. He wished "to preach Jesus, and him crucified, publicly; offering himself for death if he said or preached anything which was not contained in holy Scripture."[42] He was called before the city council and forbidden to preach in the city. The canons, priests, and monks, like foxes, were very joyful and sent for him to come into their council, on promise of good faith, to dispute and give a reason for his faith, and he did so. But the religious, like Annas and Caiaphas, sought to put him to death, saying, "What do we need from witnesses? He is guilty of death" [Matt. 26:65-66];

> to which he responded saying the words of Jesus and not of Caiaphas. They were more angry at him; and, like enraged dogs, fell upon him and his companions, striking and beating them in their synagogue, and one unfastened a firearm [*hacquebutte*] to kill and murder them. But since their time had not yet come, the weapon fell and broke in pieces on the ground, against the priests' will and choice. . . . The priests forbade him [to preach] and chased the preacher from the city, that the Word of God might be fulfilled: "They will beat and persecute you and throw you out of their synagogues" (Matt. 10).[43]

Here we see Dentière casting the story of Farel's preaching and arrest into the framework of the biblical story of Jesus' arrest and appear-

40. Ibid., 358-59. Cf. Heiko A. Oberman, "Reformation, Preaching, and Ex Opere Operato," in *Christianity Divided: Protestant and Roman Catholic Theological Issues,* ed. Daniel J. Callahan, Heiko A. Oberman, and Daniel J. O'Hanlon, S.J. (New York: Sheed and Ward, 1961), p. 225 and n. 7, where he cites comments by Luther and Zwingli that the devils begin to speak when the word is preached and Christ is present. There are no devils in Dentière's account, just human opposition.

41. *La guerre,* 358ff.

42. Ibid., 349. She calls him Faret.

43. Ibid., 349-50.

ance before the high priest and the council. She is conflating the Gospel accounts, since the quotation about the witnesses occurs only in Matthew and Mark, but the statement that Farel responded with Jesus' words must refer to John 18:19-24. Here Jesus, rather than remaining silent as in other accounts, asserts that he has always preached openly and many know his teaching. "If I have spoken wrongly, bear witness to the wrong; but if I have spoken rightly, why do you strike me?" This quotation accords well with Dentière's point that Farel wanted to preach about the crucifixion of Christ — and publicly. It also suggests that Farel made a bold and dignified reply to his accusers.

The priests play the role of the Jewish religious leaders in this account, as they often do in Reformation preaching and teaching. Like foxes, the priests deceptively offered to debate in good faith but then did their very best to kill Farel. It was against their will that the firearm broke. It simply was not the plan of God that Farel should be killed, and so even their evil plan failed. Their violent actions correspond to the warning of Jesus in Matt. 10:17, which Dentière cites, that the disciples will be delivered up to councils and flogged in the synagogues. But it is only in the parallel passage in John 16:2 that one finds the casting of the disciples out of the synagogue. Therefore Dentière's "quotation" is rather a free summary of Matt. 10 (and its synoptic parallels) and John 16:2. Dentière wishes to make clear that Farel did not refuse to deal with the Catholic priests, though he was not obliged to do so. He willingly entered into dialogue with them, but in response he was expelled by them from their church.

But there is still another point to be made. Dentière says that the civil authorities simply forbade Farel to preach and sent him off. They did not declare him innocent, as Pilate does in the biblical narrative of Jesus' arrest. There is a point beyond which Dentière will not press her narrative to conform to the biblical framework she has chosen.

On analysis, Dentière's brief and simple story proves to be not at all naive, but a carefully constructed narrative which is meaningful at several levels.[44] The form she has chosen, where the preacher is almost a symbol for Christ who recalls Christ's own ministry, underscores her belief in the present action of God in their midst: Christ's saving work continued in her own day precisely in the preaching of Christ according to the pure Word of God. This technique of a narration of an event contemporaneous to the

44. Compare the story as told by Froment, *Les actes et gestes,* 3-9. This is a narrative in chronicle style, with many of the same elements and much more detail, but lacking the literary framework of Dentière's story.

narrator in which the actions of a faithful Christian are portrayed as conforming to the pattern of Jesus' actions stands in a long tradition.[45]

Since Dentière is very much interested in preaching, she tells about other sermons. Another preacher whom she regards as a good person who came to preach about Jesus and his word was a monk, probably the Franciscan Christophe Bocquet, who preached Advent sermons in Geneva in 1532.[46] Dentière makes the point that though he was "of their sect," i.e., Catholic, his doctrine was very different from the other priests. She attributes to them the concern that if they were to allow the monk to remain, they would lose their people, their stomachs would be empty, and their bawdy women would go away. So they chased him out of town, saying "It is better that he go away and that Barabbas remain."[47] The reference to Barabbas represents a twist in the biblical story where the guilty Barabbas goes free (cf. Matt. 27:16, 26); so it functions here as an admission of their own guilt on the part of the priests and their recognition of the innocence of the preaching monk. Though Dentière has proved herself to be thoroughly antipapal and strongly biased against the priests, we see in this story that she is aware of the differences in doctrine among Catholics and capable of affirming a monk who preaches the gospel as she understands it.

Dentière is truly scandalized by the arrival of Dr. Furbity from Paris, sent to preach against the Bernese Protestants and uphold the papal law. She attributes his good reception to the custom of thieves and wolves to respect their own kind; and she contrasts his reception with that of Jesus and the apostles who were beaten, chased away, and put to death. These are the ones to be followed![48]

It is not only true and false preaching which Dentière discusses but also true and false religious practice. Dentière's objection to the Catholic practice of the reserved sacrament and the underlying teaching of Christ's bodily presence in the Mass becomes apparent where she links them to her familiar theme of Catholic idolatry. Expressing pity on the poor priests who will now have to give up their exalted position and luxurious lifestyle,

45. See, e.g., "The Martyrdom of Polycarp," in R. Knopf, *Ausgewählte Märtyrerakten,* rev. ed. G. Kruger (Tübingen: Mohr, 1929). Dentière must have had broad acquaintance with the lives of the saints during her convent years.

46. See Froment, *Les actes et gestes,* 21. Froment provides the name and the information that he was dressed as *cordellier,* and preaching Advent sermons at the convent of Rive. He describes him as *cougnoyssant la verité,* suggesting approval similar to that of Dentière. Nothing is said about his being expelled from the city, but the narrative suggests that Froment sees the monk's sermons as preparing the people to hear and understand Froment's own preaching.

47. *La guerre,* 351.

48. Ibid., 352.

she asks them about their god of the cupboard (i.e., the tabernacle on the altar) who has not defended them. She seems to be invoking once again the imagery of Elijah's mockery of the worshipers of Baal in 1 Kgs. 18:27.

> I fear strongly that you have kept him prisoner for too long, seeing that he has not helped you in your necessity. We have had more pity on him than you yourselves, for we have freed him and thrown him out of prisons, by the power of our God, who made the heaven and the earth, and by the word that his son Jesus has given us. The God who was sent for us, conceived of the Holy Spirit, born of the Virgin Mary, died for our sins, and was resurrected for our justification (Rom. 4); rose to the heavens visibly and openly (Acts 1), sat down at the right hand of God his Father (Heb. 1), till he comes to judge the living and the dead, and from there will come visibly, just as he rose openly. . . .[49] This is indeed a different God from yours: he is not asleep, not in a cupboard, but is powerful over against all his enemies, having strength and power to confound all those who rise up against him and his members. . . . This God, from his goodness and mercy, has given us the means to be delivered from you and from all adversaries.[50]

In this same context Dentière contrasts the fall of the privileged religious with the new situation of the poor, a theme reminiscent of the Magnificat which runs throughout her writing. In contrast with the false miracles of the papacy (Matt. 24), a real miracle has occurred. "Without running to St. James or to Rome, the poor have become canons."[51] The poor people of the city have been installed in the former houses of the religious, and that which used to support the priests' dogs and prostitutes is now daily distributed to the poor so that no one in the city is in need. Former priests must now earn their living by the sweat and labor of their bodies, as God has commanded.[52]

In a similar vein she speaks of the way in which all efforts to destroy the gospel in fact work to advance it. When preaching is forbidden, the people become eager to hear and speak of it. "Their curses have become

49. Though the early Protestants in Geneva were called "Lutherans" by Jeanne de Jussie, Dentière clearly shows herself to have a Zwinglian view of the Lord's Supper in another passage, *La guerre,* 353. This passage quoted above, then, is not only an attack on the reserved sacrament but also on any view of the Lord's Supper which supposes Christ's bodily presence. The resurrected Christ is not on the altar but in heaven, she believes. Given the linkage between early Genevan Protestantism and Berne, her Zwinglian view is not surprising.

50. *La guerre,* 367-68.

51. Ibid., 366.

52. Ibid., 365-66.

benedictions, excommunications absolutions, poverties riches, miseries consolations, betrayals assurances, tears joy. In brief, the evil good."[53] In the new era of peace, a new order reigns. "Injustice was done, but justice will be done as much to the small as the great; the poor were dying of hunger, thirst, and cold, but now will be supported; the poor widows and orphans dared not go to the prince, now all have access to plead their cause. The wolves were devouring and eating everything, but the true pastors will nourish all. Lies were reigning, and truth will reign. May God, by his grace and mercy, accomplish this!"[54]

There is no evidence that any objections were expressed at that time to Dentière's theological views in this first book. Why then the furor surrounding the second book, the letter to Marguerite, Queen of Navarre? Most arguments focus on Dentière's scathing remarks about the new ministers in town, and this factor must be taken seriously. What is probably equally important is the more visible feminist style and content of the second book. It is that which we shall examine.

Some clues to the context of the book can be found in notes found among the manuscripts of Froment. He writes that during the time when Farel, Calvin, and Corauld were banished from Geneva, i.e., from 1538 to 1541, the Queen of Navarre asked for news about Dentière and her new life in Geneva after leaving her convent and also asked why the ministers of the Word of God had been banished. Apparently the Queen identified Dentière as a *commère* of hers, i.e., a godmother or a good friend, and as "the first woman banished for the Gospel in our time."[55] In response Dentière wrote and published the letter. The new ministers felt, as the result of its publication, that they had been injured, offended, and humiliated, by a woman, like Pilate in the great creed or like Judas in the death of Christ, and they could not bear it. So they had the book seized by the city officials for a time, because of the divisions in the city over ceremonies, and had the printer jailed.[56]

This time indeed Dentière did not attempt to veil the fact that the author was a woman. The title page of the book announces that the author is a Christian woman from Tornay. In the cover letter Dentière justifies her writing by recognizing that women, like all lovers of truth, need to know how to live in these dangerous times with so many errors and heresies.[57] The passage following, which points out how those to whom

53. Ibid., 361.
54. Ibid., 375.
55. Herminjard, 5:295-96.
56. Ibid., 296 n. 2; pp. 456-57 (note relating to p. 301).
57. *Epistre,* in Herminjard, 5:295-96.

grace has been given by God to wish to write, speak, preach, and announce what Jesus and the Apostles did and preached are often rejected and reproved, especially by the learned sages,[58] seems in the total context of the book to refer to women. We will see shortly that similar language has been used in her "Defense for Women."[59] Dentière reminds the Queen that "that which God has given you, and revealed to us women, we should not hide and bury in the earth any more than men should. And although it is not permitted to us to preach in public assemblies and churches, it is nonetheless not forbidden to write and admonish one another, in all charity. Not only for you, my lady, have I written this letter, but also to give courage to other women held in captivity, so that they may not at all fear being banished from their country, relatives and friends, like me, for the Word of God."[60]

She writes principally, she says, for the poor little women who wish to know the truth, that instead of being tormented and afflicted, they may rather be consoled and given joy in following the truth, which is the gospel of Jesus Christ. This has been hidden from them, since it seems that women were not supposed to read or understand anything of the Scriptures. She has been moved to write in the hope that women will no longer be so despised as in the past.[61]

Ostensibly writing as a woman to women could be a device to make her work more socially acceptable. But it is obvious that she intends the conversation to be overheard by men. Furthermore, what might appear to be a sign of modesty — the woman-to-women style — appears even bolder when one takes account of the familiar and even tutorial style of her address to the Queen. Whatever her personal relationship to the Queen may have been before coming to Geneva,[62] the choice of this woman as the intended recipient of the open letter is clever. Marguerite of Navarre was a very powerful woman at the court of her brother, the King of France, ruler of her own lands, protector of the humanist reforming Catholics in France against the Sorbonne. But she was also a published author. Among her writings are poetry, religious and spiritual works, and a novel centered around the antagonisms between men and women where the spiritual leader is a woman. She is caught up in the humanist debate about the nature of

58. Ibid., 296-97.

59. *Epistre,* in Rilliet, 380.

60. *Epistre,* in Herminjard, 5:297-98.

61. Ibid., 298; cf. *Epistre,* in Rilliet, 381.

62. Evidence beyond the statements of Dentière and Froment is scarce. However there is some evidence that Froment was received by the Queen in 1542: Herminjard, 5:322 n. 6, so the claim to friendship is probably not totally fictitious.

women. One can imagine Marguerite being genuinely interested in the matters discussed in the open letter.[63]

Dentière's letter calls for a very inclusive understanding of the nature of the gospel. "I ask, did not Jesus die as much for the poor ignorant people and idiots as for my lords who are shaven, tonsured, and mitred? Did he only say: Go, preach my gospel to my lords the wise and great doctors? Did he not say: to all? Do we have two gospels, one for men and the other for women? One for the wise, and the other for the foolish? Are we not one in our Lord? In whose name are we baptized, that of Paul or Apollos, of the Pope or of Luther? Is it not in the name of Christ? Certainly he is not at all divided."[64]

Finally, we should point out that the book contains a brief section entitled, "A Defense for Women."[65] Very much in the tradition of the humanist debate about women of the late Middle Ages and Renaissance,[66] Dentière confronts the charge by adversaries but also by faithful people that for women to write one another about Scripture is too bold. She answers the charge by pointing out the bold role of women in Scripture itself. Several women are held up in Scriptures as models of behavior as well as for their faith and doctrine, like Sarah and Rebecca. The best example of all in the Old Testament, Dentière believes, is the mother of Moses who defied Pharaoh's edict to protect her son from death and to arrange for him to be cared for at Pharaoh's house (Exod. 2). Deborah, the judge of the people of Israel, should not be neglected (Judg. 4). One can hardly condemn Ruth, just because she is a woman, for having her story told in the Bible, especially since she is numbered in the genealogy of Jesus Christ (Matt. 1). Dentière notes particularly the wisdom of the Queen of Sheba. Not only is she named in the Old Testament, but Jesus also dared to name her among the other sages (Matt. 12:42; cf. 1 Kgs. 10). In the New Testament Dentière deems the Virgin Mary, the mother of Jesus who carried the son of God (Matt. 1), to have received the greatest grace ever given to a human being. Elizabeth, who was sterile but miraculously became the mother of John the Baptist (Luke 1), also received grace which was not small. "What

63. See Douglass, *Women, Freedom, and Calvin,* chap. 4. Roland H. Bainton, *Women of the Reformation in France and England* (Minneapolis: Augsburg, 1973), chap. 1, surveys her life and work. Bainton, however (cf. pp. 33-34), in his kindly manner, has missed the feminist cutting edge in Marguerite's novel, *The Heptameron.*

64. *Epistre,* in Rilliet, 383.

65. Ibid., 378-80.

66. Joan Kelly, "Early Feminist Theory and the *Querelle des Femmes,* 1400-1789," *Signs* 8 (1982): 4-28; Douglass, *Women, Freedom, and Calvin,* chap. 4; Emile Telle, *L'oeuvre de Marguerite d'Angoulême, reine de Navarre, et la querelle des femmes* (Toulouse, 1937; repr. Geneva, 1969).

woman preacher [or does she intend the comparison to any preacher?] has been made greater than the Samaritan woman who had no shame at all to preach Jesus and his word, confessing him openly before all the world, as soon as she heard from Jesus that one must worship God in spirit and truth (John 4)?"[67] Who but Mary Magdalene, from whom Jesus had cast out seven devils, can claim to have had the first manifestation of the great mystery of the resurrection of Jesus? Who but the other women learned of the resurrection from an angel rather than a human being and were commanded to preach and declare it to others?[68]

It was not women who betrayed Christ or invented ceremonies or heresies or were false prophets, Dentière argues, but men. Though women have their faults, one should not condemn them in general, as well-known textbooks do.[69] "If God then has given graces to some good women, revealing to them by his holy scriptures something holy and good, will they not dare to write, speak or declare it one to another for fear of deprecators of truth? Ah! It would be too boldly done to wish to stop them, and for us, too foolishly done to hide the talent which God has given us, who grants grace to us to persevere till the end. Amen!"[70]

This conviction of Dentière that God is now giving women grace to write about theology and preach the gospel and that they are under obligation now to use that talent and gift of grace is an essential part of her vision of God's present activity in the world.

This vision was offensive to the Genevan pastors. William Farel, in a letter to Calvin in 1539 during their exile from Geneva, reports what the replacement pastors are doing to avoid dealing with complaints from the parishioners. Among other things he says: "They affirm it unworthy and not to be tolerated that the Bible is read by other people than by experts, and the French Bible ought to be prohibited for the sake of biblical solidity, since some people and even women themselves dare to discuss these very things and to accuse the preachers."[71] This letter, though written three months before the publication of Dentière's second book, suggests that Dentière and possibly other women were publicly exercising the freedom Dentière claims for women. Such boldness seems to be inspiring thoughts of repressive action in the minds of the beleaguered new pastors.

We conclude that the power of the Word of God is at the heart of Dentière's understanding of theology. Dentière claimed for herself and

67. *Epistre,* in Rilliet, 379.
68. Ibid., 378-79.
69. Ibid., 379-80.
70. Ibid., 380.
71. Herminjard, 5:217.

other men and women the right to interpret Scripture according to the graces given them by God, a claim clearly controversial even in Reformed Geneva in that troubled time. We can also observe that Dentière has a rather broad knowledge of the Bible, since she cites a wide variety of both Old Testament and New Testament books quite appropriately. The Bible for her, however, is not a lawbook but a story of God's unmerited saving activity which provides the framework for Dentière's reading of God's actions in contemporary events in Geneva. The preaching of the Word of God is itself a powerful means of God's ruling the world, one which cannot be thwarted by any human power. The doctrines of justification by grace alone, predestination, and providence are critical hermeneutical keys for her understanding of the Bible. In this context she hears as the most fundamental message of the Bible that God cares about the poor, despised, and oppressed of this world and in surprising ways, despite their unworthiness of such vindication, liberates them through the gospel of Jesus Christ to serve God and rejoice in God's glorious ruling of the world. Finally, she believes, women are among the oppressed whom God is now freeing to new service to God.

Dentière surely stands squarely in the theological tradition of the Swiss and Genevan Protestantism of her day in her understanding of the Scripture, but she speaks with a discomforting prophetic voice, pressing the newly reformed church to continuing reformation.

15. *Bullinger's Prophets of the "Restitutio"*

Rodney L. Petersen

Heinrich Bullinger writes about prophets and prophecy in many places.[1] They appear as a part of his concern for "restitution," a term which may at first appear unusual in its association with Bullinger as the term is usually reserved for "radicality" in the sixteenth century.[2] Nevertheless, I have chosen the word *restitutio* to describe the activity of Bullinger's prophets, not so much for its frequency of appearance in his works[3] as for its descriptive power in calling us to return to a theological simplicity and spiritual immediacy which he finds in true prophets.[4] This simplicity is

1. References to Bullinger's works are to *Heinrich Bullinger Werke,* ed. Fritz Büsser (Zürich: Theologischer Verlag, 1972-); bibliographic items are cited from sec. 1, vol. 1 *(Heinrich Bullinger Bibliographie)* with the abbreviation *HBBibl* I/1, plus the no. giving Bullinger's particular work. Bullinger affirms the place of the Christian ministry, seen as containing the work of prophets and prophecy, in the following way in the *Decades:* "God indeed might by the secret illumination of the Spirit, without man's ministry (as his power is tied to no creature), regenerate the whole world, and govern the church itself: but he despiseth not his creatures, nor destroyeth the work of his own hands, and doeth all things in order; even so from the first beginning he forthwith spake to the world by patriarchs, then by prophets, afterwards by apostles; neither at this day ceaseth he to give unto the world doctors and pastors: so that it becometh us not to tempt God, that is, not to look for a secret inspiration with the heretics *Enthusiastae* [*Adv. anabt.,* 2.1]; but to acknowledge a just order, and that God speaketh unto us by men, of whom he would have us to learn religion" (*The Decades of Henry Bullinger,* V, ed. for the Parker Society [Cambridge, 1852], 94. See *HBBibl* I/1 nn. 179-82).

2. See the introductory essay on "radicality" in the 16th century in the 3d ed. of George H. Williams, *The Radical Reformation* (Kirksville, MO: Sixteenth Century Publishers, 1991), xix-xxxi.

3. The term *restituitur* is used in the sermon on Rev. 10:8-11. It appears to be set parallel to *reparandam* and *restorescet* in *Apocalypsim,* cited below (n. 5). Bullinger is critical of the doctrine of restorationism *(apokatastasis),* a view he attributes to Anabaptists in Augsburg, Basel, and Moravia (cited in Bullinger, *Antidotus,* 35).

4. Gottfried W. Locher writes of such prophets that when the Word of God is preached

characterized by a restoring, rebuilding, replacing, or reinstating associated with the covenant.

The way in which Bullinger's ideas of prophets, prophecy, and, indeed, the covenant are handled in his set of sermons on the Apocalypse, a book which he argues is a summary of biblical revelation, offers (1) an affective argument to his conception of the place of the covenant in shaping history, (2) a polemical yet effective vision of the Reformed pastor, and lays (3) an important part of the foundation for the later speculative development of the Apocalypse among Reformed churches and with implications for Protestant historiography.[5] Bullinger's debt to patristic and medieval authors for the historical vision and development of ministerial identity evident in these sermons, in particular to the tradition of Tyconius mediated through others and interwoven with Joachite themes, is a story which yet remains to be told fully. It illustrates part of the way in which texts, especially the Old Testament, were reaffirmed in Protestant scholarship, here through the filter of the *figura* of the Apocalypse.[6]

---

through rightly called preachers and prophets, Bullinger believed that God's word was itself preached. This, Locher believes, is a brief formula for the underlying sense of knowledge in the Reformation, and one might add here, with pedagogical implications ("Pradicatio verbi dei est verbum dei," *Zwingliana* 10 [1954]: 47-57; cf. Joachim Staedtke, *Theologie des jungen Bullinger* [Zürich: Zwingli, 1962], 52-79). See further on the discussion of prophecy in the sixteenth century in Locher, "Prophetie in der Reformation. Elemente, Argumente und Bewegungen," in *Charisma und Institution,* ed. Trutz Rendtorff (Gütersloh: G. Mohn, 1985), 102-9. On Zwingli's idea that his own day was similar to that of days of prophetic crisis and outpouring in the OT, see Fritz Büsser, "Der Prophet — Gedanken zu Zwinglis Theologie," *Zwingliana* 13 (1969): 7-8; cf. Gordon Rupp, "The Swiss Reformers and the Sects," in *The New Cambridge Modern History: The Reformation 1520-1559,* ed. G. R. Elton, vol. II (Cambridge, 1958), 96. The nature of this prophetic activity is described later in Bullinger's commentaries on the Hebrew prophets, e.g., *Ieremias fidelissimus et laboriosissimus Dei propheta . . .* (Zürich: Froschouer, 1575) (*HBBibl* I/1 n. 361). The exemplary prophetic activity of Jeremiah for his own day and for contemporary society is emphasized throughout, e.g., fol. 1r; note Bullinger's conclusions, fol. 8v-9r.

5. See my dissertation, "Preaching in the Last Days: The Use of the Theme of 'Two Witnesses,' as found in Revelation 11:3-13" (Princeton Theological Seminary, 1985), as revised, *Preaching in the Last Days* (New York: Oxford University Press, forthcoming). A section of chap. 3 which deals with early Reformed eschatology constitutes the basis of this article. Bullinger's sermons on the Apocalypse, *In Apocalypsim conciones centum,* might even be seen as a summary for his own corpus. The series was printed in Basel by Oporinus, 1557 (*HBBibl* I/1 n. 327). An English translation was rendered early, *A Hundred Sermons upon the Apocalypis of Jesu Christe* (London: John Day, 1561) (*HBBibl* I/1 n. 355). See in *Diarium, Annales vitae der Jahre 1504-1575,* ed. Emil Egli (Basel: Basler Buch und Antiquariatshandlung, 1904), 50. On its place in the tradition of Apocalypse commentaries, cf. R. H. Charles, *Studies in the Apocalypse* (Edinburgh: T. & T. Clark, 1913), 1:28; Wilhelm Bousset, *Die Offenbarung Johannis* (Göttingen: Vandenhoeck & Ruprecht, 1906; repr. 1966), 86-89. See Richard Bauckham for the influence Bullinger's series of sermons on the book of Revelation had upon English Protestantism, *Tudor Apocalypse* (Oxford: Sutton Courtenay Press, 1978).

6. On Tyconius's "Book of Rules" see Karlfried Froehlich, *Biblical Interpretation in*

The vignette offered by this paper into the wide domain of prophets, prophecy, and historical understanding in the sixteenth century is appropriate in itself, but especially in the light of the extensive contemporary reevaluation of the period from the perspective of social history.[7] Ideas of the Reformed ministry, developed in the light of Old Testament prophetic models in the context of a renewed sense of civic consciousness, are given polemical significance as understood through the Apocalypse, an important dimension of expanding Protestantism and Protestant conceptions of legitimate prophecy. Such views as used by Reformers aligned with the office of the magistrate will in the evolution of social history become models for later religiously disaffected and socially marginalized groups seeking further reform.[8] The study of texts, then, and of their use continues to be of central historical importance. When we turn to Bullinger, we turn to one whose advice was sought and writings read through the bulk of the sixteenth century from the Kingdom of England to the Commonwealth of Poland-Lithuania.

I. The Prophet and the Promise

Before the Apocalypse comes the Promise. There were many prophets and much prophecy in the sixteenth century. In his celebration of one such prophet, Huldreich Zwingli, Bullinger offers us an introduction to the office and function of a prophet, "For it was this one who restored the principle of the testament and the eternal covenant and renewed what was worn out.

---

the Early Church (Philadelphia: Fortress, 1984), 25-29, 104-32. Note Paula Fredrickson Landes's work as it applies to our theme, "Tyconius and the End of the World," *REAug* 28 (1982): 59-75; and the paper by Robert Bernard in this volume, pp. 88-99.

7. Several models of unfolding religious and social-political history in the 16th century present themselves: (1) a religious model, attentive to theological argument, that identifies an orthodox reformation and then further devolutions; (2) a model that draws upon the seminal works of Weber, Troeltsch, McNeill, and Williams, attentive to "sociological-theological congeries" of movements (George H. Williams, "The Radical Reformation Revisited," *USQR* 39/1-2 [1984]: 1-24); (3) a model which looks different with its focus upon unfolding social history in general, and in northern as opposed to southern German cities in particular (Heinz Schilling, ed., *Die reformierte Konfessionalisierrung in Deutschland—Das Problem der "Zweiten Reformation"* [Gütersloh: Gerd Mohn, 1986]). For a contemporary summary of these issues, see R. Po-Chia Hsia, "The Myth of the Commune: Recent Historiography on City and Reformation in Germany," *Central European History* 20 (1987): 203-15.

8. Note patterns of alienation and goal definition in Robert King Merton, *Social Theory and Social Structure* (New York: Free Press, 1968), 194-214; and as applied to religious consciousness in Barbara Hargrove, *The Sociology of Religion: Classical and Contemporary Approaches* (Arlington Heights, IL: Harlan Davidson, 1989), 270-71.

It is this one who restored to its former splendor the omnipotence and goodness and unity of God which invocation and veneration of other gods had obscured."[9] Of course, Luther was another, his work *The Babylonian Captivity of the Church* being of major influence upon the thought of Bullinger and his generation.[10]

Bullinger finds prophets among many peoples, the Greeks, Romans, Jews, and early Christians. However, the office of prophecy is particularly evident in Hebrew history and, following the examples of Jeremiah and Paul, Bullinger writes that the activities which characterize true prophets are the explanation of the sacred Scriptures and their application. It is in the Scriptures, in the patriarchs and church fathers, that one finds models for reform. Reform is needed when the visible marks of the church become obscured as in the days of Elijah. At such times the church does not cease to exist, but must give attention to the sincere preaching of God's Word and adherence to models of piety provided by the patriarchs.[11] The idea of prophets and their work in the social order lay at the heart of the Zürich Prophezei, an institution soon to be copied in other Reformed academies and universities throughout Europe. From Zürich's "bulwark of biblicism," as Büsser calls it, as well as from elsewhere came prophets (preachers, teachers, and missionaries) to carry the Reformation across Europe. The office of the prophet involved exegesis and homiletics as well as social application or politics.[12] The idea of the covenant, adherence to it or departure from it, was to guide Bullinger's historiography and prophets.[13]

9. *De prophetae officio* (Zürich: Froschauer, 1532), sig. Ei r-v (*HBBibl* I/1 n. 33). For commentary and publication of the epilogue see Fritz Büsser, " 'De prophetae officio': Eine Gedenkrede Bullingers auf Zwingli," in *Festgabe Leonhard von Muralt,* ed. Martin Haas and Rene Hauswirth (Zürich: Verlag Berichtshaus, 1970), 245-57, 253; cf. G. R. Potter, *Zwingli* (Cambridge: Cambridge University Press, 1976), 211-24.

10. Bullinger, *Apocalypsim,* sig. B2v.

11. *De prophetae officio,* sig. Aiiv-Aiiir.

12. Büsser, " 'De prophetae officio,' " 253-54; cf. Siegfrid Rother, *Die religiosen und geistigen Grundlagen der Politik Huldrych Zwinglis. Ein Beitrag zum Problem des christlichen Staates* (Erlangen: Palm & Enke, 1956), 63-72. On the spread of the Reformed movement across Europe, see Menna Prestwich, ed., *International Calvinism, 1541-1715* (New York: Oxford University Press, 1985).

13. Bullinger's definitive work on the covenant is *De testamento seu foedere Dei unico et eterno* (Zürich: Froschauer, 1534), *HBBibl* I/1 nn. 54-61; cited here, fol. 2r-3v. A sustained treatment is in *Epitome,* fol. 48 et passim. J. Wayne Baker, *Heinrich Bullinger and the Covenant: The Other Reformed Tradition* (Athens, OH: Ohio University Press, 1980), finds the covenant central to Bullinger's systematic theological understanding. He offers a useful bibliography. Note the careful nuancing of the function of the covenant and limits placed upon its systematic use in Bullinger's thought in Edward A. Dowey, "Heinrich Bullinger as Theologian: Thematic, Comprehensive, Schematic," in *Calvin Studies* 5 (1990): 41-60.

The nature of Bullinger's conception of reform lies in an apprehension of God's covenant, his *testamentum.* The covenant served as the means by which Bullinger understood humanity's relation to God. It originated in the agreement which God struck with Abraham. He believed that it was "testified in the following words of Moses which we read in Genesis 17 . . . 'I am God almighty and all-sufficient. Walk before me and be whole.' "[14] Bullinger writes of the covenant as "the source of our religion and first chapter of it."[15] God and his promises form the divine pole of what is essentially a bilateral pact.[16] Adherence or departure from the terms of the covenant gave inner structure and meaning to history. The work of the prophet, whether in the days of Elijah, Jeremiah, and Isaiah, or under the terms of the new dispensation, was the same: to call an erring people back to a saving relation with God, i.e., to the terms of the covenant.

Bullinger's interest in historical origins and their analogies in human experience is developed clearly in relation to departures from the covenant in two works written in 1528 and 1529, later printed as *On the Origin of Error* (*De origine erroris,* 1539) and cited in his Apocalypse sermons. Here he points to parallels between the idolatry and errors of earlier ages and those which grew up in Europe since the early Middle Ages. He writes of the ancient world that after a period of initial monotheism, when God had become known by many names reflecting his attributes, impious men laid the foundation for idolatry by exploiting the names of God along with those of their ancient heroes. A similar degeneration occurred among the Jews.

14. *De testamento,* fol. 5r.

15. Ibid., fol. 6v: "Haec nimirum religionis nostrae origio & illud caput primarium est." In *De prophetae officio* (sig. Aivv-Avr) Bullinger writes: "For testament, which also is the title for all of Scripture, surely stands for the content of all of Scripture. Neither is this to be wondered at as something recent and devoid of meaning. For by the word testament we understand the covenant and the agreement by which God agreed with the entire human race, to be himself our God, our sufficiency, source of good and horn of plenty. And this he would abundantly prove by the gift of the fertile earth and the incarnation of his son. Man, however, ought to pursue integrity, that he may stand before this God with a perfect and upright mind, that he may walk in his ways and commit himself totally to him, as to the highest and most loving Father."

16. *De testamento,* fol. 2-3b. Bullinger delineates the conditional nature of the covenant in this work and sets it within the context of God's promise of salvation. Baker writes: "Bullinger held to a conditional covenant on the one hand and the *sola gratia* encased within a carefully stated doctrine of a single predestination on the other" (*Heinrich Bullinger,* p. xxiii). Baker sees the covenant coming to the center of Bullinger's theological thought as early as 1528 (p. 11). The plausibility of such growing weight given the covenant follows from the nature of the Hubmaier-Zwingli debates in Zürich at this time. Both Hubmaier and Zwingli each gravitated toward different metaphors for the Christian life, the symbolism of dying and rebirth in adult baptism for the former, that of the newly covenanted Israel with civic implications for the latter and mentor of Bullinger.

They were led into the temptation of idolatry while sojourning in Egypt. Following their exodus idolatry grew rapidly until it became manifest in the Baal worship of the time of Ahab. Similarly, Roman saints were originally great martyrs or founders of particular orders. Venerated in commemoration, their images were soon worshiped and adored. Thus, abuses slowly crept into the church; they were fully evident by the eleventh century. The growth of such idolatry was furthered by barbarian invasions throughout the early Middle Ages which affected both church and society. The destruction of knowledge and education contributed to an illiterate and superstitious religion which, in turn, led to the adoration of saints.[17]

The argument and methodology developed in *The Origin of Error* is evident throughout Bullinger's sermons on the Apocalypse. Here he charts the growth of error and more clearly sets forth as an antidote God's faithful provision throughout history of true prophets. Focusing in the Apocalypse upon history in the common era, Bullinger finds a progressive growth of error marked by at least two "falls."[18] Old Rome fell around A.D. 480. Antichrist, or new Rome, originated with the claims to ecclesiastical dominion by Boniface III (607), who feared that such primacy might be given to Constantinople. An actual "fall" of the church is identified with the number "666" (Rev. 13:18), which implies a specific period from the date of John's vision (A.D. 97, for Bullinger) to the manifestation of open error in the church. Adding 666 to 97 yields the year 763, the time of the reign of Pepin the Short. Pepin gave the former exarchate of Ravenna, claimed by Byzantium, to Rome, creating the papal state by this "donation." Thus, Bullinger's conception of papal declension is tied to spiritual and temporal dominion: first property, then idolatry.[19] A further "fall" came with Boniface VIII. In his Jubilee Year, 1300, he arrogated to himself power that was not his. In causing all to worship him, he established an idolatry parallel to that of old Rome or similar to that of the days of Ahab and Jezebel.[20]

17. *De origine erroris libri duo* (Zürich: Froschauer, 1539); *HBBibl* I/1 n. 12; cited here, fol. 3r-9v. Seventy-two names are given for God, largely drawn from the OT, but pagan and classical analogies are drawn in as well. See also sections, fol. 38r-42r, 46v-52v, 164r-179r. Cf. P. Pontianus Polman, *L'Elément historique dans la controverse religieuse du XVIe siècle* (Gembloux: J. Duculot, 1932), 100-109; Baker, *Heinrich Bullinger,* 81-106.

18. On the origins and development of a "fall" theory of history, particularly in Protestantism, see Erich Seeberg, *Gottfried Arnold. Die Wissenschaft und die Mystik seiner Zeit* (Darmstadt: Wissenschaftliche Buchgesellschaft, 1964; 1st ed., 1923); note the discussion as it applies to Bullinger by Aurelio Garcia Archilla, "Truth in History: The Theology of History and Apologetic Historiography in Heinrich Bullinger" (Ph.D. diss., Princeton Theological Seminary, 1989), 245-58.

19. *In Apocalypsim,* 81-82, 172-74, 193-94.

20. Ibid., 174.

The story of the Middle Ages was one of the progressive subversion of the norms of the covenant. As the church was persecuted under old Rome, so, Bullinger believed, it was also under new Rome. The early church faced ten persecutions yet was not defeated, and so, Bullinger writes, the Lord in the Gospels prophesied this future to the church, reminding it of the consolation it would find along with the trials it would face. Through persecution the present church for the past five hundred years has been linked to the early church. Even today, "the ground is wet with the blood of martyrs." To both churches the promise is given that the witnesses of Christ, his prophets and preachers, would complete their prophesying.[21]

As reform came through Hebrew prophets following periods of Jewish idolatry, and later, in the days of Christ, through figures like Paul and Athanasius, so it was advanced by prophets and pastors in Bullinger's own day. For Bullinger, Zwingli was a part of this contemporary outburst of prophetic zeal which stood in continuity with Moses, Isaiah, Paul, and Athanasius, seeking to effect the reinstating of the covenant in social consciousness toward the establishment of a Christian Commonwealth. Bullinger referred to Zwingli as Zürich's "local" example of one filling the office of prophecy, a singular and final expression of all the qualities which one would seek in the true prophet of God.[22] Later (1557), for a different purpose, Bullinger wrote more generally that Christ always sends forth faithful preachers modeled on those prophets Enoch and Elijah, to oppose the abominations of Antichrist, "For since all times bring forth the faithful heralds of Christ, the Enochs and Elijahs, who oppose such abominations, Daniel is right in saying: 'and he waged war with the saints and prevailed against them.' "[23]

So, Bullinger writes, as Elijah called upon Israel to leave its baals and "Jezebelism," so contemporary prophets and preachers were now calling upon Christendom to leave idolatry and superstition. Jacob was blessed by God when he gave up the alien gods of Syria, burying them under the oak of Moreh in Shechem. Israel, not forsaking the gods of Egypt after her

21. Ibid., 88-91. According to Bullinger's sermon on Rev. 14:6-7, the gospel is predicted by law and prophets, fulfilled in Christ, and declared by the apostles. In the last days preachers are to preach the fear and honor of God, that the hour of judgment is near, that God alone is to be worshiped (pp. 200-201). This vision of consolation parallels other visions of consolation in chaps. 7, 10, and 11.

22. *De prophetae officio,* sig. Dviiir.

23. "Quoniam uero omnia tempora proferunt fidos Christi praecones, Enochos & Helias, qui se huiusmodi opponunt abominationibus, recte Daniel: Ac praelium, inquit, fecit cum sanctis, & praeualuit eis" (fol. 57). In *De fine seculi & iudicio venturo domini nostri Iesu Christi . . . orationes duae* (Basel, 1557); *HBBibl* I/1 n. 320. The sermon is on Dan. 7, and the reference alludes to the battle between the saints and the little horn (7:20-21).

exodus, was led to idolatry, the pollution of pure religion, and fell away from the terms of the covenant such that by the time of Ahab and Jezebel, idolatry and superstition reached an insidious level. Then Elijah appeared. He called the people to a clear decision between God and idolatry. So, today, Christian society stands in a similar situation: The development of error in the medieval church is set next to Bullinger's treatise on the fall of the Jews who had turned to the gods of Egypt and Canaan. Elijah had destroyed the prophets of Baal in his day. Now Zwingli, the "idol-smasher and impious iconoclast," performed the work of Elijah.[24]

II. Prophets and the Apocalypse

What Bullinger writes about elsewhere and in particular in *The Origin of Error,* in terms of prophets and covenants, is applied affectively to history in his sermons on the Apocalypse. However, all is not rhetoric. We learn in the preface not only of his long interest in the Apocalypse, but that it is a revelation of Jesus Christ. The doctrine found therein is the same as that taught elsewhere in Scripture. The Apocalypse, a "paraphrase" of the prophets, directs us to Christ and his work. Bullinger writes, "And I doubt whether there exists in the canonical books after the prophecy of Isaiah, after the story of the gospel, but especially after the Gospel of blessed John any other book which has more or more elegant descriptions of Christ than this book."[25]

Bullinger is aware of the affective nature of the book. The Apocalypse is simply "more painted, variable and polished" than the Gospels and epistles. Nevertheless, its doctrine is the same. The Apocalypse tells the real story of the Church by summarizing the intent of the prophets for the new dispensation. Its style is generally different from the rest of Scripture, although analogies exist. It is visionary like Daniel as well as representing a skillful exposition of Scripture itself. This concept of prophetic vision inevitably drives the expositor back to the rest of Scripture: "For this book on account of the predictions of things to come is a prophecy of the New Testament. Moreover, a prophecy, that is, an exposition which opens up and illustrates the old prophets."[26] The affective nature of prophetic vision is appropriate to times of crisis. For a community faced with the loss of coherence and identity, apocalyptic literature has offered a means of inno-

24. *De origine erroris,* fol. 94r, 46r; ref. to Zwingli, 132r.
25. *In Apocalypsim,* sig. A6v; pp. 6, 126.
26. Ibid., 8.

vating upon the past while retaining inherited Christian goals. In days threatened by imminent disaster, as Israel faced them in the time of Moses or Elijah, God makes his presence known to his Church by sending prophets. "They shall preach Christ sincerely and accuse Antichrist most severely. These he shadows by the figure of the two excellent doctors who, he says, because of their liberty of preaching and constancy of faith, must be most cruelly slain by Antichrist."[27] Strength is given to Bullinger's argument by the way in which he finds a continuity of prophets in history, a point that we cannot dwell upon here. When preachers are slain, God provides others.[28] The point is that the fate of God's prophets directs our attention back to the Old Testament and its demonstration of the character of God's work with Israel much as does Stephen's speech in Acts 7 or the argument of the author of Hebrews in 11:1–12:2.[29]

Furthermore, the style of the Apocalypse is related to its purpose: not the presentation of new knowledge but a rephrasing of what has been known since the covenant was first laid down. "The sum and end of this Scripture is this, that Jesus Christ our Lord will never fail his church on earth but will govern it with his spirit and word through the ecclesiastical ministry. But that the church itself, while it remains in the world, shall suffer many things for the confession of Christ and the truth of his gospel."[30]

The way in which Bullinger structures this series emphasizes the consolation of Christ and spiritual function of the ministry in every age, particularly the last and most severe, perhaps his own. (1) The first four sermons deal with the title and prologue of the Apocalypse. They serve as an introduction and foundation for the rest of the series. (2) The second section, sermons 5-22, develop Bullinger's central conception of Christ ruling his church (Rev. 1:12–3:22). The letters to the seven churches provide a theological checklist for what Christ desires of his church. (3) The third section, sermons 23-50 (Rev. 4–11), illustrates how God governs the world through Christ. Here the destiny of the church is presented: persecution and martyrdom are its lot as the faithful do battle with Antichrist, but consolation is envisioned through the imagery presented in chaps. 10 and 11. Here the regnant Christ is shown to stand with faithful preachers, their lot difficult in history but ultimately triumphant. (4) The conflict between such preachers and Antichrist is described in greater detail in the fourth division, sermons 51-65 (Rev. 12–14). While this section is not without its

27. Ibid., sig. A4r.
28. Ibid., sig. A2r; cf. 132-36.
29. Ibid., 102-4, 123-25; see sermon 36 on tribulation in the life of the Christian.
30. Ibid., sig. A2r; 105, 108-10, 112, 122.

own consolation (chap. 14), the emphasis is upon the nature of the Beast described therein and the parallel that Bullinger draws between old Rome and new Rome: the old political power with its manifest idolatry and the new shadow state with its idolatry centered in the papacy. (5) In the fifth division, sermons 66-95 (Rev. 15–22), Bullinger delineates the torments of the ungodly and the rewards of the righteous. (6) Finally, the last several sermons (Rev. 22:6-21) commend the book to its readers.

Although following the text, the way in which Bullinger has structured his commentary lends further affective strength to his conception of prophets and to their role in sixteenth-century society. In contrast with the three woes (Rev. 9:1ff., the greatest dangers facing the church since John's day, the papacy, the rise of Islam, and the Last Judgment), Bullinger finds three comforts in chap. 10: (1) the person and work of Christ, (2) the comfort of Scripture and preaching, and (3) the promise of restoration before the end. This restoration is said to be adumbrated under the person of the Evangelist John: "For under the person of John it is shown here that the evangelical and apostolic doctrine must be restored against Antichrist and Mohammed in the last times before the judgment."[31] This comfort lends polemical strength to the Reformed idea of the prophet or, we might say, to the preacher and pastor, without carefully delineating among these three titles at this point. John is told to preach again (10:11), a promise that he would yet preach after his exile. This is also a promise that before the Last Judgment preachers will preach before Antichrist with the spirit and doctrine of John, pictured more fully in 11:1-13. This last-named text, an occasion for the development of sermons on the characteristics of the Reformed ministry, will in later and dependent exegetes be used as warrant for even book-length monographs on emergent Protestantism.[32]

The first of such characteristics to which Bullinger draws our attention are the spiritual qualities of these prophets. Drawing attention to Rev. 11, Bullinger cites Aretas (following in the Tyconian tradition), approving of his emphasis upon the appearance of preachers, the two unnamed "witnesses" of the text, as being in the spirit of Enoch and Elijah, not of their

31. Ibid., 132.

32. See chap. 4 and the epilogue of my dissertation, "Preaching in the Last Days." Of note for American church and social history, by way of example on the importance of this text, are works by Thomas Goodwin, John Cotton, and Roger Williams on the place of such advental witnesses in early colonial history and, a little later, on the place of the advental witnesses in defining the nature of the Great Awakening for Jonathan Edwards. Finally, Moses Stuart (1780-1852), champion of Trinitarian theology at the early Andover Seminary and indefatigable biblical scholar, found pictured under the image of the advental witnesses (11:1-13) the whole history of Protestantism.

actual persons returning bodily to earth as is alleged by many common people: "Aretas . . . notes that from this text in John's book arose the opinion of the common people that John together with Enoch and Elijah would come again into the world before the judgment, i.e., corporally, and would preach earnestly and constantly against Antichrist."[33] The spiritual qualities of Enoch and Elijah, now used to provide the identity for final preachers, or adventual witnesses, in the world indicate the nature of the expected renewal.

Consider what is offered in each of these spiritual types. The person of Enoch, drawn from Genesis (given added significance in Sir. 44), was such that through him we might learn of another life for the servants of God in his deathless translation to heaven. This, we learn, was a polemic against the "Epicureans" who believe that there is no other life than this. However, Bullinger contends, while many argue that Enoch is preserved in heaven in order to return corporally in the last days: "Here Enoch is seen to come spiritually to that last age . . . similar to the one which preceded the Flood. For just as then most people despised the divine judgments, . . . even so it is in the last age, in which Enoch constantly preaches in the person of those who build up and defend eternal life and the resurrection of the body against the Epicureans. Enoch symbolizes such a warning and a witness."[34]

Elijah became a model for the work of the prophet against idolatry.[35] Bullinger's conception of the latter-day Elijah follows Aretas, thus buttressing his position with what he believes to have been patristic precedent.[36] As in the case of Enoch, there is not to be a return of Elijah the

33. *In Apocalypsim:* "Aretas Caesariensis episcopus, interpres huius libri, commemorat ex hoc Ioannis loco exortam esse uulgi opinionem, arbitrantis Ioannem cum Enoch & Helia ante iudicium in hunc mundum rediturum, nimirum corporaliter, Praedicaturumque acriter & constanter contra Antichristum. Id ipsum repetit copiosiore expositione Aretas, cum in 11 cap. ennarat uerba Ioannis de dubo. testibus, etc." (133). Aretas's commentary, frequently cited by Bullinger, was first published as a Catena of Oecumenius in 1532 and illustrates a Greek patristic influence upon Bullinger similar to that to which Susi Hausamann draws attention in her analysis of Bullinger's commentary on Romans (*Die Römerbriefauslegung zwischen Humanismus und Reformation* [Zürich: Zwingli Verlag, 1970], 66-88; cf. Polman, *L'Elément,* 95-109).

34. *In Apocalypsim*: "His Enoch uidetur spiritualiter redire ad seculum illud postremum, quod ipse Dominus simile futurum praedixit ei quod iudicia contempserunt: ita sit & in ultimo secculo, in quo Enoch constanter praedicat per illos qui uitam aeternam & resurrectionem corporum contra Epicureos astruunt atque propugnant" (133); cf. Bullinger, *Epitome,* fol. 5v-6r.

35. *In Apocalypsim*: "Spiritus ergo Heliae, & acrimonia predicationis Heliae, *ein ernsthafft, dapffer, unuerzagt scharpff prediger,* est rugitus ille leonis, qui rugit ueritatem Christi" (128). Further examples of Elijah as a model for righteous preaching are given, cf. sermons 12, 31, 33, 60, 89.

36. Ibid., 132-33. Cf. Bullinger's views with two whom he cites, the first frequently (both dependent upon Tyconius): (1) Francis Lambert, *Exegeseos in sanctam divi Joannis*

Tishbite prior to the end of the age. The historical Elijah is not "thrust out of the heavenly palace, and again subject to corruption, and given to the cruel hands of antichristians who might tear him to pieces." Rather, as Elijah appeared in strength and power in John the Baptist, the forerunner of Christ's first advent, so Elijah's preaching will be heard again before the Last Judgment. Latter-day preachers will be filled with the spirit and power of Elijah. They will call people away from idolatry in a way similar to that of Elijah the Tishbite in the days of Ahab and Jezebel: "Now the Elijahs will cry: if Christ is the perfection of the faithful, what need is there for man's inventions and constitutions in order to work perfection? If Christ is our justification, satisfaction, purification, our only intercessor and redeemer, why are these things attributed to human merit?"[37]

Similarly, a third person also frequently referred to in relation to Rev. 11 in the history of the exegesis of this text is the Evangelist John. Bullinger argues that John will not return bodily to earth, but that preachers filled with John's doctrine will preach the truth out of John's Gospel, Epistles, and Apocalypse.[38] These preachers or prophets of the Last Days will offer the consolation of Enoch, the judgment of Elijah, and be filled with the doctrine of the Evangelist John. These each become models for the new Protestant ministry.

Second, in addition to their spiritual qualities, the generality of their persons and specificity of their work leads to communal restoration. If this restoration, or restitution, appears strange, Bullinger writes, it is because of a general unfamiliarity with the book of Revelation, even condemned in recent years, by good and learned men.[39] John's call to preach against Antichrist's wickedness, found in the examples of Enoch, Elijah, and John, epitomizes the commission given to others to preach in their times. First, his call is from God; John was told to preach. In a similar way Moses was called, and so are all prophets and apostles. Second, to the one who is called a commandment is given to take the book (Rev. 10:18). This is not merely any book, but the one lying in Christ's (the mighty angel's) hand,

---

Apocalypsim (Marburg, 1528). Lambert writes on the identity of the witnesses that he neither agrees nor disagrees with the possibility that they are Enoch and Elijah or two that will come with their spirit and power. He writes speculatively that they are two clear and distinguished evangelists who appear as John appeared prior to the first advent of Christ. He prefers to find here a type of all that faithful testimony which the church needs to hear at times of satanic work. (2) Sebastian Meyer, *In Apocalypsim Iohannis* (Zürich: Froschauer, 1554). The first edition of this commentary appeared in 1539. Meyer writes that the witnesses are those who preach in the spirit of Elijah during the time of Antichrist (fol. 41r).

37. *In Apocalypsim*, 132-34; cf. *Epitome*, fol. 52r-53r.

38. *In Apocalypsim*, 133.

39. Ibid., 2, 133; an elliptical reference to Zwingli?

i.e., the holy Scriptures, the sum of faith and doctrine.[40] Ministers must obey the commandment of God to take the book and seek to understand the Scriptures. Earlier Bullinger explained that Christ stands before us with his book open although Antichrist desires to see it shut. However, Antichrist cannot shut this gospel book which lies open in these days through preaching and printing.[41]

The specificity of their work, their preaching or "prophesying," follows the lines Bullinger laid down in *De prophetae officio,* a work of his that he also cites in this series of sermons. Prophets teach, admonish, and console as did the Evangelist John, Elijah, and Enoch.[42] They are provided by God in order to rebuild his church. This message of consolation is carried over into Rev. 11 with the vision of the measurement of the temple (11:1-2).[43] As Israel's temple had been devastated by the Chaldeans, church and Christendom today lay wasted by Papists and Turks.[44] The Pope and his priests are like the heathen. Rather than explain, they impugn the Scriptures. They are permitted by God to trample over the holy city, i.e., persecute the church, but only for a limited time. This period is spoken of as lasting 42 months, a number simply indicative of the limitation to times of tribulation,[45] perhaps running from A.D. 666 (a number given mysterious significance in Rev. 13:18).[46] In commenting on Rev. 11:3-6, Bullinger writes that throughout this time the Lord will send prophets, i.e., preachers who will maintain and defend the truth of the gospel glorifying Christ. They will attack Antichrist, destroying his kingdom.[47]

40. Ibid., 134, 140-41. See Bullinger's contemporary, Theodor Bibliander, who associates our preachers (the witnesses of Rev. 11) with the Scriptures (*Ad omnium ordinum,* 138).

41. Ibid., 128, 198-99. The importance of printing in promoting the work of reform is emphasized by Bullinger and other Protestant Reformers as part of the restoration of the gospel in the latter days.

42. Ibid., 132-36.

43. This is not the old temple of Jerusalem, destroyed for good, but the church. Bullinger draws our attention to Exod. 40, the envisioned new temple and those sealed from destruction in Ezek. 9:4 and Rev. 7:3 (136). By way of comparison bearing upon ecclesiological implications, see Hans Hut's use of these texts in Gottfried Seebass, "Müntzers Erbe. Werk, Leben und Theologie des Hans Hut" (ms. Erlangen, 1972), pt. 1, 397-99.

44. *In Apocalypsim,* 136, 138.

45. Ibid., 138.

46. Ibid., 138, 193; cf. Polman, *L'Elément,* 176-77.

47. *In Apocalypsim,* 139-49. Luther had led the way in attempting to mark the development of Antichrist in the office of the bishop of Rome. Much of the speculation concerning Antichrist became summarized in the work by Lambert Daneau, *Tractatus de Antichristo . . .* (1576), published in many languages and editions (see in *Opuscula omnia theologica* [Geneva, 1583], 1049-92); cf. Olivier Fatio, *Méthode et théologie: Lambert Daneau et les débuts de la scholastique réformée* (Geneva: Droz, 1976).

Third, the nature of their moral identity gives shape to their work. The appearance of these witnesses gives visual power to the identity of Bullinger's preachers. One might reach back to Tyconius to find a precedent once again for the interpretation of these texts. For example, our preachers are spoken of as "two," implying "that the power of Christ in the world is small in the eyes of the worldly." The appearance of the prophets in sackcloth underscores their diminutive status before the world. They are dressed as penitents for mourning. Faithful ministers and pastors who resist Antichrist at all times will appear this way. We are reminded by such dress of the prophets of old, particularly Enoch or Elijah, but we are not to look for their bodily return, Bullinger again advises. Rather, as Jerome counselled Marcella, we should look for the spiritual interpretation of the text and not follow "Jewish" fables.[48]

The further imagery of the text reminds one of the renewal experienced by Israel following her return from the Babylonian captivity (Zech. 2:1-5; 4:3-14). As God remembered Israel in the closing days of the old dispensation, so he is remembering the new Israel in the sixteenth century. The images of the two olive trees and candlesticks standing before God (Rev. 11:4) reflect Zechariah (4:3-14) and his intent to describe the anointed ones (Zech. 4:14) to whom is given the task of national reconstruction.[49] Through God's Spirit Zerubbabel (godly prophet and prince) in the restored Jewish community, i.e., the golden lampstand and the two olive trees, carries with it connotations of national righteousness and renewal that reach back to Israel's earliest days (cf. Exod. 25:31-40) and carry us through the old dispensation into the new. Prophetic types point the way toward reform, the renewal of the church, and reconstruction of Christendom.[50] Such thinking draws us back to the initial covenant between God and man.

With the vision come the gifts. Our adventual witnesses are equipped with God's Word. They will speak out of the Scriptures destroying their enemies "with the fire that goes out of their mouth." Like Elijah they have the power to shut up the heavens, withholding the rain of God's grace (where preachers are not heard, God's grace is not received).[51] Like Moses

48. *In Apocalypsim*: "Duos autem producit prophetas, id est praedicatores: non quod duo duntaxat sint futuri, sed quod ita uelit innuere copias Christi in mundo fore & uideri mundanis exiguas . . . omnes omnium temporum fideles concionatores & pastores, qui se opponunt & Antichristo & haeresibus. Sunt qui haec exponant de Enoch & Helia, corporaliter uenturis ante iudicium. Caeterum Hieronymus in epistola ad Marcellam, eam opinionem refert ad fabulas Iudaicas significans spiritualiter haec de prophetis his, ut & pleraque libri huius esse exponenda" (139).

49. Ibid., 141.

50. Ibid., 136.

51. Ibid., 142; cf. 141. In his sermon on Rev. 2:1-3, Bullinger reminds us that Christ,

they have the power to turn water into blood, i.e., godly wisdom, grace, and relief. The text implies that those who do not turn to Christ at the preaching of the prophets bring down damnation upon themselves.[52] In striking the earth with plagues, our preachers, like Moses, demonstrate that God will punish sins with plagues. Finally, like Jeremiah, these witnesses are known for the strength of their preaching.[53] In ministers in whom these marks are seen one may find lawful prophets of God.

These gifts symbolize Protestant spirituality in the period lying before us: power through the Word, grace through preaching, damnation through rejection, and plagues for impenitence. It is with these formidable weapons that the new temple is to be constructed. Christ vows that in the Latter Days his church will be rebuilt through his ministers, though their number be small. Here is the measured "restitution" sought. Their work is that of Enoch and Elijah, Joshua and Zerubbabel, Moses and Jeremiah. In fulfilling their task, "they imagine nothing out of their own minds, neither add to nor take away anything from God's word, but simply declare to the church of God the things they have seen in the story of the gospels and heard from prophets and apostles."[54] One sees such, Bullinger continues, in the work of "D. Luther and D. Zwingli and other faithful witnesses of God."[55]

Fourth, we may say that contemporary history warranted a contemporary application of the text in Bullinger's view. Individual prophets may be slain (11:7-10) but new ones are raised up in order to proclaim the truth. Antichrist does not triumph by Scripture, testimony, or reason but by force. He fights using carnal weapons. Preachers will be dealt with cruelly just as Christ and his apostles suffered under old Rome. Indeed, the bodies of the faithful will be left unburied as is happening today: this is a day of martyrs comparable to the days of Constance when Hus and Jerome of Prague were burnt.[56] Today, Bullinger writes, martyrs are falling in En-

---

not the Pope, carries the keys to heaven and hell; that Christ has delegated his power to his preachers (ibid., 263-68).

52. Ibid., 142.

53. Ibid., 143.

54. Ibid., 139-40.

55. Ibid.: "Huic agemus gratias, quod diu multi praedicatores boni & hodie D. Luthurus & D. Zwinglius, & alii testes Dei fideles, in tam conscelerato seculo, & in tanta Antichristi potentia, tot annis, inuitis etiam inferorum portis, ministerio suo defungi potuerunt" (144).

56. Ibid., 144-46: "Audiuimus hodie, post Angliam relapsam ad sedem, & commotam grauissimam in membra Christi persequtionem, quanta gaudia & tripudia quantos denique triumphos ubique omnes egerint Papistae. Quoties comburuntur ministri aut fideles, illi ipsi festa mox agunt & conuiuantur in dulci iubilio, concinentes, Te Deum laudamus. Volitant ultro citroque literae gratulatoriae. Alicubi praecessionibus instructis sibi de miseria fidelium

gland. But, no matter how great the grief caused by Antichrist, God promises to continue to send his witnesses. Recent days appear to offer this consolation. The resurrection of the witnesses (11:11) illustrates God's promise of new prophets and of our future resurrection. Such was seen in John Hus, Jerome of Prague, Lorenzo Valla, and Savonarola. Now, beginning "thirty years ago, . . . Mirandola, Reuchlin, Erasmus, Luther, Zwingli, Oecolampadius, Melanchthon, and innumerable others brought light to the world. In them the spirit of life expressing itself after every man's talent, set forth the scriptures, detected the Romish wickedness, and rebuked the vices of all states, but expecially of the clergy."[57]

The kingdom of Antichrist is under full attack, Bullinger writes; the sack of Rome (1527) appears to answer to the earthquake and destruction of the tenth of the city spoken of in our text (Rev. 11:13). The faithful preachers raised up by Bullinger are in some way both illustrative of God's faithfulness in all ages yet tinged by a sense of proximity to history's end, again a tension one can discern in the patristic exegete Tyconius.[58] The Apocalypse appears to present a progression toward a final conflict. Believing the present to be in some way participant in the end brings out a tension inherent in the Tyconian tradition between the perennial spiritual truth of the Apocalypse and its specific applicability for the Last Days simply from the placement of the texts themselves. Bullinger appears to argue that his is the time above all others for the adventual witnesses. They stand at the threshold of a measure of restitution, at least the renewal of evangelical preaching prior to the Last Judgment, while error and wickedness in society intensify.[59]

---

gratulantur. At uidet haec Dominus, qui eadem in praesenti futura praedixit" (146). Robert Horn and Richard Chambers write to Bullinger (9 Sept. 1556), "all things seem to be growing worse and worse. So great is the number of martyrs, who in their cheerful profession of the word of God are most cruelly dragged to the flames and to torments," in Hastings Robinson, ed., *Original Letters Relative to the English Reformation* (Cambridge: Cambridge University Press, 1842-1847), 1:132.

57. *In Apocalypsim*, 148.

58. Ibid., 155-58, 167, and Bullinger, *Daniel,* fol. 77r-80v. While Bullinger argues against millennialism and millenarian conceptions of history associated with Joachim of Fiore (sermons 86-89), he is quite willing to use Joachim's conception of Antichrist in his polemic against the papacy. A tension in historical perspective upon the progressive development (or devolution) of history is set down here with which later apocalyptic theologians will wrestle.

59. *In Apocalypsim*, 146; cf. sig. B2v. This was held by Luther on the basis of Rev. 10:11 (WA [DB], 7:403ff.).

V. MODERN QUESTIONS OF BIBLICAL HERMENEUTICS

16. Teaching History through Preaching: Some Patterns of Historical Interpretation in the Sermons of the Lutheran Pastor Heinrich Fröhlich (1826-1881)

Klaus Fröhlich

Translated by Johanna Froehlich Swartzentruber

Thus, histories and tales contain all manner of laws, art, good counsel, warning, threat, intimidation, comfort, affirmation, instruction, caution, wisdom, prudence along with all the virtues, flowing as from a living spring. That is, histories are nothing other than an indication, memorial and sign of God's works and judgments; how he sustains, governs, hinders, promotes, punishes and honors the world and human beings in particular, according to what each one deserves — good or evil.

— Martin Luther[1]

1. From Luther's preface to "Historia Galeatii Capellae" (1538), in *D. Martin Luthers Werke* WA, 50:83ff.

My thanks are due to Princeton Theological Seminary, and to the chairmen of the symposium, Mark Burrows and Paul Rorem. My wife and I were honored to be invited as representatives of the Froehlich family from Germany. I would like to dedicate this essay to Princeton Seminary and all its scholars, who represent the expertise, collegial spirit, and generous hospitality which we so abundantly experienced in Princeton.

In every piece of memory there lies a bit of salvation.

— Jörn Rüsen[2]

I

The idea for this study originated during the symposium which was held at Princeton Theological Seminary in May 1990 on the occasion of the 60th birthday of my brother, Karlfried Froehlich. As I read the lecture texts and attempted to follow the wide-ranging discussions as well as my status as a theological layman and my limited command of the language would allow, the question arose in my mind as to what sense of history — what particular historical understanding — was presupposed by the examples of biblical interpretation being analyzed and by the various positions represented in the discussions. This is not a new question, and answers were not lacking in the contributions to the symposium: it was, after all, dedicated to the history of biblical interpretation — and the experts in this field know all too well that they are not dealing in eternal truths but in historical contingencies.

This is the question I propose to deal with here, but in a narrower, more specific framework. I will examine how historical elements are used in the articulation of the religious consciousness of a particular time and place, and how their form and content is shaped by this context. In other words, how is historical consciousness structured and how does it function in the religious interpretation of a given cultural framework? The material I will discuss bears directly on the topic of the symposium, and has a personal significance for Karlfried Froehlich. Its genre locates it in the field of biblical interpretation: sermons from the second half of the nineteenth century, which present themselves as proclamation of the Word of God and upon formal examination reveal themselves as practical biblical interpretation. A personal link to the symposium's honoree exists because these sermons were held at weekly services from 1860 to 1865 by Karlfried's great-grandfather Heinrich Fröhlich during his years as pastor of the Lutheran diaconal convent in Dresden.[3]

2. Jörn Rüsen, *Zeit und Sinn. Strategien historischen Denkens* (Frankfurt, 1990), 12.

3. The texts of thirty sermons by Heinrich Fröhlich are extant in the Fröhlich family archives in Bochum. Their length varies from 6 to 17 manuscript pages. With the exception of two sermons, they are numbered sequentially as part of a much more extensive collection, the rest of which is lost. (Cf. the index of the extant numbers in the Appendix, pp. 287-90 below.) The last sermon, preserved separately and dated September 5, 1880, seems to be the only one in Heinrich Fröhlich's own hand. The rest are all in a single hand, with the exception

The methods of this study may differ in some respects from those of a theological analysis, though I do not think they are far from those which a church historian might employ. I will not, however, be searching for theological or church-historical connections in a narrow sense; rather, I will seek to interpret these sermons from the standpoint of the history of *mentalité*, as an expression of a consciousness in which the historical imagination is mobilized to make sense of the demands of contemporary life and to guide listeners in their response to these demands. I will seek to identify the passages in which the preacher presents the events of the past and explains their significance for the present and future life of believers. For that is what historical thought consists of: it presents past occurrences as part of a temporal context, so that one's own present gains a meaningful place in a historical framework, and a future within certain parameters can be expected. "Historical thought makes sense of time. It makes [historical] contingencies conform to [contemporary] action."[4]

In this respect, any biblical interpretation, being a statement about texts from the past, contains at least elements of historical thought where the significance of these historical texts for the present and future is indicated. Such passages are not difficult to find in the sermons under discussion: they are the points at which events in the past are discussed in the form of a story (narration) which is structured according to explicit or implicit criteria of meaning.[5] Merely pointing out these formal structures, however, does not answer the question as to their actual function in the given cultural context. The practical nature of these sermons — or, to put it another way, their exemplification of a *mentalité* — becomes tangible only when they are understood as the specific expression of the desire of the pastor and his

---

of a few passages in 53. A few of the manuscripts are signed with the initials G.Z. (?) In a personal footnote to 6 the writer reveals his identity as a confirmand of the year 1821, from which a birthdate of ca. 1807 can be postulated. It seems probable that the documentation of the sermons was discontinued in 1865 because "G.Z." was no longer available.

4. Rüsen, *Zeit und Sinn*, 11. For a historical theory cf. also idem, *Historische Vernunft. Grundzüge einer Historik I: Die Grundlagen der Geschichtswissenschaft* (Göttingen, 1983); idem, *Lebendige Geschichte. Grundzüge einer Historik III: Formen und Funktionen des historischen Wissens* (Göttingen, 1989).

5. Historical passages are distinguished from dogmatic and other systematic or speculative utterances by their narrative structure. Historical thinking is articulated in the form of narrative tales in which real or supposedly real events of the past are located in a meaningful temporal structure (cf. Hans Michael Baumgartner, "Narrativität," in *Handbuch der Geschichtsdidaktik*, ed. Klaus Bergman et al., 3d ed. [Düsseldorf, 1985], 146-49). With reference to the structures of meaning, Rüsen differentiates between four types of historical narrative: the traditional, the exemplary, the critical, and the generic. Cf. in detail Jörn Rüsen, *Die vier Typen des historischen Erzählens* (1983), repr. in *Zeit und Sinn*, 153-230. In what follows, I will use this typology to classify the patterns of historical interpretation used in the sermons.

congregation to place their concrete historical situation into a larger context. To clarify this idea, I would like to introduce the concept of "piety," well known in the fields of the history and psychology of religions. What I mean by piety is that extremely subjective mental structure which encompasses knowledge and behavior and according to which all the circumstances and demands of a given life are interpreted in the light of the relationship between God and humankind. In the words of Schleiermacher, it is "the consciousness of being absolutely dependent, or, which is the same thing, of being in relation with God."[6] A "pious" or "religious" mentality, then, seeks to answer the central question of life — namely, how one is to live justly in one's own time — by reflecting on the current status of one's relationship to God. Articulations of this mindset abound in the sermons of Heinrich Fröhlich: for example, interpreting disturbing trends — such as the growing number of illegitimate births — as calls to repentance, or warning against "visual lust, fleshly lust, and vain comportment" in the light of the younger generation's appetite for pleasure. The historic dimension is apparent not only in the constant references to biblical stories, the early church, the Reformation, and Luther's teaching on justification, but also in the expression of very concrete eschatological expectations.

The sermons of Heinrich Fröhlich are particularly suited for the analysis of *mentalité*, described above, for several reasons. First, they are not "model" sermons, written to impress the general public; and they do not, as far as I can judge, exhibit any significant theological or homiletical originality. That is their greatest advantage, for they may safely be taken as testimony for the weekly Sunday practice of a Lutheran preacher in Saxony during the second half of the 19th century. Second, they were prepared with exceptional care and documented in detail, which makes their methodical analysis considerably easier. Third, we have some knowledge of the circumstances under which they were composed. To clarify this context (and also as a personal historical footnote), I will begin with a summary of the life and work of Heinrich Fröhlich, to the extent that it seems relevant to the issue at hand.

From 1856 until his premature death in 1881, Heinrich Fröhlich was pastor and rector of the diaconal convent and its adjunct institutions in Dresden.[7] He had been born in

6. Friedrich Schleiermacher, *The Christian Faith,* 2 vols. (New York: Harper, 1963), 1:12, heading for sec. 4. Cf. the summary in H. R. G. Günther, "Frömmigkeit," *RGG,* 3d ed. (1958), 2:1158-63.

7. Unfortunately, the archive of the diaconal convent was completely destroyed by fire in the bombing of Dresden on Feb. 12 and 13, 1945. Besides the sermons, no further personal documentation is extant in the family archives. Thus we are completely dependent upon the

Kamenz, where his father served in the military, in 1826. As a Saxon soldier, Heinrich's father fought in several of Napoleon's campaigns, including the fateful battle of Leipzig in 1813: this became something of a family legend for succeeding generations.[8] After his discharge in 1829 he made a modest living in various parts of Saxony as a franchised collector of crown tolls. His son Heinrich was the first of the family who had an opportunity to move up into the educated upper classes through his study of theology — a situation not uncommon in 19th-century Europe. He founded a dynasty of Saxon theologians spanning four generations of the Fröhlich family, all of whom — with the exception of Karlfried, the last in the succession — held posts as pastors in parishes of the Lutheran church in Saxony.

As a theologian, Heinrich Fröhlich was marked by the German revival movement in its Lutheran form. During his studies at Leipzig he was deeply influenced by Adolf von Harless; until the end of his life, his sermons exhibit a lively antirationalistic and literalistic streak and place great emphasis on the confessional books of the Reformation. After a few years as a private tutor, Fröhlich was called to Dresden in 1853 by Count Detlef von Einsiedel to become Secretary of the Saxon Central Bible Society. His call to the diaconal convent in 1856 was probably also due to the recommendation of Einsiedel; the position meant his promotion to the officially recognized duties of pastor and hospital chaplain. The scope of Fröhlich's pastoral work is fully encompassed by this description. He was working in the area of Christian charitable activity as it was beginning to be defined within the Saxon state church at that time through the institutions of its so-called Internal Mission branch. In organizing the work of this institution, Fröhlich looked especially to Theodor Fliedner and his institutions at Kaiserswerth.[9] For guidance in pedagogical and theological matters, Fröhlich turned to Wilhelm Löhe, the founder of Neuendettelsau, who is supposed to have said of him: "What I had intended, Fröhlich has executed."[10]

Although Fröhlich never expanded his sphere of influence beyond the confines of the church and its various institutions, and took special care to keep his distance from such "worldly matters" as the politics of the time, he was — due to his advan-

published material for our information: Gustav Molwitz, *Kirchenrat P. Joh. Karl Heinrich Fröhlich, Rector der ev.-luth. Diakonissen-Anstalt zu Dresden. Ein Lebensbild* (Dresden, repr. from "Phöbe," 1882); idem, *Zur Erinnerung an Kirchenrath P. Joh. Karl Heinr. Fröhlich* (Leipzig, 1881; repr. from "Pilger in Sachsen"); Jubiläums-Bericht der evangelisch-lutherischen Diakonissenanstalt zu Dresden, given by Pastor G. Molwitz, Dresden (1894).

8. Cf. Molwitz, *Lebensbild*, 4. Heinrich's father is presented here as having participated in the "wars of liberation" and to have distinguished himself in the battle of Leipzig by his "bravery and courage." Molwitz is suggesting that Heinrich's father played a part in liberating his fatherland from foreign tyranny; what he fails to mention is that as a Saxon soldier, Heinrich's father most certainly would have fought on the side of Napoleon — the enemy side to anyone with patriotic inclinations!

9. The founding of the Dresden house had already had Fliedner's support; he had sent two of his sisters from Kaiserswerth there. Before taking office, Fröhlich paid him a visit to gather information; afterward, he asked Fliedner for the hand of Kedwig von Zedtwitz, a young Sister of Kaiserswerth, to become his wife and the head of the Dresden house. They were married in 1857, and the pastor's wife fulfilled the office of house manager until 1884.

10. Molwitz, *Lebensbild*, 32.

tageous connections — firmly ensconced in those influential Saxon circles whose religious revivalism and political reactionism were paired with a markedly conservative social agenda.[11] Fröhlich's sermons are permeated with the sentiments of this position, which saw in the liberal and revolutionary currents of its time nothing but the interference of vainglorious Reason in the God-given order. His management of the convent shows the same consistency. Upon taking office, he and the Count von Einsiedel immediately transferred the responsibility for its administration from the committee of women which had been in charge to a board "made up of men." The women's committee continued to exist, its jurisdiction limited to "those responsibilities with respect to the convent which are particular to the calling of women."[12] The convent's cleric was an ex-officio member of the board and functioned as a sort of superintendent or general manager; he thus united in his person both spiritual and secular power over the entire institution.

It must be admitted that the patriarchal regime which Heinrich Fröhlich headed during his twenty-five years in office turned out to be extremely successful in both spheres. Under his leadership the mother house and its hospice were expanded several times and a number of daughter institutions were acquired and integrated; moreover, the field of activity of the sisters trained at the convent was considerably enlarged. Besides caring for patients in hospitals, they became parish nurses and set up "Bethesda houses" to care for those with wasting diseases, cripples, the mentally ill, and epileptics; they also ran "Magdalen sanctuaries" for the rehabilitation of homeless girls, and craft or homemaking schools for daughters of poorer families as well as day-care centers and other facilities. During Fröhlich's years in office, thirty-four permanent and sixty-nine temporary stations were set up. The Dresden convent sent its sisters to places far beyond Saxony: to Prussia and the Baltic provinces of the Russian Empire, and even to Finland and St. Petersburg. The number of sisters trained in the house increased from 22 in 1856 to 216 in 1881.[13]

Even more than for his administrative feats, Fröhlich, "hard-working and overworked,"[14] was admired for his spiritual leadership. The lasting Lutheran bent of the Dresden institute as well as the grounding of its diaconal work in God's Word and the life of the Church are ascribed to his influence.[15] The work of the house was supported

11. This is true especially of the Count von Einsiedel, who until the revolution in 1830 had been Prime Minister and chief consultant to the king; since that time he had been considered the leader of the reactionary movement in Saxony. For his pivotal role in the revival movement, see Karl Hennig, *Die sächsische Erweckungsbewegung im Anfange des 19. Jahrhunderts.* (Phil. diss., Leipzig, 1929), 150-62. Molwitz describes the close relationship with the diaconal house in *Lebensbild,* 14-20.

12. Cited in *Jubiläums-Bericht,* 34.

13. Ibid., 225ff., 135.

14. From the memorial to "the honorable fathers of our diaconal work, who rest in God," on the occasion of the anniversary of the institution at Kaiserswerth in 1886, cited in *Kleine Chronik des Diakonissen-Mutterhauses in Dresden,* 1886, 3rd quarter, p. 3.

15. See Paul Drews, *Das kirchliche Leben der Evangelisch-Lutherischen Landeskirche des Königreichs Sachsen* (Tübingen/Leipzig, 1902), 114; Franz Blanckmeister, *Sächsische Kirchengeschichte,* 2d ed. (Dresden, 1906), 425; and finally the memorial article in *Der Sonntag. Gemeindeblatt der Evangelisch-lutherischen Landeskirche Sachsen,* vol. 16, no. 18 (March 26, 1961).

by three pillars: a communal life under a Christian patriarchy which created a comfortable, familial atmosphere through nursing instruction, constant pastoral dialogue both at home and with daughter institutions, and the rhythm of common work — and which also guaranteed a large measure of spiritual and social control; a program of Bible study consisting of weekly sessions of Bible discussion according to Spener's model; and, at its center, the liturgical cycle of worship services determined by the church year, to which Fröhlich devoted particular attention.[16] The heart of these services was the sermon, understood quite literally by the pastor as the proclamation of the "pure and unadulterated Word of God," and presented accordingly. Through his sermons which Sunday after Sunday drew large numbers of worshipers from the town and the more distant villages into the small diaconal church, dedicated in 1857, Fröhlich can be said to have formed a parish — though as an offshoot of a charitable organization the diaconal institute was never officially recognized as such. His sermons, moreover, were the main channel by which the diaconal house communicated with the general public.

We will now examine these sermons in detail by considering the general question of the concept of history they exhibit and the more specific question of their *mentalité.* Here we shall consider: (1) to what extent the sermons can be called texts about history, and what patterns of historical interpretation predominate ("historical preaching as instruction in the Christian life"); (2) how the sermons perceive contemporary experience and integrate it into an assumed historical pattern ("preaching history as response to the crisis of modernization").

II

If Paul Drews's characterization of a Saxon way of preaching is accurate,[17] Heinrich Fröhlich was a Saxon preacher par excellence. All of his sermons distinguish themselves through their strict adherence to proper homiletic form. An *exordium* is almost always present; the reading of the text, which is always from Scripture, follows. A *transitus* leads into the topic of the sermon and to the *propositio* of its parts. In the interpretation, the analytic-synthetic method predominates; the topic flows directly from the text and is covered systematically, point by point. The main themes deal with the central teachings of the evangelical faith: sin and redemption, the person of Christ, and his work of

16. Besides many orders for the liturgy, Fröhlich compiled a hymnal especially for the diaconal convent, based on Roller's hymnal of 1830; in its last edition it included 1,858 hymns. See *Christliches Gesangbuch. Eine Sammlung evangelischer Kernlieder und geistlicher Gesänge,* ed. H. Fröhlich, P. Dresden (1878).

17. Drews, *Kirchliche Leben,* 165-71.

atonement. Long and frequent passages are devoted to exhorting the faithful to a holy life *(institutio vitae),* comforting them in their present troubles *(consolatio),* and correcting and guiding their behavior according to the principles of the faith *(correctio morum).* These passages demonstrate a high measure of pietistic introversion, but at the same time they contain numerous indications of how contemporary conditions were perceived. Again and again a firm distinction is made between the life of faith and the "wisdom of the world" — in particular rationalistic thought, faith in reason and Nature, and other Christian denominations such as "the Romanists," the Calvinists, and the Church of the Prussian Union. Here Fröhlich follows the Saxon tradition of preaching along denominational and dogmatic lines; the personal nature of the soul-searching message along with the overtones of pietism seem to sharpen rather than dull the cutting edge.[18]

The language of the sermons corresponds to their denominational slant: it takes its character primarily from Luther's translation of the Bible. The archaic, mannered diction lends a certain sacred aura to the sermons, almost as if they were themselves the Word of God. Preaching is understood literally to be the proclamation of God's Word in the pure linguistic dress of the Reformation, which had purged it of all the accretions of history.[19] Such language places the contents of the sermons squarely into a historical context, namely, that of the traditions of the Lutheran Reformation which in turn points back to the Old Testament and New Testament as the original expression of God's communications with his people.

These observations point to the main characteristic of Fröhlich's sermons: their strong ties to Scripture. Fröhlich was fond of saying that one cannot be too careful with the words inspired by the Holy Ghost.[20] And he took them at face value. The Christmas story as it is told in Luke 2, for example, is presented as an indubitable historical fact whose authenticity is vouched for because "the time, place and lineage of our Savior's

18. It was no coincidence that Ember Day and Reformation sermons were considered Fröhlich's particular strengths. Cf. Molwitz, *Lebensbild,* 56, 58. Good examples include 51, 102, 131, as well as 110 and 130.

19. See 110:9ff., on the image of the well in the city of God, after Ps. 46:5. Referring to Gen. 26:18, Luther is typologically described as "that Isaac" who "with his servants" purified the well that had been clogged up by the Philistines. In the following, sermons will be referred to in the text by number (see the Appendix) and page.

20. Molwitz, *Lebensbild,* 55. It seems to me that Fröhlich meant this in a rather naive, quite literal sense; he had no concern for the hermeneutical traps discussed by his great-grandson Karlfried Froehlich in "'Always to Keep the Literal Sense in Holy Scripture Means to Kill One's Soul': The State of Biblical Hermeneutics at the Beginning of the Fifteenth Century," in *Literary Uses of Typology from the Late Middle Ages to the Present,* ed. Earl Miner (Princeton, 1977), 20-48.

appearance was clearly predicted in the Old Testament" (134:6). Even the fact that it was night when the shepherds watched their flocks (Luke 2:8) finds a quasi source-critical authentication in Isa. 60:2 (134:7). The proof furnished by prophecy is generally assigned a high value in these sermons. In their methodology, prediction and fulfillment authenticate each other.[21] Predictions can even be used to flesh out the narration of the actual event, since prophecy "juxtaposes the most distant with the nearest and thereby puts everything into a larger perspective" (53:1, referring to the detailed Christ-prophecies in Zechariah). In another place, the level of detail in Luke's account of the journey to Emmaus (chap. 24) is taken on a methodological level to satisfy historical curiosity on a peripheral question: who was the second disciple besides Cleophas mentioned in v. 18? It must have been Luke himself, "because he describes it so exactly" (1865*:6). The historical arguments found in the sermons are determined primarily by the Scripture texts themselves, both on the formal and substantive levels. The essential truth of the story is found in the text dictated by the Holy Ghost. He is even presented as a model historian with special narrative talent: "The Holy Ghost likes to tell stories — in fact, He is a master storyteller" (1865*: 6). Thus, the Bible remains the true historical source, *rerum proprie gestarum narratio.*

The range of historical references found in the sermons is correspondingly small: stories from the Old Testament,[22] the history of Israel, scenes from the life of Christ (particularly the Passion), the early church described in Acts, and, a frequent topic from postbiblical times, the Reformation. According to the homiletic guidelines of the time,[23] secular history is used extremely sparingly, and then usually as a context for or contrast with the "real history" of the people of Israel. Examples include the subjugation of Israel under Rome and the destruction of the temple (127), a description of Athens in the time of Paul (108), references to Julian the Apostate (104, 127) and Constantine (138) — but nothing at all from the Middle Ages.[24] Recent history, with very few exceptions, is addressed only in the most general terms, characterizing it as a time of decline or even the end-time. The treatment of historical material demonstrates the continuing duality

21. See, e.g., 127:7-9, for the destruction of Jerusalem as fulfillment of the prophecy in Luke 13; and in reverse, Julian the Apostate's attempt to rebuild the temple to disprove the prophecy of Jesus in Matt. 24:2 failed on account of the flames that appeared on the site.

22. Fröhlich had a great fondness for the OT; in 1860 he gave an entire series of sermons, from the second Sunday after Epiphany through Palm Sunday, on texts from the OT (45-50 and 52-54).

23. Cited in *RE,* 3d ed. (1900), 8:301.

24. Molwitz, *Lebensbild,* 57, refers to a nonextant sermon on Acts 21:1-4, in which the question of the Crusades was addressed.

inherent in a view that places the history of the kingdom of God in a problematic relationship to the history of the world.

In terms of formal narrative structure, a central criterion in the analysis of historical texts, the sermons of Heinrich Fröhlich fall into two main types: teaching sermons and — as I would like to call them — historical sermons. The difference between them lies not in any distinction between *doctrina* and *historia,* but rather in the handling of narrative. In a historical sermon, the story of past events is itself the meaning of the narration. In a teaching sermon, references to past events serve to clarify a point of doctrine: the narration functions as the vehicle for meaning.

In the teaching sermons, historical references are most commonly used to make a compelling case for the validity of a particular doctrinal point. Even examples from secular history sometimes serve this function in Fröhlich's sermons. To illustrate the sentence "be glad that you are suffering with Christ" (1 Pet. 4:13), Fröhlich tells the full story, found in Arrian, of the water sacrifice performed by Alexander the Great in the Gedrosian desert in order to spur on his fainting troops. He ends by appending the rhetorical question "And now, Christians, will you not march with Jesus? Will you not suffer with Christ? . . . And yet he is a far greater king than that one. He is the Son of God, the King of Kings . . . and he did not spill a few drops of water only — no, it was his own blood that he spilled for us all" (51:4). The same sentiment — "those who believe must suffer" — is illustrated in another sermon, "On the Faith," by a reference to the great cloud of witnesses reaching from Abel in the Old Testament to Stephen in the New Testament, and on through "the whole history of the Church of the faithful in all ages, up to this very hour" (6:7). There is a sound reason behind this shift of historical levels: in order to provide one's hearers with the security of a well-grounded historical identity, a teaching sermon must place the contemporary practice of faith into the continuity of a solid religious tradition. It is not enough, however, to offer isolated historical illustrations; they do not answer the central question about the meaning of history, and of one's own place within it.

Fröhlich seems to have felt this structural deficit in his teaching sermons, for in two Good Friday sermons and one on Christmas Eve he professes not to be willing or capable of giving a teaching sermon. Instead, he says, his congregation should "become immersed in the events," "led into the story," and "hear the events of Christmas — an ancient story yet ever new — again and again." The result is a historical text whose meaning lies exclusively in its narrative structure: a true "historical sermon." The structural principle underlying these festival sermons is the retelling of those events which form the basis of believers' faith and actions: the appearance of a child in the stable at Bethlehem, the Savior's death on the cross at Golgotha, the resurrection of the Lord from the stone tomb of Joseph of Arimathea.[25] These events are narrated with the specifics of place and all the traditional details, so that their significance in the history of salvation becomes clear. At the same time, references to the historical context place them into a temporal pattern and portray them as culmination points for world history in general.[26] The story itself becomes the message of the sermon — a soteriological *mythos*.

A slightly different form of historical sermon was realized in the series of sermons on texts from Acts (104-9) given by Fröhlich in the summer of 1863. Rather than tales of mythical dimensions which encompass the totality of human history in a particular event, we find examples of certain historical situations which are then related to the problems and realities of contemporary Christian life. The preacher uses them to illustrate the far-reaching traditions of the church, or as models for an exemplary life in the faith ("traditional" and "exemplary" functions).[27] In order to determine the content and form of the 19th-century conception of a proper Christian life from the standpoint of the history of *mentalité*, it is highly interesting to note which examples are given and which traditions stressed.

In an exemplary sermon, the relationship between the historical model and contemporary reality is generally made explicit. "What can the martyr Stephen teach us about our own call to witness?" is the title of one sermon (105). The answer is given by a structured retelling of Stephen's trial and death. It is divided into three sections, each of which is preceded by a heading codifying its timeless message: "1. fight with courage, 2. suffer with patience, 3. face death with joy" (105, *propositio*). Sometimes the message is brought home through narrative and dramatic techniques which elicit a commonsense conclusion. For example, the story of Saul before Damascus is told to illustrate the point that "the greater the sinner, the greater the mercy," and Saul is depicted as evil incarnate in the telling of the details. When he is "breathing threats and murder" (Acts 9:1), "the breath coming from his nostrils is nothing less than the rage of persecution against Christ" (105:4). He prepares his campaign in Damascus with Prussian thoroughness, and as he departs, a sinister "smile parts his lips, for he had orders in his hands to persecute those who believed in a crucified Lord" (105:5). The glorious revelation of Christ appears all the brighter as

25. Since there is no sermon extant for Easter Day, see the sermon on Emmaus, cited above (1865*). It exhibits the same narrative structure as the sermons for Good Friday and Christmas.

26. 103:2 and 134:7 contain references to the interpretation of world history.

27. See Rüsen, *Vier Typen,* esp. 179-84.

it confronts the "dark figure" of Saul, striking him down and finally accepting him as a disciple. After such a presentation, the moral is abundantly clear: "If even Saul was accepted as a child of God, you too can hope for acceptance, your sins are not too great" (105:7).

Such an understanding of history clearly presupposes some continuity in the circumstances of human life. In order for the teachings of the stories to have a practical application for the present and future, the spheres of experience and action depicted in the historical narratives must coincide with those of the present. A religious mentality seeks this theoretical historical continuity in the relationship of God to humankind. Fröhlich never tires of pointing out that it is God who guides the steps of humankind and who directs the flow of history: the transformation of Saul into Paul was the work of God, meant to "furnish an example to those who believe in him unto everlasting life" (105:6, after 1 Tim. 1:16). Paul's journey from Asia to Europe was guided by the Holy Ghost (108:5, after Acts 16), and so on.

Assuming the theoretical-historical continuity of God's mercy, historical narratives with an exemplary function would seem to be particularly effective in providing guidance for "proper" conduct to those of a religious mentality in any given circumstances. They offer an opportunity to emulate the experiences of the past *(imitatio)* or, in the case of negative examples, to avoid them. This function of historical narrative corresponds to the ancient topos *historia magistra vitae.*

In one case it is even possible to document directly the effect of historical narrative as *magistra vitae* on the Dresden diaconal convent. In one of his sermons, concerning the Jewish-Christian congregation in Beroea, Fröhlich insists that it "set an example which ought to be followed everywhere even today: after the sermon was over, they examined Scripture for themselves to see if these things were so" (108:6ff., after Acts 17:11). We have reports about the diaconal church which describe the congregation as having their Bibles open during the sermon, so that they "could read for themselves the words to which [the preacher] was assigning such significance."[28] This passage also reveals Fröhlich's strong concern for grounding the life of his community in the traditions of the Church.

The instances of historical narration geared toward forming a sense of tradition are all taken from the history of the early church and from that of Luther's Reformation. Most of them concern the institutions, rituals, and customs of Protestant community life. By referring back to their origins in the distant past, these passages evoke an aura of permanence and portray

28. Molwitz, *Lebensbild,* 56.

the Protestant tradition as a historically distinct religious entity. The Protestant Christian of Fröhlich's sermons is guided by the historical authority both of the early church of the Apostles, which lived by Christ's presence "in the Word," and of Luther's Reformation, which admitted no other tradition than that of God's Word.

The early church and the Reformation are thus placed in a relationship which could be labeled origin and renewal, or departure and return. Sermon 108 describes in detail the spread of the gospel through Paul's missionary journey, beginning at Jerusalem. Fröhlich particularly emphasizes the arrival of the mission in Europe, "into our part of the world." He describes this as the work of the Holy Ghost, who "guided the victorious journey of the gospel into Europe, and through Rome even into our country, into Germany" (108:7). A sermon given only three weeks later (110, on Reformation Day 1863) echoes the same process in reverse order. Luther's act of reform, whose culmination according to popular historiography is the nailing up of his theses on October 31, 1517, now returns to Jerusalem: "And what happened to [the theses]? In a short time they spread throughout the whole world — and so astoundingly swift was their progress that the sages of that time claimed the angels themselves must have carried them. After six weeks not a city in Europe remained that had not heard of them, and Luther's theses were great news even in Jerusalem" (110:2).

The truth of this narrative lies not in its historical accuracy but in the meaning that is conveyed through its narrative structure. It is no rhetorical accident that out of all the places in the world the preacher chose Jerusalem, the gospel's birthplace, to illustrate the farthest extent of the Reformation's spread (cf. 107:1, after Acts 1:8). The message of this story is "return to the origins," and it convinces through its narrative logic. The return to origins is a pattern used by traditional interpreters of history to realize the potential of the past for the present and future. Here, in the sermons of Pastor Heinrich Fröhlich, it endows the history of the early church and the Reformation with specific significance for his congregation in the present. But return *to* the origins is not return *of* the origins. The Reformation is not the starting point of the tradition, for it has a tradition behind it; nor is it the end of a tradition, for it remains bound to the incompleteness of time. But it is one step in the universal process of the coming of God's kingdom, whose end will be marked by the return of Christ. In this process the Protestant creed of the contemporary pastor and his congregation had its own well-defined place. By locating itself within the Reformation tradition, the congregation was referred back to the tradition of the early church, and this tradition was presented as binding. The same pattern is found in 104, the first of the sermons on Acts, which uses the text of Acts 6:1-7 to narrate the story of the "Institution of the Works of Mercy, or, Love as Servant" and whose topic, of all the extant sermons, is most directly relevant to the experience of the diaconal congregation. In this sermon, the realities of diaconal service with all its hierarchical institutions and rites of initiation are firmly linked to the traditions of the first Christian community, in which the office of deacon was first distinguished from the previously unified status of Apostle, and as the office of the community was given a place after the office of proclamation of the Word. Even though this distinction was not God's doing, He did "contribute his Spirit"; and "we must all subordinate ourselves to the order which God instituted through the Holy Ghost in his Church" (104:10). Election to office, which set apart the early church from its counterpart in modern times, was possible in those days because "these communities, after all, lived in faith and love" (104:10). Today, by contrast, the motivation to charitable deeds is not faith but humanitarianism, and a chill is felt in the Church. But houses such as this, in which "love and mercy are to be practiced in the Name of Christ" (104:14) are "signs of the Lord's grace" and "His harbingers of better times to come" (104:14ff.). And on this perspective, the preacher closes with a prayer which summarizes the historical philosophy of this religious and traditional interpretation in two short lines:

> "Lord, make us rich in faith and charity,
> that the beginning as the end may be."

Return to the origins — that is the means by which a pious *mentalité* interprets history so that the end will be similar to the beginning.

But even the events transmitted in the Gospels and Acts cannot be taken as the static origin of all tradition. Following exegetical tradition, Fröhlich's sermons link these events to the narratives of the Old Testament by various typological references. Generally, the typological patterns follow those in the Scriptures themselves or in traditional exegesis: the order of the temple and synagogue stands for Christ's priesthood (102), Jerusalem for the Christian church (110), Abel for Stephen (6), the shepherd David for Christ the Good Shepherd (52), Joshua's victory over the Amorite kings for Christ's victory at Golgotha over "Sin, Death, and Devil" (103), and so on. Typological patterns are also found in passages concerning the Reformation tradition: Luther is characterized as "the Isaac" who cleared the well that had been polluted by the Philistines (110), and Melanchthon appears in connection with Solomon (56). The historical significance of these references is clear: the congregation is placed in a tradition which reaches beyond the confines of the New Testament and encompasses the entire history of Israel. The nation of Israel, God's nation, is the type; the Church, founded on God's Word, the antitype (cf. 49). These typological relationships bridge time and cultures and create a new and coherent cultural tradition, that of the one people of God. Thus, typologies can be understood as shorthand variants on traditional historical narration.[29]

Echoing Heb. 8:5-6, Fröhlich speaks of the "shadow world of the Old Testament" during his analysis of Heb. 10:19-23 (102:4). He solves the problem of explaining the access of the faithful to the Holy of Holies by telling two stories. The first concerns the order in the ancient Jewish temple and describes the curtain separating the people from the Holy of Holies as well as the yearly sacrifice performed to reconcile God to his people on account of their sins. The other deals with Jesus' road "up to Jerusalem" and Golgotha. Between the two stories Fröhlich inserts an allegorical interpretation of the curtain as the curtain of sin (cf. the typology in Isa. 59:2) and a reflection on the sad lot of children who are denied access to "the father's heart," as well as a dogmatic passage on the blood of Christ as the key to the temple. At the conclusion of the Golgotha story, the sermon continues, "And see further: he bows his head and cries, 'It is fulfilled!' — and what occurs at that moment at the temple in Jerusalem? 'The curtain of the temple was torn in two from top to bottom.' Yes, the Holy of Holies was now unlocked — no curtain could shut it off from that day forward" (102:9). The following passage elaborates, in a nonnarrative way, on the "new path" to the Holy of Holies, now accessible to anyone.

The two stories, formally separated by general and dogmatic observations, form a coherent, meaningful whole held together by the typological structure. The practices at the temple and the events surrounding Jesus' death are presented as points in a real historical process that reaches down to the present day: the history of access to the Holy of Holies. The turning point in the story is defined in precise temporal terms: it is Jesus' death at Golgotha, which continues the historical tradition of sacrifice at the temple and marks the beginning of a "new way." But at the same time, the event at Golgotha is lifted out of its temporal framework. Its meaning for history lies not simply in its continuation of a tradition, nor even in its ending of

29. Cf. Robert Hollander's term "historical recurrence." His thesis, according to which Christian typology "developed as a particular and more highly articulated application of historical recurrence," is convincing because it stresses the temporal aspect of typology (Robert Hollander, "Typology and Secular Literature: Some Medieval Problems and Examples," in Miner, ed., *Literary Uses of Typology,* 5ff.).

that tradition. Rather, its true significance is found in a transformation that transcends beginnings and endings; for it does not simply mark one step in a gradual development, or a bit of progress to be followed by others. No — the turning point of Golgotha happened once and for all: it marks the moment at which all of history comes together. The story told in this sermon exhibits exactly the same "mythical" format as that found in several other sermons discussed above. The typological narration gains its meaning from this myth, and this meaning is contained in both the "shadow world" of pre-Christian times — as the yet hidden meaning of history — and also in these post-Christian times as the true meaning of all life, revealed to us in the Scriptures. Only in this mythological framework can the historic events described in the New Testament be understood as the origin of the Protestant community's tradition.

What functions do such historical reflections fulfill in the life of the congregations to whom they are addressed? In answer to this question, contemporary homiletics turned to the concept of "edification."[30] Sermons are meant to edify, and not only the individual believer (a simple pastoral dialogue could do that), but specifically the congregation as a whole, or to put it in theological terms: the Church as "the actual community of God's people, formed and sustained as a body by faith in Jesus Christ."[31] Understood in these dogmatic terms as an existing and evolving assembly, necessarily contingent and incomplete as long as time continues, the Christian Church cannot forgo historical references in its sermons if they are to be truly "edifying," building up the community's sense of self.

In Heinrich Fröhlich's sermons it is the historical passages that are particularly community building, due to a communicative effect common to all historical narration. Historical narration is a communicative act which draws narrator and listener together in the unity of the narrative context. In the situation in which one "tells someone a true story and listens to someone tell a true story," narrator and listener create a communion between each other and also between themselves and the past which is present in the telling.[32] This commonality persists as long as a context exists in which these past events are narrated and listened to. That is why "those old and yet ever new stories" must be retold again and again; they confirm the commonality of faith within a congregation and ensure that it outlasts time and can hope for a future. It seems to me that Heinrich Fröhlich had this potential "supertem-

30. See the article "Homiletik," *RE*, 3d ed. (1900), 8:300ff.

31. Ibid., 297.

32. Kurt Röttgers, "Geschichtserzählung als kommunikativer Text," in *Historisches Erzählen. Formen und Funktionen*, ed. Siegfried Quandt and Hans Süssmuth (Göttingen, 1982), esp. pp. 30ff.

porality" in mind when he exhorted Protestant Christians in a sermon on the Reformation (110:1) "as children of the Reformation, do with Reformation history what Israel did with its history: 'Only take heed, and keep your soul diligently, lest you forget the events which your eyes have seen, and lest they depart from your heart all the days of your life; make them known to your children and your children's children' " (Deut. 4:9).

Such a communicative act can only succeed, however, when the narrated events fit into the common situation; otherwise the narrator loses his audience, and the commonality disappears. In his sermons, Fröhlich usually relates the historical reminiscences to the lives of his hearers and draws conclusions about the proper way to live a Christian life — formulating warnings, criticizing aberrant behavior, determining the prospects for reward or punishment, and proclaiming reassurance. This is done in an extremely pedagogical tone which permeates the sermons and which on the one hand places them squarely in that ancient homiletic tradition which considers the main purpose of the sermon to be *docere,* teaching;[33] on the other hand, taken as communicative acts, the tone of the sermons allows conclusions about the structure of this congregation that gathered every Sunday in the diaconal church of Dresden in the sixth decade of the last century. We see an extremely asymmetrical communicative act in which the roles of narrator and listener are firmly fixed in accordance with the differences of their spiritual offices. It is the duty of the pastor, the designated servant of God's Word, to dispense teachings or to formulate for everyone "the proper thoughts of a Christian on Good Friday under the Cross of his Redeemer" (the title of 89). It is the duty of the congregation, with their Bibles open before them, to take these teachings to heart and apply them in their daily lives. This is the assumption underlying the remark said to have been addressed to a young diaconal sister by an old regular after one of Fröhlich's sermons on repentance: "Well, if you are not saved, the pastor certainly will not be to blame."[34]

On April 22, 1860, Fröhlich dedicated an entire sermon (56) to this concept of the sermon as an authoritative teaching situation. In his analysis he presents the hearing and internalization of true teachings as the proper calling of the pious, and grounds his claims in history. The occasion was the tricentenary of the death of Philipp Melanchthon (d. April 19, 1560), who in his time had placed special emphasis on the teaching function of sermons and had even claimed a separate *genus didascalicum.* He is here portrayed as an exemplary teacher of the Lutheran church: the description of his life is an example of "the way to true discipleship in the school of heavenly wisdom"

33. Cf. *RE,* 8:299.
34. Molwitz, *Lebensbild,* 56.

(56:4). For his text, Fröhlich chose Prov. 22:17-19, and in the main body of his sermon he concentrated systematically on the exhortation in v. 17 which summarizes the role of the hearer in the communicative act: "Incline your ear and hear the words of the wise, and apply your mind to my knowledge." The theological content of this statement and its place in the history of biblical interpretation need not be discussed here. We will focus instead on the way in which these guidelines — listening to the Word of God, taking it to heart, and trusting in the Lord — are placed in the context of specifically Christian historical traditions which deal with the Christian present, the Christian past, and the Christian future. This is accomplished in three ways in the narrative passages which frame the systematic text analysis: through a historical example, through a typological interpretation, and through an eschatological prophecy. In the biography of Melanchthon, Fröhlich stresses that a proper Christian life consists of conscious daily listening for the Word of God mediated through parents (here, Melanchthon's father), teachers (his teacher Johannes Reuchlin), and friends (Martin Luther). Thereupon Melanchthon, who was Luther's helper and *praeceptor Germaniae,* is presented as the prototype of the wise teacher (56:2ff. — aside from a few human weaknesses and waverings in the face of certain Calvinist teachings, which Fröhlich does not omit); this prototype was foreshadowed in the Old Testament by Solomon himself (56:3ff., 9). Finally, the sermon, which had opened with the exhortation from Heb. 13:7 to remember one's teachers and imitate their faith, concludes with a prophecy from Dan. 12 which opens a path into the future for the remembered past: "And many of those who sleep in the dust of the earth shall awake, some to everlasting life, and some to shame and everlasting contempt. And those who are wise [the teachers] shall shine like the brightness of the firmament; and those who turn many to righteousness, like the stars for ever and ever."

The typological content of the textual interpretation in this example provides the hermeneutical key for understanding the sermons themselves as historical texts. The typology of teaching, which relates historical references to the contemporary situation, includes the present sermon within its compass, which reaches from Solomon in the Old Testament through Melanchthon to the fulfillment of Daniel's prophecy in the future. The present sermon can thus be interpreted as a further link in the typological chain; but a link which develops the typological tradition in the direction of a specific model of "edifying" the Church by teaching faith through history. The preacher appears not only as a teacher who teaches *dialecticorum more de dogmatibus,* as Melanchthon required,[35] but as an authorial

35. Cited in *RE,* 8:299.

narrator presenting meaningful stories that express the significance of the teachings of faith in their temporal dimension: namely, as continuing traditions of Christian life. The listeners "learn" the fundamentals of faith not only in the manner of a catechism but through historical experience. They are guided by the narratives and taught to orient their lives around the traditions and pious examples of history.

III

"What time is it in the Kingdom of God? And what time is it in the kingdom of this world, into which the Kingdom of God, the holy Church of our Lord Jesus Christ, is built? Who can give an answer? I look at the hour hand of the great world clock, and it ever advances, nearer and nearer it advances to the great hour of judgment for the whole world and for the Church of God — and the name of that great judgment hour? Midnight!" (128:1)

With these words Fröhlich begins a seemingly routine sermon for the 14th Sunday after Trinity, 1864. He is in fact delineating the pattern according to which he and his congregation perceive reality and integrate it into a comprehensive conception of historical time; two histories are postulated, both evolving in a single temporal framework. The two kingdoms are perceived as historical realities (cf. 129:2) and exhibit a duality which is a characteristic of historical time and will continue as long as time exists. A fusion of the two kingdoms has never existed and cannot exist today: "Behold the time of Constantine, when the gates of the Church were opened so wide that whole countries and nations could enter: at that time the world entered into the sanctuary of the Church . . . and since that time the world has sat firmly inside the Church — but what of the world? It has always been an enemy of the Lord Jesus" (128:6). In another place, Fröhlich proclaims with chiliastic exaggeration that a "Christian state" will not be possible "until the kingdom of glory arrives" (49:4).

Within this dualistic framework, contemporary experience can be located and historically interpreted. In Fröhlich's sermons, the duality of the two kingdoms determines all evaluation of the present. There is a division between the "children of God" and the "children of the world," between the "community of saints" and the worldly order — a civil society based on selfish interests, gain, and profit. It is interesting, and quite telling from a political point of view, that the state and its constitution are usually left out of these categorizations. Showing respect to those in power — even and particularly in the secular sphere — is, in good Lutheran fashion, counted among the Christian virtues. On the other side, a specifically Christian attitude toward their subjects seems to be required of those in high places (cf. 109:9ff., 14; 129:7). There is one instance (49:4) when the preacher makes it clear that since the time of the New Covenant, i.e., since the time of Christ's appearance on earth, Church and State have been two different entities; but they appear in conflict only once, and that is in a passage concerning education — or to use Fröhlich's terminology, "people's souls." Secular intervention in the schools — historically one of the most important prerequisites for the modernization of society — is roundly denounced, but not out of distaste for the state imposing its order upon the schools; rather, secular education is condemned for its stated goals of educating people as "human beings" and "for the world," which for Fröhlich is synonymous with turning away from Christ and straying from the path of righteousness — or, in general terms, with the demise of traditional Christian patterns of behavior.

The perspective on the present expressed in these sermons always includes evaluations of contemporary experience according to the biblical promises of reward and punishment; it thus draws its criteria from a historical source. The categorization of contemporary trends as leading either to damnation or to salvation is always clear-cut; it is appropriately illustrated by the concept of the broad and the narrow way (Matt. 7:13-14), a picture widely used in the revival movement and familiar from Fröhlich's writings as well.[36] No aspect of contemporary reality worth mentioning escapes categorization; gray areas *(adiaphora)* seem to be absent from this view of the world. The broad path to damnation is strewn with the monuments of Pleasure, Enjoyment, and Comfortable Living: "pleasures of the eyes and of the flesh as well as vain behavior" (129; 130); the tavern, a place of worldly joys and gluttonous festivities (48); all the delights of the dance, games, and theater (130); laughter, which drives away the serious demeanor of faith (127); the thoughtless admiration for Art, Nature, Reason, or Progress (45; 108; 130; 131); the idolization of mere mortals such as the poet Schiller (108); the greed of the businessman who finds no time for church or the sacraments (109); the disdain for using kneelers at prayer (130), and so on. The narrow way is less graphically illustrated, but its landmarks all have the glow of promised reward: daily hearing of God's Word (56); humble subordination to the

36. In the 1860s, a lithograph appeared in the circles of Württembergian pietism depicting "the broad and narrow paths"; it was highly popular at the time and can still be found today. See Martin Scharfe, *Die religion des Volkes. Kleine Kultur- und Sozialgeschichte des Pietismus* (Gütersloh, 1980), 84-87.

God-given order and authorities (46); patient suffering of the persecution and disdain of the world (51; 105; 129); the daily practice of prayer and penance (56; 57; 130); and the joyful undertaking of the service of Chtistian love for the sake of God's reward (50; 104).

Martin Scharfe convincingly calls the relocation of *adiaphora* onto the extreme ends of the spectrum the "cultural methodology" of pietism; he sees its origin in the material circumstances of the lower middle classes, whose security was threatened by industrialization.[37] The same methods, it seems to me, can be found in the sermons of Heinrich Fröhlich, though followed through in less detail and blunted by dogmatic generalities; they serve to generate and stabilize religious social patterns. But here, they function not so much to glorify the given circumstances according to a self-content ideology, but to help discipline the social and cultural life of an institution which faced threats from many directions. Within the ecclesiastical framework, the diaconate was still struggling for recognition during the 1860s, and had to defend itself from the claims of the church hierarchy (cf. the hidden references in 46 and 127). Within a larger perspective, it found itself confronted with the daily misery of a changing society; and though its calling was to alleviate that misery, it was not sufficiently endowed either by the church or by society to do so. A community whose task it was to care for all those neglected and forgotten by a society engaged in massive social change and the rapid, dog-eat-dog race to middle-class prosperity[38] could easily find itself in a marginal position fraught with contradictions. This situation could be psychologically very difficult to endure, since the community existed not just within but also through the support of society. On the one hand it was dependent on the prestigious gifts of charitable donors; on the other, it required great spiritual discipline, a willingness to sacrifice, and a large measure of inner integrity to survive. In this context, the concept of the narrow way functioned to create an ideology for this small subculture and to transform behavior that went against the norms of society into a religiously acceptable, successful pattern of living. Fröhlich's preaching about the Kingdom of God, which served at the same time to distinguish his listeners from society at large and to integrate them into a wider ecclesiastical context, played an important stabilizing role in the life and survival of this community.

In his sermons, Fröhlich applies another yardstick besides the dualistic one to his observations about contemporary life; this is the historical

37. Scharfe, *Religion,* 77-87.

38. Until the 1860s, Saxony was in the forefront of the industrialization of Germany. See the summary in Rudolf Kötzschke and Hellmut Kretzschmar, *Sächsische Geschichte* (Frankfurt a.M., 1965), 353-56.

pattern of decline and fall. Typically, positive examples from history are rhetorically contrasted with the decadent experience of the present day.

> Yes, once there were times, in the age of the Reformation, when far and wide prayers ascended to God from houses and congregations, from streets and fields and forests, from old and young, rich and poor. But now, where are those families . . . in which, upon rising in the morning and retiring at night, the parents and children ask for God's blessing, cross themselves with the holy Cross, and standing or kneeling together say the Creed and the Our Father, or Luther's evening and morning prayers? Where are the fathers who come to the table at noonday together with their children and household, soberly, hands folded in prayer, and say the *Benedicite* before and the *Gratias* after? . . . Where are now the houses and streets, the fields and the forests, where prayers and hymns can still be heard? No — silence has descended on the houses and the streets, on the fields and the forests — silence has descended on human hearts: a dead silence, the silence of the grave. . . . There is an evil smell of putrefaction; it spreads wherever there is no prayer. But where there is carrion, there the eagles gather.[39] I can already hear the whirring of their wings above our peoples. (57:1ff.)

This example is enlightening: the present is portrayed as a time when the old order and traditional forms of behavior have disappeared — but all this is only the negative shadow of a lost and golden past. Not only the decrease in prayer but also the decay of the former social structures of family and society are addressed. It is the loss of the idealized social order of a preindustrial, patriarchal society that is being lamented here (cf. also 130:12).

When the sermons address the innovations of the present day, they do so in a tone of deep mistrust. All the progress in "industry, the arts, and science" count as nothing in God's eyes (133:13). All the mouthpieces of public opinion — the press, journalism, and political agendas — are relegated to the sinful side of the scale (127; 129; 131). Democratic methods of political decision making are denounced as revolt (104, citing the example of the rebellion of Demetrius in Acts 19). The Ember Day sermons (131; 135) contain entire decalogues of the sins of modernity calculated to prove that the misery of the world is due to the breaking away from the given order of traditional piety. The preacher takes this opportunity to call for repentance — a repentance which is meant quite literally. By presenting contemporary reality in this religious-historical light, he exhorts his congregation to expect improvement only if the people go back to the traditional ways of life and religion. The internal life of Fröhlich's diaconal convent was structured accordingly; the institution saw — and presented —

39. A direct citation of Matt. 24:28!

itself as a foretaste of the Kingdom of God, a patriarchal, spiritually integrated "economy of the whole house."[40]

As gloomy as claims of the downfall and decay of the present day may have seemed, Fröhlich's sermons were anything but devoid of consolation and hope. The wings he had heard whirring over the heads of his people turned out to be not vultures' but eagles' wings — a symbol that evoked as much hope as fear in the language of 19th-century Germany. The comfort and hope sprang from a traditionalist view of Christian eschatology as it was interpreted by some of the Protestant theologians of the time.[41] They used the biblical pattern of prophecy and fulfillment to explain the *adventus Christi in iudicum* as the eschaton of historical time — the last event in history. In this sense, eschatological thought is concrete historical thought in the framework of traditional historical interpretation. The future is contained in the past; return is the guiding principle of history. Sermons about the end of the world were no rarity in German Protestantism, and were especially common in the context of pietism and the revival movement. Several of Fröhlich's sermons belong to this genre, particularly those that utilize historical forms of argument. Knowledge of the future does not arise from an analysis of human development in past and present: we are all the same in this respect, being sinners from Adam onward (89); rather, it is found in the biblical revelation texts, which are historical documents. Such a sermon admits to falling far below the modern standard of knowledge about time and the world; in fact, it takes pains to distance itself from "worldly wisdom"; but what it lacks in science it makes up in interpretive certainty, due to its adoption of the biblical model: "When the whole world stands before history and the events of the present day as before a riddle, the children of God see clearly, because Jesus reveals it to them. The further we move into the end-time, the clearer God's prophetic Word becomes" (133:12).

In this eschatological scheme, the present day has its own unique significance. "We are living at the end of time" (128:1)! The certainty of this statement, as well as of any eschatological sermon, arises from the interpretation of certain contemporary realities as fulfillments of New Testament prophecies about the end of time. There will be a massive turning away from

40. This term was introduced by Otto Brunner with reference to the "housefather-literature" of the 17th century to characterize the economic and social structures of pre-industrial life (Otto Brunner, "Das 'ganze Haus' und die alteuropäische 'Ökonomik,'" in Brunner, *Neue Wege der Sozialgeschichte* [Göttingen, 1956], 33-61).

41. See Lucian Hölscher, *Weltgericht oder Revolution. Protestantische und sozialistische Zukunftsvorstellungen im deutschen Kaiserreich* (Stuttgart, 1989), chaps. 2 and 3 — including much sermon material; Christian Walther, *Typen des Reich-Gottes-Verständnisses. Studien zur Eschatologie und Ethik im 19. Jahrhundert* (Munich, 1961).

the faith (2 Thess. 2:3), whose fulfillment the preacher sees not only in the decay of the prayer culture but also in decreased attendance at church (128; 130; 131). There will be false prophets and blasphemous teachings (Matt. 24:24; Mark 13:22): these are tangibly present in Ernest Renan's account of the Life of Jesus (128; 130; 131). The gospel will spread through the whole world: witness the mission boards, whose lively activity has placed this goal within reach. Finally, the conversion of the Jews, the last sign before the return of Christ (Rom. 11:25-26), is already well under way: "Much has happened to convert Israel, but since the first Pentecost there have not been as many converted out of the people of Israel as in the single century of our time.... The time is approaching in which God's will over us will be fulfilled. First the fulness of the Gentiles shall enter the fold, then Israel shall be converted, and then Christ Jesus shall return, as a bridegroom to the waiting bride" (127:12; 53, after Zech. 2:16). These observations about contemporary life do not, however, remain in the realm of abstract historical speculation, since they always appear in connection with the morality of the "narrow way" and thus serve as clear messages to the congregation. The sermon about the approaching eschaton addresses contemporary mores within the framework of reward and punishment, just as the biblical texts do, and opens a perspective into the future for the congregation. Two prior sermons, 51 and 72, graphically depict this future for those who keep to the ways of faith and stand fast in their sufferings as followers of Christ. Fröhlich presents a series of Christ's letters to the heads of the churches (Rev. 2 and 3), working up to a climax which ends: "To those who overcome, I shall grant a seat on my throne, just as I have overcome and sit on my Father's throne" (Rev. 3:21). The second sermon takes the scenario even further: "Then shall the angels marvel at the things which God has prepared for those who love him. Then shall the angels bow and serve those whom their King has brought to share in his rule. Mortals shall be higher than the angels — this is the magnificent reward for those who follow Christ" (72:9).

It would be too simple to take this passage as mere reassurance — putting off into the future the rewards of a community of deaconesses who were getting the short end of the stick in this life. Its true essence is its explanation of history, or to be more exact, of the meaning or purpose of life in historical time. In these passages, history is presented as a series of prophecies and fulfillments according to the same pattern we have encountered in other sermons. To be sure, their substance is a utopia which goes beyond history; but it is a utopia constructed according to the historical prophecies in the Scriptures and linked to concrete historical phenomena — the steadfastness of believers in the present and the return of Christ at the end of time. Believers who examine history trusting in the historical power of the promise will, like Stephen, "see the heavens opened" — for they become capable of "preconstructing" the future. The central lesson of this eschatological sermon, and of historical preaching in general, is the reconstruction out of history of hope for the present.

And what about the reassurance? It lies in a practical effect inherent in all remembrance. "In every piece of memory there lies a bit of salvation."[42] Within the framework of Christian salvation history presented in the sermons of Heinrich Fröhlich, the contemporary perception of the decline of the age (cf. 127:10) is endowed with positive significance. In the light of the prophecy "higher than the angels," the burden of one's own life, restricted in so many ways, became easier to bear. Thus Fröhlich's sermons, as all historical remembrance, served to free his listeners from the burden of their experience and to put a certain distance between themselves and the present. But reassurance is not a call to change. There is not the slightest attempt in these sermons to mobilize historical memory in order to make the present condition appear worthy and capable of changing; rather, they acted to stabilize a mentality that was willing to accept circumstances as God-given and to do one's best within them — with the assurance of reward.

Appendix: Index of the Extant Sermons of Heinrich Fröhlich

No.	Date	Text	Topic
6	10/02/1858 18th after Trinity	Heb. 10:38–11:6	On Faith
45	01/15/1860 2nd after Epiphany	Prov. 3:5-7	On the Arrogance of Wisdom
46	01/29/1860 4th after Epiphany	Ps. 12:1-6	The Lament of the Children of God on the Increasing Evil of the World

42. Rüsen, *Zeit und Sinn,* 12.

47	02/05/1860 Sexagesimae/ Candlemas	Jer. 9:23-24	God is the Boast of the Humble
48	02/19/1860 Estomihi	Prov. 7:2-4 (3-5)	On the Sorrow and Blessing of the Passion
49	02/26/1860 Invocavit	Ps. 85:8-14	The Prayer of Peace of the Children of Peace
50	03/04/1860 Reminiscere	Isa. 58:6-9	On Fasting
51	03/09/1860 Ember Day	1 Pet. 4:13	Christ is the Christian's Joy and Sorrow
52	03/18/1860 Oculi	Ps. 23	Christ, Shepherd and Father of His Flock
53	03/25/1860 Judica/Annunciation	Zech. 2:14-17 (10-14)	Remarks on this Prophetic Witness
54	04/01/1860 Palm Sunday	Ps. 118:15-21	A Triumph Song of the Faithful
55	04/15/1860 Quasimodogeniti	Rom. 1:4	Jesus Christ, the Son of God
56	04/22/1860 Misericordias Domini/Melanchthon's Death	Prov. 22:17-19	The Way to True Discipleship in the School of Heavenly Wisdom
57	05/13/1860 Rogate	Matt. 7:7-11	Christ's Sermon on Prayer
58	05/17/1860 Ascension	Eph. 1:20-23	The Ascension of Our Lord Jesus Christ
71	12/26/1860 Second Day of Christmas	Luke 2:15-20	Continuation of the Christmas Story
72	01/01/1861 Circumcision/ New Year	Luke 12:4-9	How Christ's Disciples Must Walk Through Time Confessing Christ
89	04/18/1862 Good Friday	1 Pet. 1:18-19	Proper Thoughts of a Christian on Good Friday Under the Cross of His Redeemer

102	03/06/1863 Ember Day	Heb. 10:19-23	On the Access to the Sanctuary, or the Father's Heart, Opened to the Poor Sinner
103	04/03/1863 Good Friday	Mark 15:25-37	The Last Hours of Suffering of Our Dying Savior
104	07/12/1863 6th after Trinity	Acts 6:1-7	The Institution of the Works of Mercy, or Love as Servant
105	07/19/1863 7th after Trinity	Acts 6:8-15; 7:55-59	What Can the Martyr Stephen Teach Us about Our Call to Witness?
106	08/02/1863 9th after Trinity	Acts 8:26-39	The Conversion of the Ethiopian Eunuch
107	08/09/1863 10th after Trinity	Acts 9:1-8	How the Lord Glorifies His Mercy in the Calling of Saul
108	10/04/1863 18th after Trinity/St. Michael	Acts 17:16-28	The Apostle Paul in Athens
109	10/18/1863 20th after Trinity	Acts 19:23-40	The Revolt in Ephesus — A Reflection of the Prejudice and Enmity toward the Gospel Still Alive Today
110	10/31/1863 Reformation Sunday	Ps. 46:5-6	"Let the City of God Rejoice"
127	07/31/1864 10th after Trinity/Destruction of Jerusalem	Luke 13:34-35	The Last Words of the Lord over Jerusalem
128	08/21/1864 14th after Trinity	Luke 9:57-62	Three Earnest Requirements of Those Who Wish to Follow Jesus as His Disciples
129	09/25/1864 18th after Trinity	Matt. 10:16-22	How the Lord Sends His Disciples out into the World

130	10/31/1864 Reformation Sunday	John 12:36	On the Light of the Reformation
131	11/18/1864 Ember Day	Eph. 4:30-32	A Call of God to His Children Sealed by the Holy Ghost, That They May Not Sadden Him
132	11/20/1864 End of Church Year/All Souls'	Phil. 1:21	Christians are Blessed People
133	11/27/1864 Advent I/New Church Year	John 15:1-16	Christ's Advent Greeting for the New Church Year: "Abide in Me!"
134	12/25/1864 Christmas Day	Luke 2:1-14	The joyful Christmas message: "Unto you is born a Savior"
135	03/17/1865 Ember Day	Luke 7:36-50	A Beautiful Story of Repentance
1865*	04/17/1865 Second Day of Easter	Luke 24:13-35	How Jesus Led the Sorrowing Disciples at Emmaus to the Consolation of Easter
1880*	09/05/1880 Anniversary of the Bethesda Hospice	Matt. 11:28	The Call of the Savior

*Not numbered.

17. *Prophecy, Millennialism, and Biblical Interpretation in Nineteenth-Century America*

James H. Moorhead

It has become something of a historical cliche to assert that postmillennialism dominated American religious thought throughout much of the nineteenth century. This eschatology, affirming that the Second Coming would occur after the millennium or thousand years of bliss foretold in Rev. 20, was trumpeted from leading pulpits and seminaries; and it held sway in popular religious magazines as well as in weighty theological quarterlies. As generally formulated, postmillennialism provided a theological rationale for a progressive view of history. God's people, under the guidance of the Holy Spirit, would gradually bring about the golden age. Thus postmillennialism expressed the dynamism of nineteenth-century evangelicalism seeking through the promotion of revivalism, missions, and social reform to make America a Redeemer Nation and to help build the Kingdom of God on earth. Yet despite all that has been written about this influential eschatology, our knowledge is relatively scanty in a crucial area. While we know much about postmillennialism as a general outlook on history, we know much less about it as a system of biblical interpretation. How did postmillennialists interpret prophetic and apocalyptic scriptures? What principles of hermeneutics and exegesis governed their approach to the biblical texts?[1] To sketch the outline of a response to these questions is the goal of this essay.

1. On the role of postmillennialism in American thought, see, e.g., Ernest Lee Tuveson, *Redeemer Nation: The Idea of America's Millennial Role* (Chicago: University of Chicago Press, 1968); Timothy L. Smith, "Righteousness and Hope: Christian Holiness and the

On first examination, one may despair of finding a single set of answers to these questions. In fact, Robert K. Whalen has insisted that it is erroneous to treat postmillennialists "as if they uniformly subscribed to an agreed upon eschatology and were conscious of forming a distinct intellectual current." He suggests that we ought rather to view postmillennialism as "a collection of various optimistic eschatologies, sacrificing uniformity to popularity, complex but without leadership or accepted traditions, and forming no integrated system or philosophy."[2] Although Whalen overstates the case, he is correct in emphasizing the diversity of opinions which flourished under the rubric of that eschatology.

At one extreme, postmillennialists included precursors of modern critical scholarship. Moses Stuart, professor of Sacred Literature at Andover Theological Seminary from 1810 until his death in 1852, provides the most notable case in point. A self-taught philologist who read German biblical scholarship with avidity (though seldom with complete approval), Stuart applied critical principles to apocalyptic and prophetic scriptures. For example, in *A Commentary on the Apocalypse* (1845), Stuart concluded that the Revelation was a tract for its own time. John wrote to the victims of persecution, probably under the reign of the Emperor Nero, in order to shore up their courage by telling them of things which would shortly come to pass. Therefore, to regard the Apocalypse as a "Syllabus of history" or "to look for the Pope, or the French Revolution, or the Turks, or the Chinese in it" was patently absurd. Yet while asserting that the events foretold in Rev. 1–19 had been accomplished in the first century, Stuart also insisted that chaps. 20ff. — the portion of the book dealing with the millennium and the final consummation — did predict future events which, even in the nineteenth century, had yet to occur: a

---

Millennial Vision in America, 1800-1900," *American Quarterly* 31 (Spring 1979): 21-45; James H. Moorhead, "Between Progress and Apocalypse: A Reassessment of Millennialism in American Religious Thought, 1800-1880," *JAH* 71 (Dec. 1984): 524-42.

Two observations on terminology may be in order. First, although most of the examples used in this paper are interpretations of the book of Revelation, exegesis of other portions of Scripture, especially the prophetic books, also appears. Here I am following the commentators of the period who did not make a sharp distinction between prophetic and apocalyptic genres. Second, I am using the term "millennialism," rather than "apocalyptic," to denote biblical visions of the end of history. While historians of earlier periods of church history often prefer the term "apocalyptic," students of the American scene have generally employed the former nomenclature. Accordingly, this paper follows that common usage. For a plea on behalf of greater terminological precision, see James H. Moorhead, "Searching for the Millennium in America," *PSB* 8/2 (1987): 17-33.

2. Robert K. Whalen, "Millenarianism and Millennialism in America, 1790-1880" (Ph.D. diss., State University of New York, Stony Brook, 1972), 120.

spiritual reign of Christ on earth, then a final unleashing of evil once again, and the raising of the dead for the Last Judgment. Stuart in effect had made the Apocalypse a postmillennial drama whose middle portion was missing. The book contained a first act detailing events of the early Christian era and a final scene explaining how the play would turn out. No one, however, could say how many intervening acts John had omitted or what would transpire during them.[3]

At Princeton Theological Seminary, the bastion of conservative Presbyterianism, a similar caution toward apocalyptic and prophetic scriptures reigned. Charles Hodge, the commanding eminence at the school from mid-century to his death in 1878, affirmed a postmillennial hope "that before the second coming of Christ there is to be a time of great and long continued prosperity." In many respects, Hodge's scheme resembled Stuart's, but there were important differences. Unlike the Andover professor, his Princeton counterpart believed that specific events, institutions, and persons between the first century and the millennium were foretold in Scripture. He supported, for example, the traditional Protestant notion that the papacy was the Antichrist. Still, Hodge was exceedingly diffident about precise identifications of historical events with particular biblical predictions. That reticence reflected no suspicion that prophecy was in any sense flawed. The inerrant Word of God would not permit such suppositions. Interpretation demanded caution because the prophecies were frequently enigmatic, sometimes telescoped widely separated events into a single portrait, and often dealt with whole classes of similar events under a single figure. Biblical prediction was "not intended to give us a knowledge of the future analogous to that which history gives us of the past. . . . Prophecy makes a general impression with regard to future events, which is reliable and salutary, while the details remain in obscurity." Thus prudence demanded that one abstain from overly precise prophetic schemes and allow future events to supply the interpretation.[4]

Not all postmillennialists were as unwilling as Stuart and Hodge to posit contemporary events as the fulfillment of specific biblical predictions. In two extended analyses in 1856 and in 1859, the Rev. Joseph Berg, one of the leading ministers of the Dutch Reformed Church, eagerly sought to

3. Moses Stuart, *A Commentary on the Apocalypse*, 2 vols. (Andover, MA: Allen, Morrill, and Wardwell, 1845), 1:159, 163, 483; 2:474-90. For further information on Stuart, consult Jerry Wayne Brown, *The Rise of Biblical Criticism in America, 1800-1870: The New England Scholars* (Middletown, CT: Wesleyan University Press, 1969), 45-59, 94-110; and John H. Giltner, *Moses Stuart: The Father of Biblical Science in America* (Atlanta: Scholars Press, 1988).

4. Charles Hodge, *Systematic Theology*, 3 vols. (New York: Scribner, Armstrong, and Co., 1872-75), 3:790-91, 797, 830, 849, 858-59.

correlate particular biblical passages with events then in process. Among his numerous conclusions were that the power of Louis Napoleon signified the pouring of the seventh vial of the Apocalypse, that contemporary evangelical efforts to convert sailors fulfilled prophecies in Isaiah (chap. 24) concerning those who "go down to the sea," and that the appearance of the United States in world history clearly corresponded to Daniel's prediction of an enduring fifth world kingdom.[5] Several years later during the Civil War a postmillennialist writing in the Methodist weekly *Christian Advocate and Journal* argued that the Scriptures foretold the American Civil War. Rev. 12, recounting the celestial battle of the Archangel Michael, was fulfilled in the Southern rebellion; and the dragon's expulsion from heaven signified the Confederacy's defeat. But the forces of tyranny would regroup among the tottering regimes of Europe, and these corrupt powers would ally to confront the United States, probably on the field of battle. That future conflict, as prophesied in Ezek. 38–39, would eventuate in American victory. Then, as a result of the triumph over European despotism, the way would be clear "for the universal spread of the Gospel, and the sublime realization of self-government among all people. . . . That long cycle of ages called the millennium will then be ushered in."[6]

In view of these diversities (and many more could be cited), one may be tempted to echo Whalen that postmillennialism indeed offered "no integrated system or philosophy"; but the conclusion would be premature. That eschatology acquired a unity as it defined itself against competing premillennial views. Of these the theories of the Baptist William Miller constituted the most notable instance. Predicting that Christ would return in 1843 or 1844, Miller generated a mass movement which at its height rated front-page coverage in the newspapers. The Millerites provided an easy mark for scoffers — at least after 1844 — and for years were regarded by many as self-evident proof of the absurdity of millenarianism. Yet other premillennialists were not so easily dismissed. Within the major denominations, a small but vocal group of advocates kept that view before the public. While eschewing the setting of specific dates, these people nevertheless expected an early end to the present world order and an imminent Second Coming. They represented a minority position at least until the last couple of decades of the century, but they nevertheless had sufficient influence to force their postmillennial counterparts to define a position

5. Joseph F. Berg, *The Second Advent of Jesus Christ, Not Premillennial* (Philadelphia: Perkinpine and Higgins, 1859), 152, 161-62; Joseph F. Berg, *The Stone and the Image, or, the American Republic* (Philadelphia: Perkinpine and Higgins, 1856), passim.

6. *Christian Advocate and Journal,* Nov. 20, 1862, 370; ibid., Nov. 27, 1862, 378.

against them. Although this minority — usually called by opponents chiliasts or millenarians — had their own internal diversities, several common themes stood out in their writings: a refutation of the postmillennial view that the thousand years would be merely a perfection of the current age, a concomitant belief that a supernatural abrogation of the present declining world order was necessary, and hence an expectation that Jesus would soon return on the clouds of heaven to establish his Kingdom. Many premillennialists also expected a political restoration of the Jewish people and a reestablishment of their religious cultus in Jerusalem. Undergirding all of these millenarian motifs, however, was a self-proclaimed adherence to a plain, literal exegesis of God's inerrant Word — a literalism which the chiliasts accused postmillennialists of spiritualizing away.[7]

Millenarians claimed as if it were their special property the historic Protestant bias in favor of the plain meaning of the biblical text — a meaning which they generally identified with the literal sense. Premillennialists also shared the prevailing commitment to the Scottish Common Sense philosophy, which dominated much of American thought until after the Civil War. That philosophy glorified the empirical method, eschewed metaphysical speculation, and stressed that the common sense of humanity offered a sure guide to truth. When the Scriptures were viewed through this philosophical lens, it was assumed that they offered a source of pure, hard "facts" — facts to be taken at face value and requiring no elaborate theory to explain them. Thus any biblical interpretation that seemed to deviate from a straightforward, factual reading of the text was at a severe disadvantage.[8]

George Duffield's *Dissertation on the Prophecies* (1842) serves as an excellent case in point. Duffield claimed to bring no preconceptions to his study. A commonsense man of no metaphysical presumptions (or so he styled

7. Ernest R. Sandeen, *The Roots of Fundamentalism: British and American Millenarianism, 1800-1930* (Chicago: University of Chicago Press, 1970), 42-58, 81-102; Whalen, "Millenarianism and Millennialism in America," 43-101, 217-49; Ruth Alden Doan, *The Miller Heresy, Millennialism, and American Culture* (Philadelphia: Temple University Press, 1987); Edwin Scott Gaustad, *The Rise of Adventism: A Commentary on the Social and Religious Ferment of Mid-Nineteenth Century America* (New York: Harper & Row, 1974); Ronald L. Numbers and Jonathan M. Butler, eds., *The Disappointed: Millerism and Millenarianism in the Nineteenth Century* (Bloomington: Indiana University Press, 1987).

8. Theodore Dwight Bozeman, *Protestants in an Age of Science: The Baconian Ideal and Antebellum American Religious Thought* (Chapel Hill: University of North Carolina Press, 1977), 124-59; George Marsden, "Everyone One's Own Interpreter? The Bible, Science, and Authority in Mid-Nineteenth Century America," in *The Bible in America: Essays in Cultural History,* ed. Nathan O. Hatch and Mark A. Noll (New York: Oxford University Press, 1982), 79-100.

himself), Duffield merely turned to the text to derive its plain meaning. "Theory is out of place and unallowable in the study of prophecy. . . . It is a simple question that in all cases must be asked, what is the fair and legitimate meaning of the words — a matter-of-fact investigation — no theorising, no speculations." This commonsense literalism did, of course, allow for metaphor in many instances. No millenarian was fool enough, said Duffield, to think that when the Apocalypse spoke of a woman who "appeared in heaven clothed with the sun, having the moon under her feet, and upon her head a crown of twelve stars, there ever, literally or in reality, was such a thing." But the burden of proof always rested on those who wished to make prophecy metaphoric. A prediction was always presumed literal unless good common sense dictated that it had to be read in a nonliteral or spiritual fashion. By this standard, he reasoned, there was nothing in human consciousness which logically forbade a supernatural rending of the present age and a premillennial coming of the Lord. Failure to take those predictions of the miraculous literally were prima facie evidence of religious unbelief, and Duffield implied with only slight qualification that some postmillennial views were verging dangerously close to infidelity.[9]

The issue of literal versus spiritual exegesis was particularly troublesome for postmillennialists. On the one hand, they did indeed argue for a spiritual reading of prophecies relative to the millennial kingdom. For example, Hodge asserted: "This whole theory of a splendid earthly kingdom is a relic of Judaism, and out of keeping with the spirituality of the Gospel." Likewise, Moses Stuart insisted that the gospel itself, through its persuasive power, would bring about the Kingdom of God on earth; and he mocked the "modern enthusiastic interpreters, who find in our text [Rev. 20] a temporal and visible reign of Christ on earth." Such carnal fantasies Stuart thought scarcely worthy to refute. Similarly, Joseph Berg insisted that scriptural images of Christ's rule on earth ought not to be read as descriptive of an actual physical or temporal sovereignty; they were symbols of a "spiritual reign" which Christ would exercise. Yet at the same time, postmillennialists were by no means willing to concede the principle of literalism to their opponents. They, too, had inherited the historic Protestant bias toward the literal sense of the biblical text and likewise had felt the influence of the Scottish philosophy. Thus postmillennialists, even as they proposed spiritual readings of prophecy, eagerly insisted that they had in no way departed from the plain or literal interpretation of Scripture.[10]

9. George Duffield, *Prophecies Relative to the Second Coming* (New York: Dayton and Newman, 1842), 63, 101, 104-5, 409.

10. Hodge, *Systematic Theology,* 3:844; Stuart, *Commentary on the Apocalypse,* 2:480;

Indeed, postmillennialists often insisted that they, not their millenarian counterparts, held clear title to commonsense, literal exegesis. Thus in January 1843, a writer in the *Methodist Quarterly Review* insisted: "We claim to be, not only rigid literalists, but unsparing iconoclasts — ruthless demolishers of all theories. We wish to strip the passage [concerning the millennium] of all the superincumbent strata which ingenious men have deposited all round it, and come down to the plainest and most obvious literal reading of the text. The advocates of Chiliasm boast of being, by eminence, *the literalists;* if therefore we detect them in unnatural figure, and show them both a more natural and more literal mode, they are bound either to give up their boast or adopt our exposition."[11] The postmillennial attack enumerated instances in which millenarians allegedly departed from their own vaunted adherence to "matter-of-fact investigation — no theorising, no speculations." That assault took the form of interminable arguments over the proper exegesis of a wide range of biblical verses and issues. Had Jesus already taken the throne of his Kingdom or was that event yet future? Did the great commission — Jesus' command to go unto all nations and make disciples of them — imply the eventual conversion of the world or rather a witness to all peoples? Did the description of the raising of the martyrs at the outset of the millennium portend an actual resurrection of some of the dead or merely a revivifying of the martyrs' values? If the former, were there, then, two resurrections — one at the beginning of the millennium and another at the end — and could one square a double resurrection with numerous scriptures appearing to recognize only one? In the matter of the political restoration of the Jewish people, which biblical verses should receive greater weight: those which promised a new Jewish kingdom or those which asserted that the old covenant had been fulfilled in the new? One could continue to list, to the point of tedium, other matters of contention. To today's readers, perhaps less familiar with the Bible than their nineteenth-century ancestors, such disputes may appear to resemble disorganized house-to-house combat in which clearly defined battle lines have dissolved; but a common front can be discerned in most of these skirmishes. Postmillennialists insisted that the major ostensive referent of prophecy was the triumph of Christ's kingdom, a kingdom which was moral or spiritual in character. To make this assertion was not to abandon the plain meaning of Scripture but rather to affirm it. In a word, the spiritual reading of the text was the literal one.[12]

Moses Stuart, *Hints on the Interpretation of Prophecy* (Andover: Allen, Morrill, and Wardwell, 1842), 140; Berg, *The Second Advent,* 128-49.

11. "The Millennium of Rev. xx.," *MQR* 25 (Jan. 1843): 87.

12. See, e.g., ibid., pp. 83-110; "Modern Millenarianism," *Biblical Repertory and*

The Rev. E. Benjamin Andrews of Granville, Ohio, presented one of the sharpest and most succinct examples of this principle at work in an 1875 essay in the *Baptist Quarterly* on the nature of prophecy. In Old Testament prophecy, Andrews noted that one could find two basic sets of images: first, predictions of a time of spiritual peace, plenitude, and prosperity; second, passages describing "the Messianic victory . . . as coming by force, strife, or bloodshed." One must not suppose that these latter verses dealt chiefly with "judgments and victories of a physical kind," although no one — except a few misguided German biblical critics — would deny that some of these predictions were in fact "fulfilled in wars and judgment" experienced by the Hebrew people. However, the primary referent of both the sanguinary and peaceful prophecies was the same: the moral triumphs of Christ's kingdom. Thus Andrews posited a fundamental hermeneutical principle: "When pictures of physical victory constitute the prophecies, spiritual and saving victories are to be the corresponding fulfillment." As if in anticipation of millenarian protests that he had illicitly "spiritualized" the literal meaning of God's Word, Andrews asserted that the New Testament itself sanctioned this interpretation. Christ taught that the Kingdom was a spiritual not a geographic or political reality, and Paul used military imagery as a symbol of spiritual rather than military crusading. Moreover, Peter's sermon on the Day of Pentecost asserted that the prophecy of Joel — a prophecy speaking not only of the pouring out of the Spirit but also of terrible supernatural portents of blood, fire, and darkness in the heavens — was fulfilled on that occasion. Similarly, the book of Revelation depicted the conquering Christ subduing the world with the sword which was in his mouth — in other words, via the proclamation of the gospel. How baseless, then, was the millenarian expectation that Christ would return in a carnal or literal sense in order to inaugurate the millennium.[13]

According to postmillennialists, their opponents' alleged literalism was a false one, resting upon a retrograde exegetical principle. Millenarians read the New Testament through the eyes of the Old Testament, rather than vice versa. To long for a thousand years during which King Jesus literally occupied a throne in Jerusalem was to confound the carnal types of prophecy with their spiritual antitype, to confuse shadow with substance. In so doing, millenarians conformed Jesus to the erroneous conceptions of his first-century contemporaries. That view, said a writer in the *Methodist*

Princeton Review 25 (Jan. 1853): 66-83; Berg, *The Second Advent,* 128-49; Hodge, *Systematic Theology,* 3:790-868.

13. E. Benj. Andrews, "The Missionary Future in the Light of Prophecy," *BQ* 9 (Oct. 1875): 430-50.

Quarterly Review in 1843, "violates the true nature of Christ's moral government." It is a return to "fables of Jewish dotage." Or as a writer in the same journal declared more than thirty years later: "After we have seen the sad and fatal mistake of the Jews in *literalizing* and *secularizing* the reign of Christ, until they have judged themselves unworthy of eternal life, is it not strange that we should swing back through the *spiritual* life and power of Christianity for eighteen hundred years, and seek to take the Son of man by force and make him an earthly king?"[14]

Deciding who came away victor in these exchanges is not an easy task. Each side scored telling points against the other. Postmillennialists could justly claim that their opponents' "literal" exegesis often pulled verses out of historical context, produced logical muddles, and subverted traditional Protestant hermeneutics in favor of rules of interpretation so novel that, in the words of the *Princeton Review* in 1853, "the Bible may almost be said to wear a new visage and speak with a new tongue — a tongue not very intelligible, in many of its utterances, to the uninitiated."[15] Yet quite apart from the merits of its specific arguments, millenarianism accurately perceived that important parts of the New Testament vibrated with apocalyptic urgency. For example, Jesus warned his disciples that they should be prepared for the coming of the Son of Man at an unexpected hour. How, on the basis of a postmillennial eschatology, could one account for this admonition? In an article in 1875, Methodist minister Daniel D. Buck pressed this point vigorously: "Indeed, assuming that the advent is post-millennial, unto whom do these warning appeals apply? Do they intend to excite apprehensions without the slightest reason to expect what is apprehended? Certainly, if the advent is post-millennial, no one who lives before the beginning of the millennium, and no one who lives during the first nine tenths of it, can have the slightest reason to apprehend the coming of the Lord. . . . Can a post-millennialist, with any show of sincerity, or any appearance of propriety, pray, preach, and exhort as our Lord did, with reference to the uncertainty, imminency, or the immediate practical use of the advent of the Lord?"[16] (The argument, of course, cut two ways: if the postmillennialist was embarrassed by the prominence of the apocalyptic hope, the millenarian had to explain why it was so long deferred. Upon the latter's hypothesis, said postmillennialists, the New Testament taught over eighteen hundred years ago the possibility of an imminent advent, and

14. "Millennial Traditions," *MQR* 25 (July 1843): 422, 435; "The Millennium and Second Advent," *MQR* 58 (July 1876): 440.

15. "Modern Millenarianism," 68.

16. Daniel Buck, "The Millennium and the Advent," *MQR* 57 (July 1875): 403.

therefore its writers were either in error or misled their readers — suppositions no devout Christian could accept.) Nevertheless, the millenarian critics exposed a fundamental weakness in postmillennial eschatology: how could the hope of an imminent apocalyptic overturning remain a vital one within a system which postponed such fulfillment by centuries?

Yet this exegesis suffered from an even deeper problem. At its heart, the postmillennial hermeneutic was profoundly ambiguous. It wanted to treat the hope of the Apocalypse partly as figurative truth and partly as literal. Against the millenarians, for example, postmillennialists fought verse by verse, insisting that prophecy had spiritual not carnal fulfillment. Prophecies of a political kingdom for the Jews were types of Christianity's religious influence, the promise of a special resurrection of the martyrs was a metaphor for the resurgence of their values, and the picture of Christ reigning in the millennium was only an emblem of his presence in the hearts of all men and women. Yet when postmillennialists came to the passages speaking of a Second Coming in which Christ would raise the dead and subject them to judgment, figurative and spiritual interpretation ceased. These prophecies were deemed literal descriptions of future events, albeit events which would occur after the thousand years. In view of the basic principle of interpretation postmillennialists had enunciated, it was not clear why such predictions should be exempt from a spiritual reading. If descriptions of an earthly millennium required a spiritual interpretation, why should not the same hermeneutic dissolve the literal facticity of a postmillennial Second Coming and end of the world?

But postmillennialists were not prepared for a step so radical. A future day of judgment, a literal Second Coming, a dramatic overturning of the present age, and the resurrection of the dead — these were motifs too deeply embedded in the Scriptures and the Protestant tradition to permit their transmutation into metaphor, at least for persons still deeply committed to the notion of an inerrant Bible whose literal sense was authoritative. The postmillennial compromise was to spiritualize those prophecies having to do with the advent of God's kingdom on earth, but to keep as nonmetaphoric or literal truths those which were expected to transpire (conveniently!) many centuries hence. As Methodist Bishop S. M. Merrill summarized in an 1879 book, a proper interpretation of the Apocalypse had simultaneously to avoid two extremes: the millenarian notion that Jesus might return at any moment "to wield an earthly scepter over the nations" and a "liberalist" view that denied altogether a literal Second Advent and Last Judgment. Merrill had, in effect, stationed the postmillennialist on a precarious exegetical tightrope.[17]

17. S. M. Merrill, *The Second Coming of Christ Considered in Its Relation to the*

By the late nineteenth century, there were signs that this tenuous exegetical balancing act could not be maintained indefinitely. In the same year as Bishop Merrill's book, Israel Warren, a Maine Congregationalist of some eminence within his denomination, authored an immensely learned work entitled *Parousia.* Warren argued that there would be no future millennium, Second Coming, end of the world, or last judgment. He did not derive these conclusions from religious skepticism. An orthodox Congregationalist, he was firmly committed to an inerrant Bible and saw himself as one who interpreted that authoritative Word according to the principles of Moses Stuart. His starting point in the endeavor was a massive catalogue of New Testament verses demonstrating that Jesus and the early Christians expected the *parousia* (the Greek word usually translated as "appearing," or "coming") in the near future. Warren ridiculed the usual devices by which orthodox interpreters obviated the natural meanings of these texts — e.g., the one which made the destruction of Jerusalem about 70 C.E. into a type of the end of the world. The plain meaning of the New Testament indicated that Jesus and his disciples expected an imminent parousia. Unwilling to admit that inspired writers could have been in error, Warren then looked for evidence that the so-called Second Coming of Christ did occur. He acknowledged that the chief obstacle to his interpretation lay in the vivid imagery used by the New Testament to describe eschatological events. Planets reeling in their courses, the heavens rolled up like a scroll, or the earth consumed with fire — these were not events which appeared to have already transpired; but the problem was obviated when one realized that the ancients used such dramatic imagery to describe political and religious upheavals. Thus all of the great eschatological events foretold in the Bible — including the Second Coming — could be attributed to historical events early in the Christian era. Thus nineteenth-century Protestants should expect no future return of Christ on the clouds, and the world moved toward no future smashup at which time the dead would be raised and judged. Each person experienced resurrection and judgment at the moment of death, and the physical universe would go on indefinitely — perhaps forever. Lest anyone think these conclusions overly radical, Warren hastened to assure his reader that they were the results of interpretive principles sanctioned by the New Testament itself:

> The material type is never fulfilled in a material antitype; bloody rite has no bloody rite as its counterpart; no Christian altar answers to Hebrew altar, no earthly Jerusalem to the Jerusalem that then was. . . . And so,

---

Millennium, the Resurrection, and the Judgment (Cincinnati: Hitchcock and Walden, 1979), 13, 282.

> by all the principles of analogy, as the ancient ritual dispensation was in all its parts symbolical of the new, which is spiritual, so [images of] its inauguration with material splendors ought to find its fulfillment in one that is spiritual. To look for one appealing to the senses is to reverse all the laws of progress and development in God's revelation to man.[18]

Few postmillennialists could have taken exception to the principle, but many must have squirmed when they saw the rigor with which Warren applied it.

Warren's theory was not significant primarily for the number of adherents it won — though it did prompt a number of favorable reviews — but rather because it disclosed the ambiguous and fragile nature of the biblical interpretation postmillennialists had created. Uncomfortable with elements of the apocalyptic mentality, they could not repudiate it entirely lest they call into question biblical inspiration as they understood it. What they did, in effect, was to spiritualize a significant portion of the Apocalypse while retaining as literal truth a Second Advent, the end of the world, and the final resurrection to judgment. Thus postmillennialism was a theological and exegetical Janus — one face looking toward the literal accomplishment of apocalyptic hopes; the other turned away, slightly embarrassed by such crudities. Warren had demonstrated how difficult it might be to maintain that dual orientation. In fact, a distinct biblically grounded postmillennialism had largely vanished from American Protestantism by the early twentieth century. But that story, of course, is another one beyond the limits of this brief essay.[19]

18. Israel Warren, *The Parousia: A Critical Study of the Scripture Doctrines of Christ's Second Coming; His Reign as King; The Resurrection of the Dead; and the General Judgment* (Portland, ME: Hoyt, Fogg, and Donham, 1879), 83, 116, and passim. A similar argument was made by George Bush, *A Treatise on the Millennium; In Which the Prevailing Theories on That Subject Are Carefully Examined; and the True Scripture Doctrine Attempted to Be Elicited and Established* (New York: J. J. Harper, 1832). The appeal of Bush's work, however, was limited by his Swedenborgianism.

19. For an account of this story, see James H. Moorhead, "The Erosion of Postmillennialism in American Religious Thought, 1865-1925," *ChH* 53 (March 1984): 61-77.

18. The Fourth Gospel as Trinitarian Source Then and Now

Cornelius Plantinga, Jr.

Introduction: Trinitarian Significance of the Fourth Gospel

A glance at the biblical text indices of major patristic treatises[1] reveals how massively the Gospel of John figured in the formation of classic trinitarianism. References to it typically overwhelm those to other biblical books. The fathers found in the Fourth Gospel a deep mine of trinity materials, and they kept returning to it not only to gather antiheretic ammunition (both modalists and Arians could be dispatched with an artful exegesis of 1:14 and 10:30),[2] but also to quarry the building blocks for their own constructive statements of the doctrine of the Trinity. Of these, Augustine's is famous and representative: "The Father is God, and the Son is God, and the Holy Spirit is God . . . yet we do not say that the very supreme Trinity itself is three Gods, but one God."[3]

1. E.g., Hilary of Poitiers, *De Trinitate;* Augustine, *De Trinitate;* Gregory of Nyssa, *Contra Eunomium.*

2. So, e.g., Hilary of Poitiers on 1:14, where the Father's only Son is παρὰ πατρός (God from God in "our creed"), concludes against Arians that "both are one nature" and, against Sabellians, that they are nonetheless "not one person" (Hilary *De Trin.* 1.17). G. Christopher Stead argues that the Johannine "of" or "from" relation is key to the meaning of the Nicene *homoousios* clause: the Son bears a relation to the Father looser than an identity relation, but tighter than mere common class membership. For the Son is of or from the Father in a quasi-genetic derivation that suggests a family relation (Stead, *Divine Substance* [Oxford: Clarendon, 1977], 247-50). On 10:30 ("I and the Father are one"), Tertullian begins a long history of using ἐσμεν to rout Sabellians (I and the Father *are* one, not *is* one) and ἕν (*unum,* not *unus*) against any who would deny unity of substance (Tertullian *Adversus Praxean* 22, 25). T. Evan Pollard has multiple instances in "The Exegesis of John X.30 in the Early Trinitarian Controversies," *NTS* 3 (1957): 334-49.

3. Augustine *De Trin.* 5.8.9. Though much debate has centered around the referent of

An innocent in these matters might be surprised to discover how much smoothing out and tidying up of biblical data Augustine had to undertake in order to get the Scriptures to yield a statement as balanced and symmetrical as the one just quoted. In particular, if the general picture of deity that emerges from the New Testament comprises three probably distinct, yet tightly yoked, divine persons, that picture is surely both sharper and richer in John's Gospel than elsewhere, and moreover sharper and richer with respect to Father and Son than with respect to the Holy Spirit. While the very terms "Father" and "Son" suggest derivation, distinction, and kinship, the Holy Spirit is a more shadowy and anonymous figure that is hardly a family member and is only arguably personal. It is instructive to note, for instance, that even in the Fourth Gospel — the most highly developed of New Testament witnesses to the *Wechselbeziehungen* within God — the Spirit is never said to love or be loved by Father and Son, and is never prayed to, doxologized, or worshiped.

Such muzzled New Testament witness undoubtedly accounts, in part, for the sluggish development of Spirit doctrine till half a century after Nicea.[4] Even then Spirit treatises sometimes show a compensating tendency to color in part of the New Testament Spirit silhouette with novel little splashes of speculation. So at one place Gregory of Nyssa charmingly defends the Holy Spirit against the Macedonians by affirming the Spirit's agency in creation. If only the Father and Son had participated in creation, says Gregory, then the Holy Spirit would have been guilty of a kind of divine freeloading: "What was the Holy Spirit doing at the time when the Father was at work with the Son upon the Creation? Was he employed upon some other works . . . ? [Was he] not employed at all, but dissociated himself from the busy work of creating by reason of an inclination to ease and rest, which shrank from toil? . . . How was it that he was inactive? Because he could not, or because he would not work?"[5]

God as predicate in the initial Father, Son, and Spirit clauses, and whether this can possibly be the same referent as in the concluding trinity clause, Augustine does clearly identify the referent of the climactic "one God" claim: the one God is the supreme Trinity itself. This clarifying reference is missing in the reproduction of Augustine's formulation in the 15th and 16th verses of the Athanasian Creed: "(15) So the Father is God, the Son is God, and the Holy Spirit is God; (16) And yet they are not [or, there are not] three Gods, but one God."

4. In accord with his theory that the Spirit itself (not just the faith kindled by the Spirit) responds to God from us (God "does not merely come to man, but encounters himself from man"), Karl Barth speculates that the lag in the development of the doctrine of the Spirit is owed to proud human reluctance to concede that even our subjective access to God is under God's control, not ours. The controversy therefore required to stimulate Spirit doctrinal development was not so much the Pneumatomachian as the Pelagian! See Karl Barth, *CD* I/1 (2d ed., 1975), 451, 467-68.

5. Gregory of Nyssa *De Spir. Sanct.*

Shorn of its rhetorical irony, Gregory's speculation still reveals his awareness of the relevant clues (certain titles, functions, and formulas) and his resultant habit of thought: the Spirit is a divine figure and a personal one. Such titles as "Spirit of God" and "Spirit of Christ" are capsular for a general New Testament distinction-within-unity description of the Spirit in relation to the Father and Son. Moreover, the Spirit performs certain uniquely divine functions, is vulnerable to blasphemy, and is included in those bi- and triadic formulas, some of them liturgical, that link the names of the three persons as if they are similarly divine and similarly personal.[6] So the case for moving beyond binitarianism to full three-personed trinitarianism could and can be made, even if with due caution and misgiving.

In making it, why were major fourth-century trinitarian theorists drawn like a magnet to John? Among all New Testament documents the Fourth Gospel provides not only the most raw material for the church doctrine of the Trinity, but also the most highly developed patterns of reflection on this material — particularly, patterns that show evidence of pressure to *account* somehow for the distinct personhood and divinity of Father, Son, and Spirit without compromising the unity of God.

How are such accounts attempted? Within the Fourth Gospel's general program of life giving and life disclosing, Father, Son, and usually Spirit/Paraclete appear as distinct role players. Yet they are also unified in John's scheme by (let us say) six central phenomena: common will, work, word, and knowledge, plus reciprocal love (excluding the Spirit) and glorifying.[7] A functional subordination relation among the three (the Father sends, the Son sends and is sent, the Spirit is simply sent) insures that the same phenomena that distinguish the persons also unite them, for in the divine missions just one will or work, for instance, gets presented. In fact, John appears to treat the six phenomena as manifestations — possibly as reinforcements — of some mysterious, superlative unity expressed by the use of εν or ἕν, i.e., "in" or "one." Father and Son are *in* each other; they are also *one* with each other.[8] Though the relation of "in-ness" and oneness is never explained, the two concepts are, for John, obviously close, transcendent, and primordial.

6. Functions: regenerating (John 3:5), judging (John 16:8-11), dispensing God's love (Rom. 5:5); vulnerability to blasphemy: Mark 3:29; Luke 12:10; presence in triadic formulas: Matt. 28:19; Rom. 14:17-18; Gal. 4:6; 2 Cor. 13:14. The Johannine Paraclete references (14:16, 26; 15:26; 16:7) seem strikingly personal.

7. Will: 4:34; work: 5:19-22; 15:26; word: 3:34; 16:14; knowledge: 10:14-15; love: 3:35; glory: 16:14; 17:22.

8. Cf. 10:30 and 10:38. In chap. 17, in a mass of reciprocity statements, the in-ness and oneness relations are extended from divine life to human life, and then set forth as a model for the continuing life of the new community. See esp. 17:20-22.

John's combination of transcendent unity and functional subordination in the life of God virtually assured later debate (not least the Arian debate of the 4th century) and has offered theologians along the centuries endless opportunity for testing various hermeneutical skills and theories in the attempt to draft trinity statements.

Of course, it is mere anachronism to burden the Fourth Gospel with an obligation to answer later trinitarian questions, or at least to answer them in the terms in which they are asked.[9] For one thing, what John says of Jesus is often soteriologically or eschatologically motivated and functionally, not metaphysically, cast.[10] For another, modern translations of John 1:14, 18; and 3:16, 18 have largely emasculated these verses as intratrinitarian eternal generation prooftexts. The "only-begotten Son" has been trimmed to the "only Son" (RSV) or "one and only Son" (NIV) in order to render μονογενής more accurately, if with less metaphysical specificity and ambitiousness.[11]

Still, there may be less doctrinal loss here than meets the eye. Beyond reading out of it a mysterious, nontemporal derivation relation of Son to Father, nobody ever knew what "only-begotten" meant anyhow. Its traditionally modest doctrinal yield can probably be harvested just as well from

9. Theologians in every age have found temptation in this area hard to resist. Two examples, one patristic and one contemporary: In *De Trin.* 2.2.4, Augustine ponders John 7:16 ("My teaching is not mine, but his that sent me") and wonders which provision of his "double rule" applies to the interpretation of this text, namely, Jesus' equality with God given his divine status (his *forma dei*) or Jesus' inequality with God given his human status (his *forma servi*). Augustine concludes that if this Johannine statement is to be referred to Jesus in his divine status, what it means is simply that God has begotten his Son. For in a divine person (given Neoplatonic simplicity theory) to have something and to be that thing are equivalent. Hence for God to give doctrine or teaching to his Son is simply to beget him, since "the Son is not one thing and his doctrine another."

In considering a number of Johannine texts suggestive of Jesus' preexistence, Rudolf Bultmann assures us that "Jesus is not presented in literal seriousness as a preexistent divine being who came in human form to earth to reveal unprecedented secrets." According to Bultmann, preexistence language is used only to underscore the life-and-death urgency of Jesus' call to decision. The author of the Fourth Gospel turns out, reassuringly enough, to be an existentialist demythologizer. See Rudolf Bultmann, *Theology of the New Testament,* trans. Kendrick Grobel, 2 vols. in 1 (New York: Scribner's, 1955), 2:62.

10. E.g., "Son of God" appears to function as an obedience title in John. One can see this by noting that, for Jesus, "Father" and "the one who sent me" are largely equivalent designations (7:16; 14:10b). Though the title's obedience function does not remove its divine redolence (indicated, e.g., at such places as 5:18), it does show that divinity ascriptions by title are typically complex and oblique.

11. The translation history here includes Jerome's choice of *unigenitus* (rather than *unicus* or *solus*) as the Vulg. rendering of μονογενής, the influence of the Vulg. on AV and other translations, and the contemporary rejection of "only-begotten" and equivalents on the basis of philological conclusions. The pioneering treatment is D. Moody, " 'God's Only Son': The Translation of John 3:16 in the RSV," *JBL* 72 (1953): 213-19.

the sheer pairing of Father and Son language and imagery in John's Christological preexistence contexts.

The fact is, while making cautionary allowances for the nonmetaphysical motive and cast of many of John's central claims, such twentieth-century theologians as Karl Barth, Jürgen Moltmann, and Leonardo Boff still find much of interest in them. This is so despite the solemn warnings sometimes issued against using the Fourth Gospel as a trinitarian happy hunting ground — warnings that such use precritically ignores the conclusions of scholarship since at least Strauss's *Leben Jesu,* namely, that John is late, nonhistorical, and highly interpretive theologically.[12]

What is seldom noticed by those who assume the historical-critical disenfranchisement of the Fourth Gospel as a trinity source is that answers to the question whether John reproduces, say, any of Jesus' words, or only Jesus' voice, or even something much less, are typically relevant only to the reconstruction of Jesus' consciousness of his status vis-à-vis God, not to that status itself or to our knowledge of it. Even if the most radically skeptical assessment of the Fourth Gospel were true,[13] it would hardly follow that John is not an open mine for trinity material. All that would follow is that the canonically accepted testimony to Jesus' divine status is presented not autobiographically as Jesus' but theologically as John's.[14]

I. Method Contrasts

Though, as we shall see, patristic and contemporary approaches to John as a trinity source sometimes converge in interesting ways, nobody who reads representative examples of each can miss certain revealing differences.

12. See, e.g., Maurice Wiles, "Christianity Without Incarnation?," 4, and John Hick, "Jesus and the World Religions," 172-73, 175-76, both in *The Myth of God Incarnate,* ed. John Hick (Philadelphia: Westminster, 1977).

13. See, e.g., Kirsopp Lake: "John may contain a few fragments of true tradition, but in the main it is fiction," in *The Albert Schweitzer Jubilee Book,* ed. A. A. Roback (Cambridge, MA: Sci-art, 1945), 431.

14. This distinction is sometimes acknowledged and sometimes ignored by the same theologian. E.g., Karl Barth often assumes a certain amount of temporal compression in the Fourth Gospel so that John 17 may be seen as a prayer of the exalted Lord and the whole Gospel as almost "one long story of the transfiguration" (*CD* IV/1, 314; IV/2, 139). Moreover, he explicitly states that the NT presentation of Jesus Christ as divine "would still be true even if it could be proved and not merely suspected that Jesus Himself did not expressly speak of His majesty, His Messiahship, His divine Sonship" (IV/1, 161-62). Nonetheless, Barth pointedly treats 14:6 (I am the way, the truth, and the life) as *ipsissima verba Jesu* in using this text as an antidote to natural theology (II/1, 177).

Most obvious are contrasts in theological method, including division or distribution of labor. Contemporary Christian trinitarianism subcontracts to a host of specialists including biblical scholars; historians of doctrine, theology, liturgy, and confession; philosophers and historians of philosophy; motif researchers;[15] sociologists and phenomenologists;[16] ethicists; and, of course, other dogmatic or systematic theologians. With the notable exception of Karl Barth, few contemporary systematic theologians exhibit the fruit of their own exegesis. Some do not even exhibit the fruit of other people's exegesis: process trinitarians, for example, typically do not linger long over John because they do not linger long over Scripture.[17]

The fathers were more versatile. The major fathers present trinity studies that weave exegesis, hermeneutical theory, polemics, philosophy, dogmatics — sometimes meditation, prayer, preaching, and even numerology — seamlessly together.

As in most matters patristic and trinitarian, Augustine is the paradigm case. In *On the Trinity* one finds a powerful and subtle statement of the doctrine of the Trinity that self-consciously derives trinitarian principles largely, though not wholly, from Scripture. For instance, from his analysis of John 10:30 and the alternation in John 14:26 and 15:26 between Father and Son as senders of the Paraclete, Augustine derives the principle that, where trinitarian persons are concerned, what is said of each is said of all. The alternation passages also provide him with one of several supports for his *filioque* teaching.[18] Meanwhile, Augustine uses his hermeneutical double rule, mentioned above, to handle those "apparently contrary and mutually repugnant sayings" in John (esp. 10:30 and 14:28) and elsewhere that have misled heretics and confused the faithful.[19] True, in the sometimes acutely difficult middle books, largely aimed at the "cunning argument" of the Arians, Augustine subjects his trinity statement to a searching conceptual analysis that appears to owe more to Plotinus and Marius Victorinus than to the Fourth Gospel and that yields a formal trinity statement so tightly unified as to prompt endless suspicions of modalism.[20] Still, a

15. E.g., G. Christopher Stead, *Divine Substance.*

16. See, e.g., the references in Joseph A. Bracken, "The Holy Trinity as a Community of Divine Persons," *Heythrop Journal* 15 (1974): 166-82, 257-70; and in Geevarghese Mar Osthathios, *Theology of a Classless Society* (Maryknoll, NY: Orbis, 1980).

17. Examples: Joseph A. Bracken, *The Triune Symbol: Persons, Process, and Community* (Lanham, MD: University Press of America, 1985); Norman Pittenger, *The Divine Triunity* (Philadelphia: United Church Press, 1977); Marjorie Hewitt Suchocki, *God — Christ — Church: A Practical Guide to Process Theology* (New York: Crossroad, 1982).

18. *De Trin.* 1.12.25; 4.20.29.

19. Ibid., 1.11.2; 1.7.14; 1.9.18.

20. The key places in *De Trin.* are 5.10.11, where Augustine has each of Father, Son,

comparison of books 5-7 with the more Hilary-like books 1-4 and especially 15 (which draws much from pluralist statements of the Fourth Gospel) shows that Augustine's overall statement is mixed.[21]

Along the way, Augustine offers patches of pious entreaty and meditation,[22] a brief and wonderfully obscure treatment of ternary and senary numbers in relation to the timing of the Incarnation in the "sixth age,"[23] and a closing prayer of considerable beauty.[24]

What impresses the modern reader is the constant, visible blend of exegesis, dogmatics, polemics, and piety, and the chastening evidence throughout of Augustine's conviction that even difficult and technical theology is always done from and for catholic faith. Accordingly, after turning again and again to John's prologue as the center of his incarnation theory, Augustine at one point suggests a rehabilitation program for those who struggle with the doctrine of incarnation. They must gain understanding and love by faithfully purging their minds, by abstaining from sin, by doing good works, and "by praying with the groaning of holy desires."[25]

This is a regimen seldom prescribed in contemporary trinitarianism. Though contemporary trinitarians do draw on Scripture and surely on the Fourth Gospel as one base for their trinity theories, they sometimes leave broad hints that concerns other than piety, knowledge of God, or the building of catholic faith have become important, possibly primary. Especially in the recent wave of liberation trinitarianisms, one often finds trinity theories shaped significantly by socio-political motives and goals, and self-conscious from the outset that "our unjust society and our perverted

---

and Spirit identical with the divine essence; 6.1.2, where each of the essence attributes is identical with each of the others, and esp. 7.6.11 where Augustine (by contrast with Gregory of Nyssa) refuses the relevance of the genus/species/individual apparatus in the Trinity since there can be utterly no reproduction or multiplication in the divine life. The "persons" are really only self-relations of the one divine essence to itself. Harnack's complaint of modalism in Augustine is premiere among many: Augustine, says Harnack, "only gets beyond Modalism by the mere assertion that he does not wish to be a Modalist, and by the aid of ingenious distinctions between different ideas" (Adolf von Harnack, *History of Dogma,* trans. Neil Buchanan, 7 vols. repr. in 4 [New York: Dover, 1961], 4:130-31 n. 1).

21. Even his favorite and final trinitarian analogy — that of an individual human mind remembering, understanding, and loving God within itself — is not quite conclusive for trinitarian monism in Augustine. For in comparing, e.g., 14.8.11 with 14.12.15, we can see the (possibly deliberate) ambiguity in Augustine's thought between self-reflexive and mutual love, sometimes expressed with plays on *diligere se.* See Oliver O'Donovan, *The Problem of Self-Love in St. Augustine* (New Haven: Yale University Press, 1980), 131-34.

22. *De Trin.* 1.3.5; 2.1.1; 8.1.1.

23. Ibid., 4.4.7.

24. Ibid., 15.28.51. So also Hilary, *De Trin.* 12.52-57.

25. Ibid., 4.21.31.

idea of God are in close and terrible alliance."[26] Thus the calls to justice and to trinitarian theory revision get issued simultaneously. Joseph Bracken is explicit in endorsing this contemporary tendency to shape trinity theories to reflect social needs and realities: "Human beings are more aware than ever before of the need for community, of the fact of change or development, often accompanied by deep suffering, in human life, and finally of the distinctively bisexual character of all human relations. If the concept of God, specifically of God as triune, does not in some way reflect these all-pervasive human concerns, then it will cease to be truly relevant to present-day men and women."[27]

Whether mildly or aggressively proposed, the principle of trinitarian relevance to human needs and realities — sacramental, liturgical, ethical, social, political — has become a twentieth-century staple. Virtually every contemporary trinitarian theorist would endorse for trinity theory what Walter Kasper observes with respect to Christology, namely, that even if trinity doctrine is not "derived *from* human and social needs," we must at least demand that it be constructed "*in the light of* human questions and needs."[28]

II. John and the Social Analogy

No twentieth-century trinity theory meets Kasper's demand more self-consciously than the various species of social analogies. These are theories that have Father, Son, and Spirit as distinct centers of love, will, and act (and, accordingly, of knowledge and consciousness) who are tightly enough joined to each other so as to make plausible the claim that they are a (complex) social unit.[29] Though variously motivated, social trinity theories can plausibly claim to follow the trajectories not only of the incarnational

26. Juan Luis Segundo, *Our Idea of God,* trans. John Drury, Theology for Artisans of a New Humanity, 3 (Maryknoll, NY: Orbis, 1974), 8.

27. Joseph Bracken, *What Are They Saying about the Trinity?* (New York: Paulist, 1979), 81.

28. Walter Kasper, *Jesus the Christ,* trans. V. Green (London: Burns and Oates, 1976), 20.

29. Examples: Joseph Bracken, *What Are They Saying?;* Jürgen Moltmann, *The Crucified God: The Cross of Christ as the Foundation and Criticism of Christian Theology,* trans. R. A. Wilson and John Bowden (New York: Harper & Row, 1974); idem, *The Trinity and the Kingdom,* trans. Margaret Kohl (San Francisco: Harper & Row, 1981); Geevarghese Mar Osthathios, *Classless Society;* David Brown, *The Divine Trinity* (LaSalle, IL: Open Court, 1985); Leonardo Boff, *Trinity and Society,* trans. Paul Burns (Maryknoll, NY: Orbis, 1988).

and divine pluralism lines found in Paul, Hebrews, and John (esp. chap. 17), but also of certain suggestive tendencies in, among others, Hilary, Augustine, and especially Gregory of Nyssa — tendencies themselves often explicitly grounded in Fourth Gospel references. For instance, Hilary has a robust states-of-Christ Christology in each phase of which the Son appears fully personal and distinct from the Father.[30] Augustine draws heavily on those places in the Fourth Gospel in which Father, Son, and Spirit/Paraclete appear as distinct divine centers of love, will, knowledge, and purposeful action — indeed, as *mutually* knowing, loving, glorying entities.[31] The divine persons share a unity (not an identity) of will akin to that of humans, and a "society of love."[32] "For," says Augustine, "if the many souls that draw nigh to God are one through charity . . . is it not still truer that the Trinity is one God?"[33] After trying a host of psychological analogies for the Trinity, Augustine concedes in *De Trinitate* 15 that we shall be quite misled if we think of Father, Son, and Spirit as three faculties of one divine person. For each is "living"; none lacks perception or knowledge.[34]

But it is really Gregory of Nyssa who offers the most direct link from the Fourth Gospel to contemporary social theories. For though his theory is formally similar in many respects to Hilary's and Augustine's, Gregory draws pluralist lines out from John's Gospel without a competing and aggressive simplicity theory that might tangle or fuse them. Moreover, he is relatively consistent in the use of a three-man analogy: Father, Son, and Spirit are to godhead or godness what Peter, James, and John are to

30. Hilary *De Trin.* 3.16 gives the parabola-shaped pattern of three states of Christ (preexistence, incarnation, exaltation). At 4.17 Hilary has companionship *(consortium)* of Father and Son in the uttering of the Gen. 1:28 cohortative, and throughout book 4 he has OT theophanies by the Son — a topic on which Augustine is more circumspect. At 9.37 Hilary rejects typical fountain/stream, and light/light analogies because they do not sufficiently allow for the distinct reality of the Son *in se.* Revealingly, he describes the Son as a person (the same person in incarnation as in preexistence) and the heresy of the Sabellians as belief in only one person (9.14; 2.23). This suggests that for Hilary *persona* meant something much more substantial than mode, mask, or role.

31. E.g., John 10:14-15; 16:14-15; 17:24; 16:14.

32. *De Trin.* 4.8.12.

33. *In Ioann. Evang. Tract.* 39.5.

34. *De Trin.* 15.23.43; 15.5.7. However, at 15.23.43 Augustine abandons both the love analogy of books 8 and 9 and the various psychological analogies that follow as symmetrically inadequate. This, plus the remarkably monist tone of books 5-7, makes it hard to judge the overall status of Augustine's theory. Jean-Baptiste Du Roy, "L'expérience de l'amour et l'intelligence de la foi trinitaire selon saint Augustin," *Récherches augustiniennes* 2 (1962): 441-43, claims that Augustine was enough of a Christian churchman to be attracted to ecclesiastical intersubjectivity from John 17 as a love-analogy for the Trinity, but too much of a Neoplatonist to make anything of it.

manhood or manness (τό ἄνθρωπος). Though there are, in fact, many hypostases of the one man (or "manness"), there are precisely three of the one God.[35] Throughout his work, Gregory's three-man analogy supports his consistently personal language with respect to Father, Son, and Spirit — often in contexts in which they are being distinguished. His language shows that he thinks of the persons as distinct agents; his analogy — however dependent on certain Platonic coalescences of concrete and abstract objects — tries to show how the three can still be one God.[36] John's Gospel, Gregory of Nyssa, and, in the West, Richard of St. Victor — whose elaboration of Augustine's abandoned love analogy distressingly resembles a *ménage à trois*[37] — these plus certain predominately Anglo-Catholic theories of the first half of the twentieth century[38] give us tracers in the social trinity trajectory from the first century to the present.

In recent theory, the fruit of the rudimentary social analogies in John, especially 17:20-22, is sometimes combined with reflection on human suffering and on human community and solidarity in the face of it. Challenging the traditional, Hellenistic doctrine of God's impassibility, social trinity theologians often treat the divine life as a model of suffering love and of solidarity in the face of the evil that love suffers.

In *The Crucified God,* Jürgen Moltmann sharply distinguishes the Father and the Father's suffering from the Son and the Son's suffering in the trinitarian event of the cross — an event from which a spirit of love emerges. In this event, and for all *theologia crucis,* Moltmann finds vast socio-political implications of a communitarian kind. For in the crucial trinitarian distinctions which liberate us from "philosophical and political monotheism," we find a "deep community of will" between Father and Son and an inner oneness of surrender and suffering love. All this motivates us toward a "political hermeneutic of liberation," including socialist, democratic, ecological, and cultural liberations.[39]

35. *Ad Graecos* (Jaeg. 3.1, p. 29).

36. For more, see Cornelius Plantinga, Jr., "Gregory of Nyssa and the Social Analogy of the Trinity," *The Thomist* 50 (1986): 325-52.

37. Richard's theory includes not only the conviction that all love needs both a giver and receiver, but also that any good being would be willing to share two-personed love with a third. His conclusion: "In order for love to be true, it demands a plurality of persons; in order for it to be perfect, a trinity of persons" (*De Trin.* 3.13).

38. E.g., J. R. Illingworth, *The Doctrine of the Trinity* (London: Macmillan, 1907); Francis J. Hall, *The Trinity* (New York: Longmans, Green & Co., 1910); Clement C. J. Webb, *God and Personality* (London: George Allen & Unwin, 1918); Leonard Hodgson, *The Doctrine of the Trinity* (London: James Nisbet & Co., 1943); Charles W. Lowry, *The Trinity and Christian Devotion* (New York: Harper and Bros., 1946).

39. Moltmann, *Crucified God,* 216, 243-55, 332-35. Beyond the speediness of his

In his more recent *The Trinity and the Kingdom,* Moltmann suggests that Father, Son, and Spirit are open not only to one another, but also to the human community that is eschatologically progressing toward God. Reflecting on John 17:21, Moltmann compares the "perichoretic at-one-ness" depicted here[40] not only to "the experience of the community of Christ" (to which John extends it), but also to "any order of society which deserves the name of 'human' in the Christian sense," i.e., where love and acceptance prevail. A properly framed doctrine of the Trinity will in fact "compel us to develop social personalism or personal socialism in which individual and social rights converge."[41]

Leonardo Boff has recently developed some of these themes in a particularly forceful and appealing way. In *Trinity and Society,* Boff derives just as much mutuality, reciprocity, liberating intersubjectivity, and other communitarian impulses from the Fourth Gospel's presentation of in-ness and oneness among distinct persons in the divine life as does Jürgen Moltmann, but Boff exhibits more exegesis and takes more care with the tradition. One of the special features of his social-liberation trinitarianism is the discussion of divine *perichōrēsis,* a lovely theologoumenon deriving from the in-ness motifs of the Fourth Gospel, and represented by medieval Latins as either *circuminsessio* or *circumincessio.*[42] *Perichōrēsis* is a sort of intra-trinitarian hospitality concept according to which the divine persons engage in a constant intercourse of mutual love and knowledge, an endless dance of overture and acceptance. *Circuminsessio,* the more passive concept, suggests mutual enveloping; *circumincessio,* the more active, suggests interpenetration. Altogether, the idea for Boff is that in the divine life (John as our witness) a constant, zestful communion of life is carried on, overflowing with self-giving and other-receiving, and mediated to creatures

moves from the trinitarian suffering of the cross to socialism and other commitments, Moltmann marks himself as a modern trinitarian by the use of language that sounds at least as Hegelian as Johannine. E.g., the author claims that "God" is a retrospective description of "the unity of the dialectical history of Father and Son and Spirit in the cross of Golgotha. . . . In that case 'God' is not another nature or a heavenly person or a moral authority, but in fact an 'event'" (p. 247, p. 286 n. 106).

40. Moltmann settles for perichoretic, or mutual in-ness, unity as his oneness principle — a settlement critics have scored as weak and tending to tritheism in comparison with the oneness of nature that the fathers read out of John 10:30 and 17:20-22.

41. Jürgen Moltmann, *Trinity and Kingdom,* 157-58, 199-200. Here and in *Crucified God,* Moltmann's trinity sources and norms are rich and various, including suffering, fellowship, liberating praxis, doxology, history of doctrine, ecumenical dialogue, theological feminism, church order, Jewish and Spanish passion mysticism, Scripture, Luther, Hegel, and the wonderful world of Joachim of Fiore.

42. Boff, *Trinity,* 134-37.

through the Word, Spirit, and communion of the church: "The united society that exists in the Trinity is the foundation of human unity; the latter is inserted in the former. Persons are not annulled, but empowered. Unity is composed of actual persons, both in the Trinity and in humanity, inasmuch as persons are essentially related. . . . The Trinity seeks to see itself reflected in history, through people sharing their goods in common, building up egalitarian and just relationships among all, sharing what they are and what they have."[43]

In an evenhanded drawing of social and ethical implications from his social theory of the Trinity, Boff concludes, with Moltmann, that such a theory calls to account ecclesiastical and political aberrations of both individualist and collectivist sorts. As Jesus' high priestly prayer teaches us, the church is the best analogue of the Holy Trinity. The church is model, agent, and witness to society of the perfect communion within God the Trinity. Rejecting narcissist individualism and massifying collectivism alike, we must grasp the beauty of this distinction-within-unity of the life of God.[44]

III. Social Analogy Conclusion

The development of a full-blown social trinitarianism in contemporary Christian theology shows us one model of development — perhaps an organic model of embryo and plant. John presents a rudimentary social analogy in which Father and Son are one in some mysterious sense that prominently includes mutual love. Augustine offers and withdraws a love analogy for the divine life which then becomes the centerpiece in the medieval trinitarianism of Richard of St. Victor. Meanwhile, Gregory of Nyssa presents a consistent and aggressive three-man analogy that finally amounts to a logical and theological base on which a fuller social theory could be built.

But, of course, Gregory does not speak of "centers of consciousness" or of "personalities" in God. He does not call the Trinity a "society." He shows little interest in the sorts of mutuality and intersubjectivity themes that have become regnant in a part of the twentieth-century tradition. And, predictably, he has nothing to say to the particular interest of liberation trinitarians in grounding a redeeming political praxis in a social view of God. Indeed, Gregory says very little generally about the broader implica-

43. Ibid., 134.
44. Ibid., 148-54.

tions of his theory.[45] The deliberate use of pluralist divinity themes in the Fourth Gospel for liberating social and political conclusions is a contemporary *novum.*

IV. Perils of Economic and Immanent Trinity Identification

If the social analogy offers us one model of Fourth Gospel use in patristic and contemporary perspective — an organic or developmental model — quite a different one may be shown in considering the nest of issues that surrounds the question of immanent and economic trinity identification. Here we find much less by way of clear development of a theme. Instead, it can be shown that a certain trinitarian methodological problem that haunted some of the fathers continues, in virtually the same form, to afflict important twentieth-century theories. In both cases the Fourth Gospel is a main source of the raw material that resists easy assimilation into a coherent trinity theory; in both cases we see a conflict emerge between two of the most basic of all theological principles.

In trinitarian theology we often distinguish the immanent or ontological Trinity from the economic Trinity. That is, we distinguish the patterns and relations of the inner life of God from the patterns and relations of God exhibited in the economy of redemption — centrally the incarnation and the work of the Spirit.

But a stubborn, perhaps an irresolvable question persists: Is this a real distinction? Is there actual and important difference between immanent and economic trinities, or is this mostly an academic distinction drawn for, say, pedagogical purposes? Karl Rahner seems to weigh in on the latter side with what is surely one of the most often-quoted of twentieth-century trinitarian claims: "The 'economic' Trinity *is* the 'immanent' Trinity and the 'immanent' Trinity *is* the 'economic' Trinity."[46]

The question of immanent and economic trinity identification, especially when raised with reference to some specific body of biblical material

45. The most one can say is that Gregory's doctrine of the image of God is pluralist, or, at least, not merely individual. Roger Leys, *L'Image de Dieu chez Saint Grégoire de Nysse: Esquisse d'une doctrine* (Paris: Brouwer, 1951), 64-78, 93, 120-21, observes that for Gregory the image of God is not merely the human individual possessing various faculties, but also humanity ("le plérômé de l'humanité"); i.e., the whole *genre.* Gregory also thinks the church is the image of God, but he develops neither of these ideas as particular implications of his pluralist trinitarianism.

46. Karl Rahner, *The Trinity,* trans. Joseph Donceel (New York: Herder & Herder, 1970; repr. New York: Seabury, 1974), 22 (my emphasis).

such as the Fourth Gospel, at once becomes an exhibit of the tension between two contrary methodological principles that seem equally basic and equally plausible. On the one hand, God *in se* must be the same God as God *ad nos,* or we have no revelation link and no dependable knowledge of God. On the other hand, given that God is transcendent, sublime, and past finding out, we need an accommodation principle that allows a certain amount of slippage between how God appears to us and how God actually is in the supreme freedom and transcendence of the divine life, or God is transparent, predictable, and obvious — none of which preserves the sovereign mystery of God's relation to creatures.

Though a full consideration of these principles, and the tension between them, is far beyond the scope of this essay, a hint of the role they play in representative patristic and contemporary trinity theories will be revealing. Let us briefly consider some samples of the tension in Augustine and Karl Barth's use of John's Gospel.

As noted above, Augustine relies on John 10:30 as an anchor for his claim that what is said of each of the trinitarian persons is said of all. For him "the general rule" is that "each person in the Trinity is mentioned by name in such a way that the others are also understood to be there."[47] Of course, Augustine knows and states at the outset that only the Son was incarnate, only the Spirit poured out at Pentecost, only the Father audible from heaven in the "You are my Son" identifications at Jesus' baptism and transfiguration. These events economically distinguish the persons, and Augustine is willing to draw the immanent conclusion: "He who is the Father is not the Son. . . . He who is the Son is not the Father; and the Holy Spirit is neither the Father nor the Son."[48]

Still, appearances can be deceiving. For in Augustine's overall thought, the oneness statements of John 10 and 17 (which, however mysterious, include oneness of work) plus Augustine's remorseless philosophical tendency to unify and simplify the divine life — these things lead him to a general indivisibility-of-work principle that, in ranging speculatively far beyond any ordinary sense of Scripture, sometimes reaches heroic proportions. Accordingly, he has the whole Trinity (including the Son) working the conception in and birth from Mary.[49] In fact, not content with

47. *De Trin.* 1.10.21. Cf. 6.7.9: "It is difficult to see how one can speak of the Father or the Son alone . . . not that both are the Father or both the Son, but because they are always mutually in one another and neither is alone." Here it is clear that Augustine has in mind the in-ness statements from John 17 as well as the oneness statements from there and from chap. 10.

48. *De Trin.* 1.4.7.

49. Ibid., 2.5.8-9.

the anti-subordination claim that "the Son and Spirit are not less because sent," Augustine uses a fancy paralogism, loosely based on the Fourth Gospel, to argue that the Son actually sends himself: "Wherefore, since the Father sent him by a word, His being sent was the work of both the Father and his Word; therefore the same Son was sent by the Father and the Son, because the Son Himself is the word of the Father."[50]

Finally, the Son's handing over of the Kingdom to the Father in 1 Cor. 15:24 turns out at the end of the day to include handing it over to himself: "He himself is not excluded; because he is one God together with the Father."[51] In the immanent life of God things are tighter and more unified than they appear in the economy of revelation and redemption.

One of the most interesting signs of methodological strain along these lines may be found in Augustine's use of a central Western theological conviction, namely, that the Fourth Gospel missions (the Father sends the Son and the Spirit; the Son also sends the Spirit) are elongations of the intratrinitarian relations.[52] One would suppose that this is a classic case of positing an identity relation between immanent and economic trinities. Indeed, like Hilary, Augustine uses the principle this way for the *filioque* conclusion. If in the economy of redemption the Johannine Jesus alternates in saying that he will send the Spirit from the Father (15:26) with saying that the Father will send the Spirit "in my name" (14:26), then we may conclude that the Spirit proceeds from both. The missions extend an eternal heavenly trajectory.[53]

Yet in considering whether the missions reveal eternal subordination relations in God, Augustine demurs. For here we have to factor in the double rule that distributes texts about Jesus into two categories — those

50. Ibid., 2.5.9.

51. Ibid., 1.8.16.

52. Augustine telescopes the μονογενής texts (John 1:14, 18; 3:16, 18) and certain "coming from" texts (e.g., 8:42; 13:3; 16:28; 17:8) in the movement from missions in books 1-3 of *De Trinitate* back to processions in 4.20.28: "Therefore the Word of God is sent by Him, of whom He is the Word; He is sent by Him, from whom He was begotten; He sends who begot, That is sent which is begotten."

53. Ibid., 4.20.29. Augustine adds that the Spirit is sometimes called the Spirit of the Son, and sometimes the Spirit of the Father, and that in the "small insufflation" of John 20:22 Jesus declares "by a fitting sign" that the Spirit proceeds from him as well as from the Father. Hilary *De Trin.* 2.29 concentrates on the scriptural alternation between such locutions as "Spirit of God" and "Spirit of Christ" for his conclusion on the Spirit that both the Father and Son "begot Him." For Eastern objections to the Western "confusion" of missions with intra-trinitarian relations, esp. keyed to John 15:26, see Jaroslav Pelikan, *The Christian Tradition: A History of the Development of Doctrine,* 5 vols. (Chicago: University of Chicago Press, 1971-1989), 2:193-96. Pelikan observes that the West needed the *filioque* in part because the third person, not the first as in the East, is the typical Latin unity figure.

that describe him according to the form of God and those that attach to him according to the form of a servant. Any subordination relations of Jesus to the Father — surely any statement to the effect that the Father is greater than he — belong to the latter category.[54] Moreover, the sending relations imply no superiority on the part of the sender nor inferiority on the part of the one sent. For one thing, the Son and Spirit really were not sent at all, since in being divine they were already omnipresent. For another, the Son was sent only according to the form of a servant, not according to the form of God. Finally, as above, because he is himself the Word by which God sends, the Son actually sends himself.[55]

By these maneuvers Augustine resists a conclusion yielded by the same principle that gave him the *filioque,* namely, that God *in se* is the same as God *ad nos,* that the economic Trinity discloses the immanent one. Economic subordination is inconclusive for subordination in the precincts of heaven. The most Augustine will concede is that, between two equal persons, it is fitting that the Father send and the Son be sent. After all, "the Son is from the Father, not the Father from the Son."[56]

In Karl Barth's massive, fascinating, and exasperating trinitarianism we find evidence of similar ambivalence on the relation of economic and immanent trinities. The early Barth wants a sharp distinction between them to protect the concept of God's radical freedom and grace. God's Word is always hidden even while revealed: "It is . . . absolutely essential that along with all older theology we make a deliberate and sharp distinction between the Trinity of God as we may know it in the Word of God revealed, written and proclaimed, and God's immanent Trinity, i.e., between 'God in Himself' and 'God for us,' between the 'eternal history of God' and His temporal acts."[57]

This distinction, which Barth regards as a hedge against the *speculatio Maiestatis* that Luther repudiated, leads him to pious agnosticism about the Johannine and Nicene image of the Father and Son: "All the associations which might be meaningfully suggested by the image are legitimate, and none is legitimate. . . . All . . . may be expressed and on all . . . we must be able to be silent again. The knowledge expressed in the metaphor is a non-knowing knowledge. It should regard itself as a knowing non-knowledge. . . . We can speak of the truth only in untruth. We do not know what we are saying when we call God Father and Son."[58]

54. *De Trin.* 1.7.14; 2.1.2.
55. Ibid., 2.5.7-9.
56. Ibid., 4.20.27.
57. Barth, *CD* I/1 (2d ed.), 172.
58. Ibid., 432-33.

Still, the same Barth who speaks so eloquently of our learned ignorance on the relation of Father and Son insists a few pages earlier that "the concealed God is no other than the revealed God and *vice-versa.*" For "as Christ is in revelation, so He is antecedently in Himself . . . the begotten of God and not His creature." Indeed, "we have to take revelation with such utter seriousness that in it as God's act we must directly see God's being too."[59]

It is this insistence on the revelation principle that leads Barth to follow Augustine and others in seeing the divine missions as extensions of the intratrinitarian relations. Accordingly, Barth defends the *filioque* clause of the Latin text of the Nicene Creed, since "statements about the divine modes of being antecedently in themselves cannot be different in content from those that are to be made about their reality in revelation."[60] Complaining that Eastern theologians isolate John 15:26 (where the Spirit is from the Father) from other texts that plainly have the Holy Spirit as the Spirit of the Son, Barth objects precisely to Eastern reservations about the identity of economic with immanent trinities and rejects them as a speculative abridgment of revelation.[61]

But of course speculation is a two-sided mirror. A formal problem with Barth's complaint is that it reflects back on his own confidence. Why should it be less speculative to assert that God *in se* is identical with God *ad nos* than to reserve judgment on this possibility?

Further, in following Augustine's theory of the Spirit as the fellowship or love that binds together the Father and the Son, Barth is obliged to abandon Scripture (which is wholly vague on this point) and base his claim on the neuter gender of πνεῦμα and the adjectival use of κύριος in the Nicene Creed's main Spirit clause, and on some quotes from Augustine, John of Damascus, and Anselm![62] In fact, Barth uses these things to shore up and reaffirm an old Western weakness: as a "bond" or "something in common" between Father and Son, the Holy Spirit, in distinction from the Father and Son, can hardly be called a person: "He is not a third spiritual Subject. . . . He is a third mode of being of the one divine Subject or Lord."[63]

Still further, anyone who affirms the revelation principle, anyone who endorses a strong identity relation of immanent and economic trinities, will

59. Ibid., 428. Barth later adds regarding the Holy Spirit that "what He is in revelation He is antecedently in Himself" (p. 466).

60. Ibid., 479.

61. Ibid., 480.

62. Ibid., 469.

63. Ibid.

have to deal with the synoptic picture of the Spirit's relation to Jesus vis-à-vis that of the Fourth Gospel. The latter suggests that the Son sends the Spirit. But in the synoptic Gospels the Spirit conceives (Matt. 1:18), compels (Mark 1:12), and inspires (Luke 10:21) the unexalted Jesus. This contrast raises an acute question of revelation: Which portrait — synoptic or Johannine — gives us purchase on the eternal life of God?

Here Barth is not content to point out the distinction between the states of Christ, humiliated to exalted. Instead, to ease the tension between John and the synoptics Barth takes refuge in a remarkably Nestorian-sounding distinction: In the synoptics, "it is this man Jesus, not the Son of God, who becomes the Son of God by the descent of the Spirit."[64] Somehow the synoptics are able to tell us about Jesus without telling us anything revealing about the eternal life of God.

When it comes to the question of subordination, however, Barth gamely accepts the consequences of an economic/immanent identity principle. As stated above, Augustine hedges on it in order to resist subordination within God. But in IV/1 Karl Barth deals with the same Johannine passages as Augustine did (e.g., 8:50; 10:18; 14:28, 31), applies the revelation principle, and accepts the conclusion: "The true God — if the man Jesus is the true God — is obedient."[65] Rejecting the possibility that the subordination of Son to Father is an ad hoc arrangement for the exigencies of the economy of redemption (for this would destroy our knowledge of "the proper being of God"), Barth explicitly affirms that there is "in God Himself," or in "the inner life of God" obedience and subordination: "We have . . . actually to affirm and understand as essential to the being of God [*dem Sein Gottes wesentlich*] the offensive fact that there is in God Himself an above and a below, a *prius* and a *posterius,* a superiority and a subordination."[66]

Why does Barth reject the ad hoc nature of subordination as an emergency requirement of incarnation and redemption? Beyond his general (though not exclusive) loyalty to the revelation principle, Barth wishes to find some space even further out to the monist side of the trinitarian threeness-oneness spectrum than is occupied by his own modalist-tending position. Accordingly, the ad hoc theory is what Barth wants to reserve as description of what he calls modalism.[67] It is *modalists* who distinguish the revealed God from the real God. Barth therefore feels obliged to affirm

64. Ibid., 485.
65. Ibid., IV/1, 164.
66. Ibid., 200-201.
67. Ibid., 196-97. This same claim is made in I/1, 311, 353, and elsewhere.

that the one-personed God (a theory Hilary rejects as modalism) has *essential* internal subordination (a theory Augustine would probably have rejected as Arian), and that such essential subordination is no more an abridgment of equality or dignity than is a wife's "second" or "subordinate" place vis-à-vis her husband.[68] At a stroke, Barth thus manages to embrace two ancient heresies and one contemporary one.

Most of the angularities of Christian trinitarianism — subordination, *filioque,* indivisibility of work, social monotheism, the revelatory significance of the missions — derive in one way or another from the Fourth Gospel. For the doctrine of the Trinity, this deceptively complex Gospel is a continuing source of great riches and great difficulties.

68. Ibid., IV/1, 202. For Hilary, see above, n. 30.

19. *Historical Criticism and Dogmatic Interest in Karl Barth's Theological Exegesis of the New Testament*

Bruce McCormack

Karl Barth's two commentaries on Paul's epistle to the Romans marked a revolution in biblical hermeneutics. Hans-Georg Gadamer is quite right in seeing the less well-known first edition of 1919 as already constituting a "hermeneutical manifesto."[1] The revolution consisted in this: Barth was seeking to show the limits of historical-critical study of the Bible in the interests of a more nearly theological exegesis. He was not at all interested in setting historical-critical study aside, as some of his early critics thought. In fact, he was quite convinced that historical criticism could itself play a role in establishing its own limitations. Just as Kant's *Critique of Pure Reason* paid the highest possible compliment to reason (by showing that reason itself could establish its own limits), so Barth was in a very real sense paying a compliment to historical-critical study.

It was not perceived that way by the guild of New Testament scholars, of course. Adolf Jülicher spoke for many when he wrote of the first edition that it gave expression to "a period in the history of culture that is not historically oriented." He noted that such an attitude is typical of times of societal collapse, when discontent over what the reigning culture had produced was widespread.[2] He saw in Barth a *Pneumatiker*.

> Those before him have attained only to the historical. He does not oppose the historical, but passes through it to the Spirit. This is exactly the

1. Hans-Georg Gadamer, *Truth and Method* (New York: Crossroad, 1975), 463.

2. Adolf Jülicher, "A Modern Interpreter of Paul," in *The Beginnings of Dialectic Theology*, ed. James M. Robinson (Richmond, VA: John Knox, 1968), 81.

> standpoint of Origen, except that Barth declares the former's spirit to be an unspirit; it is exactly the standpoint of the Gnostics, except that they, to be sure, were not at all concerned with the historical. One of them, however . . . Marcion, about A.D. 150 in Rome, held the same position as Karl Barth in his exegesis of Paul. He proceeded with the same sovereign arbitrariness and assurance of victory, with the same one-sided dualistic approach of enmity to all that comes from the world, culture, or tradition, and never tired of tossing a few pet ideas in front of us. And this has the same effect — that when we give ourselves to these tones without interruption, we finally hear only them and nothing else.[3]

Barth's exegesis of Paul was everywhere determined by his own problems and concerns; the result was that Paul was made to conform to Barth's dogmatic a priori (in Jülicher's view, to Barth's peculiar understanding of the Kingdom of God). Jülicher concluded that Barth's book would have far less significance for the history of interpretation than it would one day for the history of Christianity. "Much, perhaps even very much, may someday be learned from this book for the understanding of our age, but scarcely anything new for the understanding of the 'historical' Paul."[4]

Jülicher was only capable of seeing the relation between scientific (historical-critical) exegesis and what he was calling Barth's "practical" (pneumatic and edifying) exegesis as two mutually exclusive alternatives. For him, practical exegesis is an exposition which has its center of gravity in the present day, in the desire to recast Paul's message in terms which would address contemporary problems. Such an exposition was seen as needful, especially in times of cultural collapse. It was a largely prophetic task, for which (he was happy to concede) Barth had outstanding gifts. But practical exegesis was no substitute for historical exegesis. Jülicher's attitude was characteristic of an entire generation of biblical scholarship which saw in the historical method the only guarantee of the scientific character of theology generally. Theology was celebrated as a science because it had a definite historical object and a method appropriate for the study of that object. To claim to have understood Paul without any obvious signs of having engaged in the necessary historical work (as seemed to be the case with Barth) constituted a tacit rejection of historical science, and that could only open the door to enthusiasm, subjectivism, and relativism.

Jülicher's dichotomizing of historical and dogmatic exegesis demonstrated quite forcefully his failure to comprehend a central feature of Barth's revolution. Barth was not at all unwilling to acknowledge that he approached the task of exegesis with certain dogmatic assumptions. What he

3. Ibid., 78.
4. Ibid., 81.

was seeking to make clear to the guild of New Testament scholars was that he was not alone in approaching exegesis with a dogmatic interest. The "scientific" exegetes had failed to recognize that they too had their dogmatic assumptions, assumptions which were strictly historicist in character. A dichotomy between historical and dogmatic exegesis could therefore not be sustained in practice. Had that been acknowledged, the more interesting and important question as to whether some dogmatic interests might not be more suitable and appropriate for New Testament exegesis than others might have been debated. But the older generation of biblical scholars could not bring themselves to that basic acknowledgment.

Barth was never willing to accept the widespread charge that he was an enemy of historical criticism. To his mind, historical study of the "historical Paul" was not irrelevant to theological exegesis. It was a first and indispensable stage in attaining a true understanding of the subject matter of which Paul was speaking. Moreover, he was adamant in refusing to accept Jülicher's description as valid: "I am no 'pneumatic' . . . "[5]

Still, the suspicion that Barth was engaged in a flight from history in favor of a dogmatic handling of biblical texts continued to follow him. If anything, the issue of Barth's attitude to history is even more pressing today than it was in the 1920s. Today it is certain would-be friends of Karl Barth who are finding parallels between Barth's hermeneutics and certain schools of literary criticism which, by set determination, have no interest in the author of a text or the historical world behind a text.[6] All the more reason to ask

5. Karl Barth, *Der Römerbrief 1922* (Zürich: TVZ, 1984), xiii. ET, *The Epistle to the Romans* (Oxford: Oxford University Press, 1968). Cf. with this Barth's later, fuller explanation of his rejection of this title: "There is no method by which revelation can be made revelation that is actually received, no method of scriptural exegesis which is truly pneumatic, i.e., which articulates the witness to revelation in the Bible and to that degree really introduces the Pneuma" (*CD* I/1, 183).

6. Mark I. Wallace's recent statement is illustrative of this tendency: "We see a fundamental affinity between Barth's antihistoricist hermeneutic and current literary interpretations of the Bible: the Bible's meaning is not located in the historical realities or authorial intentions *behind the text, but in the language-specific realities spoken of within* the text. Barth stands alongside both New Critical and current deconstructive critics of the Bible in maintaining that all literary creations, the Bible included, are primarily works of art, not by-products of history — as such, they possess a life of their own, a life relatively independent from the cultural and authorial milieus that produced them. Possessing semantic autonomy, the 'literary work exists, in a sense, outside of history, in a kind of aesthetic preserve' where the text's surplus of meaning escapes the finite conditions that gave rise to it in the first place" ("Karl Barth's Hermeneutic: A Way Beyond the Impasse," *JR* 68 [1988]: 403). Wallace's essay does demonstrate sufficiently that the parallel he is trying to draw has limitations. Still, the passage here cited can only be regarded as a misleading and anachronistic reading of Barth's concerns. Barth in no way regarded the attempt to understand the author's intentions as a fallacy, as do many contemporary schools of hermeneutics.

anew: just what is the role played by historical criticism in Barth's hermeneutics? And if Barth has strictly delimited the role of historical study, what controls remain to prevent the free flow of arbitrariness in interpretation?

Previous attempts to defend Barth from the charge of enmity toward historical study of the Bible have all suffered from a common weakness: a failure to give adequate attention to the relationship between what we might call "historical sense" and "revelatory significance," between the meaning established by historical criticism and the meaning which is alleged to accrue to a text as the result of a revelation-event.[7] If it could be shown that revelatory significance has *no* relation to historical sense, then the claim to take historical-critical study seriously would be rendered hollow. The argument here will be that it is Barth's much-discussed *analogia fidei* which provides a vehicle for the coherent conceptualization of the relationship in question. Furthermore, it will be shown that it is the ecclesial framework within which the *analogia fidei* functions that provides Barth's final response to the charge of unleashing the forces of subjectivism.

I. More Critical than the Historical Critics!

In the foreword to the second edition of *Der Römerbrief,* Barth defended himself at some length against the charge that he was the enemy of historical criticism. This passage is of great importance for understanding the structure of Barth's hermeneutics. What emerges is a hermeneutical edifice with three stages. Before looking at the basic structure of Barth's hermeneutics in detail, it must be noted at the outset that that structure did not change after the writing of the second edition of *Der Römerbrief.*[8] What did change

7. In response to Gerhard Ebeling's warning that historical exegesis and theological exegesis must not be allowed to become two tracks which run alongside of one another but never touch, Georg Eichholz asserted that Barth was not guilty of such a two-track approach. Historical exegesis must be integrated into theological exegesis. Unfortunately, Eichholz's defense is more assertion than explanation. See Georg Eichholz, "Der Ansatz Karl Barths in der Hermeneutik," in *Antwort: Karl Barth zum siebzigsten Geburtstag am 10. Mai 1956,* ed. Ernst Wolf, Charlotte von Kirschbaum, and Rudolf Frey (Zollikon-Zürich: Evangelischer Verlag, 1956), 52-68. Other defenses of Barth have really fared no better. The following should be noted: Rudolf Smend, "Nachkritische Schriftauslegung," in *Parrhesia: Karl Barth zum achtzigsten Geburtstag am 10. Mai 1966,* ed. Eberhard Busch, Jürgen Fangmeier, and Max Geiger (Zürich: EVZ, 1966), 215-37; James A. Wharton, "Karl Barth as Exegete and His Influence on Biblical Interpretation," *USQR* 28 (1972): 5-13; and Mark I. Wallace, *JR* 68 (1988): 397-402.

8. Barth's mature treatment of the three stages of interpretation is to be found in *CD* I/2, 722-40. There he identifies the three stages as *explicatio, meditatio,* and *applicatio.* The nomenclature is new; the content of the stages under discussion is largely the same.

was the framework in which that hermeneutical strategy did its work — a point to which we will return in conclusion. It will therefore be legitimate to draw on material from later phases of Barth's development for describing the contours of his biblical hermeneutics.

Barth begins by asserting that he is more than happy to learn from the historical critics. Historical criticism, he notes, is concerned with establishing "what stands in the text." It does so by means of philological and archeological investigation of the meaning of Greek words and word groups and the translation of them into modern equivalents. Barth understands that this work is not easy and he freely acknowledges that there are others with better gifts and training for it than he possesses. "So long as it is simply a question of establishing what stands in the text, I have never dreamed of doing anything else than sit attentively at the feet of such learned men as Jülicher, Lietzmann, Zahn, and Kühl."[9] Barth goes on to add, however, that to establish the historical sense (that which stands in the text) is not yet to explain the meaning of a text. It is only a first "primitive" attempt at an explanation.[10] Genuine understanding begins where the critics are content to stop. It is at this point that the nature of Barth's hermeneutical revolution emerges clearly.

Historical science contented itself with historical explanation because it understood its object as a purely historical phenomenon. The object of investigation in this case was the "historical Paul" — *his* self-understanding, *his* piety, *his* religion. The problem, from Barth's point of view, was that the "historical Paul" had no such interest in himself and his religion. The attention of Paul was totally absorbed by something (Someone!) other than himself. In his Aarau lecture of March 1920, Barth likened the writers of biblical texts to people outside our windows who suddenly stop in the middle of the street and look up, shading their eyes against the sun and straining to see something which is hidden from our view by the roof.[11] Or again, they are like John the Baptist in Grünewald's painting of the crucifixion, pointing in a strange way to something beyond themselves, something otherworldly, something wholly other.[12] Barth was convinced that historical study of Paul ought to be able to make that clear;[13] if it does

9. Karl Barth, *Der Römerbrief,* x.

10. Ibid., xi.

11. Karl Barth, "Biblical Questions, Insights, and Vistas," in Barth, *The Word of God and the Word of Man* (Gloucester, MA: Peter Smith, 1978), 62.

12. Ibid., 65.

13. Karl Barth, *Credo* (New York: Scribner's, 1963), 188: "The Bible is a *human* document, having its place in the whole history of religion. The modern science of history makes it possible for us to understand this human document on its human side, and consequently to understand it as *witness.*"

not, the fault does not lie with the historical method so much as it does with the theological prejudgment of the critics which is determining what they are able to see. Historical criticism ought to be able at least to help in establishing its own limits.

The difference between Barth's view of Paul and that of the critics was fundamental. The reigning biblical science saw him as an object of interest in his own right; Barth saw him as a *witness.* This did not mean that the historical sense had become irrelevant to genuine understanding in Barth's view. What does Paul's witness consist of if not his own understanding of the object to which he bears witness? How can access to the object be gained otherwise than through the historical sense? But as Barth would put it later, "The essential content of the New Testament is a unique event, a truly singular occurrence, with a significance far beyond anything the New Testament writers themselves or their contemporaries ever dreamed of."[14] The significance of the object to which Paul witnesses exceeds his ability to grasp. Therefore, the interpreter must not stop with the historical sense. Real understanding only arises where the interpreter, too, is confronted by the same object as the first witness; where that which had been hidden from view now comes into view.

To establish what stands in the text (the witness of the historical Paul) is the "starting-point"[15] for Barth's hermeneutics; it constitutes the first stage of the enterprise.[16] At this first stage, some provisional understanding of what the text is about may be formed. Such a "provisional clue" provides a kind of working hypothesis with which one then proceeds to further work.[17] The second stage consists in penetrating through the text to the mystery which lies concealed within. Exegetes must think along with and after Paul, wrestling with his subject matter

14. Karl Barth, "Rudolf Bultmann — An Attempt to Understand Him," in *Kerygma and Myth,* ed. Hans-Werner Bartsch (London: SPCK, 1962), 2:85.

15. Barth, *Der Römerbrief,* xi.

16. Barth would later call this initial stage *explicatio,* and would define it as the attempt to understand the sense of the words of Scripture in their historical setting: "I must try to hear them [the words of the prophets and apostles] as documents of their concrete historical situation. They speak through it; I must see them in that situation, if I am to hear them speaking intelligibly. . . . I attempt to bring into the most likely inner connexion the words and phrases of which a certain biblical text is composed. For this purpose I use the methods of source-criticism, lexicography, grammar, syntax and appreciation of style. My aim is to convey the subject-matter or reference of what the author says in this particular text" (*CD* I/2, 723).

17. Barth, "Rudolf Bultmann," 108: "Surely, if we want to understand any given text, the provisional clue to its understanding must be sought from the text itself, and moreover from its spirit, content and aim. . . . I do not mean to suggest that this canon should be applied rigidly; it is only a flexible rule for further research."

until they, too, are confronted by the same object (or Subject!) which once confronted Paul.

> So far as possible, the blocks of merely historical, merely given, merely accidental conceptions should fade into the background; so far as possible, the relation of the words to the Word in the words must be discovered. As the one who seeks to understand, I must be thrust forward to the point where I almost stand only before the mystery of the *subject-matter,* where I almost no longer stand before the mystery of the *document* as such, where I almost forget that I am not the author, where I have understood him so well that I allow him to speak in my name and can myself speak in his name.[18]

In claiming to understand Paul so well that he almost forgets that he is not the author of the epistle, Barth is no longer focusing on the historical sense. He is not claiming to understand Paul's meaning better than Paul himself did. He has already acknowledged that establishing what stands in the text is exceedingly difficult. Barth is not at all so naive as to think that he can simply jump over Lessing's "wide, ugly ditch" and attain to a perfect understanding of Paul's intended meaning. Something rather different is meant. Barth thinks he has understood Paul this well only because he thinks he has caught sight of the object of which Paul was the witness. It is no longer a question of historical sense; the interpreter has penetrated to the real subject matter. It is at this point that the transition from the second to the third stage occurs, and it is here that theological exegesis becomes truly critical.

Having penetrated to the subject matter, the third and last step in the interpretive process is to return to the text, to seek to understand it anew, this time in the light of the subject matter.

> For my money, the historical critics must become *more critical.* For how "what stands *there*" is to be *grasped* is not decided by the occasional *valuation* of the words and word-groups, a valuation which is determined by the accidental standpoint of the exegete. Rather, it is decided through participation in the inner tension of the concepts which are presented more or less clearly by the text, a participation that is as relaxed and willing as possible. *Krinein* vis-à-vis a historical document means for me the measuring of all the words and word-groups contained in it by the subject-matter of which, if I am not completely deceived, they are clearly speaking; the relating-back of all the answers given in it to the questions which stand unmistakeably over against them and the latter

18. Barth, *Der Römerbrief,* xii.

> once again to the cardinal question which contains all questions in itself; the interpretation of everything which it says in the light of that which alone *can* be said and therefore also really *must* be said.[19]

To become more critical than the historical critics involves not only becoming self-critical (with regard to one's own standpoint), though that clearly is involved. But much more is at stake. What is required is really a criticism of one's preliminary work on the historical level in the light of what Barth would later characterize as a fresh hearing of the Word of God through the text. The goal of this stage is an "*objective* reworking of the text" — one which gives expression to the exegete's understanding of the text in the light of its subject matter in his or her own words. Barth's commentaries, we might point out before proceeding, typically offer only the results of this third step. The first stage, in which he has listened to the results of the best historical work available, is something which has occurred behind the scenes. In defense of this procedure, it must be said that a book which tried to present this entire interpretive process would be much too long and unwieldy.

Now the hardest step in this interpretive process is the second one. Indeed, to penetrate to the subject matter is something which Barth everywhere described as a human impossibility. To hear the Word in the words, to bring the Word into play, is not something which lies in the power of the exegete to bring about. If it comes about at all, it does so as a divine possibility, as the result of a divine speaking through the text. Barth would later express this point by saying,

> . . . [I]n the face of this subject-matter there can be no question of our achieving, as we do in others, the confident approach which masters and subdues the matter. It is rather a question of our being gripped by the subject-matter — not gripped physically, not making an experience out of it and the like, although (while maintaining one's sense of humor!) that can happen — but really gripped, so that it is only as those who are mastered by the subject-matter, who are subdued by it, that we can investigate the humanity of the word by which it is told us.[20]

That Barth expected to be gripped by the subject matter as he wrestled to catch sight of it is clear. Certainly, he gave every indication in the foreword to the second edition of *Der Römerbrief* that he had caught sight of it. The walls separating the twentieth century from the first had become transparent; he had seen what Paul saw. Therefore, he was able to describe the theme of the Bible in the following terms.

19. Ibid.
20. Karl Barth, *CD* I/2, 470.

> But what do I mean when I call the *inner dialectic of the subject-matter* and its recognition in the wording of the text the decisive factor in understanding and explanation? I am told (a Swiss reviewer said it with particular bluntness) that I could only mean my "system" with these words. The suspicion that here more is read into the text than read out of it is, of course, the most obvious one which can be brought against this attempt. To that, I have the following to say: If I have a "system," then it consists in the fact that I persistently keep in view what Kierkegaard called the "infinite qualitative difference" between time and eternity, in its negative and its positive significance. "God is in heaven and you are on earth." The relation of *this* God to *this* human being, the relation of *this* human being to *this* God, is for me the theme of the Bible and the sum of philosophy in one. The philosophers call this crisis of human knowing the Origin. The Bible sees at the same crossroads, Jesus Christ.[21]

The theme of the Bible, once envisioned, can then be employed to correct the working hypothesis with which the interpreter began. The result is still only a provisional clue; it never attains the level of an infallible criterion for exegesis because the interpreter's understanding of his or her theme is always imperfect. That Barth places the word "system" in quotation marks gives notice that he does not see his understanding of the subject matter as a system at all. In fact, it scarcely has any positive significance. "God is God" — that is what all talk of an infinite qualitative distinction between time and eternity is intended to bear witness to. "God is God" says simply that whatever God is, he is not world. An ontological chasm distinguishes the Creator from the creature. Barth's provisional understanding of the theme of the Bible is that it concerns the relation of the Creator to the creature and the relation of the creature to the Creator. It is in the light of this theme that Paul is to be understood.

Barth's hermeneutical edifice is now clearly before us, but the question which still needs to be addressed is, what is the relation between the results of the first stage and the results of the final stage? Can the meaning of a text, once established by historical-critical study, be simply left behind and ignored? Will God's address through the text to the Church in our day bear no relation to that historical sense? Can that address even contradict the meaning intended by the writer and/or redactor? *Der Römerbrief* left these problems unresolved, but it would not be long before Barth would be operating with a conceptual vehicle which would open the way to an answer. In appealing to the so-called analogy of faith as the answer to our

21. Barth, *Der Römerbrief,* xiii.

questions, we must candidly admit that we are here pressing Barth to give answers to questions which he did not put to himself in this form. We are here operating on the boundaries of Barth's thought, seeking to address a problem which he himself passed by in silence. And yet, it is surely not inappropriate to make use of the analogy of faith — an idea which Barth developed for explaining how our dogmatic statements could be enabled to refer adequately to their object — to also explain how Paul's witness was related to its object. On the face of it, such a transferal would seem most natural.

II. The Critical Value of the *Analogia Fidei*

Where analogical thinking first emerges in Barth's development has long been a subject of debate among Barth scholars. The dominant view for almost forty years now has been that of Hans Urs von Balthasar. Von Balthasar posited a "turn from dialectic to analogy" with the publication of Barth's book on Anselm in 1931.[22] In recent years, however, attempts have been made to uncover "analogical moments" in the earlier, so-called dialectical phase.[23] The subject would require too much space to be entered into here. For our purposes, the assumption will be made that analogical thinking of the same structural form as what Barth would later call the *analogia fidei* was already at work from around 1924 on.

"Analogy of faith," as Barth employs it, refers most fundamentally to a correspondence between an act of God and an act of a human subject. The act in question on the divine side is God's act of self-revelation; on the human side, it is faith in that revelation (or the knowledge of faith). "Analogy of faith" means that in the event of revelation, an analogical relationship is established between the content of the divine speaking and the content of the human hearing in faith. The analogy works strictly from above to below. It is not that the divine Word is like our human understanding of it; rather, human understanding is made to conform to the divine Word. The analogy is finally highly actualistic in character. That means

22. Von Balthasar, *The Theology of Karl Barth* (New York: Holt, Rinehart & Winston, 1971).

23. I have sought to demonstrate this at some length. See Bruce L. McCormack, "A Scholastic of a Higher Order: The Development of Karl Barth's Theology, 1921-31" (Ph.D. diss., Princeton Theological Seminary, 1989). The following are also important: Ingrid Spieckermann, *Gotteserkenntnis: Ein Beitrag zur Grundfrage der neuen Theologie Karl Barths* (Munich: Chr. Kaiser, 1985), 140-43; and Michael Beintker, *Die Dialektik in der "dialektischen Theologie" Karl Barths* (Munich: Chr. Kaiser, 1987), 259-86.

that it is effective only in the event of revelation. The analogy, once established, does not become the attribute of the human subject.

Applied to the problem of God's speaking through the witness of Scripture, the analogy of faith has the following consequences. In and of itself, human language is entirely unsuitable to be a vehicle of the divine Word; it has no intrinsic capacity for becoming a bearer of revelation.[24] Human language is developed by humans for human purposes, to speak of objects, ideas, or experiences given to us in everyday life. Such words can only mislead when applied without further ado to God. To apply the word "Father" to God, for example, is misleading if we think in doing so that God is like a human father. Even the word "love" can only be inappropriately applied to God if it is allowed to retain connotations of human love (with all of its imperfection). We will not be able to remedy the problem simply by trying to strip our words of what we think are their negative connotations. There will be a solution only if God teaches us how to apply our language to himself. And that is precisely what God has done. God has spoken in Jesus Christ, and in doing so, engendered the witness of the prophets and apostles.

But a problem still remains. The gracious action in which God teaches his people how to speak rightly of him is not something which is completed once and for all with the engendering of the scriptural witness. In and of itself, even the biblical language cannot teach us how to speak rightly of God. In and of itself, the biblical language is simply ordinary human language — language which awakens in readers all the connotations which they ordinarily ascribe to it. Barth's view is that this problem is overcome in that God continually takes up the witness of the biblical writers and bears witness to himself in and through their witness. In that he does so, the human words of Scripture are made to conform or correspond to the divine Word. A relationship of analogy between the Word and the words is established. But only in the event of the divine speaking! The language is not altered by the event; revelation does not become a predicate of the biblical text. If God did not speak again and again through these words in an active way, they would snap back into their old connotations. Again, it is the biblical language which is made to conform to God's speech about himself. It is not that God's speech conforms itself to this language. Since the shape of the analogy is determined from above, and not on the basis of ordinary usage, we cannot anticipate what it will look like. That being so, we cannot "build up" from the historical sense of sacred texts to a knowledge of the divine Word.

The impossibility of building up from the historical sense of biblical

24. See Karl Barth, "The Word of God as the Task of Ministry," in Barth, *Word of God and Word of Man,* 210-11.

language to its significance in the revelatory event is further guaranteed by the fact that revelation is not an absolutely stable quantity. By this is meant that what God has said through the prophets and apostles to the Church in the past may give hints of what he will say through the same to the Church in our own day, but he is not bound to repeat himself. It is the freedom of God to address himself to the Church in new and different ways through the witness of Scripture which gave rise, in Barth's view, to the possibility that a text could bear a plurality of meanings. Note well: that Barth could accept the possibility that biblical texts could bear a number of valid meanings had nothing to do with a general literary-critical theory. It had everything to do with his conviction that God is a living agent, who continues to speak anew through these ancient texts.

But granted that God is free to address himself in new and different ways through the sacred text, are there limits to the use made of this freedom? It is here that the problem of the relation of revelatory significance to historical sense becomes most acute. The answer is that the analogy of faith itself provides a critical delimitation. If the word "analogy" in the phrase *analogia fidei* means what it says (and is not simply a misnaming of what in fact is equivocation), then revelatory significance will have to stand in an analogical relation to historical sense. To be sure, the exegete will not be able to anticipate the shape of the analogy. One must constantly be open to surprises. But because the analogy in question will truly be an analogy, historical-critical work will provide a limiting horizon against which to measure any alleged new revelatory event in the Church. What is being suggested here is that *at a certain point* historical-critical exegesis has much the same value for Barthian exegesis as it has for the historical critics. It provides a safeguard against subjectivistic excess. Now again, Barth himself never made this explicit. Nevertheless, this use of historical study is certainly consistent with the notion of analogy which guided Barth's own reflections on the relation of Word and words.

Historical criticism can thus be seen to perform two functions in Barth's hermeneutics. First, in reflecting on the historical sense of ancient texts, it provides a starting point for the interpretive exercise. Here, it must be emphasized: this is a starting point only, it is not an unshakable foundation. This preliminary understanding may in fact be corrected by the revelatory event. The shape of the analogy cannot be anticipated. But correction will not entail contradiction or equivocation. This suggests a second, critical function for historical criticism. Historical study can be brought in after the fact, after a proposal has been made for how a revelatory event should be understood, to exercise a human and relative control over that proposal. Historical criticism may not be able to establish a revelatory event, but it can help to prevent subjective excess by falsifying the more outrageous claims that have arisen from time to time. The interpretive *process* in which the hearing of the Word through the text is allowed to correct preliminary historical understanding and historical understanding in turn is allowed to challenge and perhaps even correct claims to a hearing of the Word is a never-ending dialectical process. The historical critic must be open to surprises, but the theologian who wishes to make use of the scriptural witness for authorizing dogmatic proposals must be equally open to challenges from the historians.

Thus far, we have considered the issue of dogmatic interest and subjectivism in Barth's hermeneutics solely in relation to his attitude to historical study of the Bible. But there is a further element in his hermeneutics which provides his final answer to his critics. In the years 1923/24, Barth underwent a subtle shift from seeing the Church as the locus of divine judgment (the critique of religion in *Der Römerbrief*) to seeing the Church as the locus of authority.[25] As noted earlier, this shift did nothing to alter the basic shape of his hermeneutics, but it did provide a different understanding of its context. Biblical exegesis, Barth would henceforth insist, occurs in the Church and for the Church, and that too places restrictions on the claims made by exegetes to having heard the Word in and through the sacred text. Individualism in exegesis is replaced by a communal reading of the Scriptures.

III. Hermeneutics in an Ecclesial Context

In their famous debate in January 1923, Adolf von Harnack chided Barth for his claim that the Bible could only be understood in the power of the Spirit with the observation that such a claim is indistinguishable from a theory of an "exclusive inner word."[26] The question being raised here was an important one. Is the appeal to the inner testimony of the Spirit anything more than a legitimation of privatized and exclusivistic exegesis? The question was not given an adequate answer until the following year.

In the summer semester of 1924, Barth delivered his first lectures on dogmatics in Göttingen. The subject was prolegomena — the first version of what would eventually become *Church Dogmatics* I/1 and I/2. Most

25. See McCormack, "A Scholastic of a Higher Order," 376-77.

26. Adolf von Harnack, "An Open Letter to Professor Karl Barth," in Robinson, ed., *Beginnings of Dialectic Theology*, 172.

noteworthy for our purposes is the very large role which was now granted to the authority of the Church in mediating the event of the Word to the interpreter.[27] The interpreter, it was now stressed, is not alone in a field somewhere, waiting for revelation, constantly in danger of turning the internal testimony of the Holy Spirit into an exclusive inner word. The interpreter is (ideally, at least) a member of the *communio sanctorum* and the testimony of the Spirit is something which occurs — and has always occurred! — in that context.

"No one reads the Bible directly; we all read it through a pair of glasses, whether we wish to or not."[28] From the very beginning of his hermeneutical revolution, Barth was thoroughly convinced that a neutral, disinterested exegesis was an impossibility.[29] Many factors, both historical and cultural, condition our attempts to understand the meaning of Scripture. Barth was also convinced, however, that although these factors can never be completely eliminated, we do enjoy a freedom within limits to choose

27. The effect of this shift was felt in Barth's published essays of the 1920s as well as in his unpublished student lectures. Consider the following statement from June 1925: "There is a third entity between, on the one hand, the Word of God which is spoken in revelation by the Word who was in the beginning and is authentically witnessed to in the Scriptures alone, which is to be heard through the Church and to which obedience is to be required through the Church; and on the other hand, human religious opinions and convictions. The Church has not only the Scripture and receives not only the Spirit, but also the Church has and receives through the Scripture and the Spirit, from generation to generation, the truth which as God's truth is whole and unchangeable, but which, as received and possessed by men and women is fragmentary and changeable — but none the less truth for all of that. According to the Reformed conception, this third entity is *dogma, doctrina vera et pura*" (Karl Barth, "The Desirability and Possibility of a Universal Reformed Creed," in Barth, *Theology and Church* [London: SCM, 1962], 114).

28. Karl Barth, *Unterricht in der christlichen Religion: Prolegomena* (Zürich: TVZ, 1985), 279.

29. From the many passages which could be cited in support of this contention the following will suffice: "No one simply reproduces 'what stands there' [in the text]; no one simply describes the events and figures as they were. . . . In that [the interpreter] understands the text objectively, she is also present subjectively. In that she allows it to speak, she herself speaks. Through what she sees in the text and what she does not see, through what she says and does not say concerning it, she can do nothing else but betray the fact that . . . she has a definite philosophy. . . . We all wear some such glasses — if we did not wear them, we would not be able to see anything — and it is really a comical piece of theatre whenever anyone thinks she is in a position to point with outstretched finger to all the rest as if only they were conditioned by this or that philosophy, whereas she relies on her two healthy eyes and lives completely in reality. No one does that. Of no one may it be truly said that she does not mingle the gospel with philosophy. . . . In this sense, we all pursue allegorical exegesis; that is, we make use of some key, some schematism of thought, in order to 'come along' [with the text]" (Karl Barth, *Die christliche Dogmatik im Entwurf,* ed. Gerhard Sauter [Zürich: TVZ, 1982], 522-25). The passage may also be found in a slightly more abbreviated form in the earlier version of the prolegomena. See Barth, *Unterricht,* 314-17.

which among them we would like to hear above all others. For the interpreter of the Scriptures of the Church, the choice was clear: it is the voice of the Church which was to provide that one conditioning factor above all others to which the interpreter should happily look for guidance. For Barth, this guidance took the form of doctrinal decisions made by the Church in ages past.

> How should it be possible to hear the Word of God in Scripture today in any other way than that thereby is *also* heard what the Church of God, the fellowship of believers in the various centuries, has laid down in the public documents [confessions] as the unanimously acquired result of *their* hearing? Again, this factor could only be ignored if one were to conceive the time lying between the prophetic and apostolic witness and the present *only* as history, *not at all* as Church history in the pregnant sense of the word, as the history of the one — perhaps hidden but at no time not present — Church of God. It is impossible for faith in the efficacy of the Holy Spirit in the *present* to be reconciled with a fundamental *denial* of His efficacy in the past."[30]

The history of the Church — "Church history in the pregnant sense" — is a history of an encounter with the witness of the prophets and the apostles as interpreted by the Holy Spirit. "The way taken by the Church, the history of the Church in time is the history of the exposition of Holy Scripture."[31] The result of that interpretive encounter has been set down from time to time in the form of authoritative decisions. Where the Church has not yet received better instruction (so that it might be in a position to revise or even revoke those prior decisions), they remain in force.

The dogmas of the Church now provided Barth with guidance for the attempt to seek a fresh hearing of the Word as witnessed to in Scripture. The authority proper to dogmas and the creeds and confessions which embodied them was only a human and relative authority. It was not the absolute authority which is proper to Scripture alone. Dogmas are by their very nature reformable. Still, the authority of the Church's doctrinal decisions — so far as they remain unrevised and in force — have to be taken with strict seriousness. "It is a tumultuous, illegitimate and senseless use of the Protestant *Scripture-principle* whenever one thinks it may be employed to set aside the authority of the Church."[32]

The inner testimony of the Spirit — so far from being a license for

30. Barth, *Unterricht,* 291-92.

31. Karl Barth, *The Knowledge of God and the Service of God* (London: Hodder and Stoughton, 1938), 179.

32. Barth, *Unterricht,* 299.

"uncontrollable fanaticism"[33] — was something which was to be received in the Church, under the guidance of the Church, and ultimately, validated or rejected by the Church.[34] Herein lay Barth's final answer to the problem of subjectivism in biblical interpretation.

The appeal to the ecclesial context in which exegesis is to take place had gotten Barth off the hook where the charge of "uncontrollable fanaticism" was concerned. But had an answer to that charge been purchased at too great a price? What then is the effect of this new framework for exegetical work on Barth's previous contention that it is historical-critical study which is to provide the starting point of exegesis? Has historical study of the Bible been so imprisoned by the dogmatic tradition that it is no longer really the starting point of the exegetical process? The answer must be a tentative no. The guidance provided by the tradition is a relative guidance. It can only be employed legitimately where it is employed flexibly and with openness to correction. Historical study remains the initial stage of Barth's hermeneutics. But because Barth was also convinced that historical study never takes place otherwise than under the control of some interest or other, it is best to be self-conscious about one's controlling interests and, so far as it lies within one's powers to do so, to place oneself under the guidance of that teaching of the Church which has resulted from critical testing and correction in the past, viz., creeds and confessions.

Conclusion

> There is a notion that complete impartiality is the most fitting and indeed the normal disposition for true exegesis, because it guarantees a complete absence of prejudice. For a short time, around 1910, this idea threatened to achieve almost canonical status in Protestant theology. But now we can quite calmly describe it as merely comical.[35]

33. Harnack, "An Open Letter," 165.

34. Barth did explicitly recognize something like a Protestant equivalent to the teaching office in the Roman Catholic Church. The major difference between his version of it and that which was found in the Roman Catholicism of his day is that for him, the authority to teach is something which belongs to the whole of the *communio sanctorum.* Teaching authority becomes visible in certain individuals who are set apart by the faithful as teachers of the Word. But such authority does not belong to them and cannot be limited to them (or to one teacher, the Pope). The teaching office is fundamentally a function of the entire Church of God. See Barth, *Die christliche Dogmatik im Entwurf,* 498. On the role played by the Church in approving confessions see Barth, *Theology and Church,* 116-17.

35. Barth, *CD* I/2, 469.

Barth's theological exegesis of the Bible never pretended to be impartial. It was just the opposite. It set out to be partial, to operate from the standpoint of a definite dogmatic interest. Years of "impartial" exegesis had taught Barth (as it was teaching others at the time, most notably Rudolf Bultmann) that "impartiality" was no guarantee of objectivity. "Impartiality" was just a lack of critical self-awareness, a failure on the part of historical critics to see the extent to which their historicism was shaping and determining their exegesis. The results of such "impartiality" had been subjectivism, and it was precisely for the sake of a more genuine objectivity that Barth now sought to be partial. Every exegete operates with some kind of dogmatic interest. The question is, which dogmatic interest is appropriate to the New Testament? Which is most likely to produce a faithful understanding of the sacred texts of the Church? Barth was aware of the dangers which surrounded his choice and, as has been shown, sought to build into his hermeneutic certain safeguards which would stem the flow of an unchecked subjectivism.

Was he guilty of imposing a dogmatic a priori on the New Testament? He himself would have said that his dogmatic interest was derived in an a posteriori manner. It was something which he thought he had learned, in a provisional form at least, from the New Testament itself. It was something which was also reinforced in him by his attempts to hear the voice of the Church in the past. The dogmatic assumption which Barth found most fruitful for understanding the witness of the New Testament was simply this: *Deus dixit* —God has spoken (past tense). That was the great fact on which all exegesis which seeks at least an approximate objectivity must rest.[36] The question which Barth's hermeneutics poses for us today is, can the Church, should the Church, read its Scriptures with any other guiding assumption than that in Jesus Christ, God has himself appeared in human history? We must not be too quick to answer. The question is not a purely theoretical one, to be decided dispassionately. It is a question which reaches to the very heart of the Christian faith.

36. Barth's early attempt to describe the theme of the Bible in terms of the "infinite qualitative difference between time and eternity" very quickly gave way to a different description. Already in his prolegomena lectures of 1924, Barth was describing the subject matter of the Bible in terms of the formula *Deus dixit* —thereby giving evidence of the fact that the focal point of his attention was now increasingly on the incarnation of God in history. See Barth, *Unterricht,* 53-54.

Postscript

Karlfried Froehlich

Those who are engaged in teaching probably know the discouragement of depression and loneliness. Is anyone listening? Is it worth the effort? Is there any relevance for a new generation which will have to carry on but already has its own agenda? Teachers seem to shout into the forest with only a slim chance of an echo coming back. As a rule, they see their students for a few months or years and then never again. They receive anonymous course evaluations but little constructive feedback, and the results of their work over the long haul remain hidden to them. Teaching, it seems, must be its own reward; but this thought affords little comfort for those who struggle along in the dark.

For any teacher who is able to sympathize with this professional predicament, a symposium like the one whose fruits are published in the present volume would be an amazing experience. How should one describe what happened? Was it the echo of the shouts of thirty years finally becoming audible? Was it a rare opportunity to measure the actual growth of seeds sown over a long period of time against subjective expectation? One could perhaps use a more appropriate metaphor and submit, more modestly and more accurately, that it was the exhilarating experience of seeing a text taking on a life of its own, unexpected in its depth and its beauty, exciting and challenging in its promise. It is my conviction that the participants did not come primarily to celebrate a person but to experience once more the joy of working together on a common *Sache*. It has always been an embarrassment for my professional rhetoric that this useful German word has no precise equivalent in English. The *Sache* which commanded the full attention of the group was not only a particular "subject matter," "topic," or "theme." The term signals a deeper dynamic; it points to the dialectic of the classical triangle of truth which builds itself up in the lively encounter and mutual search of passionately engaged human minds. Συμπόσιον was one of Plato's terms for this kind of festal occasion — searching, exacting, fulfilling in its intellectual activity, delightful and intimate in its table fellowship.

The *Sache* which united the members of this group had a long history of asserting itself in the collegial relationships of teaching and learning, in seminars on such seemingly unrelated topics as Augustine's hermeneutics, Jerome as an exegete, the Letters of Augustine and Jerome, Boethius, Bernard of Clairvaux: De Consideratione, the school of Saint Victor, Abelard as a theologian, the Romanesque ceiling of Zillis, Aquinas on the Sacraments, the prosecution of heresy in the Later Middle Ages, Pelagius and Pelagianism in the Middle Ages, Marsilius of Padua, and others. Over the years, it has guided much of my own research which was begun under a generation of great teachers in the University of Basel — Walter Baumgartner, Walther Eichrodt, Karl Ludwig Schmidt, Ernst Staehelin, Fritz Buri, Eduard Thurneysen, Karl Barth, and especially Oscar Cullmann — and it has continued ever since.

In the inaugural lecture of 1977 which the editors decided to reprint at the head of the present volume, I wrestled with the definition of the *Sache.* I began with the assumption that a description such as "the discipline of the history of scriptural interpretation" would be satisfactory, following the lead of Gerhard Ebeling's seminal essay of 1947. My consideration of the fate of the Ebeling thesis over the thirty years of its life, however, uncovered very quickly the deficiencies of this definition. First of all, *Auslegungsgeschichte,* contrary to the pronouncements of its early advocates, could not claim to be a "discipline" in the true sense of the word. It had no clear parameters, no specific methodology, and no defined goals. The disappointment on the part of exegetes and theologians who had given it a chance furnished eloquent witness to this dilemma. The promise that they would be helped in their tasks was not, and probably could not be, delivered. Moreover, the role of several components in the total enterprise such as the history of biblical hermeneutics and the diachronic history of specific biblical texts needed clarification. It dawned on me that the pretentious definition of the *Sache* to which I wanted to devote my energies as "the discipline" of *Auslegungsgeschichte* was too ambitious and too precise. Thus, my deliberations resulted in a much more modest, tentative description: *Auslegungsgeschichte,* the history of the interpretation of Scripture, is not an independent specialty but one entrance point into church history, providing no more than an "interpretive horizon" for the comprehensive task of doing church history in its universal dimensions. What gives this particular entrance point its unique significance, I argued, is the immense power of biblical language (understood or misunderstood) which has shaped a great deal of human life and action in a decisive manner, in the past and in the present as well.

Looking back on this clarification today, I realize that the conviction of the power of the biblical word as a perceptible phenomenon in history, and thus as the *Sache* of my central scholarly interest, has grown on me even more. It is as much a historical given as it is a theological judgment. This power is not a palpable entity, but it can be observed in its results. Oscar Cullmann's *Heilsgeschichte* was not the object of historical observation either; but it was the observable result of a conviction of faith expressed in a multiplicity of historical sources. In 1977 I cited the development of Mariology as an instance of the creative power of biblical language in the history of Christianity. I have argued more recently that much of the agenda of medieval "theology" in its formative stage was provided by the terminology of the Pauline Epistles in its Vulgate form. The examples could be multiplied.

The description of the *Sache* as the power, the δύναμις, of the biblical word corresponds, I believe, to another conviction that has imposed itself on my thinking in recent years. In my inaugural lecture I admitted problems with the expectation that diachronic histories of specific biblical passages would yield a reliable picture of development according to discernible patterns. It had become clear that every effort in this direction had to cope with quite unpredictable meanderings without intrinsic rhyme or reason. I was less pessimistic about arriving at a credible construct of development in the case of biblical hermeneutics. But many historical treatments of hermeneutics suffer from the same difficulty which I encountered with my original assumption about *Auslegungsgeschichte:* hermeneutics is seen as a clearly defined "discipline" constituted by its subject, method, and goal. The concern for method is dominant. The history of hermeneutics seeks to answer the question: what rules govern a particular interpretation of Scripture and what changes in the rules need to be explained? I have argued elsewhere that this seemingly objective, descriptive approach may lead to a reduction which allows for no more than a superficial understanding of hermeneutical dynamics. A distinction must be made between "principles" and "rules," between the governing theological assumptions about purpose, nature, origin, and function of Scripture in the divine economy in the broad sense, and the specific techniques, often derived from literary practices in the surrounding culture, by which an interpreter seeks to lead his or her Bible-reading audience into the horizon of deeper theological understanding. The eminently practical *middôt* of Rabbi Hillel in the Jewish tradition or the traditional terms of the fourfold sense of Scripture are not just one set of tools to be applied to a text at will; they reflect and presuppose specific decisions about the nature of *this* text, about principles which determine the theological horizon into which Scripture must be interpreted. "Principles" precede "rules."

The dialectic set up in the inaugural lecture between church history as a theological and a historical discipline, in this order, reflects this distinction. Church history as a *theological* discipline has priority for me inasmuch as it concerns the principles, not the rules. I tried to link this theological aspect to an ecclesiological horizon in the history of interpretation: the churches, the historic communities of faith in all their variety and with all their sectarian prejudice, are the primary audience for the *Sache.* In a very real sense they are all creatures of the biblical word whose power has shaped and in most cases still is shaping their separate existence as well as their ecumenical commitment. This is the reason why I consider my personal vocation as a church historian to be properly exercised in a seminary of the church rather than in a university setting.

The theological priority does not imply, however, that the "rules" do not count. The commitment to the tasks of "dull but solid scholarship," the respect for evidence, for document and monument, was and is a methodological and thus even a chronological priority, especially for those who aspire to doing church history in the context of theological education. The reason is that the truth which is open for all to investigate with the tools of historical scholarship is one and the same. I continue to hold that there is no shortcut to relevance, and that only the patient work on primary sources in constant touch with historical scholarship everywhere will allow us to avoid the blinders of a restrictive sectarianism and open our eyes for the unpredictable otherness of all historical experience. The logical priority of the "principle" will insure that we see this otherness in the context of a shared faith and a common commitment, especially if we use the history of biblical interpretation as our point of entry into church history. But our endeavor always proceeds according to the rules shared by all historians who practice their craft with equal devotion in different communities of commitment.

In its deliberate concentration upon the *Sache* of the history of biblical interpretation, the symposium presented a unique opportunity to learn, to assess the situation, and to find new perspectives on the work that lies ahead. There was plenty of confirmation and rearticulation of insights and intuitions which I could recognize as part of my own commitment. There were numerous incidental discoveries which I know I will want to integrate into my thinking in the future. There were also new horizons which opened up to be pursued by anyone interested in the *Sache.* It is impossible to do justice to the richness of insights, suggestions, and challenges represented by the essays of this volume. Out of the abundance of the offering I would like to lift up, and reflect upon, some themes which struck me as particularly important or fruitful for the work of the future.

It was something of a surprise and certainly a delight to encounter the name of Karl Barth so prominently at several points in the proceedings. Bruce McCormack focused on Barth directly; Cornelius Plantinga treated him as a serious discussion partner. For me, one of the most important discoveries was the realization that the Ebeling thesis which guided my inaugural deliberations had already been formulated by Barth much earlier. McCormack gave the quotation: "The way taken by the Church, the history of the Church in time is the history of the exposition of Holy Scripture." Reading his analysis of Barth's process of biblical interpretation made me aware how much more deeply than I thought I may be indebted to this master teacher of my Basel years. I certainly resonate with the three steps outlined by McCormack which begin with the historical-critical work and describe a hermeneutical circle: from the text, through the promise of the word-event, back to the text in its radical historicity, a text which now, "with a gain in language" (Jüngel), becomes open again for God's gracious use. I concur with the location of the inner testimony of the Spirit in community, in the Church which remains the primary audience for biblical interpretation, and I find the suggestion worth pondering that it is Barth's *analogia fidei* (which appears much earlier than commonly believed), not just his dialectic, which provides the bridge between *Auslegungsgeschichte* as a theological and a historical discipline. With such challenges on the table, I am convinced that a new generation will not allow the interest in Barth's contribution to the *Sache* to wane.

The way a particular text was heard in the Church is, of course, part and parcel of the historian's concern when the power of biblical language to shape Christian life is being considered. The exegesis of any text, certainly of a biblical text, needs more than the exploration of its prehistory and its *Sitz im Leben* in order to allow it to be heard in its full meaning today. "To ask what a text means should also involve the question what it has meant" (Heffner). Like other critics, I was not really sure in the face of past experience how one might encourage a fruitful approach to the need for a posthistory of as many biblical texts as possible. The laudable attempt to incorporate the history of exegesis into biblical commentaries (I am thinking, e.g., of the series, *Evangelisch-katholischer Kommentar zum Neuen Testament,* published in Germany by the Neukirchner Verlag since 1970) has not yet produced fully convincing results; the integration of the material remains problematic. But in a field so vast, how does one select a "good" passage and avoid the hit-and-miss potential of a random choice? Apparently, not every passage in which we might be interested has also had an interesting history of interpretation. It has become clear to me that it may be better to follow the lead of the historical material itself and allow the quest for an exegetical history of a particular text to arise from this matrix, so to speak.

Several papers bear out this rule of thumb. Blake Heffner studied late medieval mystical texts and found that his study would profit by an understanding of the history of interpretation of a central passage, Luke 10:38-42 on Mary and Martha — the topic of his colorful tapestry of dialogical vignettes. Elsie McKee provides a striking object lesson about the unhappy results of the neglect of exegetical history in modern Calvin studies: "A chief source of the confusion about Calvin's 'eisegesis' is ignorance of the exegetical tradition on the part of modern readers." Finally, Cornelius Plantinga does in an exemplary fashion what should be the practice of every historian of doctrine who discusses doctrinal development in its internal logic. Rather than arguing for a proper model of the Trinity simply on the basis of modern systematic requirements, he also examines the patristic options and their obvious roots in the exegetical tradition of Johannine texts. One would hope that his example finds imitators elsewhere.

In the broader context of exegetical history, the changing image of Paul and the different reading of his letters throughout the centuries continue to fascinate me. We should be wary of assuming that there was one Paul only. There were many, and it is difficult to say which one was legitimate and which one was not. Paula Fredriksen points to the bewildering open-endedness of this issue in her wide-ranging and deep-reaching comparison between Paul and Augustine: "Paul had his greatest influence among Christian dualists, Gnostics and Manichaeans," and Augustine was "more classically Pharisaic than Paul himself" in his understanding of the resurrection of the body. The image of Paul in medieval minds was that of the normative teacher of revealed truth, the epitome of a professor of theology. The centrality of Paul's texts, his very terms and phrases in their Latin translation, for the formulation of Latin theology becomes clear when one reads David Steinmetz's careful analysis of three historical interpretations of Rom. 8–9. I am glad that the author comes out where he does: Calvin is *not* a Thomist. In a deeper sense, however, what is really at issue is not Thomas Aquinas but the options in understanding *Paul's* normative terminology.

Since the forceful reaffirmation of the "apocalyptic" Paul in recent years (J. C. Beker), one major source of apocalyptic thought forms in early Christianity has claimed our attention again. The definitional debate about "apocalypticism" has not yet led to a general consensus. I am still impressed by Philipp Vielhauer's observation that apocalyptic literature does not focus on last times, but on second-to-last times. In this sense, the apocalyptic message establishes the framework for the prophetic call to action before it is too late, for renewal, reform, restoration, along with its consolatory function. I have noticed this pattern in unusual reformers: Charlemagne, Bernard of Clairvaux, Jean Gerson. They all saw the urgent challenge of their time as affording one more chance for needed changes. For all of them, much of the timeless power of biblical apocalypticism rested on the overcoming of ancient Christian millennialism by the hermeneutical notion of continuous fulfillment during the time of the Church. Having written on Tyconius herself, Paula Fredriksen presents a concise summary of the idea's most influential adaptation in Augustine's eschatology. Rodney Petersen demonstrates the immense power with which this "Catholic" vision, locating the fulfillment of the millennial expectation in the experience of the Church, asserted itself even in early Protestant theology: the Church of the book of Revelation is the Church of the Reformation. For Bullinger, Enoch and Elijah, the "two faithful witnesses" of Rev. 11:3, are models of the new Reformed ministry. Petersen also points to a "process of literalization" which begins to take over with John Foxe at the end of the century. The American religious scene in the nineteenth century shows the deep impact of this development on modern biblicism. James Moorhead's essay not only addresses with exemplary lucidity the terminological confusion of pre- and postmillennialism in this period but also for the first time describes the full extent of the hermeneutical difficulties into which the classical postmillennial position in particular maneuvered itself. How literal does literalism have to be?

One element closely related to Christian apocalypticism is the interest in numerology. Augustine was convinced of the revelatory nature of biblical numbers, and under his dominance number symbolism became a major preoccupation among a variety of Western interpreters, from exegetes such as Hrabanus Maurus in the ninth century to the painter of the ceiling at Zillis (Graubünden) in the twelfth down to the musician Johann Sebastian Bach in the eighteenth. John Fleming, whose ingenious "reading" of pictorial art has inspired much of my own interest in Christian iconography, surprises his readers once more — should it be a surprise? — with the delightful discovery of Christopher Columbus as a rather imaginative biblical numerologist. Fleming's masterful portrait of Columbus dabbling in exegesis with a Franciscan passion and an avid mind "as porous and fissured as a sponge" makes the enigmatic person of the admiral much more credible as a child of an age where "exegetical habits had penetrated popular culture." One even is tempted to follow the author in his further suggestion that it is the power of biblical images which informs and illumines the self-interpretation of this amateur exegete in the famous report of his diary that he founded the first Christian settlement in the New World under the name "Nativity" from the bowels of his ship "Mary" on Christmas day of 1492! "He did not come to write exegesis until about 1500, but he was clearly *living* exegesis a good deal earlier."

With this remark, we are touching on the issue of the "principles" of interpretation. For what purpose do people read the Bible? What are the assumptions with which they approach it? What do they expect to hear? What is the horizon into which they want to move the text's meaning through their exegesis? My interest in the development of biblical hermeneutics has centered around these questions, and several of the essays raise them directly. Kathleen McVey is probing the beginnings. Her argument that Theophilus of Antioch's interpretation of the *Hexaemeron* was not simply an instance of early Christian allegorization, a technique or a set of "rules," but rather rested on the principle that commonly accepted Stoic science should be read from the text of the Bible rather than from the epic tradition of classical literature, raises intriguing questions about apologetics and hermeneutics in second-century Christianity. Apologetics may well have been at the origin of a specifically Christian interpretation of the Bible. But do we perhaps too easily assume a natural primacy of the truth of the biblical text for these writers? Do they (or at least some of them) make their case more for a superior literature than for a superior truth? How "Christian" are these early Christian apologists? Robert Bernard looks at a specific hexaemeral text in Augustine's interpretation, Gen. 1:6, and develops from there his analysis of the heart of Augustine's hermeneutics. He spells out this center in terms of the trinitarian and incarnational principle of "divine eloquence." God is "the master rhetorician" whose Word must be read by fallen humanity in Scripture through the protective mediation of indirect language. Bernard's proposed term for this principle, "figuration," is Augustinian and precise enough to deserve wide reception.

Some of my own recent work concerns the shifts in medieval hermeneutics before the time of the Reformation. I have become increasingly critical of the thesis that progress in late medieval hermeneutics should be measured by the responsiveness to a "scientific" value of the literal sense of the Bible. The history of the literal sense after Hugh of St. Victor is a fascinating subject, but the backbone of a convincing developmental picture would have to be a close study of the hermeneutical "principles" behind its use by specific theologians. To my great joy, two contributions in the volume take on this task directly and break new ground in areas where my own research has left me with unanswered questions. Christopher Ocker's richly documented study uses the phenomenon of the "fusion of papal ideology and biblical exegesis" in the minds of mendicant theologians to articulate sharply the needed corrections to the confused picture of biblical studies in the fourteenth century which has been *terra incognita* for most of us. The store of unpublished materials in his notes invites intensive study and will greatly assist our understanding of a puzzling set of "principles" which defy neat classification by the remarkable cohesiveness of their eclecticism. "There were profound conceptual reasons for this mish-mash in fourteenth-century exegesis which have been scarcely understood."

Mark Burrows probes another terrain which has been of interest to me ever since my M.A. thesis at Drew University: the twilight zone between medieval and Reformation hermeneutics in the thought of the Paris theologians of the early fifteenth century. For his study of the late Gerson, Burrows read the treatises which I always wanted to read, and now has advanced the discussion in a decisive way. His description of a *sensus a patribus traditus* as Gerson's answer to the hermeneutical ambiguity of his day, a sense pointing back to the historic church, not only does justice to the position of Gerson which is in constant danger of being misunderstood, but has far-reaching implications for church and theology today. "The canonical texts stand in need of a canonical interpretation, or a 'traditioned sense.' " I hear in this pregnant sentence the call for *Auslegungsgeschichte* as a historical enterprise as well as the theological challenge of the quest for authority as it has been pursued by theologians from John Henry Newman to George Lindbeck. Nothing could be more contemporary.

One example for the contemporary relevance might suffice: "Scripture and Tradition" is the topic of the present round of the Lutheran–Roman Catholic National Dialogue in the United States. A colleague of many years in this dialogue, Eric Gritsch, entertained all of us with a sparkling treatment of the role of humor in Luther's exegesis. In his wide-ranging display of wonderful texts he drives home the truth of a "principle": Luther's humor points to the God who is infinitely incongruous with human nature but took upon himself this nature in order to overcome "our ancient foe." "Wit becomes a witness to the God who sits in heaven and laughs."

Principles do not come without their enfleshment in "rules." For instance: How does one deal with deliberate alteration of an original in the scribal tradition (one could add here the problems created by the ancient translations)? Bart Ehrman's essay, which sparked a lively debate, not only alerts readers to the possibility of such deliberate corruption which can give the history of a passage a direction not endorsed by the original; it also asks the wider questions: What *is* a "text"? Who or what gives it meaning? Must an original always have priority? His careful answer formulates a methodological axiom, a hermeneutical triangle which must be taken seriously: "Texts are never read in isolation but always in interpretive contexts, and the contexts in which interpreters live determine the meaning of the texts they read." Deliberate corrections are also the focus of David Johnson's paper, which reads like a commentary on Ehrman's axiom. Johnson demonstrates that the revision of Pelagius's Pauline commentaries by selective correction and the insertion of quotations from Augustine did not achieve the intended purge because the "theological acumen" of Cassiodorus and his students "was not astute enough." Quite clearly, we have here one major reason why Pelagianism continued to exercise its influence so powerfully alongside Augustine throughout the Middle Ages.

Pelagius's commentary on Romans belongs to an intriguing group of similar exegetical writings which appeared almost simultaneously at the end of the fourth century in the Latin Church. The phenomenon of biblical "commentaries" as a literary genre needs historical investigation. I have argued that, apart from Origen, the classical genre was not represented in the exegesis of the first three centuries. Kathleen McVey provides support for this conclusion by showing that the well-known section of Theophilus's apology which follows Gen. 1:1–3:19 verse by verse (II.10-28) is precisely not a commentary which respects the biblical word as the "text" to be interpreted. Again, Amanda Berry Wylie raises "critical questions about the usual boundaries of genre" in looking at John Chrysostom's "commentary" on the Acts of the Apostles. Her questions are fully justified, not only because the work is actually a series of homilies but also because Chrysostom preaches the text of Acts as *history;* it is the latter which he interprets under the rules of Hellenistic historiography, not its biblical literary form.

It is a thought-provoking experience to find so much of Chrysostom's interest in the utility of history, the apostolic models for contemporary Christian life, or the proof of God's providence echoed in the sermons of the nineteenth-century preacher whose portrait Klaus Fröhlich presents in his provocative essay. The fact that this preacher was one of the author's and my own ancestors adds an unexpected personal touch to this volume which any historian would gladly welcome. I knew of this great-grandfather, but he seems present now in a much more real, perhaps also more disturbing, manner. I am impressed by the author's meticulous source work. Sifting through a stack of unpublished sermons may have needed the extra incentive of the family relation. But Klaus Fröhlich succeeds in tracing from his reticent sources a bourgeois mentality which may well be representative, as he claims, of many nineteenth-century preachers in Germany, informing popular biblical interpretation to a far greater extent than one might wish. Also disturbing could be the insight that Heinrich Fröhlich, as so many of his colleagues, seems to have perceived the power of the biblical word as more or less restricted to its consolatory function — only one of the foci of the apocalyptic message. On the other hand, the preacher himself obviously did hear the call to action. For me, his deep involvement in the social work of the Church carries a message no less important than that of his sermons.

Another surprising new acquaintance is made through the powerful portrait of Marie Dentière, the Genevan Reformer, which Jane Dempsey Douglass paints for the reader with finely nuanced strokes. Here, too, the immediacy of biblical language in the interpretation of contemporary Christian life is striking. The Bible *is* history, and this history, especially from the books of the Old Testament, gives Dentière the categories for understanding and interpreting her own time. It is fascinating to see how the "discomforting prophetic voice" issuing from an articulate, politically astute, and courageous woman of the sixteenth century becomes the channel for the power of the biblical word claiming attention in the corporate life of the Reformed community, even against the conventions of the time. The discovery of such a woman is a precious gift to the history of biblical interpretation. Are there more such women whom we all should know?

No more than a few themes could be mentioned in these brief pages. As I reflect on each of the contributions once more, they all seem to have one thing in common. Each one in its own way provides an inroad into the vast maze of coherence which a life with and under the biblical word has created, and still is creating, in the soul and mind of Christian people throughout the history of the Church. To explore, experience, and express ever more deeply this coherence in our common endeavor as historians and theologians is a task which none of us will ever outgrow.

Chronological Bibliography of the Works of Karlfried Froehlich

Compiled by Amanda Berry Wylie

"The Libri Carolini and the Lessons of the Iconoclastic Controversy." In *The One Mediator, the Saints, and Mary,* ed. Joseph A. Burgess, Lutherans and Catholics in Dialogue, 8, forthcoming.

"Interpretation of the Bible in the Early Church." In *The Oxford Companion to the Bible,* ed. Bruce M. Metzger (Oxford/New York: Oxford University Press), forthcoming.

(editor) with Margaret T. Gibson. *Biblia Latina cum Glossa Ordinaria: Facsimile Reprint of the Editio Princeps by Adolf Rusch of Strassburg, c. 1480* (Turnhout, Belgium: Brepols), forthcoming.

"The History of the Printed Editions of the Glossa Ordinaria." In *Biblia Latina cum Glossa Ordinaria: Facsimile Reprint of the Editio Princeps by Adolph Rusch of Strassburg, c. 1480,* ed. Karlfried Froehlich and Margaret T. Gibson (Turnhout, Belgium: Brepols), forthcoming.

"Romans 8:1-11: Pauline Theology in Mediaeval Interpretation." In *Faith and History: Essays in Honor of Paul W. Meyer,* ed. John T. Carroll, Charles H. Cosgrove, and E. Elizabeth Johnson (Atlanta: Scholars Press, 1991), pp. 239-60.

"Justification Language and Grace: The Charge of Pelagianism in the Middle Ages." In *Probing the Reformed Tradition: Historical Studies in Honor of Edward A. Dowey, Jr.,* ed. Elsie Anne McKee and Brian G. Armstrong (Louisville: Westminster/John Knox, 1989), pp. 21-47.

"Saint Peter, Papal Primacy, and the Exegetical Tradition, 1150-1300." In *The Religious Role of the Papacy: Ideals and Realities, 1150-1300,* ed. Christopher J. Ryan, Papers in Mediaeval Studies, 8 (Toronto: Pontifical Institute of Mediaeval Studies, 1989), pp. 3-44.

"Summary Observations." In *The Leuenberg Agreement and Lutheran-Reformed Relationships: Evaluations by North American and European Theologians,* ed. William G. Rusch and Daniel F. Martensen (Minneapolis: Augsburg, 1989), pp. 123-25.

(co-author) with Gary Gilbert. "Early Christianity." In *The Best in the Literature of Philosophy and World Religions,* ed. William L. Reese, The Reader's Adviser: A Layman's Guide to Literature, 4, ed. Barbara A. Chernow and George A. Vallasi (New York/London: Bowker, 1988), pp. 527-76.

"Pseudo-Dionysius and the Reformation of the Sixteenth Century." In *Pseudo-Dionysius: The Complete Works,* trans. Colm Luibheid, foreword, notes, and translation collaboration by Paul Rorem, Classics of Western Spirituality (New York/Mahwah, NJ: Paulist, 1987), pp. 33-46.

"Crusades. Christian Perspective." In *The Encyclopedia of Religion,* Mircea Eliade, editor-in-chief (New York: Macmillan, 1987), 4:167-71.

"Bibelkommentare — Zur Krise einer Gattung." *Zeitschrift für Theologie und Kirche* 84:4 (1987): 465-92.

"Luther's Hymns and Johann Sebastian Bach." *Lutheran Theological Seminary Bulletin* (Gettysburg, PA) 66:1 (1986): 3-29. "Discussion," pp. 30-33. — Repr. in *Encounters With Luther,* Vol. 4: *Lectures, Discussions and Sermons at the Martin Luther Colloquia 1985-1989,* ed. Eric W. Gritsch, Institute for Luther Studies, Gettysburg Lutheran Seminary (Gettysburg, PA: GAM Printing, 1990), pp. 1-31.

"Justification Language in the Middle Ages." In *Justification by Faith,* ed. H. George Anderson, T. Austin Murphy, and Joseph Burgess, Lutherans and Catholics in Dialogue, 7 (Minneapolis: Augsburg, 1985), pp. 143-61, nn. 348-50.

Biblical Interpretation in the Early Church. Sources of Early Christian Thought, William G. Rusch, series ed. (Philadelphia: Fortress, 1984).

(editor) *Ökumene: Möglichkeiten und Grenzen Heute* (Tübingen: Mohr, 1982).

"Einführung." In *Ökumene: Möglichkeiten und Grenzen Heute,* ed. Karlfried Froehlich (Tübingen: Mohr, 1982), pp. VII-XXII.

(editor) *Testimonia Oecumenica in Honorem Oscar Cullmann Octogenarii Die XXV Februarii* A.D. *MCMLXXXII* (Tübingen: Refo-Druck Hans Vogler, 1982).

"Oscar Cullmann — Ein Leben für die grössere Ökumene. Zugleich ein Vorwort." In *Testimonia Oecumenica in honorem Oscar Cullmann Octogenarii Die XXV Februarii* A.D. *MCMLXXXII,* ed. Karlfried Froehlich (Tübingen: Refo-Druck Hans Vogler, 1982), pp. 1-22.

"Biblical Hermeneutics on the Move." *Word and World: Theology for Christian Ministry* 1:2 (1981): 140-52. — Repr. in *Ex Auditu: An Annual of the Frederick Neumann Symposium on Theological Interpretation of Scripture, Princeton Theological Seminary* 1 (1985): 3-13; and in *A Guide to Contemporary Hermeneutics: Major Trends in Biblical Interpretation,* ed. Donald K. McKim (Grand Rapids: Eerdmans, 1986), pp. 175-91.

Review of *The Secret Book of Revelation: The Last Book in the Bible,* by Gilles Quispel. *TToday* 37/4 (1981): 538-39.

"The Plan of St. Gall." *TToday* 38/1 (1981): 84-91.

"Crusades"; "Inquisition." In *Academic American Encyclopedia,* 1980 edition.

"Problems of Lutheran Hermeneutics." In *Studies in Lutheran Hermeneutics,* ed. John Reumann in collaboration with S. H. Nafzger and H. H. Ditmanson (Philadelphia: Fortress, 1979), pp. 127-41.

"Church History and the Bible." *PSB* n.s. 1/4 (1978): 213-24.

(collaborator) *Mary in the New Testament: A Collaborative Assessment by Protestant and Roman Catholic Scholars,* ed. Raymond E. Brown, Karl P. Donfried, Joseph A. Fitzmyer, and John Reumann (Philadelphia/New York: Fortress/Paulist, 1978).

"Charismatic Manifestations and the Lutheran Incarnational Stance." In *The Holy Spirit in the Life of the Church, from Biblical Times to the Present,* ed. Paul D. Opsahl (Minneapolis: Augsburg, 1978), pp. 136-57.

"Fallibility Instead of Infallibility? A Brief History of the Interpretation of Gal. 2:11-14." In *Teaching Authority and Infallibility in the Church,* ed. Paul Empie and Austin Murphy, Lutherans and Catholics in Dialogue, 6 (Minneapolis: Augsburg, 1978), pp. 259-69, nn. 351-57.

" 'Always to Keep the Literal Sense in Holy Scripture Means to Kill One's Soul': The State of Biblical Hermeneutics at the Beginning of the Fifteenth Century." In *Literary Uses of Typology from the Late Middle Ages to the Present,* ed. Earl Miner (Princeton: Princeton University Press, 1977), pp. 20-48.

"The Hours of Catherine of Cleves. The Farnese Hours." *TToday* 34/1 (1977): 111-18.

(collaborator) "Concordia Seminary (Missouri)." Report of the Committee on Issues of Academic Freedom and Academic Tenure, *AAUP Bulletin* 61/1 (1975): 49-59.

(co-author) with Howard C. Kee and Franklin W. Young. *Understanding the New Testament,* 3d ed. (Englewood Cliffs, NJ: Prentice-Hall, 1973).

(collaborator) *Peter in the New Testament: A Collaborative Assessment by Protestant and Roman Catholic Scholars,* ed. Raymond E. Brown, Karl P. Donfried, and John Reumann (Minneapolis/New York: Augsburg/Paulist, 1973). Also translated into German, French, Spanish, Japanese.

"Montanism and Gnosis." In *The Heritage of the Early Church: Essays in Honor of the Very Reverend Georges Vasilievich Florovsky,* ed. David Neiman and Margaret Schatkin, Orientalia Christiana Analecta, 195 (Rome: Pontificium Institutum Studiorum Orientalium, 1973), pp. 91-114.

"The Ecology of Creation." *TToday* 27/3 (1970): 263-76. — Repr. in *PSB* 63/2-3 (1970): 13-23. — Excerpted in *The Church Woman* 37/8 (1971): 14-16.

(managing editor) *Journal for Theology and the Church,* ed. Robert W. Funk in association with Gerhard Ebeling et al. (Tübingen/New York: Mohr/Harper & Row, 1965–1968).

Vol. 5: Herbert Braun et al. *God and Christ: Existence and Providence* (TB 255; 1968).

Vol. 4: Wolfhart Pannenberg et al. *History and Hermeneutic* (TB 254; 1967).

Vol. 3: Ernst Käsemann et al. *Distinctive Protestant and Catholic Themes Reconsidered* (TB 253; 1967).

Vol. 2: Rudolf Bultmann et al. *Translating Theology into the Modern Age* (TB 252; 1965).

Vol. 1: James M. Robinson et al. *The Bultmann School of Biblical Interpretation: New Directions?* (TB 251; 1965).

"Die Mitte des Neuen Testaments: Oscar Cullmanns Beitrag zur Theologie der Gegenwart." In *Oikonomia. Heilsgeschichte als Thema der Theologie,* ed. Felix Christ (Hamburg: Herbert Reich Evangelischer Verlag, 1967), pp. 203-19. — Excerpted in *Evangelischer Digest* 5 (1967): 62-65.

(editor) *Oscar Cullmann: Vorträge und Aufsätze, 1925-1962* (Tübingen/Zürich: Mohr/Zwingli, 1966).

"Vorwort." In *Oscar Cullmann: Vorträge und Aufsätze, 1925-1962,* ed. Karlfried Froehlich (Tübingen/Zürich: Mohr/Zwingli, 1966), pp. 7-14.

(co-author) with Howard C. Kee and Franklin W. Young. *Understanding the New Testament,* 2d ed. (Englewood Cliffs, NJ: Prentice-Hall, 1965). — German translation: *Das Geschehen Ohnegleichen. Panorama des Neuen Testaments,* trans. Helmut Zechner (Stuttgart: Quell-Verlag, 1967).

"Oscar Cullmann: A Portrait." *Journal of Ecumenical Studies* 1 (1964): 22-41.

Formen der Auslegung von Matthäus 16,13-18 im lateinischen Mittelalter (Teildruck). Excerpt of doctoral dissertation (Tübingen: Fotodruck Präzis, 1963).

"Spinola, Christoph Royas de." In *RGG,* 3d ed., ed. Kurt Galling et al. (Tübingen: Mohr, 1962), 6:249.

Formen der Auslegung von Matthäus 16,13-18 im lateinischen Mittelalter. Dissertation zur Erlangung der Doktorwürde der theologischen Fakultät der Universität Basel, 1960.

Review of *Das Geschichtsverständnis des Markus-Evangeliums,* by James M. Robinson. *Theologische Zeitschrift* (Basel) 14/3 (1958): 224-25.

Translations into German of all articles submitted in French and some in English for *RGG,* 3d ed., 6 vols., ed. Kurt Galling et al. (Tübingen: Mohr, 1956-62).

Translation into German of James M. Robinson, *The Problem of History in Mark,* Studies in Biblical Theology, 1/21 (Naperville, IL: Allenson, 1957). = *Das Geschichtsverständnis des Markus-Evangeliums,* Abhandlungen zur Theologie des Alten und Neuen Testaments, 30 (Zürich: Zwingli, 1956).

Contributors

Robert W. Bernard Adjunct Professor, Southwestern Baptist Theological Seminary (Fort Worth, TX)

Mark S. Burrows Associate Professor of the History of Christianity and Historical Theology, Wesley Theological Seminary (Washington, DC)

Oscar Cullmann Professor Emeritus of New Testament and Early Christianity, The Universities of Basel, Paris, and Strasbourg

Jane Dempsey Douglass Hazel Thompson McCord Professor of Historical Theology, Princeton Theological Seminary

Bart D. Ehrman Assistant Professor of Religious Studies, The University of North Carolina at Chapel Hill

John V. Fleming Fairchild Professor of English, Princeton University

Paula Fredriksen William Goodwin Aurelio Professor of the Appreciation of Scripture, Boston University

Karlfried Froehlich Benjamin B. Warfield Professor of Ecclesiastical History, Princeton Theological Seminary

Klaus Fröhlich Akademischer Rat, Ruhr-Universität Bochum

Eric W. Gritsch Maryland Synod Professor of Church History, Gettysburg Lutheran Seminary

Blake R. Heffner Pastor of St. John's United Church of Christ (Easton, PA)

David W. Johnson Assistant Professor of Church History, Brite Divinity School, Texas Christian University (Fort Worth, TX)

Bruce McCormack Associate Professor of Theology, Princeton Theological Seminary

Elsie Anne McKee Associate Professor of Church History, Andover Newton Theological School

Kathleen E. McVey Associate Professor of Church History, Princeton Theological Seminary

James H. Moorhead Mary McIntosh Bridge Professor of American Church History, Princeton Theological Seminary

Christopher Ocker Assistant Professor of Church History, San Francisco Theological Seminary (San Anselmo, CA)

Rodney L. Petersen Executive Director, The Boston Theological Institute

Cornelius Plantinga, Jr. Professor of Systematic Theology, Calvin Theological Seminary (Grand Rapids, MI)

Paul Rorem Associate Professor of Church History, The Lutheran School of Theology at Chicago

David C. Steinmetz Amos Ragan Kearns Professor of the History of Christianity, The Divinity School, Duke University (Durham, NC)

Amanda Berry Wylie Ph.D. candidate, Princeton Theological Seminary

Pictured on the steps of Stuart Hall at Princeton Theological Seminary on the final morning of the Symposium are Karlfried and Ricarda Froehlich, along with most of the contributors to this volume. From left to right: Mark S. Burrows, Robert W. Bernard, Daniel Migliore (of Princeton Theological Seminary, and convenor of the Modern section), Amanda Berry Wylie, Paul Rorem, Christopher Ocker, Blake R. Heffner, Bart D. Ehrman, David W. Johnson (in rear), John V. Fleming, Cornelius Plantinga, Rodney L. Petersen, David C. Steinmetz, Bruce McCormack, Ralph Quere (of Wartburg Theological Seminary, and convenor of the Reformation section), Elsie Anne McKee, and James H. Moorhead.

Index of Biblical References

Index of Names

Index of Subjects